GOSPEL TRUTH OF JUSTIFICATION

GOSPEL TRUTH OF JUSTIFICATION

PROCLAIMED

DEFENDED

DEVELOPED

DAVID J. ENGELSMA

Printed in the United States of America

All scripture quotations by the author are taken from the Authorized (King James) Version

Reformed Free Publishing Association
1894 Georgetown Center Drive
Jenison, MI 49428
www.rfpa.org
mail@rfpa.org
616-457-5970

Book cover by Christopher Tobias / www.tobiasdesign.com
Interior design and typesetting by Katherine Lloyd / www.theDESKonline.com

ISBN 978-1-944555-18-4
Ebook ISBN 978-1-944555-19-1
LCCN 2017936250

To the work of Jesus Christ through Martin Luther—
humblest of the children of God,
mightiest of the men of God,
and greatest of the reformers (heroes all)

The truth of the Gospel is this, that our righteousness comes by faith alone, without the works of the Law. The falsification or corruption of the Gospel is this, that we are justified by faith but not without the works of the Law...If the doctrine of justification is lost, the whole of Christian doctrine is lost.—Martin Luther[1]

Christian freedom...consists of [this]...that the consciences of believers, in seeking assurance of their justification before God, should rise above and advance beyond the law, forgetting all law righteousness. For since...the law leaves no one righteous, either it excludes us from all hope of justification or we ought to be freed from it, and in such a way, indeed, that no account is taken of works. For he who thinks that in order to obtain righteousness he ought to bring some trifle of works is incapable of determining their measure and limit but makes himself debtor to the whole law. Removing, then, mention of law, and laying aside all consideration of works, we should, when justification is being discussed, embrace God's mercy alone, turn our attention from ourselves, and look only to Christ. For there the question is not how we may become righteous but how, being unrighteous and unworthy, we may be reckoned righteous. If consciences wish to attain any certainty in this matter, they ought to give no place to the law.—John Calvin[2]

---

1 Martin Luther, commentary on Galatians 2:4–5, in *Luther's Works*, vol. 26, *Lectures on Galatians 1535*, ed. Jaroslav Pelikan (Saint Louis, MO: Concordia, 1963), 88.

2 John Calvin, *Institutes of the Christian Religion*, ed. John T. McNeill, trans. Ford Lewis Battles, 2 vols., Library of Christian Classics 20–21 (Philadelphia: Westminster Press, 1960), 3.19.2, 1:834.

CONTENTS

PREFACE

Such is the importance of the truth of justification both for the gospel and for the salvation of the chosen people of God that a defense of it is always in order, if not necessary.

Justification is God's pardon of the guilty sinner—the forgiveness of sins—delivering the sinner from eternal damnation. It is also the gift to the sinner of a righteousness that makes the sinner worthy of eternal life and glory.

Paul indicates the importance of the truth of justification for the gospel in Galatians 1:6: "I marvel that ye are so soon removed from him that called you into the grace of Christ unto another gospel." Loss of the truth of justification, or more precisely, corruption of the truth of justification (for this is the evil of the Galatians to which the apostle is referring), results in "another gospel" than God's gospel of grace. The one who preaches the other gospel, by corrupting the truth of justification, is accursed of God: "If any man preach any other gospel unto you than that ye have received, let him be accursed" (1:9).

David expresses the importance of the truth of justification for the salvation of the sinner in Psalm 32:1: "Blessed is he whose transgression is forgiven, whose sin is covered," that is, blessed is he who is justified. Forgiveness, or justification, is the fundamental blessing of salvation. Without it no one is blessed, whether spiritually or materially. For the man or woman who is not justified, there is only divine curse. With justification one receives all the blessings of salvation, as well as the blessing of God in all the circumstances of earthly life. For the justified man or woman, there is no curse.

The apostle quotes Psalm 32:1 in Romans 4, where he is teaching justification as the imputation of righteousness by faith, apart from works. "Even as David also describeth the blessedness of the man, unto whom God imputeth righteousness without works, saying, Blessed are they whose iniquities are forgiven, and whose sins are covered" (Rom. 4:6–7).

As its centrality in the epistle to the Romans shows, justification with its ground in the atoning death of Jesus Christ is the heart of the church's proclamation of the gospel of grace. Justification is also the Christian's peace in life and death (5:1) and the wellspring of his life of holiness (12:1).

There are several reasons that a thorough treatment and an uncompromising defense of justification by faith alone ought to be published in 2017.

One reason is that the doctrine of justification by faith alone is so fundamental to the gospel of grace that an exposition and defense of this truth are in order always. The true church of Christ in the world simply cannot keep silent about this doctrine. To keep silent about justification by faith alone would be to silence the gospel. The true church certainly cannot allow the false churches and the heretics to corrupt this gospel truth without sounding the alarm and defending the faith.

A second reason is that the present day sees the most serious assault on the gospel of justification probably since the time of the Reformation. The enemy is within. It appears, launches its attack, and is protected and defended within the Reformed and Presbyterian churches that have a reputation for orthodoxy, the Orthodox Presbyterian Church and the Presbyterian Church in America among others. The name of the enemy is federal vision. Adding to the gravity of the assault is that these churches are the main players in the ecumenical movement called North American Presbyterian and Reformed Council (NAPARC) that is popular with any number of conservative denominations, including the Protestant Reformed Churches. Churches that tolerate, refuse to condemn, and even approve the federal vision and its heretical proponents at their broadest assemblies are not conservative but churches that take on the mark of the false church.

This book exposes the federal vision for the gospel-denying heresy that it is. It is the contemporary form of the false doctrine condemned in Romans, especially chapters 3–5, and in the epistle to the Galatians. It is the doctrine of justification by works.

A third reason why this book is timely is that 2017 marks the five hundredth anniversary of the Reformation of the church of Jesus Christ. In 1517 the reformer Martin Luther affixed the ninety-five theses to the door of the church in Wittenberg, Germany, the act by which Jesus Christ began his reformation of his church. Essential to this Reformation was the gospel truth of justification by faith alone. This book on justification is intended by the Reformed Free Publishing Association to celebrate that glorious work of Christ.

But the purpose both of the Reformed Free Publishing Association and of the author is more than a celebration of the beginning of the Reformation. It is the purpose of both to maintain, defend, and promote the Reformation in the perilous times for the church at present. This too we have learned from Luther. At one stage in the progress of the Reformation, Luther addressed the German nation, whose ear he had. God has given you the gospel, he proclaimed, with special reference to the truth of justification by faith alone. Hold on to it, he continued, for if you corrupt it, or allow it to be taken from you, God himself will take it away from you, and you [the German people] will never have it back again.

Germany has not heeded the warning of its great prophet and teacher. Germany has let the gospel go. It is now a spiritual and theological wasteland of unbelief and liberalism. Upon the German churches lies the awful judgment of God.

The same apostasy is today far advanced in the United States. Most churches proclaim the false gospel, that is no gospel, of righteousness and salvation by the works and will of the sinner (see Rom. 9:16). Today the churches with the most exalted reputation for Reformation orthodoxy are helpless, apparently, before the onslaught of the federal vision.

At such a time as this, a work that echoes Luther's "here I stand" with specific regard to the fundamental doctrine of the Reformation is not only appropriate, but necessary. Clearly, unequivocally, creedally, biblically, the gospel truth of justification by faith alone, without works—any works, all works! Only the alien, perfect work of the Son of God in our flesh, Jesus the justifying Christ of God! Received by faith *alone*!

Protestantism, Protestantism in North America, Protestantism worldwide, especially Reformed and Presbyterian Protestantism, again *hear* this gospel, *believe* it, *confess* it, and *defend* it!

—David J. Engelsma
2017, the five hundredth anniversary
of the Reformation of the church

Chapter One

DOCTRINAL BACKGROUND: ROMAN CATHOLIC AND ARMINIAN HERESIES

Controversy with Rome

The sixteenth-century Reformation of the church was Christ's deliverance of his church from the heresy of justification, and therefore salvation, by the works of the sinner himself. The apostate church of that day taught that guilty sinners are justified partly by Jesus Christ through faith and partly by their own good works. Their own good works are the decisive factor in justification.

That church rigorously applied its false doctrine of salvation by works to the lives of the people. In the sacrament of penance, the people paid the price of the "temporal punishment" of their sins by their own deeds of "satisfaction," that is, satisfaction of the justice of God. The church taught the people to expect dreadful suffering after death in a place called purgatory. This suffering would be the people's further payment of the "temporal" debt of their sins.

In addition, the lively ecclesiastical traffic in indulgences bound the doctrine of justification by works upon the people. By all kinds of deeds, including the purchase of indulgences with money, the people could work their way out of purgatory into heaven by their own payment for sin.

The institute that thus manifested the mark of the false church—denial of the gospel of salvation by grace—also oppressively bound its works doctrine on the people by denying that any of them could be assured of everlasting justification and therefore of salvation, a terror far worse than the fear of the fires of purgatory. A justification that is dependent on the sinner's own works is necessarily highly uncertain.

This apostate church, which hardened herself against Christ at the Reformation, is the Roman Catholic Church. Rome made her heretical doctrine of justification creedal in the Canons and Dogmatic Decrees of the Council of Trent (1563).

The Roman Catholic Church has not changed her doctrine of justification. She has not repented of and retracted the doctrine of justification that occasioned the Reformation. She has not withdrawn the anathemas she pronounced at Trent on the Protestant doctrine of justification by faith alone. Indeed, Rome has reaffirmed her heretical doctrine of justification in the dogmatical decrees of Vatican II (1962–65), including the sacrament of penance, purgatory, and indulgences.

We know Rome's teaching about justification from the condemnation of it in the Reformed confessions, particularly the Heidelberg Catechism, questions and answers 57–64; the Belgic Confession, articles 22–24; and the Westminster Confession of Faith, chapters 11 and 16. We know the Roman doctrine of justification also from Rome's official statements, especially the Canons and Dogmatic Decrees of Trent, Sixth Session, Decree on Justification.

The doctrine of the Roman Catholic Church concerning justification is that the guilty sinner becomes righteous in the judgment of God partly by his own good works. Rome is quick to add, especially in controversy with Protestant defenders of justification by faith alone, that the sinner performs these works only with the help of grace. The good works that justify are those that proceed from true faith in Christ. With appeal to Galatians 5:6, "faith which worketh by love," Rome contends that justification is by faith and by the deeds of love that faith performs. But the sinner is righteous in the divine act of justification by his own deeds.

The righteousness of a sinner before God therefore is partly the work of Christ for him, especially the atoning death of the cross, and partly the sinner's own good works. A sinner earns, or merits, and *must* earn forgiveness and eternal life by his efforts (with the help of grace, Rome is quick to add, especially in controversy). In Roman Catholic doctrine, the good works of the sinner are a cause of God's act of justification.

Two additional features of Rome's doctrine of justification are noteworthy as basic to the teaching. First, Rome teaches that justification is a renewing, sanctifying work of God within the sinner, and not a strictly legal declaration by God the judge upon the sinner. According to Rome, in justification God *makes* the sinner righteous, rather than *declaring* the sinner righteous. God *infuses* righteousness into the sinner, rather than *imputing*, or *reckoning*, righteousness to him.

This doctrine of justification makes room for the sinner's good works to play a role—a *decisive* role—in the matter of his justification. When God judges the sinner (and for Rome too there is in justification this element of judging), he takes into account what the sinner himself has done and what the sinner himself actually is (with the help of grace, Rome is quick to add, especially in controversy). In justification, according to Trent, God "maketh us just" by renewing us, so that "we are not only reputed, but are truly called, and are just, receiving justice within us." The righteousness of justification is "inherent" in those who are justified.[1]

---

1 Canons and Decrees of the Council of Trent, Sixth Session, Decree on Justification 7, in Philip Schaff, ed., *The Creeds of Christendom with a History and Critical Notes*, 6th ed., 3 vols. (New York: Harper & Row, 1931; repr., Grand Rapids, MI: Baker Books, 2007), 2:95–96.

The second feature of Rome's doctrine of justification that is basic to its heresy is Rome's teaching that the sinner has a "free will," that is, the natural, spiritual ability to choose God and the good when these are offered to him. Although fallen men and women are sinful and unable to save themselves, they do retain a free will. It is the proper exercise of free will that gives the sinner's good works their merit and that distinguishes those whom God justifies from those whom God condemns. If a sinner merits in the matter of justification, he must have something of his own that he contributes to his righteousness. That which he contributes is the proper exercise of his free will. In the first chapter of its confession concerning justification, Trent declared that "free-will," although "attenuated…in its powers" in all men because of Adam's sin, "was by no means extinguished in them."[2] Later, Trent cursed those who deny that "man's free-will…co-operates towards disposing and preparing itself for obtaining the grace of Justification."[3]

The Protestant churches, Reformed and Lutheran, condemned Rome's doctrine of justification as heresy, as the radical and total corruption of the gospel, so that her doctrine of justification marks Rome as a false church. In their condemnation of Rome's doctrine of justification, the reformers, Calvin as well as Luther, and the Protestant churches, Reformed as well as Lutheran, judged the Roman Catholic doctrine of justification as essentially the false doctrine of justification by the works of the law that Paul exposes and condemns in Romans 3–5 and in the book of Galatians.

The evidence that nothing other and nothing less than this was the Reformation's condemnation of Rome's doctrine of

2 Canons and Decrees of the Council of Trent, Sixth Session, Decree on Justification 1, in ibid., 2:89.

3 Canons and Decrees of the Council of Trent, Sixth Session, [Canons] on Justification 4, in ibid., 2:111.

justification is again the Protestant creeds. These creeds condemn the Roman Catholic doctrine of justification with the language that Paul used against the teachers of justification by works in Romans and Galatians. They raise against the Roman Catholic doctrine the passages of scripture that Paul wrote against those teaching righteousness by works in his day. In support of the Protestant doctrine of justification, which the Roman Catholic Church curses, they appeal to the texts in Romans and Galatians that affirm justification by faith.

Having exposed the Roman Catholic doctrine of justification as the teaching that "something more is required besides him [Christ]," the Belgic Confession declares, as the Protestant doctrine of justification: "Therefore we justly say with Paul, *that we are justified by faith alone,* or *by faith without works.*"[4]

In article 23 of the Belgic Confession ("Our Justification Consists in the Forgiveness of Sin and the Imputation of Christ's Righteousness"), the Reformed church confesses that "our salvation consists in the remission of our sins for Jesus Christ's sake, and that therein our righteousness before God is implied." Therefore, the Reformed church rejects as presumption the Roman Catholic doctrine that the people of God are to trust "in any thing in ourselves, or in any merit of ours." In support of this Reformed belief concerning justification, *and in condemnation of the Roman Catholic doctrine*, the creed appeals to Psalm 32:1–2; Romans 4:6–8; and Romans 3:24: "As David and Paul teach us, declaring this to be the happiness of man, that God imputes righteousness to him without works. And the same Apostle saith, *that we are justified freely by his grace, through the redemption which is in Jesus Christ.*"[5]

---

4 Belgic Confession 22, in Schaff, *Creeds of Christendom*, 3:408. The heading of the article is "Of Our Justification through Faith in Jesus Christ." The emphasis is that of the confession.

5 Belgic Confession 23, in ibid., 3:409. The emphasis is that of the confession.

The Protestant and Reformed doctrine of justification is biblical. The doctrine of Rome is the false doctrine condemned in Romans and Galatians.

Controversy with Arminianism

Within a mere fifty years or so after the death of Martin Luther and only thirty years after the death of John Calvin (and after the writing of the Heidelberg Catechism and of the Belgic Confession), a heretical doctrine of justification caused schism in the Reformed churches in the Netherlands and eventually in the Reformed churches in all of Europe. The ministers and professors of these churches who taught the heresy are known as Arminians after the leading theologian of their faction, James Arminius. They are also called Remonstrants because of a remonstrance, or protest, they lodged against the orthodox doctrine of the Reformed churches.

The error of the Arminians concerning justification is often overlooked because of the emphasis on the struggle over five other cardinal truths of the Christian faith. These truths are predestination, the atonement, the spiritual condition of fallen mankind, regenerating grace, and the preservation of saints—the well-known five points of Calvinism. Nevertheless, Arminian theology included a distinct, erroneous doctrine of justification.

Regardless that the Arminian doctrine of justification is often ignored by both defenders and opponents of Arminianism, and regardless that justification is not listed among the main points that were (and still are) at issue between the Arminian heresy and Reformed orthodoxy, the Arminian doctrine of justification was (and still is) a crucially important aspect of the Arminian perversion of the gospel of grace. John L. Girardeau was right when he stated:

> In nothing, except in its assertion of the supremacy of the sinner's will in the matter of practical salvation, and its consequent rejection of the sovereignty of God's

> electing grace, is the Arminian theology more conspicuously defective than in its denial of the great principle, that God requires in the sinner, in order to justification, the possession of a real, substantive, perfect righteousness of works [the righteousness of the works of Christ in the stead of and imputed to the elect believer].[6]

That Arminianism included a false doctrine of justification and what this false teaching was are evident from the condemnation of the Arminian heresy by the orthodox Reformed churches in the Canons of the Synod of Dordt (1618–19). Even though this creed of the Reformed churches does not devote a separate head, or chapter, to a defense of justification in opposition to Arminianism's false teaching regarding justification, it does explicitly refer to and describe the Arminian doctrine of justification.

The main reference to the Arminian doctrine of justification occurs in the rejection of errors section of the second head of the Canons. In the context of a rejection of the Arminian teaching that the death of Christ "acquire[d] for the Father the mere right to establish with man such a covenant as He might please, whether of grace or of works" (the necessary implication of Arminianism's doctrine of universal atonement), the Canons condemn those, that is, the Arminians,

> who teach that the new covenant of grace, which God the Father, through the mediation of the death of Christ, made with man, does not herein consist that we by faith, inasmuch as it accepts the merits of Christ, are justified before God and saved, but in the fact that God, having revoked the demand of perfect obedience of the law, regards faith itself and the obedience of faith, although imperfect, as the

---

6 John L. Girardeau, *Calvinism and Evangelical Arminianism: Compared as to Election, Reprobation, Justification and Related Doctrines* (1890; repr., Harrisonburg, VA: Sprinkle Publications, 1984), 553.

> perfect obedience of the law, and does esteem it worthy of the reward of eternal life through grace.[7]

The crucial phrase in determining the Arminian doctrine of justification is "regards faith itself and the obedience of faith, although imperfect, as the perfect obedience of the law, and does esteem it worthy."

The Canons analyze the Arminian doctrine of justification similarly in the rejection of errors section of the first head of doctrine. Refuting the Arminian teaching of conditional election, the Canons note that in Arminian thinking election consists in this, that God chose not certain persons rather than others, but "the act of faith, which from its very nature is undeserving, as well as its incomplete obedience, as a condition of salvation, *and that He would graciously consider this in itself as a complete obedience and count it worthy of the reward of eternal life*." This understanding of faith, charge the Canons, is "injurious" to the "truth of gracious justification."[8]

As the Canons accurately describe their doctrine of justification, the Arminians taught (and teach) that the sinner's act of believing is itself his righteousness with God and therefore his worthiness to obtain eternal life. Obviously, a sinner's faith is not, in actuality, the equivalent of perfect obedience to the law, much less the payment of the debt of sin to an offended God. But, said the Arminian theologians, God graciously waives the requirement of perfect obedience to the law and likewise graciously is willing to esteem the activity of believing as the sinner's righteousness.

Appealing to Genesis 15:6, "And he [Abraham] believed in the LORD; and he counted it to him for righteousness," the Arminians rejected the Reformed explanation that Abraham's

---

7 Canons of Dordt 2, error 4, in *The Confessions and the Church Order of the Protestant Reformed Churches* (Grandville, MI: Protestant Reformed Churches in America, 2005), 164–65. Schaff does not include the rejection of errors section of the Canons in English translation.

8 Canons of Dordt 1, error 3, in ibid., 160; emphasis added.

faith was counted, or reckoned, to him for righteousness *inasmuch as the object of Abraham's faith was Christ crucified, so that the righteousness reckoned to Abraham was, in fact, the obedience of Christ in his stead, which faith always looks to, embraces, trusts in, and receives.* Rather, the Arminians explained the text, which Paul quotes as fundamental to the doctrine of justification he sets forth in Romans 4, as teaching that Abraham's activity of believing itself, *as an activity*, was counted to him by God for his righteousness.

Although James Arminius was exceedingly crafty in disguising his real opinion regarding justification, as also regarding all his departures from the great doctrines of grace recovered at the Reformation, he made his aberrant doctrine of justification known clearly enough. Defending himself against the charge that he taught that "faith is not the instrument of Justification," Arminius appealed to Genesis 15:6. He explained: "Faith, not as it is *an instrument*, but as it is *an act*, is imputed for righteousness." Confusing the issue, but not at all retracting what he had just asserted, Arminius added, "although such imputation be made on account of Him whom it apprehends."[9]

Arminius was more candid in explaining his doctrine of justification to his theological friend Uitenbogard than he was in defending it to his theological foes. Regarding the biblical phrase "faith is imputed for righteousness," Arminius wrote Uitenbogard: "If I understand it at all, I think this is the meaning of the phrase, *God accounts faith for righteousness*: And thus justification is ascribed to faith, not because it accepts, but because it is accepted." The great heretic went on to express his disagreement with the orthodox explanation of Genesis 15:6, that faith is counted for righteousness inasmuch as the object of faith is

9 James Arminius, "Apology against Thirty-One Theological Articles," in *The Works of James Arminius*, trans. James Nichols (repr., Grand Rapids, MI: Baker, 1991), 2:49–51.

Christ: "For, *not the object which he apprehends by faith*, but *his believing*, is said to be imputed to him for righteousness."[10]

According to the Arminian doctrine of justification, not only is faith a human work by which a sinner distinguishes himself as worthy of God's justifying verdict and by which he earns this verdict, but faith, that is, the sinner's act of believing, is also itself the sinner's righteousness with God. In justification God does not reckon the obedience of Christ to the account of the guilty sinner by means of the sinner's faith. But God reckons the act of believing as the sinner's righteousness.

In the language of Romans and Galatians, Arminianism teaches justification by work. The work is faith. Arminianism teaches justification *on account of* faith (something scripture does not teach), rather than the biblical justification *by (means of)* faith.

Yet works of obedience to the law are not excluded from the Arminian doctrine of justification. As the Canons remark, the Arminian doctrine of justification is that God "regards faith itself *and the obedience of faith*" as the sinner's righteousness. The "obedience of faith" is the good works that faith performs.

Therefore, justification for Arminianism is by works, *with a vengeance*. Arminianism's doctrine is worse than Rome's. Rome at least makes the obedience of Christ part of the sinner's righteousness in justification, indeed the greater part (in theory, if not in practice). For Arminianism, the sinner's righteousness is *all* his own works: his faith as a human work and his obedience to the law. Christ is not the sinner's righteousness whatsoever. Christ merely made it possible for the sinner to justify himself by believing and obeying.

As the Canons point out in their rejection of the error, the Arminian doctrine of justification is closely related to Arminianism's teachings regarding Christ's death and regarding the new covenant. First, denying the substitutionary efficacy of the cross by its theory of universal, ineffectual atonement, Arminianism

---

10 Ibid., 2:50.

taught (and teaches) that Christ's death merely obtained for God the right to offer all humans salvation on the condition that they believe. Faith, then, for Arminianism is not the instrument (earned for the elect sinner by the cross and bestowed on him by the Spirit) by which the sinner receives the perfect righteousness of Jesus Christ by imputation. Faith is the work of the sinner's fulfilling the prescribed condition and thus becoming the sinner's righteousness with God.

Second, the Arminian heresy of justification on the basis of faith and good works is an aspect of Arminianism's erroneous doctrine of the covenant. The Canons' description and condemnation of Arminianism's doctrine of justification, in Canons 2, errors 2, 4, are part of the Canons' repudiation of the Arminian doctrine of a conditional covenant. Arminianism denied that the death of Christ "confirmed the new covenant" for and with "all those, and those only, who were from eternity chosen to salvation, and given to him by the Father." It denied that this confirmation of the covenant included Christ's purchase for the elect of both salvation and the faith by which they receive salvation.[11]

Rather, Arminian theology taught that Christ's death earned for God the right to establish the covenant with all humans, conditioned upon their faith and obedience. In such a conception of a conditional covenant, justification is necessarily also conditional, that is, dependent upon the work of the sinner, whether faith or good works or both.

Basic to the Arminian doctrine of justification, as it is also basic to the Roman Catholic doctrine, is the notion of the free will of the sinner. By their free will, sinners are able to distinguish themselves as worthy of justification and to contribute something of their own in the matter of justification.

Necessarily involved in this doctrine of justification is the admission that the grace of justification can be lost. A

11 Canons of Dordt 2.8, in Schaff, *Creeds of Christendom*, 3:587.

righteousness consisting of the sinner's works is highly uncertain, indeed fickle. An act of justification dependent on the sinner is precarious to the very last breath of the sinner.

The Synod of Dordt—that grandest and most important assembly of the ecumenical church for the Christian faith from the time of Nicea/Constantinople and Chalcedon to the present day—condemned the Arminian doctrine of justification with all its related teachings, particularly those concerning the death of Christ and the covenant, as heresy. In fact, in the context of its condemnation of the Arminian doctrine of justification the Canons damn Arminianism, root and branch, the Arminianism of John Wesley as much as that of James Arminius, as the "bring[ing] again out of hell the Pelagian error."[12]

That the Canons judge the Arminian teaching as essentially the false doctrine concerning justification that the apostle condemns in Romans and Galatians is proved by the biblical passages adduced by the Canons against the Arminian teaching. In the critically important article concerning the Arminian doctrine of justification, the Canons quote against it Romans 3:24–25: "[The Arminian doctrine of justification] contradict[s] the Scriptures: *Being justified freely by his grace through the redemption that is in Christ Jesus: Whom God hath set forth to be a propitiation through faith in his blood* (Rom. 3:24–25)." In a further, searing indictment, the creed adds, "And these [Arminians] proclaim, as did the wicked Socinus, a new and strange justification of man before God, against the consensus of the whole church."[13]

12 Canons of Dordt 2, error 3, in *Confessions and Church Order*, 165.

13 Canons of Dordt 2, error 4, in ibid.

Chapter Two

DOCTRINAL BACKGROUND: FEDERAL VISION HERESY

In a development that almost defies belief, this "new and strange justification of man before God" now appears in conservative Reformed and Presbyterian churches. These include the Orthodox Presbyterian Church, the Presbyterian Church in America, the United Reformed Churches, and the Confederation of Reformed Evangelical Churches. The heresy that Romans 3–5 exposes as destructive of the gospel of grace and that the apostle calls "another gospel" in Galatians 1:6 now works at subverting the gospel from within the conservative churches. In the case of the Orthodox Presbyterian Church, it has already accomplished this subversion by official decisions of presbyteries and general assembly protecting and approving the heresy.[1] The

1 In proof of these assertions, see O. Palmer Robertson, *The Current Justification Controversy* (Unicoi, TN: Trinity Foundation, 2003); A. Donald MacLeod, "A Painful Parting, 1977–1983: Justifying Justification," in *W. Stanford Reid: An Evangelical Calvinist in the Academy* (Montreal: McGill-Queen's University Press, 2004), 257–79; Paul M. Elliott, *Christianity and Neo-Liberalism: The Spiritual Crisis in the Orthodox Presbyterian Church and Beyond* (Unicoi, TN: Trinity Foundation, 2005); W. Robert Godfrey, "Westminster Seminary, the Doctrine of Justification, and the Reformed Confessions," in *The Pattern of Sound Doctrine: Systematic Theology at the Westminster Seminaries*, ed. David Van Drunen (Phillipsburg, NJ: P&R, 2004), 127–48; and Guy Prentiss Waters, *The Federal Vision and Covenant Theology: A Comparative Analysis* (Phillipsburg, NJ: P&R, 2006). Waters, himself a member of the Presbyterian Church in America, writes: "Recognized proponents of the F[ederal] V[ision] are

leading theologians of the Confederation of Reformed Evangelical Churches are bold and noisy champions of the doctrine of justification by faith and works.

Prominent, influential advocates or defenders of justification by faith and works in these churches include Norman Shepherd; Richard B. Gaffin Jr.; Steve Wilkins; Peter J. Leithart; John Barach; Douglas Wilson; and Steve Schlissel. Shepherd, formerly a member of the Orthodox Presbyterian Church and a longtime professor at Westminster Seminary in Philadelphia, is now a minister in the Christian Reformed Church. Schlissel is an independent.

The heresy concerning justification gains entrance into the conservative Reformed churches as a fundamental tenet of the theological movement that calls itself the federal vision.[2]

By affirming that James 2 is "talking about justification by faith in the [same] forensic, soteric sense that Paul talks about it in Romans and Galatians," Shepherd, in an important respect the father and leading theologian of the federal vision, confesses justification by faith and works in the sense condemned as Roman

---

cross-denominational (within the Presbyterian Church in America, the United Reformed Churches, the Confederation of Reformed Evangelical Churches, as well as independent churches)" (1). Oddly, Waters omits the Orthodox Presbyterian Church from his list. With the seminary in Philadelphia with which it is closely associated, the Orthodox Presbyterian Church has been the fountainhead of the federal vision heresy of justification by works in the conservative Reformed and Presbyterian churches in North America, as the other books mentioned above make plain.

2 For the federal vision's teaching regarding justification by the men of the movement themselves, see Norman Shepherd, *The Call of Grace: How the Covenant Illuminates Salvation and Evangelism* (Phillipsburg, NJ: P&R, 2000); E. Calvin Beisner, ed., *The Auburn Avenue Theology Pros and Cons: Debating the Federal Vision* (Ft. Lauderdale, FL: Knox Theological Seminary, 2004); and Steve Wilkins and Duane Garner, eds., *The Federal Vision* (Monroe, LA: Athanasius Press, 2004). Contributing writers in the last volume include Steve Wilkins, John Barach, Rich Lusk, Peter J. Leithart, Steve Schlissel, and Douglas Wilson.

Catholic heresy by the Reformation and the Reformed creeds.[3] If justification in James 2 has the same forensic sense that it has in Romans 3 and 4, James 2:24 teaches forensic justification by faith *and works*, as Rome has always contended against the Reformation's doctrine of (forensic) justification by faith alone, altogether apart from any work of the sinner. The text reads: "Ye see then how that by works a man is justified, and not by faith only."

Shepherd adopts the Roman Catholic interpretation of James 2:21: "Was not Abraham our father justified by works, when he had offered Isaac his son upon the altar?" "Abraham was considered righteous for what he did when he offered his son Isaac on the altar."[4] Deliberately, Shepherd does not explain the text as teaching that Abraham was *shown* to be righteous by his work of offering Isaac, as is the explanation by the Reformation. But God "considered" Abraham to be righteous because of what he did, in a forensic sense of *considered*. This is the standard Roman Catholic explanation of James 2:21 and the full, naked, Roman Catholic doctrine of justification by faith and works.

By rejecting Luther's understanding of Romans 3:28 ("Therefore we conclude that a man is justified by faith without the deeds of the law") as teaching justification by faith *alone*, Shepherd embraces Rome's doctrine of justification by faith and works. Justification by faith *and works* is the only alternative to justification by faith *alone*.

> Luther inserted "alone" into his translation of Romans 3:28 to make it read "For we hold that one is justified by faith *alone* apart from works of the law." This is the origin of the dogmatic formula, justification by faith alone. However, his insertion actually distorts Paul's meaning.[5]

---

3 Norman Shepherd, "Justification by Faith Alone," *Reformation & Revival Journal* 11, no. 2 (Spring 2002): 80.

4 Shepherd, *Call of Grace*, 16.

5 Shepherd, "Justification by Faith Alone," 87.

Criticism of Luther's understanding of the key text in the Reformation's controversy with Rome over justification is, of course, criticism of Calvin as well. Calvin too explained Romans 3:28 as teaching justification by faith *alone*. The "shift" by which the Roman Catholic theologians attempt to exclude "this adjective" ("alone" in the phrase "justified by faith *alone*"), Calvin judged "false" and "obviously ridiculous." Calvin asked rhetorically, "Does not he who takes everything from works firmly enough ascribe everything to faith alone? What, I pray, do these expressions mean: 'His righteousness has been manifested apart from the law' [Rom. 3:21...]; and, 'Man is freely justified' [Rom. 3:24...]; and, 'Apart from the works of the law' [Rom. 3:28]?"[6] The last biblical reference is specifically to Romans 3:28. By understanding the text as teaching justification by faith *alone*, Calvin too, according to Shepherd and the federal vision, was guilty of "distorting" Paul's meaning.

Criticism of the Creeds

Not Luther, not Calvin, not the Reformation, but the Roman Catholic Church got Paul's meaning right (according to Shepherd), and Paul's meaning is justification by faith *and by works of obedience to the moral law*—justification by faith *and works*. Indeed, Shepherd's criticism of Luther's (and Calvin's) interpretation of Romans 3:28 falls as well on the Reformed confessions. Largely on the basis of the understanding of Romans 3:28 that Shepherd criticizes as a distortion of Paul's meaning, the Reformed confessions teach justification by faith *alone*. The Heidelberg Catechism is representative of all the Reformation creeds.

> Why sayest thou that thou art righteous *only* by faith?
>
> Not that I am acceptable to God on account of the worthiness of my faith; but because only the satisfaction,

---

6 John Calvin, *Institutes of the Christian Religion*, 3.11.19, 1:749.

> righteousness, and holiness of Christ is my righteousness before God, and I can receive the same and make it my own in no other way than by faith only.[7]

Shepherd's indirect but definite criticism of the Reformed confessions is another aspect of the sin of the men of the federal vision, and not the least. They break the vow they have taken to uphold and defend the confessions. All have sworn agreement with all the doctrines contained in the confessions, whether the three forms of unity or the Westminster standards, promising not to contradict or criticize any of the doctrines publicly or privately. Among the doctrines they have vowed not to criticize is justification by faith *alone*.

Against the Reformation, the Roman Catholic Church explained the "deeds of the law" in Romans 3:28, which are excluded from justification, as merely works of obedience to the Jewish, ceremonial law. Steve Schlissel agrees with Rome.

> When Paul says in [Romans] 3:28, "Therefore we conclude that a man is justified by faith without the deeds of the law," he is not speaking of faith versus obedience. Such a thought is nonsense in every sense. He means one is reckoned among the righteous—not by merit, not by presumption, not by being a Jew, but—by faith. Whatever specific Paul might have in mind when speaking of the "deeds of the law" in Romans 3:28, it clearly has reference to a *Jewish thing*, and not to a Lutheran conception of the Law.[8]

Both for Rome and for Schlissel, the significance of explaining "deeds of the law" in Romans 3:28 as merely Jewish, ceremonial

---

7 Heidelberg Catechism Q&A 61, in Schaff, *Creeds of Christendom*, 3:327; emphasis added.

8 Steve Schlissel, "Justification and the Gentiles," in Wilkins and Garner, *The Federal Vision*, 260–61.

works is huge. This enables them to read the text as allowing for justification by genuine good works—works of obedience to the *moral* law. Like Rome, the federal vision reads Romans 3:28 this way: "Therefore we conclude that a man is justified by faith without Jewish deeds of the ceremonial law, but with Christian deeds of the moral law."

Another crucial text in the controversy whether justification is by faith *alone* or by faith *and works* has always been Romans 2:13: "For not the hearers of the law are just before God, but the doers of the law shall be justified." Does the Holy Spirit teach here what would be required if justification is by the law, namely, that one must be a doer of the law—something that the following verses and chapters make abundantly clear is an utter impossibility? Or does he teach what is actually the case: justification is by the doing of the law? The Reformation and the Reformed creeds gave the former explanation; Rome gave the latter.

The men of the federal vision side with Rome in their explanation of Romans 2:13.

> This statement [Romans 2:13] is not a theoretical proposition concerning some meritorious method of being righteous before God. The presuppositions undergirding Paul's statement include the facts that the Law is "obeyable," that truly responding to the Law (the Word) in faith does justify.[9]

Richard B. Gaffin Jr. also explains Romans 2:13 as teaching what is actually the case, although he refers the justification by works that the text teaches (on his understanding) to the justification of the final judgment. That future justification, Gaffin insists, will be essentially the same as present justification by faith. At stake will be "nothing less than its ultimate issue, the

---

9 Ibid., 260.

all-or-nothing of their [Christians'] final, eternal destiny." Romans 2:13 teaches that that coming, decisive justification will take into account works of obedience to the law. "Romans 2:5ff., at least in verses 5–11, if not verses 12–13 as well, is best seen as describing what will be true of Christians at the final judgment."[10]

Peter J. Leithart boldly criticizes the Reformation's (and the Reformed creeds') doctrine of justification. "The Reformation doctrine of justification has illegitimately narrowed and to some extent distorted the biblical doctrine."[11] The distortion, according to this spokesman for the federal vision, was the Reformation's sharp distinction between justification and sanctification. "The Protestant doctrine has been too rigid in separating justification and sanctification."[12] The Reformation's distortion of justification was also its explanation of justification, especially in Romans and Galatians, as strictly a legal, or judicial, act of God—a verdict from the heavenly tribunal. "'Justifying' is never *merely* declaring a verdict."[13] The divine act of justifying is also a sanctifying work that enables the sinner to perform good works. These good works then become part of the

---

10 Richard B. Gaffin Jr., *By Faith, not by Sight: Paul and the Order of Salvation* (Bletchley, Milton Keynes, Bucks, UK: Paternoster Press, 2006), 97. Gaffin vigorously defended Shepherd's denial of justification by faith alone during the years 1975–82, when men at Westminster Seminary in Philadelphia tried to have Shepherd's heresy exposed and condemned. Gaffin also wrote a glowing recommendation of Shepherd's book *The Call of Grace* on the back cover: "valuable instruction on what it means to live in covenant with God." The book denies not only justification by faith alone, but also all the doctrines of grace.

11 Peter J. Leithart, "'Judge Me, O God': Biblical Perspectives on Justification," in Wilkins and Garner, *The Federal Vision*, 209.

12 Ibid., 211. "Separating" distorts the doctrine of the reformers and of the Reformed creeds. The Reformation did not "separate" justification and sanctification. It rather related them inseparably. But it sharply *distinguished* the two great saving works of God. This is objectionable to Leithart, as it is objectionable to Rome.

13 Ibid., 213. The emphasis is Leithart's.

sinner's righteousness with God in justification. This is the doctrine of justification of the Council of Trent.

In the federal vision's theology of justification, the sinner's righteousness with God is his faith, *viewed as the activity of believing*. The activity of believing can be reckoned by God as the sinner's righteousness, because believing is the condition on which the covenant and its main benefit—justification—depend.

> Thus, the promises made to Abraham had to be believed if they were to be fulfilled. We must not discount faith as a condition to be met for the fulfillment of promise. In fact, Genesis 15:6 says that Abraham's faith was so significant that it was credited to him as righteousness! If so, then righteousness was a condition to be met, and faith met that condition.[14]

Not faith strictly regarding its object—the obedient Messiah—not faith as the embrace of the perfect obedience of Christ in the sinner's stead and on the sinner's behalf, not the lifelong obedience to the law and atoning death of Jesus Christ, which faith receives and makes its own, but Abraham's activity of believing, as his fulfillment of the required "condition," is Abraham's, and by implication every believer's, righteousness with God. This is the Arminian doctrine of justification, and Shepherd's rehashing of it is as rank as anything Arminius ever uttered.

If the activity of believing is one's righteousness with God, it must further be suggested (albeit cautiously, since the men of the federal vision still profess to be Reformed) that the activity of believing is one's own contribution, one's own work, perhaps not meriting righteousness but at least rendering the conditional promise of righteousness effective. Shepherd continues: "These are the two parts of the covenant: grace and faith, promise and

---

14 Shepherd, *Call of Grace*, 15.

obligation."[15] Faith, according to Shepherd and the federal vision, is not of grace. Nor is it included in the divine promise. Faith is a human activity *contrasted* with grace and promise. It is the obligation that the sinner himself must perform. Upon this obligation grace and promise depend, for grace, according to Shepherd and the men of the federal vision, "is not without conditions."[16]

It is not enough for the federal vision, as it is not enough for Rome and Arminianism, that the sinner's righteousness consists of his activity of believing. Obedience to the moral law, the love by which faith works (Gal. 5:6), must also be part of the righteousness of justification. With reference to the obedience God required of Israel in the Old Testament, Shepherd writes, "Obedience is simply faithfulness to the Lord; it is the righteousness of faith (compare Rom. 9:32)."[17] In fact, Romans 9:32 *contrasts* the righteousness of faith with Israel's obedience: "[Israel] sought it [righteousness] not by faith, but as it were by the works of the law." Shepherd *defines* the righteousness of faith as Israel's obedience.

Shepherd repeats the heresy: "The righteousness of faith is the obedience of faith (Rom. 1:5; 16:26)." Lest anyone still fail to grasp that this obedience is the sinner's own works, Shepherd adds, "and is therefore simultaneously covenant privilege *and responsibility*."[18]

A righteousness that depends on and consists of the sinner's activity and works is always in jeopardy. The federal vision teaches, indeed seems to take a special delight in teaching, that the blessing of justification is losable and often lost. One can be justified and saved for a time, only eventually again to fall under condemnation, so as to perish everlastingly.

---

15 Ibid., 63.

16 Ibid.

17 Ibid., 39.

18 Ibid., 76; emphasis added.

> Those who ultimately prove to be reprobate may be in covenant with God. They may enjoy for a season the blessings of the covenant, including the forgiveness of sins [justification], adoption, possession of the kingdom, sanctification, etc., and yet apostatize and fall short of the grace of God...*The apostate doesn't forfeit "apparent blessings" that were never his in reality, but real blessings that were his in covenant with God.*[19]

Thus the federal vision contradicts both the Westminster Confession of Faith, which declares that justified sinners "can never fall from the state of justification,"[20] and the Canons of Dordt, which confess the perseverance of justified and sanctified saints.[21]

Distinctive Heresy

The federal vision's doctrine of justification is distinguished from that of the Roman Catholic Church and of Arminianism, if at all, mainly in two respects. Neither of these mitigates the heresy in the slightest. One distinction is the federal vision's rejection of merit. Although the sinner's righteousness with God consists of his own activity of believing and of his obedience to the law, the federal vision denies that this believing and obedience are meritorious.

This rejection of merit is of no consequence. First, the significant fact remains: the sinner is justified by his own working and works. His righteousness is his own activity (believing) and his own deeds (obedience to the moral law). This is the issue in the controversy of Dordt, the Reformation, and the gospel with the doctrine of justification by "deeds of the law."

---

19 Steve Wilkins, "Covenant, Baptism, and Salvation," in Beisner, *The Auburn Avenue Theology*, 264.

20 Westminster Confession of Faith 11.5, in Schaff, *Creeds of Christendom*, 3:627.

21 Canons of Dordt 5, in ibid., 3:592–95.

Second, the federal vision's rejection of the sinner's merit in justification is an aspect of the federal vision's rejection of *all* merit in salvation, including the merit of the obedient life and atoning death of Jesus Christ. The federal vision's denial of the meritorious character of Christ's life and death is yet another flagrant contradiction of the Reformed confessions. The article in the Belgic Confession that treats of justification through faith in Jesus Christ declares that "faith...embraces Jesus Christ with all his merits."[22] Denial of the meritorious nature of Christ's life and death is an undermining of the mediatorial work of Christ as substitutionary satisfaction to the justice of God.

Third, the rejection of merit, while affirming a conditional justification whose righteousness consists of man's works, is a distinction without a difference. To condition justification on an activity of the sinner and to make the righteousness of justification the sinner's own activity and obedience are to teach the false doctrine that the defenders of grace have always opposed, regardless that the false doctrine no longer flies the odious and impious banner of "merit." Indeed, to strike the banner of "merit" only makes the false doctrine more deceptive, and therefore more dangerous.

A second distinction is that the federal vision's doctrine of justification is an integral aspect of its doctrine of the covenant. *Federal* means "covenant." The federal vision is, and advertises itself as, a development of the doctrine that the new covenant of God in Christ is conditional. That is, at baptism God graciously promises salvation to every child of believers alike, graciously establishes his covenant with every child alike, graciously unites every child alike to Jesus Christ, and begins to bestow on every child alike the blessings of the covenant. However, whether the promise avails to the everlasting salvation of any child, whether the covenant continues with any child, whether any child abides

---

22 Belgic Confession 22, in ibid., 3:408.

in Christ, and whether any child finally inherits eternal life and glory in the new world depend upon conditions the child must perform. These conditions are believing and obeying or, as the men of the federal vision like to say, the covenantal faithfulness of the child.

With reference to members of the church who eventually fall away into everlasting damnation, federal vision theologian John Barach has written:

> God truly brings those people into His covenant, into union with Christ. They are "in Him," to use Jesus' words in John 15. They share in His blessings (think of Hebrews 6). They experience His love, but that covenant relationship is conditional. It calls for repentance and faith and new obedience. God's *choice* was not conditional, but life in the covenant is.[23]

Because the covenant itself is conditional, so also is the great benefit of the covenant—justification—conditional.

In the theology of the federal vision, the doctrine of justification by faith and works is the necessary implication of the conception of a conditional covenant. Shepherd spells this out with candor and clarity in the space of a few pages in his *The Call of Grace*. On page 13, he denies that the covenant of grace with Abraham was (and is) "unconditional." On page 14, he affirms that the Abrahamic covenant was (and is) conditional. On page 15, he draws the conclusion concerning justification in this conditional covenant that Abraham's righteousness consisted of Abraham's performance of the condition of believing. On page 16, Shepherd adds that Abraham's righteousness in justification was also his performance of the condition of obeying.

---

23 John Barach, "Covenant and Election," in Wilkins and Garner, *The Federal Vision*, 37.

Justification by works comes into the conservative Reformed and Presbyterian churches on the wings of the conditional covenant.[24]

Embedding the teaching of justification by works in a doctrine of a conditional covenant in no wise lessens the enormity of the heresy. The Arminian teaching of justification was also grounded in its conception of a conditional covenant. But the covenantal approach of the federal vision does make its doctrine of justification extremely dangerous to the conservative Reformed and Presbyterian churches. Most of them are committed to the doctrine of a conditional covenant, of which justification by works is an integral element.

The federal vision's doctrine of justification is essentially and unmistakably the heresy of Roman Catholicism and of Arminianism. Therefore, as the Reformation and Dordt judged, the teaching of the federal vision concerning justification is the false doctrine of justification by the works of the law condemned by the apostle in Romans and Galatians. In the judgment, if not the very words, of Martin Luther, it is the article of a falling church. In the words of the Holy Spirit, it is "another gospel, which is not another" (Gal. 1:6–7).

24 For the only critique heretofore of the theology of the federal vision, including its doctrine of justification, regarding its fundamental teaching of a conditional covenant of grace, see David J. Engelsma, *The Covenant of God and the Children of Believers: Sovereign Grace in the Covenant* (Jenison, MI: Reformed Free Publishing Association, 2005), and *Federal Vision: Heresy at the Root* (Jenison, MI: Reformed Free Publishing Association, 2012).

Chapter Three

DOCTRINAL BACKGROUND: THE NEW PERSPECTIVE ON PAUL

The current attack on the doctrine of justification by faith alone in the conservative Reformed and Presbyterian churches by the men of the federal vision and their theological allies has a history. As the previous chapters have shown, this history includes the controversy of Dordt with the Arminians and the controversy of the Reformation with Rome. Later chapters will demonstrate that this history goes back to the controversy of the apostle Paul with the Judaizing proponents of justification by the works of the law and to the controversy of Jesus Christ with the Pharisees.

The contemporary falling away from the gospel truth of justification by grace in the Reformed and Presbyterian churches by the federal vision also has an ecclesiastical and a theological milieu. The federal vision flourishes in the present-day ecclesiastical atmosphere of ecumenicity, especially the ecumenicity of the reunion of the Protestant churches with the Roman Catholic Church. Ecumenical relations with Rome require the Protestant sacrifice of justification by faith alone (and with this fundamental truth, all the doctrines of grace). A prominent, powerful agent of the reunion of evangelical Protestantism with the Roman Catholic Church is the organization that calls itself Evangelicals and Catholics Together. I will examine this organization and movement in the next chapter.

New Perspective on the Reformation Gospel

Regarding its theological environment, the federal vision is heavily influenced by the theology of the new perspective on Paul. As the name indicates, the new perspective is a recent theology of the writings of the apostle Paul. The New Testament scholars who teach the new perspective are non-Reformed, higher-critical liberals. E. P. Sanders wrote the book in 1977 that brought the new understanding of Paul's theology to the foreground.[1] James D. G. Dunn coined the phrase new perspective on Paul.

The new perspective charges that Luther and the Reformation misunderstood Paul's teachings especially in Romans and Galatians concerning justification. Basic to this world-shaking charge (which judges the sixteenth-century Reformation of the church a gigantic mistake) is the discovery by these scholars that the Jews whom Jesus Christ and the apostle Paul condemned were not, in fact, guilty of the sin of works-righteousness. The scholars refer to these Jews and their beliefs as "second temple Judaism." The new perspective scholars have studied extra-biblical documents of that day. These documents, the scholars assure us, reveal that the Jews of the first century AD believed that salvation is by grace.

> E. P. Sanders...demonstrated that Judaism has always been first and foremost a religion of grace, with human obedience understood as response to that grace. The covenant had been given by divine initiative, and the law provided the framework for life within the covenant.[2]

---

1 E. P. Sanders, *Paul and Palestinian Judaism* (London: SCM/Philadelphia, PA: Fortress Press, 1977).

2 James D. G. Dunn, *The Theology of Paul the Apostle* (Edinburgh: T&T Clark, 1998), 338.

The conclusion is that Paul could not have been combating the heresy of salvation by meritorious works, particularly justification by one's own good works. Protestantism's portrayal of the teaching of the Pharisees who opposed Jesus and of the beliefs of the Jews who opposed Paul has been a "caricature (and worse)."[3] Luther therefore was mistaken in basing his opposition to the Roman Catholic doctrine of salvation on Paul's teaching. Luther erroneously read his own opposition to the Roman Catholic doctrine of justification by faith and works back into Paul's teaching and then used his own mistaken reading of Paul to oppose Rome.

In the new perspective, Luther is the villain, indeed the schismatic, that Rome has always accused him of being. Luther split the church because of his grave misunderstanding of the doctrine that was at the heart of the dispute. The influence of the new perspective on the federal vision is evident in the sharp criticism of Luther by the men of the federal vision. This criticism is directed specifically at Luther's understanding of justification. Condemning Luther's understanding of justification apart from works and defending the new perspective view of justification apart from works in the book of Galatians (without mentioning the new perspective), Steve Schlissel has written, "Anyone not thoroughly infected with Luther's malady can see that Galatians is not about the Law as God gave it, but the law as misappropriated by and misapplied in Jewish traditions, and especially about Sinai distinctives being foisted upon Gentiles."[4]

By this judgment of Luther's perspective on justification in Romans and Galatians, the new perspective overthrows the entire sixteenth-century Reformation of the church, for the heart of the Reformation, as all the world knows, was Luther's doctrine of justification by faith alone.

---

3 Ibid.

4 Schlissel, "Justification and the Gentiles," in Wilkins and Garner, *The Federal Vision*, 255.

It is not only the Reformation's doctrine of justification on which the new perspective has a new perspective. With the Reformation's doctrine of justification fall away also its entire doctrine of salvation, its doctrine of Christ, and its doctrine of God. Such is the relationship between the doctrine of justification by faith alone and the work of Christ that if justification is not the divine declaration imputing to the believing sinner the merits of Christ, the life and death of Jesus Christ cannot have been Christ's meritorious obedience on behalf of elect humans. Particularly, Christ's death cannot have been penal satisfaction to divine justice in the place of others, God imputing to him the guilt of the others.

Predestination, the source of justification and salvation in Paul, likewise must now be viewed with a radically different perspective from that of Luther and Calvin. Predestination is not an eternal decree appointing some humans to salvation in sovereign grace and appointing the others to damnation in sovereign justice.

The new perspective is radical. Viewing the fundamental truth of justification differently from the Reformation, it views everything differently. The new perspective is a radically different religion from that of the Reformation.

Justification in Paul, according to the new perspective, is God's recognition that someone is a member of the covenant, or New Testament church. Whereas the Reformation thought that justification is a saving act of God, delivering the justified from the guilt of sin and from the eternal damnation to which guilt exposes him and constituting him worthy of eternal life, the new perspective sees justification as having to do primarily, if not exclusively, with church membership. Prominent new perspective theologian James D. G. Dunn writes: "[In justification] the covenant God counts the covenant partner as still in partnership, despite the latter's continued failure. But the covenant partner could hardly fail to be transformed by a living relationship with the life-giving God."[5] As Dunn points out, inasmuch as justification (in new perspective theology) consists of a transformation of life, it is an act of God that "*make[s]* righteous" (as the Roman Catholic Church has always taught) and not exclusively an act that "*reckon[s] as* righteous" (which was the teaching of the Reformation).[6]

Paul's teaching on justification in Romans and Galatians was directed not against a perennial human determination to be righteous by one's own works and thus earn one's salvation, but against the Jewish error of barring Gentiles who did not observe the Jewish ceremonial laws from the new community of the covenant. "It is difficult to sustain the claim that Paul was polemicizing against 'self-achieved righteousness.'"[7] Rather,

> Paul [was] fiercely resisting his own earlier pre-Christian assumption that God's righteousness [which for the new perspective is not forgiveness of sins but membership in the covenant] was only for Israel, and only for Gentiles if they became Jews and took on the distinctive obligations of God's covenant with Israel.[8]

"Deeds of the law" in the Pauline polemic in Romans and Galatians, then, are not all works of obedience to the whole law of God, including the moral law, by which a sinner attempts to accomplish his righteousness with God. "Paul evidently did not associate 'works of the law' with 'good works.'"[9] Rather, "deeds of the law" are works of observing Jewish ceremonial laws, especially circumcision, Old Testament dietary regulations, and keeping the Old Testament Sabbaths. Such deeds were "markers" of covenantal membership by which those Jewish Christians

---

5 Dunn, *Theology of Paul*, 344.
6 Ibid., 344. The emphasis is Dunn's.
7 Ibid., 370.
8 Ibid., 371.
9 Ibid., 365.

whom Paul opposed intended to exclude Gentile believers. "The 'works' he [Paul] had in view were not deeds done to attain righteousness, but commandments of the law practiced in order to maintain covenant righteousness, not least by separation from Gentiles."[10] Dunn specifies "circumcision, food laws, and Sabbath."[11]

The new perspective explains the faith by which one is justified as both the way to become a member of the covenant and the sign that identifies one as a member of the covenant. That God justifies by faith means that he regards one's faith as the evidence, indeed the ground, of his being "in the right," that is, a member of the covenant. In opposition to the Jewish error of demanding obedience to the ceremonial laws as the sign and basis of membership in the new covenant, Paul demands faith. "It is faith and not works which is the sole basis of acceptance in Christ and which therefore should be sufficient basis also for mutual acceptance by those in Christ."[12]

On the view of the new perspective, justification, which the Reformation saw as the gracious act of God, becomes a matter of human work and worth, literally from beginning to end. Justification depends on one's faith, that is, for the new perspective one's activity of believing. The activity of believing is the "basis" of God's recognizing someone as "in the right," that is, in the covenant. The divine act of justifying a person is merely God's recognition of what is true of him because he believes: he is a member of the covenant. It is not an act of God that reckons someone to be what he is not, namely, innocent, and by this very act constituting him what God reckons him to be. The new perspective is not able to penetrate to the heart of Paul's doctrine of justification: God justifies "the ungodly" (Rom. 4:5).

---

10 Ibid., 360.

11 Ibid.

12 Ibid., 359.

Whether the justified person remains in the covenant depends on his continuing to believe, as well as his continuing to obey God, thus showing himself covenantally faithful. At the end of the day, in the final judgment, God's justification of some, recognizing them as still in the covenant and worthy of eternal life by their own lifelong, covenantal faithfulness, will depend on their faith and obedience.

Since justification by faith alone (as taught not by the new perspective but by Paul, and as rightly confessed by the Reformation) is the heart of the gospel of salvation by grace, the perversion of this gospel truth necessarily results in the loss of the certainty of salvation. The new perspective teaches the real possibility of apostasy *in the sense of the falling away of true believers into spiritual death and eternal damnation.*

> *Apostasy* remains a real possibility for the Pauline believer...There is evidently the real possibility that believers may live *kata sarka* [according to the flesh]; and if they do so they will die...Paul envisages the possibility of "destroying" the work of salvation in a person...the loss [for a believing saint] of the prospect of resurrection life.[13]

The influence of the new perspective on the federal vision regarding the falling away of believing, covenantal saints is unmistakable.

The new perspective is murky regarding the relationship of justification to the cross of Christ, and even murkier in its doctrine of the cross. Dunn is content to say that all the biblical descriptions of the cross of Christ, including that of a sacrifice, are merely "metaphors." They do not indicate "literal facts, as though, for example, Christ's death were literally a sacrifice provided by God."[14] Dunn does not know, and evidently

13 Ibid., 497–98.
14 Ibid., 231.

no one can know, what the death of Christ was in literal fact. Apparently, knowledge of what the cross was, in literal fact, is unnecessary for the Christian faith. Therefore, Dunn can make the truly astounding statement that "it is also doubtful whether the death of Christ can be dispensed with in any theology calling itself Christian."[15]

Uncertain itself as to the meaning of the cross, the new perspective is certain that the Reformation's doctrine of the cross is wrong. Rejecting the Reformation's doctrine of justification as the imputation of the merits of Christ's life and death to the sinner by means of faith, the new perspective rejects also the Reformation's teaching that the cross was God's imputation of the guilt of all the elect to Jesus Christ. It rejects the doctrine of substitutionary atonement by the meritorious satisfaction of divine justice on behalf of the elect. Dunn denies that "Paul's doctrine of atonement [was] one of substitution (Jesus died and the sinner went scot-free)."[16]

This is rejection of the doctrine of the cross confessed in article 21 of the Belgic Confession of Faith:

> Jesus Christ...presented himself in our behalf before his Father, to appease his wrath by his full satisfaction, by offering himself on the tree of the cross, and pouring out his precious blood to purge away our sins...feeling the terrible punishment which our sins had merited...and hath suffered all this for the remission of our sins.[17]

In some inexplicable, unknowable way (other than the Reformation's substitutionary atonement), according to the new perspective, Jesus' death destroyed sin for the entire human race. "Christ's death...[was] the death of all, of sinful flesh...The

15 Ibid., 233.
16 Ibid., 386.
17 Belgic Confession 21, in Schaff, *Creeds of Christendom*, 3:406–7.

cancer of sin in the human body is destroyed in the destruction of the cancerous flesh."[18] If this means anything, it means that the crucified Jesus was "cancerous flesh," indeed the "cancerous flesh" of all humans without exception, which is both heretical and blasphemous. On this basis—the unexplained destruction of the cancer of sin in the cancerous flesh of Jesus—God can now accept all humans into the covenant, making available to them the enjoyment of the blessings of the covenant, on the condition of faith (rather than on the condition of observing the Jewish ceremonial regulations).

Upon close examination, the new perspective on the death of Christ and its relationship to justification does not appear new at all. It bears an uncanny resemblance to the old perspective of Arminianism.

Every believer with enough education to read Romans 1–5 and Galatians and having a modicum of the illumination of the Holy Spirit can and will easily determine that this new doctrine of justification is a false, indeed absurd, interpretation of Paul's doctrine. Nevertheless, the new perspective, particularly the new perspective on the doctrine of justification in Paul, has a powerful influence within conservative Reformed and Presbyterian churches. It strongly influences the men of the federal vision. The chief agent of this influence is the Anglican bishop N. T. Wright.

The Wrongs of Wright

Wright is the spokesman of the new perspective to evangelicals, particularly to theologians in conservative Presbyterian and Reformed churches. He has their ears, if not their hearts. I witnessed Wright's popularity with these theologians. A few years ago, Calvin Theological Seminary in Grand Rapids, Michigan, sponsored an all-day seminar taught by Wright. The house was

---

18 Dunn, *Theology of Paul*, 386.

packed with several hundred Reformed and Presbyterian ministers and professors of theology from virtually every seminary and denomination in North America.

Wright took us through the book of Romans. Clearly, though cleverly, winsomely, and ostensibly exegetically, he denied, doctrine by doctrine, the Reformation's understanding of every cardinal teaching in the book of Romans, from total depravity to predestination. Especially the Reformation's doctrine of justification by faith came under Wright's velvet-clothed hammer. At the outset, he explicitly stated that the practical result, indeed the practical purpose, of his and the new perspective's doctrine of justification is to establish "table-fellowship," that is, communion at the sacrament of the Lord's supper, between Protestants and Roman Catholics. At the conclusion of this unrelenting undermining of everything that the men and women of the Reformation fought for, and in hundreds of thousands of instances gave their lives for, several hundred ministers and theologians of conservative Presbyterian and Reformed churches throughout North America gave the heretic a standing, enthusiastic ovation.

The men of the federal vision have Wright as a speaker at their conferences, read his books, quote from his books as authoritative on the great doctrines of the Christian faith, explicitly approve many of his important insights into the theology of Paul, and, often without attribution, make his interpretations of important passages in Paul's writings their own.

One thing they do not do. They do not condemn Wright's new perspective on Paul as heretical; as unlawful public criticism of the Reformation creeds, including the Thirty-Nine Articles of the Church of England (which are binding on Anglican bishop N. T. Wright); and as the undoing of Christ's reformation of his church in the sixteenth century. Reformed and Presbyterian believers should know from Wright's writings (one is tempted to say, "Wright's 'wrongings'") what he teaches about the fundamental gospel truth of justification by faith alone.

The Reformation doctrine that "one can only be saved by the sheer unmerited grace of God, appropriated not by good works but by faith" is "not entirely misleading." Nevertheless, this doctrine "does not do justice to the richness and precision of Paul's doctrine, and indeed distorts it at various points." In fact, with this view of justification "you may actually lose sight of the heart of the Pauline gospel."[19]

Justification in Paul does not refer to "how human beings come into a living and saving relationship with the living and saving God."[20] Reading Romans as "a description of how persons become Christians, and [supposing] that justification is central there...[have] systematically done violence to that text for hundreds of years."[21] Rather, justification for Paul was "God's eschatological definition...of who was, in fact, a member of his people...It wasn't so much about soteriology as about ecclesiology; not so much about salvation as about the church."[22] Justification is "the declaration that they [believers] *have become* a Christian."[23]

Paul's polemic in the book of Galatians against justification by the law was not against the error of "legalism" (as the Reformation thought and explained). Similarly, in the book of Romans "Paul has no thought...of warding off a proto-Pelagianism, of which in any case his contemporaries were not guilty."[24] Rather, his controversy was with the mistaken notion of certain Jewish Christians that circumcision and other observances of the ceremonial law were required if Gentile Christians were to be

19 N. T. Wright, *What Saint Paul Really Said: Was Paul of Tarsus the Real Founder of Christianity?* (Grand Rapids, MI: Eerdmans, 1997), 113. This book comes highly recommended by leading new perspective scholar James D. G. Dunn.

20 Ibid., 116.

21 Ibid., 117.

22 Ibid., 119.

23 Ibid., 125.

24 Ibid., 129.

admitted to the Lord's supper. Justification in Galatians is "'how you can tell who is a member of the covenant family.'" It is "the doctrine which insists that all who share faith in Christ belong at the same table, no matter what their racial differences."[25]

The doctrine of the "imputed righteousness of Christ," which was fundamental to the Reformation's teaching of justification by faith alone and thus to the Reformation, has no basis in the text of scripture. The Reformation's understanding of the phrase is "nonsense."[26] Wright repudiates imputation as the explanation of justification. "It makes no sense whatever to say that the judge imputes…his righteousness to…the defendant. Righteousness is not an object, a substance or a gas which can be passed across the courtroom."[27] Therefore, the righteousness that those who are justified possess is not "*God's own righteousness.*" "God's own righteousness [in the passages in Paul that treat of justification] is his covenant faithfulness."[28]

Righteousness in Paul's writings is "a covenant status," not the pardon of sins and the imputed, meritorious obedience of Jesus Christ. The "righteousness which is of God by faith" (Phil. 3:9) is not a legal standing before God of perfect conformity to the law, which God has worked out in the life and death of Christ and bestows upon the guilty sinner by imputation. It is rather "the status of covenant *membership*."[29]

Faith, then, cannot be the instrument by which the sinner receives the imputed righteousness of God in Christ. Nor is it, according to Wright and the new perspective. "Faith is the badge of covenant membership."[30]

---

25 Ibid., 122.
26 Ibid., 123.
27 Ibid., 98.
28 Ibid., 99.
29 Ibid., 124.
30 Ibid., 125.

In terminology that escapes the mild critics of the federal vision and the new perspective, but that is enormously significant in expressing that one obtains and makes himself worthy of justification (as Wright conceives it and as Paul supposedly teaches it) by his own efforts, Wright describes faith as the "basis" of justification. "Present justification declares, *on the basis of faith*, what future justification will affirm publicly (according to [Romans] 2:14-16 and 8:9-11) *on the basis of the entire life*."[31]

In the theology of Wright, faith is the *basis* of justification. We will see later in this book that scripture never refers to faith as the "basis" of justification. The "basis" of justification is the cross of Jesus Christ. Faith is the means, or instrument, of justification. If faith is the basis of justification, the sinner can and will take credit for his justification, as is the teaching of Roman Catholicism and Arminianism. It is exactly this boasting in self that the apostle is determined to destroy with the doctrine of justification *by* (not *on the basis of*) faith in Romans and Galatians (and in Ephesians, Philippians, and all his other writings). "God forbid that I should glory [that is, boast], save in the cross of our Lord Jesus Christ" (Gal. 6:14).

As is evident from the last quotation of Wright, this proponent of the new perspective also teaches justification by good works: "future justification...on the basis of the entire life." Although justification is not by works of obedience to the *ceremonial* law, it *is* based on works of obedience to the *moral* law. Especially will the public justification at the final judgment be based on good works. This is Wright's explanation of Romans 2:13, a crucial text in the contemporary controversy over justification in the Reformed and Presbyterian churches. The text reads: "For not the hearers of the law are just before God, but the doers of the law shall be justified." Whereas Luther and Calvin explained the text as teaching what would be required

---

31 Ibid., 129; emphasis added.

if sinners were justified by the law, but which cannot possibly be the case because a doer of the law is one who keeps the law perfectly, Wright explains the text as teaching what is actually the case: sinners will be justified by the law. "The first mention of justification in Romans is a mention of justification by *works*—apparently with Paul's approval (2:13)...The right way to understand this, I believe, is to see that Paul is talking about the *final* justification...on the last day."[32] The decisive justification will be by works!

What of the cross of Christ, which is the foundation of justification in Romans and Galatians and apart from which there is no justification? What of the cross of Christ, which is the object of justifying faith? What of the cross of Christ, which the Reformation regarded as the obedience of Christ that becomes ours by means of faith: "relying and resting upon the obedience of Christ crucified alone, which becomes ours when we believe in him"?[33]

In the theology of Wright, as I have already pointed out, the cross of Christ is not the righteousness of God, worked out and worked up for elect sinners by Christ's suffering the punishment demanded by divine justice for their sins, and credited to the account of the guilty sinner through faith. Wright denies imputation. "The 'obedience' of Christ is not designed to amass a treasury of merit which can then be 'reckoned' to the believer, as in some Reformed schemes of thought."[34]

> *It is therefore a straightforward category mistake, however venerable within some Reformed traditions including part of my own, to suppose that Jesus "obeyed the law" and so obtained "righteousness" which could be reckoned to those who believe in him.* To think that way is to concede, after

32 Ibid., 126.

33 Belgic Confession 23, in Schaff, *Creeds of Christendom*, 3:409.

34 N. T. Wright, *Justification: God's Plan & Paul's Vision* (Downers Grove, IL: IVP Academic, 2009), 228.

> all, that "legalism" was true after all—with Jesus as the ultimate legalist.[35]

Regarding the nature of the cross, Wright is noticeably vague. He likes to speak in generalities: "the undoing of Adam's sin"[36]; "the means whereby the reign of sin and death is replaced with the reign of grace and righteousness"[37]; "dealt with sin on the cross."[38]

The question is how? *How* did the cross deal with sin so as to undo it? What was the *nature* of the death of Christ?

As the primary meaning of the crucifixion, Wright proposes "the decisive victory over the 'principalities and powers.'"[39] This is the doctrine of the cross known as "*Christus Victor*" (Christ the Conqueror). In contemporary theology, it is put forward not as an explanation of the cross that expresses the effect of the more basic satisfaction of divine justice by Christ's paying to God the penalty of sin in the stead of others, but as an explanation that replaces the doctrine of substitutionary, penal satisfaction.

The question remains: *How and why* did the cross of Christ conquer the principalities and powers? What was the *nature* of the cross that brought about such a great and glorious victory? Wright and the new perspective will not answer this question. Their refusal is damning.

Wright does make plain that he rejects the Reformation's doctrine of the cross as substitutionary satisfaction of divine justice—God's punishment of Jesus Christ in the stead of Jesus' elect church. This doctrine of the cross, Wright dismisses as a crude theory:

> It is therefore true to Paul to speak of the punishment which all have deserved being enacted, instead, on the

35 Ibid., 232.
36 Wright, *What Saint Paul Really Said*, 48.
37 Ibid., 47.
38 Ibid., 49.
39 Ibid., 47.

> cross. But Paul has here nuanced this view in two ways which distance it from the cruder theories made familiar in some branches of theology. First, he is careful to say that on the cross God punished (not Jesus, but) "sin."... Second, his argument functions within the whole matrix of thought according to which the death of Jesus can be interpreted in this way because he represents Israel and Israel represents humankind as a whole.[40]

As this quotation indicates, Wright's rejection of the doctrine of substitutionary, penal satisfaction goes hand-in-hand with the false doctrine of the cross of Christ as universal atonement (although for Wright the cross was not really atonement): "humankind as a whole." The spokesman of the new perspective to conservative Presbyterian and Reformed churches makes his advocacy of universal atonement unmistakably plain:

> God has deliberately given the Torah [Law] to be the means of concentrating the *sin of humankind* in one place, namely, in his people, Israel—in order that it might then be concentrated yet further, drawn together on to Israel's representative, the Messiah—in order that it might there be dealt with once and for all.[41]

The men of the federal vision also promote the theory of universal atonement. Norman Shepherd is critical of the "Calvinist" who "hedges on the extent of the world" in John 3:16, on account of the doctrine of election. Against this hedging, Shepherd is bold to affirm that "the Reformed evangelist can and must preach to everyone on the basis of John 3:16, 'Christ died to save you.'"[42]

---

40 N. T. Wright, *The Climax of the Covenant: Christ and the Law in Pauline Theology* (Minneapolis, MN: Fortress Press, 1991), 213.

41 Ibid., 196; emphasis added.

42 Shepherd, *Call of Grace*, 84–85.

Justification and the cross are intimately related. To err concerning justification is necessarily to deny the cross.

It is never enough that the heretic denies the truth. He must also rail against it. Wright rails against the Reformation's doctrine of justification by faith alone with its basis in the great, legal exchange in the death of Christ ("He hath made him to be sin for us, who knew no sin; that we might be made the righteousness of God in him" [2 Cor. 5:21]): "a legal transaction, a cold piece of business, almost a trick of thought performed by a God who is logical and correct but hardly one we would want to worship."[43]

Rejection of the truth of justification by faith alone as confessed by the Reformation is, by virtue of this fact, rejection of the Reformation in its entirety. Wright is frank regarding his and the new perspectives's complete abandonment of the Reformation: "The stray lambs [Wright and the other proponents and disciples of the new perspective] are not returning to the Reformation fold…It is time to move on."[44]

Back to Rome

Repudiation of the Reformation necessarily has the men of the new perspective and their followers heading back to the Roman Catholic Church—from the fold of the Great Shepherd to the fold of the pope.

> Paul's doctrine of justification by faith [as explained by Wright] impels the churches, in their current fragmented state, into the ecumenical task. It cannot be right that the very doctrine which declares that all who believe in Jesus belong at the same table (Galatians 2) should be used as a way of saying that some, who define the doctrine of justification differently, belong at a different table. The

43 Wright, *What Saint Paul Really Said*, 110.

44 Wright, *Justification*, 29.

> doctrine of justification, in other words, is not merely a doctrine which Catholic and Protestant might just be able to agree on, as a result of hard ecumenical endeavour. It is itself the ecumenical doctrine, the doctrine that rebukes all our petty and often culture-bound church groupings, and which declares that all who believe in Jesus belong together in the one family...The doctrine of justification is in fact the great *ecumenical* doctrine.[45]

Shepherd expresses the same ecumenical purpose of the theology of the federal vision, particularly its doctrine of a conditional covenant implying justification by works.

> Is there any hope for a common understanding between Roman Catholicism and evangelical Protestantism regarding the way of salvation? May I suggest that there is at least a glimmer of hope if both sides are willing to embrace a covenantal understanding of the way of salvation [as taught by Shepherd and the men of the federal vision].[46]

Contrast with this answer to the question, "Is there any hope for a common understanding between Roman Catholicism and evangelical Protestantism regarding the way of salvation?" the answer that a true son of the Reformation would give: "Absolutely none, so long as the Roman Catholic Church continues to maintain justification by faith and works and thus salvation by man's will and works from beginning (conditional election) to end (perseverance to purgatory by man's will and works and deliverance from purgatory by dint of man's own payment for his sins)."

The new perspective frankly acknowledges its ecumenical attraction to the Roman Catholic Church. "Two factors made

---

45 Wright, *What Saint Paul Really Said*, 158. The emphasis is Wright's.
46 Shepherd, *Call of Grace*, 59.

it impossible for that situation ['the Catholic-Protestant debate,' centering on the doctrine of justification] to persist. One was Vatican II, and in effect the removal of most of the old Catholic-Protestant agenda as no longer at issue."[47]

The ecumenical purpose of the men of the new perspective, as of the federal vision, and indeed the inherent ecumenical tendency of the theology of both these movements, especially regarding reunion of the Protestant churches with the Roman Catholic Church, comports well with the spirit of the age. Which way this gale-force wind is blowing in the churches was recently indicated by the forming of an ecumenical organization that calls itself Evangelicals and Catholics Together. Leading evangelicals and prominent Roman Catholics have banded together in order to cooperate in a common mission. Basic to this union and its common mission is oneness regarding justification—oneness achieved by giving up the Reformation's doctrine of justification for the doctrine of the Roman Catholic Church.

---

47 Dunn, *Theology of Paul*, 338. The other factor is the Nazi effort to exterminate the Jews. This evil caused the Protestant scholars of the new perspective to abandon the old perspective on Paul as anti-Semitic.

Chapter Four

DOCTRINAL (AND ECCLESIASTICAL) BACKGROUND: EVANGELICALS AND CATHOLICS TOGETHER

In recent years leading evangelicals, including J. I. Packer and Charles Colson, have been cooperating with prominent Roman Catholics, including Avery Dulles and Richard John Neuhaus, to unite evangelicals and Roman Catholics. They call their organization and movement for union Evangelicals and Catholics Together (ECT). It is endorsed by such influential Protestants as Os Guinness, Nathan Hatch, Richard Mouw, Mark Noll, and Pat Robertson. The evangelical magazine *Christianity Today* supports the organization. Obviously, it attracts, and will attract, large numbers of evangelical Protestants.

The document that announced and described the union was published in March 1994. The document, which refers to itself as the "ECT Statement," is titled, "Evangelicals and Catholics Together: The Christian Mission in the Third Millennium."[1] The opening line of the statement reads: "We are evangelical Protestants and Roman Catholics who have been led through

1 The "ECT Statement," "Evangelicals and Catholics Together: The Christian Mission in the Third Millennium," is published in Charles Colson and Richard John Neuhaus, eds., *Evangelicals & Catholics Together: Toward a Common Mission* (Dallas, TX: Word, 1995), xv–xxxiii.

prayer, study, and discussion to common convictions about Christian faith and mission."[2]

The stated purpose of this coming together and cooperating of evangelicals and Roman Catholics is threefold: "cobelligerency" in a war against the ongoing depraving of Western culture; cooperation in evangelism; and the uniting of the church. Cobelligerency in the culture war refers to the cooperation of evangelicals and Roman Catholics in resisting abortion; assisted suicide; sexual depravity; and the antichristian education of the state schools, in Western society. Cooperation in evangelism especially aims at defusing the hostility between evangelicals and Roman Catholics in Latin America. It intends to discourage "sheep-stealing" on the part of the two religious communities. Evangelicals and Roman Catholics ought rather to cooperate in evangelizing the unsaved.

The efforts of the organization on behalf of reuniting evangelical churches and the Roman Catholic Church are motivated by sorrow over the divided state of Christianity. ECT is an ecumenical movement. Its spokesmen describe their work of reuniting the churches as "ecumenism of the trenches": "It is the 'ecumenism of the trenches'...which 'Evangelicals and Catholics Together' is intended to cement and encourage."[3] By this they refer to the uniting of the churches not by official consultations and negotiations on the part of the officials of the churches, but by the fellowship and cooperation of the people themselves. Evangelicals involved in the organization defend this ecumenicity by calling attention to the fact that members of evangelical churches have been active in such "grass roots" ecumenicity for a long time. The people have joined with Roman Catholics in Promise Keepers, in the Billy Graham crusades, in non-denominational Bible

2 Ibid., xv.

3 Charles Colson, "The Common Cultural Task: The Culture War from a Protestant Perspective," in ibid., 31.

studies, and in other, similar spiritual and evangelistic groups, organizations, and movements. ECT is simply building on such ecumenical organizations and movements.

One in the Faith

For ECT's threefold "mission," a solid basis is necessary. Obviously, cooperation in evangelism, that is, the preaching of and witnessing to the gospel and reuniting the churches demand that the basis be oneness in the faith. Evangelicals and Roman Catholics cannot witness to Christ together or unite in one church if they are not one in the faith.

But also cobelligerency in the culture war demands oneness in the faith. The men of ECT recognize that the enemy in the culture war is a mighty spiritual power. Only the power of the Christian faith can withstand and overcome it. If evangelicals and Roman Catholics are to be victorious in the culture war, they must oppose the dominating spirit in Western society with the faith of Jesus Christ. If they are to cooperate in fighting the culture war, they must be one in this faith.

In an intriguing account, Charles Colson explains that ECT deliberately rejected the doctrine of a "common grace" of God as the basis of the organization, particularly regarding the alliance of evangelicals and Roman Catholics for contending together in the culture war. A common grace of God is widely accepted among evangelicals as a beneficent, though non-saving, operation of the Spirit of God in both ungodly and godly. This influence of the Spirit is supposed to keep the ungodly from becoming totally depraved and to enable them to perform good works in the sphere of earthly society. Because the ungodly share this gracious operation of the Spirit with the godly, common grace has been proposed and utilized as the basis of union and cooperation of believers and unbelievers on behalf of a good, even godly, culture. That is, common grace has been proposed as the basis for exactly the kind of project that has been launched by ECT.

The theory of a culture-forming common grace uniting evangelical Christians and Roman Catholics in the task of fighting a culture war and establishing a decent, if not godly, culture originated with the nineteenth-century Dutch Reformed theologian Abraham Kuyper. Kuyper gave popular expression to this theory in the book *Lectures on Calvinism*.[4] Kuyper rode the union of Roman Catholics and Reformed evangelicals realized by his theory of culture-renewing common grace into the office of prime minister of the Netherlands. For many years evangelical churchmen and scholars in Europe and North America have looked to common grace as the power to create a godly culture and as the basis of the cooperation of believers and unbelievers as agents of common grace in this task. A recent instance of this appeal to common grace as the power of good, godly, even "Christianized" culture is Richard Mouw's *He Shines in All That's Fair: Culture and Common Grace*.[5] Mouw is one of the prominent evangelicals who have endorsed ECT.

The evangelical members of the organization are well aware of Kuyper and his doctrine of common grace. They are also well aware that, on the basis of common grace, the renowned Dutch theologian and politician pleaded for union of Reformed (evangelical) Christians and Roman Catholics in a cooperative effort very much like that of ECT. Defending ECT's union of evangelicals and Roman Catholics, Colson calls on Kuyper. He quotes Kuyper as affirming what today is described as "cobelligerency in the culture war."

> Our call to cooperation is itself part of our heritage as evangelicals. For example, on the threshold of the

---

4 Abraham Kuyper, *Lectures on Calvinism* (Grand Rapids, MI: Eerdmans, 1953). This is the translation of the Dutch original, *Het Calvinisme: Zes Stone-Lezingen* (Amsterdam: Hoveker & Wormser, n.d.). Kuyper delivered the lectures that are the content of the book in 1898.

5 Richard J. Mouw, *He Shines in All That's Fair: Culture and Common Grace* (Grand Rapids, MI: Eerdmans, 2001).

> twentieth century, the noted Dutch Calvinist, Abraham Kuyper, succinctly described for European Christians the very situation all Christians now face in America: "Now, in this conflict [against liberalism] Rome is not an antagonist, but stands on our side, inasmuch as she recognizes and maintains the Trinity, the Deity of Christ, the Cross as an atoning sacrifice, the scriptures as the Word of God, and the Ten Commandments. Therefore, let me ask if Romish theologians take up the sword to do valiant and skillful battle against the same tendency that we ourselves mean to fight to death, is it not the part of wisdom to accept the valuable help of their elucidation?"...In his own struggle against modernism in its manifestations at that time, Kuyper forged a coalition of fellow Calvinists and Dutch Roman Catholics led by Hermanus Schaepman. Together, they helped bring moral and social reform to the Netherlands.[6]

Nevertheless, Colson and his evangelical cohorts deliberately rejected common grace as the basis for the union and cooperation of ECT. The reason was not that they were opposed to the doctrine of common grace. Rather, they judged that common grace is an inadequate basis for such a weighty work as the ECT has set itself to accomplish. Fighting the demonic powers now unleashed in North America and then forming Western culture after a godly pattern are a monumental task. For such a titanic struggle and heavy labor, common grace is far too frail and shallow a basis and far too feeble a power.

Explaining why Christians cannot "simply forge political alliances with Catholics...on the basis of common grace," Colson writes:

---

6 Colson, "The Common Cultural Task," in Colson and Neuhaus, *Evangelicals & Catholics Together*, 38–39.

> While cooperation on the basis of common grace might suffice for merely political alliances among different religious communions, it can not suffice in reestablishing Christian influence in our increasingly secular and even increasingly hostile culture. Indeed, the urgent task before all Christians today far transcends victories in political campaigns. Our task is nothing less than to articulate convincingly the biblical worldview to a culture awash in nihilism and hedonism.[7]

Surely this decision was wise. One does not fight Goliath with Saul's armor. In Colson's words, "Common grace does not hold soldiers fast in their trenches during battle."[8] ECT grounded itself therefore, regarding its culture war as well as the other two aspects of its mission, in the Christian faith: "The mission that we embrace together is the necessary consequence of the faith that we affirm together."[9]

This brief, matter-of-fact declaration is astounding. Evangelical Protestants and Roman Catholics together confess one and the same Christian faith! They are therefore one in Jesus Christ. The "ECT Statement" goes on to assert: "Evangelicals and Catholics are brothers and sisters in Christ."[10] Apparently, the Roman Catholic theologians in ECT contradict the creed of their church, the Canons and Decrees of the Council of Trent, which anathematizes the evangelical confession of the faith and all those who confess it. The evangelical theologians in ECT certainly take issue with all the Reformation confessions, which condemn the Roman confession as heresy. Indeed, by this declaration the evangelical theologians in ECT judge the Reformation to have been not merely an unfortunate mistake, but the

7 Ibid., 37.
8 Ibid.
9 "ECT Statement," in ibid., xvii.
10 Ibid., xviii.

grievous sin of schism. If Roman Catholics affirm the Christian faith together with evangelical Protestantism, if Roman Catholics and evangelical Protestants are brothers and sisters in the one family of God, the Reformation sinfully divided the body of Christ, unless Rome has changed, which no one claims, least of all the notable and astute Roman Catholic theologians in ECT.

Why the Roman Catholic and evangelical theologians in ECT could make the astounding declaration that they are one in the faith becomes immediately evident in the "ECT Statement." Following the declaration of oneness in the faith is a section headed "We Affirm Together." This section mentions and briefly describes the fundamental doctrines of the faith that evangelicals and Roman Catholics affirm together. The first is the doctrine that Jesus is lord and savior. This affirmation is characteristically crafty deception on the part of the Roman Catholic theologians and sheer duplicity on the part of the evangelicals. Rome effectively nullifies the lordship of Jesus by its blasphemous attribution to its pope of sovereign lordship over heaven, hell, and purgatory and over the church and each member, and the evangelicals know this full well. Nor does Rome regard Jesus as the only savior. Mary, the saints, and the free will of every sinner are also saviors for Rome, and this too is well known by the evangelicals in ECT.

One Regarding Justification

But it is the common affirmation of the second fundamental doctrine that makes everything plain. The second fundamental doctrine affirmed together by the evangelicals and the Roman Catholics in their organization is justification. Justification was the doctrine at the very heart of the sixteenth-century Reformation of the church. The gospel truth of justification was the evangel, or good news of grace, that the Reformation proclaimed for the comfort of guilty sinners and for the glory of the God of grace in Jesus Christ. The truth of justification warranted, indeed demanded, the Reformation. The Reformation charged that it was Rome's perversion of the biblical truth of justification that exposed her as a false church. Rome on her part cursed the Reformation, its gospel, its churches, and its children on account of the Reformation's doctrine of justification.

If evangelical Protestants and Roman Catholics are to affirm the Christian faith together, they must, above all, agree in their confession of justification. The men of ECT do agree in their doctrine of justification: "We affirm together that we are justified by grace through faith because of Christ."[11]

The doctrine of justification in which the evangelicals and the Roman Catholics are agreed is the Roman Catholic doctrine, for the affirmation of justification omits *only*, the one word that distinguishes the Reformation's confession of justification from the Roman Catholic confession. The affirmation deliberately does not state, "We affirm together that we are justified...through faith *only* and thus by grace *only* because of Christ *only*." Richard John Neuhaus freely acknowledges that the omission of *only* was deliberate: "The *solas* [plural in Latin of *only*] are conspicuous by their absence [from ECT's affirmation concerning justification], and it is not by accident that they are absent."[12]

The issue dividing the Reformation from Rome, distinguishing the genuine evangelicalism of the Reformation from the Roman Catholic teaching of salvation by works, and preserving the gospel of grace from the perversion of it is bound up with and expressed by *only* in the confession, "justified by faith *only*." Rome's confession has always been, "justified by faith *and by the good works of the sinner*." As if to emphasize that the omission of *only* in the affirmation of justification betokens the Roman

---

11 Ibid.

12 Richard John Neuhaus, "The Catholic Difference," in Colson and Neuhaus, *Evangelicals & Catholics Together*, 200.

Catholic doctrine, the offending statement is immediately followed by "living faith is active in love."[13] What is suggested and intended is that justification is by faith and by the loving deeds that proceed from faith.

The truly evangelical confession of the Reformation has always been "justified by faith *only*, that is, apart from all works of the sinner, including the works of love that proceed from true faith." Faith works by love, but in the grand act of justification the loving deeds of faith are excluded. In the divine act of justification, only the work of Christ in the place of and on behalf of the elect, believing sinner is in view. Omitting *only* from their affirmation of justification, the evangelicals in ECT betrayed the Reformation, perverted the gospel of God, and made themselves responsible for the destruction of all those evangelicals who will embrace the Roman Catholic heresy of justification and eventually return to Rome because of ECT's treacherous affirmation of justification.

That the ECT's joint affirmation on justification was, in fact, no expression of real agreement between those confessing the Reformation's doctrine of justification and the Roman Catholics, and that the evangelicals who signed the "ECT Statement" knew it, was publicly acknowledged by those evangelicals a few years after the appearance of the "ECT Statement." In their magazine *Christianity Today*, the evangelicals defended ECT's affirmation of justification by faith, specifically the omission of *only*. The evangelical defense frankly admitted that there is no agreement between the evangelical and Roman Catholic participants in ECT on "the language of justification as it relates to *imputed…righteousness*."[14] But imputation is basic to biblical justification. Justification *is* imputation.

---

13 "ECT Statement," in ibid., xviii.

14 "ECT: The Gift of Salvation," *Christianity Today* 41, no. 14 (December 8, 1997): 38; emphasis added.

If evangelicals and Roman Catholics do not agree on imputation, they do not agree on justification. To affirm oneness on the doctrine, in spite of this fundamental disagreement, is a lie at best. At worst, it is the evangelical capitulation to the Roman Catholic doctrine of justification as *infusion*.

In fact, the basis of ECT is oneness in Roman Catholic faith, especially Roman Catholic faith concerning justification.

Both the evangelicals and the Roman Catholics in ECT are fully aware not only of the importance of justification, but also of the evangelicals' compromise of the Reformation's doctrine in ECT's affirmation of justification. Both parties to the infamy therefore try to excuse, soften, or justify it. Neuhaus, who as a convert to Rome from Lutheranism knows better, attempts to disparage the Reformation's doctrine of justification by faith alone as merely the theological peculiarity of a few "professional theologians," especially Martin Luther.

> The arguments surrounding the *sola fide* [by faith only] formula are the preserve of a relatively small number of professional theologians, mainly Lutheran and Calvinist, in North America and Western Europe. That does not mean the arguments are wrong; it does mean that they are not, and cannot be, at the center of the global proclamation of the gospel and the Christian mission in the third millennium...Luther's motif of righteousness before God, with its attendant insistence upon justification by faith alone—a motif and insistence that is historically much more Lutheran than Calvinist, although today it is pressed upon evangelicals in the name of Calvinist orthodoxy—has been embraced by many Christians as the most powerful construal of the gospel and the most faithful to Paul's understanding of salvation. But to declare it to be the article by which the Church stands or falls in a manner that excludes other

> ways of saying the gospel is to turn it into a sectarian doctrine.[15]

Every such attempt to minimize the importance of justification shatters on the book of Romans. That fullest revelation of the gospel in the compass of one book has justification as its main theme, as any reader discovers for himself. In addition, the book of Galatians is devoted to the defense of the gospel truth of justification by faith, apart from deeds of the law, that is, apart from all good works. Such is the fundamental importance of justification for the gospel, not merely to a few professional theologians, according to Galatians, that to corrupt the truth of justification is to pervert the gospel (1:7) and to concoct "another gospel, which is not another" (1:6–7). To believe and act on the corruption of the truth of justification, as they do who embrace the teaching of justification by faith and by good works, is to be "fallen from grace" (5:4).

Neuhaus' shrewd effort to play Luther off against Calvin in the matter of the confession of justification by faith alone is shown to be utterly false simply by reading Calvin on justification in his *Institutes* and by referencing the Reformed confessions. There was no difference whatever between the two reformers regarding either the meaning or the importance of the doctrine of justification by faith alone. It is noteworthy that the men of the federal vision also try to drive a wedge between Luther and Calvin regarding justification. Their efforts are as false, foolish, and futile as Neuhaus'.

The learned, jesuitical Avery Dulles, S. J., tries a different tactic. He disarms alarmed evangelicals by putting "to rest any suspicions that Catholics consider it possible to be justified by good works without grace and faith."[16] No knowledgeable Prot-

15 Neuhaus, "The Catholic Difference," in Colson and Neuhaus, *Evangelicals & Catholics Together*, 204, 207.

16 Avery Dulles, S. J., "The Unity for Which We Hope," in ibid., 138.

estant ever entertained these suspicions. Besides, opposition to the Roman Catholic doctrine of justification does not now depend, and never has depended, upon ungrounded "suspicions." The genuine Protestant knows with certainty, from Rome's official creeds, that Rome considers it not only possible, but also necessary, that sinners are justified by grace and faith *plus their own good works*. The addition of good works is the denial of justification by faith and by grace. The Reformation's objection was not to a teaching of justification by works "without grace and faith," but to Rome's refusal to teach that justification is by grace and faith *without works*.

If Neuhaus' defense of the "ECT Statement" on justification is puerile and Dulles' defense is subtle, J. I. Packer's defense is discouraging and deplorable. This erstwhile champion of the Reformation and its gospel of the sovereign grace and incomparable glory of God admits that the ECT affirmation of justification is deliberate evangelical compromise of the gospel truth of justification in the interests of the evangelicals' union with Roman Catholics in ECT. "Neither evangelicals nor Roman Catholics can stipulate that things they believe, which the other side does not believe, be made foundational to partnership at this point; so ECT *lets go Protestant precision on the doctrine of justification*."[17]

Letting go "Protestant precision" on the doctrine of justification is to approve the precise Roman Catholic doctrine of justification. Letting go "Protestant precision" on the doctrine of justification is precisely to let go the gospel, grace, Christ, and God—is to let them go entirely (Gal. 1:6–7; 5:1–4).

Compromise of God's truth for the sake of man's ecumenicity is bad enough. Still worse is Packer's defense of the compromise. He has recourse to sheer doctrinal indifference.

---

17 J. I. Packer, "Crosscurrents among Evangelicals," in ibid., 167; emphasis added.

Packer confronts the criticism of ECT's compromise statement on justification, that the Reformation's doctrine of justification by faith alone and the Roman Catholic doctrine of justification by faith and works "express two different gospels, one of which is not a true gospel." He responds that "evangelism seeks to lead people into salvation, and what brings them salvation is not any theory about faith and justification, but trusting Jesus himself as Lord, Master, and divine Savior."[18]

The wording of Packer's response is glaringly deficient in two respects. First, justification by faith alone is not a Protestant "theory," proposed for scholarly debate against the equally defensible Roman Catholic "theory" of justification by faith and works. It is inspired divine truth. It is fundamental gospel truth. "Therefore we conclude that a man is justified by faith without the deeds of the law" (Rom. 3:28).

Second, "what brings [sinners] salvation" is not simply "trusting Jesus himself." What brings sinners salvation is trusting Jesus himself *only*. To trust in Jesus *and Mary*, or in Jesus *and some saint*, or in Jesus *and one's good works*, or in Jesus *and an indulgence* is to be condemned and, if there is no repentance, eternally damned. "There is…one mediator between God and men, the man Christ Jesus" (1 Tim. 2:5).

Exactly because the Spirit of Christ uses the doctrine of justification by faith alone to cause elect sinners to trust alone in Jesus Christ for forgiveness and eternal life, the Reformation's doctrine of justification is indeed "what brings [sinners] salvation." Because the Roman Catholic doctrine of justification causes sinners to trust for righteousness and eternal life in Mary, the saints, the sinners' own works, indulgences, and what not more besides, as in Paul's day it caused the Galatians to trust in circumcision, the Roman Catholic doctrine of justification consigns all those who believe and practice it to perdition.

18 Ibid., 168.

Packer's defense of the evangelicals' compromise, indeed surrender, of the truth of justification implies the unimportance of any and every doctrine of the Christian faith. As he counseled a compromise statement concerning the deity of Jesus and therefore concerning the Trinity, in the interests of accord with Arius and his party, Athanasius might have said, "What brings our people salvation is not any theory about the full Godhead of Jesus, or any theory about three persons in one divine being, but trusting Jesus himself as lord, master, and divine savior." This is not what Athanasius counseled. On the contrary! Therefore, the creed that is named after him reads radically differently concerning the importance of believing and confessing right doctrine than does Packer's defense of the "ECT Statement" on justification.

> Whosoever will be saved: before all things it is necessary that he hold the Catholic Faith: Which Faith except every one do keep whole and undefiled: without doubt he shall perish everlastingly. And the Catholic Faith is this: That we worship one God in Trinity, and Trinity in Unity...Furthermore it is necessary to everlasting salvation: that he also believe rightly [faithfully] the Incarnation of our Lord Jesus Christ...This is the Catholic Faith: which except a man believe faithfully [truly and firmly], he can not be saved.[19]

Ecumenical Evil

Even though our interest in ECT in this chapter concerns its affirmation of justification, several related truths should be noted, if only briefly. First, at this stage of church history all efforts by genuine evangelicals, that is, those who embrace and confess the gospel of grace recovered by the Reformation, on

19 Athanasian Creed, in Schaff, *Creeds of Christendom*, 2:66–70.

behalf of ecumenical relations with either the Roman Catholic Church or Roman Catholics are forbidden. Committed as it is to the heresy of justification by faith and works, to the denial of the one sacrifice of Christ by its doctrine of the mass, to its worship of and trust in Mary, to the abomination of transubstantiation issuing in the worship of a piece of bread, and to a host of other unbiblical teachings and practices (to say nothing of its murder of multitudes of saints for their witness to Jesus Christ, for which the Roman Catholic Church has never repented), the Roman Catholic Church must be condemned, rather than recognized as a worthy partner in the spiritual work of manifesting the unity of Christ's church.

By virtue of being a member in the Roman Catholic Church, every Roman Catholic is responsible for all of Rome's teachings and practices. Specifically, he is guilty of continual idolatry and denial of the one sacrifice of Christ by his participation in the required practice of the mass; of continual denial of the sole mediatorship of Jesus Christ by his prayers to Mary and the saints; and of continual rejection of the truth of justification by faith alone by his participation in the sacrament of penance (involving as it does his works of satisfaction). The evangelical may not cooperate with Roman Catholics in any activity *on the basis of a common Christian faith*, but must rather call them to repentance and to faith alone in Jesus Christ.

Indeed, a Reformed evangelical would be reluctant to cooperate with Roman Catholics in fighting for a decent culture on any basis whatever, including a common humanity under the providence of God. A decent culture is certainly one in which boys are protected from sexual molestation by perverts. The current scandal of the sexual abuse of boys by Roman Catholic priests and especially the unconscionable protection of the priestly perverts by the Roman Catholic hierarchy, reaching to the pope himself (whose concern is exclusively the standing and power of the Roman Catholic Church in the world), does not encourage Reformed Christians to suppose that Roman Catholics have any real interest in the morality of society. Calling to mind that this widespread, appalling buggery is the direct result of, indeed the divine judgment on, Rome's insistence on priestly celibacy, contrary to both nature's and scripture's demand for marriage and in disregard of the Reformation's solemn warning against the celibacy of the clergy, Reformed Christians conclude that they must make their own evangelical protest against the lawlessness of contemporary, Western culture.

It is ironic that the public press reports that the leading figure in ECT—Richard John Neuhaus—was also the most outspoken defender of the prominent Roman Catholic clergyman Marcial Maciel. The *Los Angeles Times* describes Maciel as a "lifelong sexual predator who molested numerous seminarians and fathered at least one child." Pope John Paul II shielded Maciel for years. When finally the evidence against the pervert and fornicator became public and incontrovertible, the current pope—Benedict XVI—ordered Maciel to retire and "spend the rest of his days in prayer and penance," although he remained a priest.

The *Times* observes:

> What's interesting about all of this is that a list of Maciel's most vociferous defenders reads like a who's who of the conservative Catholic intellectuals...Among Maciel's defenders [has] been the late Father Richard John Neuhaus...When the Vatican ordered Maciel into retirement, Neuhaus—who earlier had written that he knew the man's innocence as "a moral certainty"—told the New York Times: "It wouldn't be the first time that an innocent and indeed holy person was unfairly treated by church authority."[20]

20 Tim Rutton, "A troubling order for the Catholic Church," the *Los Angeles Times*, Wednesday, March 31, 2010.

Second, leaving aside the unlawfulness of evangelical ecumenicity with Rome and Roman Catholics, the method of ecumenicity employed by the men of ECT is wrong. They try to accomplish unity by playing with words, crafting misleading statements, and adopting deceptive documents that paper over real, substantial, and abiding divisions. Their ecumenical method is not that of frankly facing up to doctrinal differences and then honestly debating these issues in order, under the blessing of the Spirit of Christ, to arrive at oneness consisting of real agreement in the truth of the word of God.

In this respect, ECT resembles the notable ecumenical conference between Protestants and Roman Catholics at Regensburg in 1541. Just as the Regensburg conference labored for church union under the pressure of the emperor, who needed that union for his earthly, political ends, so also ECT works for union under the pressure of the admittedly grave, threatening developments in the increasingly antichristian culture of the West. Packer acknowledges this pressure, indeed applies it to those who dissent from ECT: "The present needs of both Church and community in the Western world…cry out for an alliance of all who love the Bible and its Christ to stand together against the slide into secularism and paganism that is so much a mark of current culture."[21] Invariably, the result is the sacrifice of the truth of the gospel.

The evangelical heavyweights at the Regensburg conference, Philip Melanchthon and Martin Bucer, sold out the Reformation by their compromises with Roman Catholic heresies. They agreed to a statement on justification that failed to affirm justification by faith alone; approved a declaration stating that the church is the authoritative interpreter of scripture; produced a draft article that taught transubstantiation; and acknowledged

---

21 Packer, "Crosscurrents among Evangelicals," in Colson and Neuhaus, *Evangelicals & Catholics Together*, 171.

that the adoration of Christ in the bread of the Lord's supper need not be rejected as a matter of principle. Only the pope's uncompromising insistence on still more Protestant concessions and the adamant opposition of Luther, who was not invited to the conference, wrecked the ecumenical enterprise and saved the Reformation.

Regensburg is a warning to the true church in all ages that false, if well-intentioned, ecumenicity is as great a danger to the gospel and therefore to the church as is heresy. The truth, which has been won by dint of struggle, sacrifice, suffering, and blood on the battlefield, over the course of centuries, can be lost at the conference table by means of friendly, smiling, peace-loving ecclesiastical diplomats, in one week.

No genuine church unity will ever be realized by ignoring, disparaging, or manipulating sound doctrine. This is not the way of the Spirit of the truth, and the Spirit of the oneness and catholicity of the church is the Spirit of the truth.[22]

The third truth relating to the ecumenicity of ECT and bearing more directly on ECT's common affirmation concerning justification is the real oneness of many evangelicals with the Roman Catholic Church in a doctrine that not only implies agreement with Rome on justification but also requires reunion with the Roman Catholic Church. This is the doctrine of the free will of sinners. According to this doctrine, God's offered salvation depends finally on the decision of the sinner, so that salvation is not the gift and work of sovereign grace, but the

---

22 On the Diet of Regensburg, also known as the Colloquy of Ratisbon, see Philip Schaff, *History of the Christian Church*, vol. 7: *Modern Christianity: The Swiss Reformation* (New York: Charles Scribner's Sons, 1892), 381–83; David F. Wright, "Martin Bucer 1491–1551: Ecumenical Theologian," in *Common Places of Martin Bucer*, trans. and ed. David F. Wright (Appleford, Abingdon, Berkshire, England: Sutton Courtenay Press, 1972), 42–46; and David J. Engelsma, "Martin Bucer: 'Fanatic of Unity,'" *Mid-America Journal of Theology* 4, no. 1 (Spring, 1988): 40–42.

cooperation of God and the sinner. Indeed, the sinner saves himself, God helping him.

The doctrine of free will is fundamental to the Roman Catholic teaching of justification by faith and works, indeed to the whole of Roman Catholic theology. Free will therefore is basic to the Roman Catholic Church. Much of contemporary "evangelical" Protestantism (in distinction from the truly evangelical Protestantism of the Reformation) likewise embraces and preaches free will and its decisive role in salvation. Agreeing with Rome in this fundamental doctrine, evangelicals are, in fact, one with Rome regarding the gospel, including justification. If they are one with Rome regarding the gospel, there is no reason they should not also unite with Rome, not only in fighting the culture war, but also by membership in the Roman Catholic Church.

Neuhaus makes this very observation. He defends ECT's affirmation of justification against the criticism by some evangelicals that the affirmation fails to confess the Reformation's "only": justification by faith *only*. He reminds these evangelicals that "the great majority of evangelicals in America and the world do not believe" what the Reformation taught about sovereign grace, as expressed in the phrase "justification by faith alone." On the contrary, "Wesleyan, Arminian, Holiness, Pentecostal, and other evangelical traditions are much closer to the Catholic understanding" of justification in particular and of the gospel in general.[23]

To his list of churches that today are closer to the Roman Catholic understanding of justification than they are to the Reformation's doctrine, inasmuch as they deny the sovereignty of grace, Neuhaus could have added all those Reformed and Presbyterian churches that teach a (saving) grace of God in Christ

23 Neuhaus, "The Catholic Difference," in Colson and Neuhaus, *Evangelicals & Catholics Together*, 199.

toward all who hear the gospel, which nevertheless fails to save many of them. Basic to every form of the attack on justification by faith alone, from the open denial of the doctrine by the Roman Catholic Church to the subtle compromise of ECT, is the rejection of sovereign, particular grace.

The federal vision attacks the doctrine of justification from within the conservative Reformed and Presbyterian churches. The new perspective has a radically different perspective on the doctrine of justification from that of the Reformation. ECT fatally compromises the doctrine of justification in the interests of ecumenicity.

These contemporary threats to the doctrine of justification call for a fresh explanation and renewed defense of the gospel truth of justification by faith alone, not only on behalf of Reformed and Presbyterian believers and their children, but also on behalf of all Protestants.

Chapter Five

THE REFORMED CONFESSIONS ON JUSTIFICATION: AN INTRODUCTION

I begin this explanation and defense of the gospel truth of justification with a brief examination of the Reformed confessions regarding the doctrine.

The reason for beginning with the confessions is not a misapprehension that the confessions are equally authoritative regarding sound doctrine with the inspired scriptures. As a Reformed officebearer, I have affirmed that I receive the sixty-six books of the Old and New Testaments "as holy and canonical, for the regulation, foundation, and confirmation of our faith."[1] These inspired and therefore holy books are the only "infallible rule" of right doctrine and the godly life that proceeds from orthodoxy. "Neither may we compare any writings of men, though ever so holy, with those divine Scriptures."[2]

Holy scripture is the source of the doctrine of justification by faith, as of the godly life of thankful obedience to the law of God that is the fruit of the doctrine of justification. Holy scripture must be the ultimate rule that establishes justification by faith alone as the truth in the present controversy and that judges the teaching of justification by works as the lie.

1 Belgic Confession 5, in Schaff, *Creeds of Christendom*, 3:386.
2 Belgic Confession 7, in ibid., 3:388.

Nevertheless, there are good reasons for settling the controversy in the Reformed and Presbyterian churches over justification by appealing first to the Reformed confessions.

One reason is that for some two thousand years the Spirit of truth has guided the Christian church into a clear understanding of most of the cardinal doctrines of scripture. The ecumenical and Reformation confessions are the outstanding products of this divine guidance. The Reformed confessions, which address the truth of justification specifically and at length, have been a blessing to Reformed churches and Christians for nearly half a millennium. Especially in circumstances of controversy over justification, the Reformed churches must avail themselves of the Spirit's work in the churches in the past.

It is no credit to the men of the federal vision and of the new perspective or to the evangelicals involved in Evangelicals and Catholics Together that they simply ignore the confessional statements concerning justification. At the very least, they thus disparage the Spirit's work on behalf of the truth in the history of the church and despise the wisdom of the church of the past.

The sin of the men of the federal vision regarding the Reformed confessions is still greater. These men are almost without exception officebearers—ministers of the gospel, professors of theology, and ruling elders—in Reformed and Presbyterian churches. In these churches the Reformed confessions—the three forms of unity (Belgic Confession of Faith, Heidelberg Catechism, and Canons of Dordt) or the Westminster standards (Westminster Confession of Faith, Larger Catechism, and Shorter Catechism)—have binding authority, particularly regarding the teaching and the oversight of the teaching by the officebearers. This is another reason for beginning this defense of justification by faith alone with an examination of the Reformed confessions.

Bound to the Confessions

Reformed churches have adopted the confessions as the official, authoritative expression of the churches' belief concerning the teachings of scripture. To the confessions the churches bind their officebearers by a solemn promise, or vow. According to this vow, Reformed officebearers declare that they believe that all the doctrines taught in the confessions are in harmony with scripture; that their preaching and teaching will conform to the confessions; that they will not teach contrary to the confessions, whether publicly or privately; that they reject all teachings that contradict the confessions; and that they will defend the doctrines of the confessions against all errors that militate against the confessions.

The instrument by which Reformed churches in the tradition of the Synod of Dordt bind their officebearers to the three forms of unity is the Formula of Subscription. This formula, which derives from the Synod of Dordt, reads as follows.

> We, the undersigned, professors of the...Reformed Churches, ministers of the gospel, elders and deacons of the...Reformed congregation of..., of Classis...do hereby sincerely and in good conscience before the Lord declare by this, our subscription, that we heartily believe and are persuaded that all the articles and points of doctrine contained in the Confession and Catechism of the Reformed Churches, together with the explanation of some points of the aforesaid doctrine made by the National Synod of Dordrecht, 1618–'19, do fully agree with the Word of God.
>
> We promise therefore diligently to teach and faithfully to defend the aforesaid doctrine, without either directly or indirectly contradicting the same, by our public preaching or writing.

> We declare, moreover, that we not only reject all errors that militate against this doctrine, and particularly those which were condemned by the above mentioned synod, but that we are disposed to refute and contradict these, and to exert ourselves in keeping the church free from such errors. And if hereafter any difficulties or different sentiments respecting the aforesaid doctrines should arise in our minds, we promise that we will neither publicly nor privately propose, teach, or defend the same, either by preaching or writing, until we have first revealed such sentiments to the consistory, classis, and synod, that the same may be there examined, being ready always cheerfully to submit to the judgment of the consistory, classis, and synod, under the penalty in case of refusal to be, by that very fact, suspended from our office.
>
> And further, if at any time the consistory, classis, or synod, upon sufficient grounds of suspicion and to preserve the uniformity and purity of doctrine, may deem it proper to require of us a further explanation of our sentiments respecting any particular article of the Confession of Faith, the Catechism, or the explanation of the national synod, we do hereby promise to be always willing and ready to comply with such requisition, under the penalty above mentioned, reserving for ourselves, however, the right of an appeal, whenever we shall believe ourselves aggrieved by the sentence of the consistory, the classis, or the synod, and until a decision is made upon such an appeal, we will acquiesce in the determination and judgment already passed.[3]

Presbyterianism has a similar document binding officebearers in a Presbyterian church to the Westminster standards.

3 Formula of Subscription, in *Confessions and Church Order*, 326.

The men of the federal vision, almost all of whom belong to confessional Reformed or Presbyterian churches, may not dissent from the confessional doctrine of justification by faith alone, with its ground in the meritorious obedience of Jesus Christ; may not even privately question the confessional doctrine; may not subtly cast doubt on the confessional doctrine; indeed, may not fail to defend the doctrine of justification by faith alone when it is attacked. They are under vow to God not to do so. For them to deny the confessional doctrine of justification by faith alone, apart from all the good works of the justified sinner—*as they do*—is wickedly to break their vow. Thus they show themselves faithless men.

Although N. T. Wright, a proponent of the new perspective, and J. I. Packer, participant in Evangelicals and Catholics Together, are officebearers in the Anglican Church, they too are bound by a Reformed confession, the Thirty-Nine Articles of the Church of England. Regardless that this confession has become virtually a dead letter in the apostate Anglican Church, it remains the official and therefore binding confession of that church. It is binding upon Bishop Wright and upon Dr. Packer. The Thirty-Nine Articles both confess justification by faith alone and condemn the Roman Catholic teachings that oppose justification by faith alone.[4] Wright may not reject the Reformation doctrine of justification by faith alone as the mistaken perspective of Martin Luther. Packer may not compromise the doctrine for the sake of ecumenicity with Rome. Their own church's confession binds these two men.

Reformed churches thus bind their officebearers to the confessions because the churches are directed by the Spirit of truth to esteem the confessions as right and sound expressions of the main teachings of holy scripture. The confessions are orthodox.

4 See the Thirty-Nine Articles of the Church of England 10–14, in Schaff, *Creeds of Christendom*, 3:493–95.

As faithful systematizations and summaries of holy scripture, the confessions are the standard of orthodoxy for Reformed churches. By binding their officebearers to the confessions, Reformed churches purpose a perfectly orthodox confession of the truth by the churches, whether in the congregations, in the seminary, or in evangelism and missions. Reformed churches, like the prophets, the apostles, and Jesus Christ, are zealous for doctrinal purity.

Unity and Peace

By this doctrinal purity throughout the church federation, Reformed churches ardently desire the unity and peace of the congregations and their members. If every minister and professor of theology were at liberty to teach whatever he judges to be the truth, especially regarding the cardinal doctrines of the gospel (among which is justification), the churches would soon be racked by strife and division.

The precious unity of the one body of Christ is founded on and rooted in oneness of doctrine. The "unity of the Spirit" in the church is the unity of "one faith" (Eph. 4:3–5). Binding officebearers to the confessions safeguards and promotes unity.

Already the faithless violation by the men of the federal vision of their vow to uphold the confessions, particularly the confessional (not merely Lutheran or Reformation) doctrine of justification by faith alone, has caused schism in the Reformed and Presbyterian churches where these men have their membership and exercise their offices.[5]

---

5 In proof of these schisms, for which the heretics are responsible, see the books mentioned in chapter 2. In addition, see John W. Robbins, *A Companion to the Current Justification Controversy* (Unicoi, TN: Trinity Foundation, 2003) and Paul M. Elliott, *A Denomination in Denial: An Evaluation of the Report of the Committee to Study the Doctrine of Justification of the Orthodox Presbyterian Church* (Westminster, MD: Teaching the Word, 2006).

Yet another reason for beginning an examination of the doctrine of justification with a study of the Reformed confessions, especially in controversy, is that the confessions enable the members of the congregations to judge the teachings of their officebearers. Every false teacher claims, loudly, even indignantly, to be teaching the truth. Invariably, he couches his false doctrine in careful, clever, deceptive, and biblical language. Like the serpent in the garden of Eden, he is subtle. As the Dutch proverb puts it, in the heretic Satan does not come noisily in wooden shoes, but stealthily in slippers. As scripture puts it, Satan's ministers transform themselves as "ministers of righteousness," just as "Satan himself is transformed into an angel of light" (2 Cor. 11:14–15). Usually, the heretic manifests himself as a jovial, friendly, loving, sweet Christian besides.

Without the confessions, the members of the Reformed churches are virtually at the mercy of the false teachers and their spiritual master. With the confessions, the Reformed laity are able to discern and withstand heretical teachings.

When a Norman Shepherd teaches that justification, *in the Pauline sense of Romans 3–5 and Galatians*, is by faith and the works of faith,[6] the Presbyterian man or woman compares this teaching with chapter 11 of the Westminster Confession of Faith and condemns Shepherd's teaching as heresy. When the same Norman Shepherd writes that a missionary may tell every human that God loves him with the love of John 3:16 and that "Christ died to save you,"[7] the Reformed man or woman compares this teaching with heads 1 and 2 of the Canons and condemns Shepherd's teaching as heresy.

When a John Barach proclaims that all baptized children

6 Shepherd, "Justification by Faith Alone," 80; see also his *Call of Grace*, 50–51.

7 Shepherd, "Justification by Faith Alone," 84–85.

are alike in covenantal union with Christ so that they all share Christ's covenantal love and blessings, but that some fall away from Christ, the covenant, covenantal love, and covenantal blessings, because the covenant and its salvation are conditional—the condition being faith—[8]the Reformed man or woman compares this message with Canons 2, rejection of errors 2–6, and Canons 3–4.14 and condemns Barach's teaching as heresy.

When a Steve Wilkins contends that persons who have enjoyed the grace of God and the blessings of the covenant, including the forgiveness of sins, can nevertheless fall away to perdition,[9] the Reformed man or woman compares this doctrine with head 5 of the Canons and condemns Wilkins' teaching as heresy.

When a heresy is brought for judgment to the major assemblies of Reformed and Presbyterian churches—classis or presbytery and synod or general assembly—the Reformed confessions can and must function as the bulwark of the truth. Delegates to the broadest assembly—the synod—of Reformed denominations in the tradition of the Synod of Dordt are required to decide all matters that come before the assembly on the basis of and in agreement with the three forms of unity. The instruction given delegates to the synod of the Protestant Reformed Churches is representative:

> With instruction and authority to take part in all deliberations and transactions regarding all matters coming legally before the meeting and transacted in agreement with the Word of God *according to the conception of it embodied in the doctrinal standards of the Protestant*

8 Barach, "Covenant and Election," in Wilkins and Garner, *The Federal Vision*, 15–44.

9 Wilkins, "Covenant, Baptism and Salvation," in ibid., 62.

> *Reformed Churches, as well as in harmony with the Church Order of the Protestant Reformed Churches.*[10]

Especially are the confessions the strength at the major assemblies of pastors, who might be overawed by the formidable professor of theology, and of the ruling elders, who are inclined meekly to defer to the phalanx of ministers.

Such is the necessity of the authority of the confessions at the major assemblies, especially regarding judgment in doctrinal controversy, that an assembly's failure to defend and uphold teaching that accords with the confessions and to condemn teaching that contradicts the confessions thereby constitutes the church represented by the assembly as Reformed merely in name, not in reality. A Reformed church is a confessional church, and a confessional church is a church that honors the confessions in deed, not merely in empty words.

The Reformed and Presbyterian confessions can and ought to be the salvation of Reformed and Presbyterian churches and their members in the current controversy over justification by faith alone.

There is a prescribed procedure in Reformed churches by which the churches can correct the confessions according to the ultimate standard of truth, holy scripture. Reformed churches acknowledge that confessions can err and that the Spirit may shed more light on some doctrine of scripture than is reflected in the confessions. The procedure that an enlightened theologian, or layman for that matter, must follow, in correcting or even repudiating a teaching of the confessions, consists of presenting an official objection to the confessional teaching in question to the major assemblies of his denomination.[11] Thus the objecting

---

10 "Decisions pertaining to Article 33," in The Church Order of the Protestant Reformed Churches, in *Confessions and Church Order,* 390; emphasis added.

11 The technical name of this formal objection against the confessions is

theologian or layman submits the matter to the judgment of the church.

Not one of the proponents of the federal vision has followed this honorable, honest, and required course regarding the federal vision's objection to the confessional doctrine of justification by faith alone (and to the related five points of Calvinism). All inveigh against "scholastic theology" and plead for a more "biblical theology," which are thinly veiled attacks against the doctrines of the confessions and equally thinly disguised excuses for their wanton insubordination to the confessions. But not one has followed the orderly way of official objection against the teaching of the confessions. Even if their doctrine is right, therefore (which it is not), God will not bless it. They promote it lawlessly.

There is still another reason that a defense of justification by faith alone against its contemporary assailants within the Reformed churches does well to begin with a consideration of the Reformed confessions. This reason concerns a benefit of the confessions that is often overlooked. The confessions contain succinct but thorough and penetrating analysis of many of the false doctrines that trouble the Reformed church throughout the ages. As the fruit of the profound study of specially gifted and godly Reformed theologians, in the case of the Canons of Dordt and the Westminster standards the fruit of the deliberations of large bodies of extraordinary servants of Jesus Christ, and the fruit of the special guidance of the church by the Spirit of Christ, the confessions lay bare the essential errors of perennial heresies.

---

gravamen. The word derives from the Latin word meaning "burdened." "Gravamen means *objection*...In the strict sense a gravamen is an objection by an officebearer or member of the congregation against one or another article of faith of the confession of his church" (*Christelijke Encyclopaedie voor het Nederlandsche Volk* [Christian encyclopedia for the Dutch people], ed. F. W. Grosheide, J. H. Landwehr, C. Lindeboom, and J. C. Rullmann, vol. 2 [Kampen: J. H. Kok, 1925], 389. The translation of the Dutch is mine).

This exposure of false doctrines is of great help to Reformed churches and Christians. Heretics are always deceptive, as Jesus warned in Matthew 24:11: "Many false prophets shall rise, and shall deceive many." The false teachers adorn their errors with orthodox terminology, bury the errors under mountains of verbiage (especially today when the Internet permits them to babble interminably), and hide the errors in ambiguity.

Arch-heretic Arius, who denied the deity of Jesus Christ, affirmed that Jesus is "a god." The Greek term by which Arius denied Jesus' Godhead—and the Trinity and therefore the Christian faith—differed from the orthodox term in one small letter of the Greek alphabet. The heretical Michael Servetus, condemned by church and state for denying that Jesus is the eternal son of God, went to the stake calling upon Jesus as "the son of the eternal God." All the while heretics are promoting false teachings in the churches, they are crying out to high heaven that they are sound, orthodox, spiritual men of God and that their theological adversaries are cruel "heresy-hunters."

The confessions cut through all the deception, ambiguity, and verbiage of the heresies, as well as through the heretics' claims of fidelity and piety, to the fundamental errors. The confessions make the errors plain not only to learned theologians, but also to every member of the church—man, woman, and child.

Since these exposures of the doctrinal errors are confessional, they are binding on all members of the Reformed churches.

Question and answer 80 of the Heidelberg Catechism exposes the grievous errors of the Roman Catholic doctrine of the mass: "a denial of the one sacrifice and passion of Jesus Christ [and an accursed idolatry.]"[12]

Articles 14 and 15 of the Belgic Confession expose two basic errors of the Pelagian heresy, which repeatedly appear to trouble the Reformed churches (although the contemporary Pelagians

---

12 Heidelberg Catechism Q&A 80, in Schaff, *Creeds of Christendom*, 3:336.

are at pains to deny their identity). Both errors corrupt the truth of the consequences of the disobedience of Adam for the human race. Article 14 condemns as false doctrine the teaching of the "free will of man."[13] Article 15 rejects "the error of the Pelagians, who assert that sin proceeds only from imitation."[14]

Of particular importance to the Reformed and Presbyterian churches and their members regarding the contemporary controversy over justification is the confessions' careful, clear, pointed analysis of the Roman Catholic and Arminian doctrines of justification. Included is the Canons of Dordt's condemnation, in the rejection of errors section of the second head, of the Arminian doctrine of a conditional covenant, whence the Arminian heresy of justification by works arises.

With the Reformed confessions, therefore, I begin this explanation and defense of the biblical, Reformed gospel truth of justification. Because some readers may not have easy access to the confessions and because a reading and study of the confessions should be an important part of the instruction of this book, I quote in full the sections of the Reformed and Presbyterian confessions that express and defend the orthodox doctrine of justification.

The reader is urged to study these confessional statements carefully. These statements themselves, without any further explanation, clearly expose and sharply condemn the teachings of justification by the federal vision, the new perspective, and Evangelicals and Catholics Together. Part of the blame for the spread of the heresies of the federal vision, the new perspective, and ECT in evangelical and Reformed churches is that the members of these churches are ignorant of their own confessions.

---

13 Belgic Confession 14, in ibid., 3:399.
14 Belgic Confession 15, in ibid., 3:401.

Chapter Six

THE REFORMED CONFESSIONS ON JUSTIFICATION: THE STATEMENT

This chapter gives the statement of the gospel truth of justification by the main Reformed and Presbyterian confessions. I speak of "statement" rather than of "statements," because the Reformed confessions make their declaration concerning justification with one voice.

To these confessions and their statement, the doctrine of justification of the federal vision, of the new perspective, and of Evangelicals and Catholics Together must be brought for testing and judgment. On these confessions and their statement, every Reformed and Presbyterian church must stand. By these confessions and their statement, every Reformed and Presbyterian minister, ruling elder, deacon, professor of theology, and missionary is bound. To these confessions and their statement, every Reformed and Presbyterian man, woman, and child must go for clear, authoritative instruction concerning justification.

Belgic Confession

One of the earliest Reformed confessions is the Belgic Confession of Faith (1561). The Belgic Confession expresses the Reformed faith concerning justification in articles 22 and 23.

Significantly, these articles immediately follow the article on the death of Jesus Christ as "full satisfaction" of the justice of

God in the place of his people, "this only sacrifice, once offered, by which believers are made perfect forever."[1]

> We believe that, to attain the true knowledge of this great mystery, the Holy Ghost kindleth in our hearts an upright faith, which embraces Jesus Christ with all his merits, appropriates him, and seeks nothing more besides him. For it must needs follow, either that all things which are requisite to our salvation are not in Jesus Christ, or if all things are in him, that then those who possess Jesus Christ through faith have complete salvation in Him. Therefore, for any to assert that Christ is not sufficient, but that something more is required besides him, would be too gross a blasphemy; for hence it would follow that Christ was but half a Saviour. Therefore we justly say with Paul, *that we are justified by faith alone,* or *by faith without works.* However, to speak more clearly, we do not mean that faith itself justifies us, for it is only an instrument with which we embrace Christ our Righteousness. But Jesus Christ, imputing to us all his merits, and so many holy works, which he hath done for us and in our stead, is our Righteousness. And faith is an instrument that keeps us in communion with him in all his benefits, which, when they become ours, are more than sufficient to acquit us of our sins.[2]

> We believe that our salvation consists in the remission of our sins for Jesus Christ's sake, and that therein our righteousness before God is implied; as David and Paul teach us, declaring this to be the happiness of man, that God imputes righteousness to him without works. And the same Apostle saith, *that we are justified freely by his*

1 Belgic Confession 21, in Schaff, *Creeds of Christendom*, 3:406–7.
2 Belgic Confession 22, in ibid., 3:408–9. The emphasis is the confession's.

> *grace, through the redemption which is in Jesus Christ.* And therefore we always hold fast this foundation, ascribing all the glory to God, humbling ourselves before him, and acknowledging ourselves to be such as we really are, without presuming to trust in any thing in ourselves, or in any merit of ours, relying and resting upon the obedience of Christ crucified alone, which becomes ours when we believe in him. This is sufficient to cover all our iniquities, and to give us confidence in approaching to God; freeing the conscience of fear, terror, and dread, without following the example of our first father, Adam, who, trembling, attempted to cover himself with fig-leaves. And, verily, if we should appear before God, relying on ourselves or on any other creature, though ever so little, we should, alas! be consumed. And therefore every one must pray with David: *O Lord, enter not into judgment with thy servant: for in thy sight shall no man living be justified.*[3]

I add the last part of article 24 of the Belgic Confession, which treats of sanctification, because it speaks directly to the terrifying doctrine of the Roman Catholic Church, Arminianism, the federal vision, the new perspective, and ECT that we are justified now and will be justified (or condemned) in the final judgment partly on the basis of our own good works:

> In the mean time we do not deny that God rewards good works, but it is through his grace that he crowns his gifts. Moreover, though we do good works, we do not found our salvation upon them; for we can do no work but what is polluted by our flesh, and also punishable; and although we could perform such works, still the remembrance of one sin is sufficient to make God reject them.

---

3 Belgic Confession 23, in ibid., 3:409–10. The emphasis is the confession's.

> Thus, then, we should always be in doubt, tossed to and fro without any certainty, and our poor consciences would be continually vexed if they relied not on the merits of the suffering and death of our Saviour.[4]

Thirty-Nine Articles

The Thirty-Nine Articles of the Church of England (1562) say this:

> We are accounted righteous before God, only for the merit of our Lord and Saviour Jesus Christ by Faith, and not for our own works or deservings. Wherefore, that we are justified by Faith only, is a most wholesome Doctrine, and very full of comfort, as more largely is expressed in the Homily of Justification.[5]
>
> Albeit that Good Works, which are the fruits of Faith, and follow after Justification, can not put away our sins, and endure the severity of God's judgment; yet are they pleasing and acceptable to God in Christ, and do spring out necessarily of a true and lively Faith; insomuch that by them a lively Faith may be as evidently known as a tree discerned by the fruit.[6]

Heidelberg Catechism

The Heidelberg Catechism's statement is perfectly clear, exceedingly thorough, and simply glorious. It is more proclamation than statement.

> But what does it help thee now that thou believest all this [that is, all that is confessed in the Apostles' Creed, as explained by the Reformed faith]?

---

4 Belgic Confession 24, in ibid., 3:412.

5 Thirty-Nine Articles of the Church of England 11, in ibid., 3:494.

6 Thirty-Nine Articles of the Church of England 12, in ibid.

That I am righteous in Christ before God, and an heir of eternal life.[7]

How art thou righteous before God?

Only by true faith in Jesus Christ; that is, although my conscience accuse me that I have grievously sinned against all the commandments of God, and have never kept any of them, and that I am still prone always to all evil, yet God, without any merit of mine, of mere grace, grants and imputes to me the perfect satisfaction, righteousness, and holiness of Christ, as if I had never committed nor had any sin, and had myself accomplished all the obedience which Christ has fulfilled for me, if only I accept such benefit with a believing heart.[8]

Why sayest thou that thou art righteous only by faith?

Not that I am acceptable to God on account of the worthiness of my faith; but because only the satisfaction, righteousness, and holiness of Christ is my righteousness before God, and I can receive the same and make it my own in no other way than by faith only.[9]

But why can not our good works be the whole or part of our righteousness before God?

Because the righteousness which can stand before the judgment-seat of God must be perfect throughout, and wholly conformable to the divine law; whereas even our best works in this life are all imperfect and defiled with sin.[10]

---

7 Heidelberg Catechism Q&A 59, in ibid., 3:326.
8 Heidelberg Catechism Q&A 60, in ibid., 3:326–27.
9 Heidelberg Catechism Q&A 61, in ibid., 3:327.
10 Heidelberg Catechism Q&A 62, in ibid.

How is it that our good works merit nothing, while yet it is God's will to reward them in this life and in that which is to come?

The reward comes not of merit, but of grace.[11]

But does not this doctrine make men careless and profane?

No; for it is impossible that those who are implanted into Christ by true faith should not bring forth fruits of righteousness.[12]

Two other sections of the Heidelberg Catechism bearing on justification should be noted. One is question and answer 126, on the fifth petition of the model prayer:

What is the fifth petition?

And forgive us our debts as we forgive our debtors. That is: Be pleased, for the sake of Christ's blood, not to impute to us, miserable sinners, our manifold transgressions, nor the evil which still always cleaves to us; as we also find this witness of thy grace in us, that it is our full purpose heartily to forgive our neighbor.[13]

The other section of the Catechism that sheds light on the truth of justification is question and answer 56. Here the Catechism explains the Reformed believer's confession of the forgiveness of sins in the Apostles' Creed.

What dost thou believe concerning the *forgiveness of sins*?

That God, for the sake of Christ's satisfaction, will no more remember my sins, neither the sinful nature with which I have to struggle all my life long; but graciously

11 Heidelberg Catechism Q&A 63, in ibid.
12 Heidelberg Catechism Q&A 64, in ibid., 3:328.
13 Heidelberg Catechism Q&A 126, in ibid., 3:353–54.

> imparts to me the righteousness of Christ, that I may nevermore come into condemnation.[14]

Three elements of this brief treatment of justification are especially significant regarding the heresies now assailing the Reformation's doctrine of justification. First, the forgiveness of sins, which is the basic aspect of justification, is the divine act of not remembering the sins of the believer. Not remembering is a strictly legal act regarding sin's guilt and punishment. It is a forensic judgment of God, that is, his verdict as judge in the courtroom of the sinner's own consciousness. It is radically different from an activity that cleanses the sinner from the pollution of his sins, or that renews the sinner to live a holy life. Not remembering does not infuse a spiritual power into the believer, so that he performs good works. But it is a divine overlooking of sin's deservingness of punishment, so that the sinner is of good cheer.

The second noteworthy element is the assertion that the sole basis of the divine act of justification is "Christ's satisfaction." In this respect, the doctrine of question and answer 56 is exactly the same as that of question and answer 126, which affirms that the sole basis of justification, as the non-imputation of sin, is "Christ's blood." Excluded as the basis, or even part of the basis, of justification is the sanctifying work of Christ within the sinner and therefore the sinner's good works.

Third, the effect and benefit of present justification, or forgiveness, for the believing sinner are that he "may nevermore come into condemnation." The German original of the Catechism reads literally: "that I shall nevermore come into the judgment" ("*in's Gericht nimmermehr kommen*").

At first glance, the Catechism seems to teach that the forgiven sinner will not even appear in the final judgment. If this were the doctrine of the Catechism, the Catechism would

---

14 Heidelberg Catechism Q&A 56, in ibid., 3:325.

contradict scripture. Scripture teaches that also the elect, justified believer will be judged in the final judgment (Matt. 25:31–46; 2 Cor. 5:10). That the Catechism does not intend to deny the final judgment of the believer is evident from the Catechism's explanation of the final judgment, in question and answer 52. The comfort of the believer regarding Christ's coming again to judge the quick and the dead is not that the believer will avoid the final judgment altogether. Rather, the judge of the believer in the final judgment will be "the self-same One who has before offered himself for me to the judgment of God, and removed from me all curse."[15]

By "nevermore come into condemnation" (German: *Gericht*, "judgment"), the Heidelberg Catechism means that the justified believer will never be judged on the basis of his own works, whether his imperfectly good works or his completely evil works. He therefore will never be condemned. The reference is especially to the final judgment that impends. Thus the Catechism denies the contemporary, terrifying doctrine, particularly the doctrine of the federal vision, that believers face a final judgment in which their works will be the basis, in part, of the verdict of the judge.

Voetius' explanation of question and answer 56 of the Heidelberg Catechism is correct.

> What benefit and profit do you have from the forgiveness of sins?
>
> That now I shall nevermore come into the judgment of God (Dutch: "*in't gerichte Godts*").
>
> Shall then the true believer not be judged in the last day?
>
> Yes: II Corinth. 5. 10. For we must all appear before the judgment seat of Christ, etc.

15 Heidelberg Catechism A 52, in ibid., 3:324.

> Why then do you say that you shall nevermore come into the judgment of God?
>
> That is, that I shall indeed be judged, but I shall not be condemned.[16]

Westminster Confession of Faith

The Westminster Confession of Faith (1647) has the following on justification, in chapter 11.

> Those whom God effectually calleth he also freely justifieth; not by infusing righteousness into them, but by pardoning their sins, and by accounting and accepting their persons as righteous: not for any thing wrought in them, or done by them, but for Christ's sake alone; nor by imputing faith itself, the act of believing, or any other evangelical obedience to them, as their righteousness; but by imputing the obedience and satisfaction of Christ unto them, they receiving and resting on him and his righteousness by faith; which faith they have not of themselves, it is the gift of God.[17]
>
> Faith, thus receiving and resting on Christ and his righteousness, is the alone instrument of justification; yet is it not alone in the person justified, but is ever accompanied with all other saving graces, and is no dead faith, but worketh by love.[18]
>
> Christ, by his obedience and death, did fully discharge the debt of all those that are thus justified, and did make

---

16 Gisbertus Voetius, *Voetius' Catechisatie over den Heidelbergschen Catechismus* [Voetius' catechism on the Heidelberg Catechism], ed. A. Kuyper (Rotterdam: Gebroeders Huge, 1891; originally published 1662), 567. Translation of the Dutch is mine.

17 Westminster Confession of Faith 11.1, in Schaff, *Creeds of Christendom*, 3:626.

18 Westminster Confession of Faith 11.2, in ibid.

> a proper, real, and full satisfaction to his Father's justice in their behalf. Yet inasmuch as he was given by the Father for them, and his obedience and satisfaction accepted in their stead, and both freely, not for any thing in them, their justification is only of free grace; that both the exact justice and rich grace of God might be glorified in the justification of sinners.[19]
>
> God did, from all eternity, decree to justify all the elect, and Christ did, in the fullness of time, die for their sins, and rise again for their justification: nevertheless, they are not justified until the Holy Spirit doth, in due time, actually apply Christ unto them.[20]
>
> God doth continue to forgive the sins of those that are justified; and although they can never fall from the state of justification, yet they may by their sins fall under God's fatherly displeasure, and not have the light of his countenance restored unto them, until they humble themselves, confess their sins, beg pardon, and renew their faith and repentance.[21]
>
> The justification of believers under the Old Testament was, in all these respects, one and the same with the justification of believers under the New Testament.[22]

Further concerning justification in the Westminster Confession of Faith, chapter 16, article 5, on good works, states that our good works "can not endure the severity of God's judgment," because we defile them with our imperfection.[23] This statement is important against the teaching of the men of the

19 Westminster Confession of Faith 11.3, in ibid., 3:626–27.
20 Westminster Confession of Faith 11.4, in ibid., 3:627.
21 Westminster Confession of Faith 11.5, in ibid., 3:627–28.
22 Westminster Confession of Faith 11.6, in ibid., 3:628.
23 Westminster Confession of Faith 16.5, in ibid., 3:635.

federal vision (to which I will return) that the justification of the believer in the final judgment will be conditioned by the good works of the believer, that is, the justification of the final judgment will be by faith and by works. It was particularly this false teaching of the Orthodox Presbyterian elder John Kinnaird that the general assembly of the Orthodox Presbyterian Church approved in 2003.[24]

Also, the Westminster Confession of Faith denies that true believers are "under the law as a covenant of works, to be thereby justified or condemned."[25]

Canons of Dordt

It has always struck me as peculiar that the Canons of Dordt do not include a chapter, or head, on justification, inasmuch as it was an integral part of the Arminian heresy that it denied the Reformation doctrine of justification and taught a novel doctrine of justification. The explanation, no doubt, is that the Synod of Dordt responded to the Arminians' statement of their heretical doctrines, and the Arminians stated their heresy in five points of doctrine that did not include justification as a separate point.

Nevertheless, the Canons of Dordt do take notice of the Arminian error regarding justification, refer to it explicitly in the course of their treatment of the five controverted doctrines, and refute it. Even though the pertinent articles in the Canons have already been referred to in chapter 1 in connection with the Arminian heresy, I quote them here, so that the reader may have all the passages on justification in the leading Reformed confessions before him.

---

24 See Robbins, "The Kinnaird Case," in *A Companion to the Current Justification Controversy*, 53–58; Elliott, "The Kinnaird Case and Its Aftermath," in *Christianity and Neo-Liberalism*, 175–237; and Elliott, *A Denomination in Denial.*

25 Westminster Confession of Faith 19.6, in Schaff, *Creeds of Christendom*, 3:641.

The Canons of Dordt condemn the teaching of the Arminians that election is merely God's choice of faith as a condition of salvation. The Canons charge that this error amounts to an attack on "the truth of gracious justification."[26] The error is an attack on justification inasmuch as it teaches that the act of faith itself is one's righteousness with God, rather than that faith is the instrument that receives the obedience of Christ as righteousness by a legal act of imputation. This is worth noting, because the error of the Arminians at Dordt condemned by the Canons is that of the men of the federal vision today. Norman Shepherd explains Genesis 15:6, "And he [Abraham] believed in the LORD; and he counted it to him for righteousness," as teaching that Abraham's act of believing itself was Abraham's righteousness with God, inasmuch as it was a condition Abraham was required to fulfill for salvation in the covenant.[27]

Especially significant is the Canon's condemnation of the Arminian doctrine that teaches

> the new covenant of grace, which God the Father, through the mediation of the death of Christ, made with man, does not herein consist that we by faith, inasmuch as it accepts the merits of Christ, are justified before God and saved, but in the fact that God, having revoked the demand of perfect obedience of the law, regards faith itself and the obedience of faith, although imperfect, as the perfect obedience of the law, and does esteem it worthy of the reward of eternal life through grace.[28]

The doctrine of justification condemned here is the teaching that God graciously regards faith itself and the imperfect obedience that proceeds from faith as a sinner's righteousness before

---

26 Canons of Dordt 1, error 3, in *Confessions and Church Order*, 160.
27 Shepherd, *Call of Grace*, 15.
28 Canons of Dordt 2, error 4, in *Confessions and Church Order*, 165.

him. The sinner's own works—his believing and his obeying—are his righteousness upon which his eternal salvation depends.

The Canons refute and reject this teaching thus:

> For these contradict the Scriptures: *Being justified freely by his grace through the redemption that is in Christ Jesus: whom God hath set forth to be a propitiation through faith in his blood* (Rom. 3:24–25). And these proclaim, as did the wicked Socinus, a new and strange justification of man before God, against the consensus of the whole church.[29]

It should be noticed that in its description of the Arminian error concerning justification, this article of the Canons succinctly describes the orthodox, Reformation doctrine of justification: "that we by faith, inasmuch as it accepts the merits of Christ, are justified before God and saved."

Article 6 of the fifth head of doctrine of the Canons, on perseverance, denies that, although a saint may fall deeply into sin for a while, God ever allows an elect saint to "forfeit the state of justification."

> But God, who is rich in mercy, according to his unchangeable purpose of election, does not wholly withdraw the Holy Spirit from his own people, even in their melancholy falls; nor suffer them to proceed so far as *to lose the grace of adoption and forfeit the state of justification*, or to commit the sin unto death; nor does he permit them to be totally deserted, and to plunge themselves into everlasting destruction.[30]

All of these creeds of many Reformed and Presbyterian churches all over the world agree as to what justification is and as

---

29 Canons of Dordt 2, error 4, in ibid.

30 Canons of Dordt 5.6, in Schaff, *Creeds of Christendom*, 3:593; emphasis added.

to its central importance both in the proclamation of the gospel and in the work of salvation. This creedal doctrine of justification is attacked today by the federal vision, the new perspective, and Evangelicals and Catholics Together, without protesting against the creeds, which bind them.

Chapter Seven

THE REFORMED CONFESSIONS ON JUSTIFICATION: AN OVERVIEW

The statement of justification by the Reformed confessions establishes the following truths as the right understanding of the biblical doctrine and, of course, as Reformed orthodoxy. Subsequent chapters in this book will further explain these truths, develop them, apply them to the contemporary heresy in the Reformed and Presbyterian churches, and indicate their biblical basis.

The confessions establish that justification is fundamental to the gospel. Article 23 of the Belgic Confession declares that "our salvation consists in the remission of our sins for Jesus Christ's sake" and in "our righteousness before God," which is "therein... implied." The remission of sins with the implied gift of righteousness before God is justification.[1] The very first, and evidently fundamental, benefit of believing the gospel as summarized in the Apostles' Creed, according to the Heidelberg Catechism, is justification: "But what does it help thee now that thou believest all this? That I am righteous in Christ before God."[2]

Therefore, to go wrong on the doctrine of justification is utterly to corrupt and thus to lose the gospel. When the

1 Belgic Confession 23, in Schaff, *Creeds of Christendom*, 3:409.

2 Heidelberg Catechism Q&A 59, in ibid., 3:326.

Westminster Confession of Faith states that "both the exact justice and rich grace of God [are] glorified in the justification of sinners," the implication is that false doctrine concerning justification destroys the gospel regarding both the justice and grace of God.[3] The most reprehensible aspect of this destruction of the gospel, as Westminster suggests, is its robbing God of his glory.

Such is the relationship between justification and the death of Christ, according to the Belgic Confession, that to err concerning justification is to make Christ "but half a Savior." This, adds the Confession, is "too gross a blasphemy."[4]

The effect of the preaching of false doctrine concerning justification, specifically the lie of justification by the sinner's works, is that, trusting for righteousness in his or her own works, a man or woman will be condemned and damned. This is the warning of the Belgic Confession: "Verily, if we should appear before God, relying on ourselves or on any other creature, though ever so little, we should, alas! be consumed."[5] In support of this heart-shrinking warning, the Confession appeals to Psalm 143:2: "O Lord, enter not into judgment with thy servant: for in thy sight shall no man living be justified."[6]

The Reformed confessions establish what the divine act of justification is. The confessions are crystal clear as to the nature of justification. Contributing to this clarity is the confessions' description of the errors that oppose the gospel truth of justification and that the Reformed confessions repudiate. No Reformed teacher has any excuse for deviating from the right doctrine of justification. No Reformed church member has any excuse for being misled by heretical teachers. No Reformed church has any excuse for approving or even tolerating a false doctrine of justification.

---

3 Westminster Confession of Faith 11.3, in ibid., 3:627.
4 Belgic Confession 22, in ibid., 3:408.
5 Belgic Confession 23, in ibid., 3:410.
6 Belgic Confession 23, in ibid.

Imputation, Not Infusion

Justification, according to the Reformed confessions, is God's act of imputing, or reckoning, to the account of the elect sinner the perfect righteousness of Jesus Christ. This imputation includes as its first element the forgiveness of sin.

Justification is a legal act of God. It is *strictly* a legal act of God. By the act of justification God changes the sinner's standing, or legal position, before himself as judge. Whereas the sinner is guilty, the act of justification renders him not guilty. Whereas the sinner stands before the divine bar of justice as one who has transgressed all the commandments of God, justification constitutes him innocent. Whereas the sinner appears in the divine courtroom as one who has not kept the law of God and is therefore worthy of damnation, justification gives him the state or status, that is, the legal standing, of one who has perfectly satisfied all the demands of the law, including its demand of the punishment of everlasting damnation, and is therefore deserving of eternal life.

All the Reformed confessions use legal terms, and only legal terms, to describe justification. The Belgic Confession states that "God *imputes* righteousness."[7] The Heidelberg Catechism says the same: "God…*grants and imputes* to me the perfect satisfaction, righteousness, and holiness of Christ," the meaning of which is that God grants by imputing.[8] The Thirty-Nine Articles use a different term, the sense of which, however, is as legal as "imputes": "We are [in justification] *accounted* righteous before God."[9]

The Heidelberg Catechism describes the effect of justification as a dramatic change in the justified sinner's standing

---

7 Belgic Confession 23, in ibid., 3:409; emphasis added.

8 Heidelberg Catechism A 60, in ibid., 3:326; emphasis added.

9 Thirty-Nine Articles of the Church of England 11, in ibid., 3:494; emphasis added.

before God the just judge, thus making plain that justification, which brings about this change, is a strictly legal act of God as judge. In the moment of justification, the sinner stands before God as guilty and damnworthy: "My conscience accuse[s] me that I have grievously sinned against all the commandments of God, and have never kept any of them, and that I am still prone always to all evil." The result of justification is that the justified sinner now stands before God "as if I had never committed nor had any sin, and had myself accomplished all the obedience which Christ has fulfilled for me."[10] "As if I had never committed nor had any sin" is a judicial verdict, a decree from the bench, and one's position before the judge and his law.

According to the confessions, which affirm that justification is strictly a legal act of God, justification is not the *infusion* of righteousness into the sinner. Justification is not an act of God that makes a depraved sinner holy. Justification is not the change of the sinner's actual, spiritual condition. Justification is not the inner, renewing work of the Holy Spirit causing a bad man to become good and thus producing good works.

The Westminster Confession expressly denies that justification is the infusion of righteousness: "Those whom God effectually calleth he also freely justifieth; not by *infusing* righteousness into them." Driving home the truth that justification is strictly legal—the change of one's state, rather than the change of one's actual, spiritual condition—Westminster adds, "but by pardoning their sins, and by accounting and accepting their persons as righteous."[11]

The importance of the Reformed faith's rejection of the teaching that justification is the infusion of righteousness cannot be stressed too strongly. The truth of justification and therefore of the gospel of grace simply depends on this rejection. Basic

10 Heidelberg Catechism A 60, in ibid., 3:326–27.
11 Westminster Confession of Faith 11.1, in ibid., 3:626.

to the heresy of justification by works as proclaimed both by the Roman Catholic Church and by the federal vision is the teaching that justification is, at least partly, the infusion of righteousness. This doctrine of justification enables both Rome and the federal vision to conclude that God justifies sinners partly by their own good works, which they perform by virtue of the infusion, and that the righteousness of justified sinners, upon which eternal life depends, both now and in the final judgment, is at least in part the sinners' own good works.

Faith, Not Works

The Reformed confessions establish that the means of justification, that by which the sinner is justified, is faith. The Thirty-Nine Articles speak for all the Reformed confessions when they affirm that "we are accounted righteous before God... by Faith."[12] The confessions make explicit that their insistence on faith as the means of justification is intended to exclude the sinner's works as the means. The Thirty-Nine Articles immediately add to their affirmation of faith as the means of justification this denial: "and not for our own works or deservings."[13]

The confessions conclusively exclude the sinner's works from the divine act of justification by declaring that justification is by faith *only*. "How art thou righteous before God?" the Heidelberg Catechism asks in question 60. The answer is, "Only by true faith in Jesus Christ."[14] "Faith," says the Westminster Confession of Faith, "is the alone instrument of justification."[15]

If this were not foolishly being challenged by the men of the federal vision today, it would not even enter into the mind of a Reformed man to observe that by the word *only* the Reformed

12 Thirty-Nine Articles of the Church of England 11, in ibid., 3:494.
13 Thirty-Nine Articles of the Church of England 11, in ibid.
14 Heidelberg Catechism Q&A 60, in ibid., 3:326.
15 Westminster Confession of Faith 11.2, in ibid., 3:626.

confessions express their full agreement with Martin Luther on justification. Specifically, the confessions express their agreement with Luther's understanding and translation of Romans 3:28: "Therefore we conclude that a man is justified by faith without the deeds of the law." By this expression of agreement with Luther's understanding of justification, they make his understanding, specifically of Romans 3:28, binding on all Reformed churches, theologians, and Christians. It is binding doctrine in all Reformed churches that in Romans 3:28, as well as many other places, the apostle Paul teaches that justification is by faith *only*, apart from all works of the sinner. The Reformed confessions forbid and condemn the effort of the men of the federal vision to drive a wedge between Luther and Calvin, in effect between Luther and the Reformed faith, regarding justification.

When the Belgic Confession states, "Therefore we justly say *with Paul, that we are justified by faith alone*, or *by faith without works*," the Confession expresses the Reformed faith's understanding of Paul in Romans 3:28—an understanding that is the same as Luther's.[16] This is binding on all Reformed theologians. It is violation of his subscription vow, therefore, for Norman Shepherd to criticize Luther's understanding and translation of Romans 3:28.

> Luther inserted the word "alone" into his translation of Romans 3:28 to make it read "For we hold that one is justified by faith *alone* apart from works of the law." This is the origin of the dogmatic formula, justification by faith alone. However, his insertion actually distorts Paul's meaning.[17]

The criticism of Luther is also criticism of article 22 of the Belgic Confession (which Shepherd has sworn to uphold), as

16 Belgic Confession 22, in ibid., 3:408; emphasis on the words "*with Paul*" is added.

17 Shepherd, "Justification by Faith Alone," 87.

well as of all the Reformed confessions, which embrace justification by faith *alone* on the basis, in large part, of "Luther's" understanding of Romans 3:28.

Affirming justification by faith *alone*, the Reformed and Presbyterian confessions expose Presbyterian theologian Peter A. Lillback as completely mistaken in distinguishing Calvin from Luther in his doctrine of justification. "In regard to the relationship of justification and good works, Calvin occupies a middle ground between Luther and the Schoolmen...There really is a 'works' righteousness that will stand before God." This alleged difference of Calvin from Luther and purported agreement of Calvin with the medieval (Roman Catholicizing) theologians leads Lillback straight to the conclusion that "mature Reformed covenant theology," no doubt in Lillback's mind the covenantal theology of the federal vision, is linked positively with "medieval covenant theology."[18]

There is no middle ground between justification by faith and works, as taught by "medieval covenant theology," and justification by faith *alone*, exclusive of all human works of any kind and in any way, as taught by Luther, Calvin, *and the Reformed confessions.* Bound by the Westminster Confession of Faith, Lillback is not at liberty to suggest a middle way regarding justification, *as a Presbyterian option.* "Faith...is the *alone* instrument of justification."[19]

In addition to casting aspersions on the work of the Holy Spirit in every child of God that consists of giving him the knowledge of his misery as long as he lives, federal visionist Steve Schlissel assails the Reformed confessions when he ascribes Luther's belief of justification by faith alone to "Luther's

---

18 Peter A. Lillback, *The Binding of God: Calvin's Role in the Development of Covenant Theology* (Grand Rapids, MI: Baker, 2001), 200.

19 Westminster Confession of Faith 11, in Schaff, *Creeds of Christendom*, 3:626; emphasis added.

malady."[20] By "Luther's malady," Schlissel means Luther's thorough knowledge of himself as a guilty sinner before God in light of the testimony of Galatians and Romans. For Schlissel this knowledge of one's misery, which regards justification by faith alone as one's only salvation, is a "malady," a deplorable sickness. This sickness accounts for Luther's doctrine of justification by faith *alone.*

Regardless whether Luther was right in his understanding of justification and the law in Galatians and Romans, to attribute the doctrine of justification by faith alone to a sickness is to charge the Reformed confessions with the same sickness. All the confessions teach justification by faith alone. All the confessions regard this doctrine as beneficial to those who rightly and thoroughly know their misery of sin, particularly the *guilt and shame* of sin.

On the reckoning of Schlissel and the federal vision, question and answer 126 of the Heidelberg Catechism, *which explains a petition commanded by Jesus Christ,* is nothing but the disagreeable symptom of a "malady" of the Reformed confession: "Be pleased...not to impute to us, miserable sinners, our manifold transgressions, nor the evil which still always cleaves to us."[21]

The works of the justified sinner that are excluded in justification, the Reformed confessions identify as *all* the sinner's works, especially the good works that proceed from a true faith by the operation of the indwelling Spirit of Christ.

Just as the men of the federal vision are prohibited by the confessions from teaching justification by faith and works, so Anglican bishop N. T. Wright is prohibited by his confession, the Thirty-Nine Articles, from teaching that justification is something

20 Schlissel, "Justification and the Gentiles," in Wilkins and Garner, *The Federal Vision*, 255.

21 Heidelberg Catechism Q&A 126, in Schaff, *Creeds of Christendom*, 3:353–54.

other than the forgiveness of sins and the imputation of righteousness. Specifically, he is forbidden to teach that justification in Paul is rather a declaration of membership in the church and acceptance at the Lord's table. The Thirty-Nine Articles authoritatively define justification as God's accounting a sinner righteous before him.[22]

Likewise, Anglican J. I. Packer is not at liberty to confess and describe justification by a formula that omits *only*. Least of all is he at liberty to omit *only* in ecumenical discussions with Roman Catholics. His confession binds him to affirm and defend that "we are justified by Faith *only*."[23] The confession was formulated precisely against the Roman Catholic omission of *only* in its doctrine of justification.

The Reformed confessions establish that the works of the sinner that are excluded in justification are *all* his works, especially the good works that proceed from his true faith by the operation of the indwelling Spirit. With reference to works that are "good and acceptable in the sight of God," inasmuch as "they proceed from the good root of faith," the Belgic Confession states that these works—*these* works—are "of no account towards our justification." That the gospel truth of justification by faith alone intends above all to exclude the good works of the child of God from justification, the Confession makes plain when it immediately adds, "For it is by faith in Christ that we are justified, even before we do good works."[24]

When the Heidelberg Catechism defends its exclusion of works from justification, by the doctrine of justification by faith only, it asks, "But why can not our *good works* be the whole or part of our righteousness before God?"[25] The works

22 Thirty-Nine Articles of the Church of England 11, in ibid., 3:494.

23 Thirty-Nine Articles of the Church of England 11, in ibid.; emphasis added.

24 Belgic Confession 24, in ibid., 3:411.

25 Heidelberg Catechism Q 62, in ibid., 3:327; emphasis added.

of the sinner chiefly in view in the exclusion of works from justification are the truly good works of the believer. Similarly, the Thirty-Nine Articles of the Church of England identify the works that the doctrine of justification by faith alone excludes from justification as the "Good Works, which are the fruits of Faith...pleasing and acceptable to God in Christ, and [works that] do spring out necessarily of a true and lively Faith."[26]

When therefore the men of the federal vision and the new perspective explain the works excluded from justification, for example in Romans 3:28 and in Galatians 3, as merely Jewish works, performed in order to merit with God, not only do they grossly, indeed ludicrously, corrupt the scriptures, but they also contradict the Reformed confessions. The Reformed confessions understand the works excluded by Paul from justification as *all* the works of the sinner, especially the good works that the regenerated sinner performs by the Spirit of Christ in him. The Reformed confessions emphasize that the works excluded from justification are the truly good works of the justified sinner, *because the Roman Catholic heresy teaches justification by the good works of the sinner—works performed by the grace of God in him.* This understanding of the Pauline doctrine excluding works from justification is binding on all those who have the Reformed confessions as the creeds of their churches.

Means, Not Condition

The Reformed confessions establish that the role of faith in justification is that of the means, or instrument, by which the justified sinner receives the righteousness of another. The Westminster Confession of Faith teaches that "faith, *thus receiving and resting on Christ and his righteousness*, is the alone *instrument* of justification."[27] The Canons of Dordt declare that "we

26 Thirty-Nine Articles of the Church of England 12, in ibid., 3:494.
27 Westminster Confession of Faith 11.2, in ibid., 3:626; emphasis added.

by faith, *inasmuch as it accepts the merits of Christ*, are justified before God and saved."[28]

The confessions deny that the sinner's activity of believing is itself his righteousness with God, is regarded by God as the sinner's righteousness, or functions as a condition that the sinner performs to make himself worthy of justification. The confessions deny that justification *by* faith means justification *on the condition of* faith, because the latter was (and still is today) the heresy of Arminianism.

> Why sayest thou that thou art righteous only by faith?
>
> *Not that I am acceptable to God on account of the worthiness of my faith*; but because only the satisfaction, righteousness, and holiness of Christ is my righteousness before God, *and I can receive the same and make it my own in no other way than by faith only.*[29]

> However, to speak more clearly, we do not mean that faith itself justifies us, for it is only an instrument with which we embrace Christ our Righteousness.[30]

> The true doctrine having been explained, the Synod [of Dordt] *rejects* the errors of those...who teach that the new covenant of grace, which God the Father, through the mediation of the death of Christ, made with man, does not herein consist that we by faith, inasmuch as it accepts the merits of Christ, are justified before God and saved, but in the fact that God, having revoked the demand of perfect obedience of the law, *regards faith itself and the obedience of faith, although imperfect, as the*

28 Canons of Dordt 2, error 4, in *Confessions and Church Order*, 165; emphasis added.

29 Heidelberg Catechism Q&A 61, in Schaff, *Creeds of Christendom*, 3:327; emphasis added.

30 Belgic Confession 22, in ibid., 3:408.

> *perfect obedience of the law, and does esteem it worthy of the reward of eternal life through grace.*[31]

Thus his own confessions forbid leading federal vision theologian Norman Shepherd to teach as he does that

> the promises made to Abraham had to be believed if they were to be fulfilled. We must not discount faith as a condition to be met for the fulfillment of promise. In fact, Genesis 15:6 says that Abraham's faith was so significant that it was credited to him as righteousness! If so, then righteousness was a condition to be met, and faith met that condition.[32]

The Canons of Dordt 2, error 4 exposes and condemns Shepherd's doctrine as the Arminian heresy of conditional justification and salvation.

The Reformed confessions establish that the sole ground, or basis, of justification is the obedience of Jesus Christ on behalf of and in the stead of the justified sinner during Christ's earthly ministry. The sole ground of justification is the obedience of Christ *outside* the sinner, especially the obedience of suffering the shame and agony of the cross. Explaining the fifth petition of the model prayer, "And forgive us our debts as we forgive our debtors," the Heidelberg Catechism puts in the mouth of the believer beseeching God for the grace of justification these words: "Be pleased, *for the sake of Christ's blood*, not to impute to us, miserable sinners, our manifold transgressions."[33] The Westminster Confession of Faith teaches: "God…freely justifieth…

---

31 Canons of Dordt 2, error 4, in *Confessions and Church Order*, 165; emphasis added.

32 Shepherd, *Call of Grace*, 15.

33 Heidelberg Catechism A 126, in Schaff, *Creeds of Christendom*, 3:353; emphasis added.

not for any thing wrought in them, or done by them, but for Christ's sake alone."[34]

According to the confessions, justification is always grounded solely in the work of Christ for the elect sinner. It is never grounded in the sinner's own works. Therefore, when Orthodox Presbyterian ruling elder John O. Kinnaird taught that the "forensic justification" in the final judgment will require the sinner's good works as a "condition," he contradicted and stood condemned by the Reformed confessions: "These good works are a required condition if we would stand in the Day of Judgment...Who are these people...who stand on the Day of Judgment? They are those who obey the law who will be declared righteous."[35]

When the 2003 General Assembly of the Orthodox Presbyterian Church exonerated Kinnaird and approved his teaching of justification grounded in part—the *decisive* part—in the sinner's own good works, *in defiance of its own creed*, the Orthodox Presbyterian Church ceased being a Presbyterian church. A genuinely Presbyterian church is a confessional church. Indeed, by approving the heresy of justification grounded in the sinner's own good works, the Orthodox Presbyterian Church rejected the fundamental gospel truth of justification by faith alone and thus manifested the dreadful mark of a false church.[36]

The Reformed confessions also explicitly establish the implication of the truths that justification is by faith alone and that the obedience of Christ is the sole ground of the sinner's justification. The implication of these two truths is that the righteousness of the justified sinner before God the judge, which

34 Westminster Confession of Faith 11.1, in ibid., 3:626; emphasis added.

35 Cited in Elliott, "The Kinnaird Case and Its Aftermath," in *Christianity and Neo-Liberalism*, 189–90.

36 For the proceedings and decision of the 2003 General Assembly of the Orthodox Presbyterian Church on Kinnaird's denial of justification by faith alone, see ibid., 221–30.

makes him worthy of eternal life, is exclusively the obedience of Jesus Christ in the sinner's stead. The righteousness of the sinner in the divine act of justification does not include any obedience to the law of God on the part of the sinner—not his faith; not his love for God and the neighbor; not his feeding the hungry; not his visiting the prisoner and the sick; not so much as one small sigh of repentance.

> [In justification] God, without any merit of mine, of mere grace, grants and imputes to me *the perfect satisfaction, righteousness, and holiness of Christ.*[37]

> Why sayest thou that thou art righteous only by faith?
>
> Because only the satisfaction, righteousness, and holiness of Christ is my righteousness before God.[38]

> But why can not our good works be the whole or part of our righteousness before God?
>
> Because the righteousness which can stand before the judgment-seat of God must be perfect throughout, and wholly conformable to the divine law; whereas even our best works in this life are all imperfect and defiled with sin.[39]

> *Jesus Christ*, imputing to us all his merits, and so many holy works, which he hath done for us and in our stead, *is our Righteousness.*[40]

Therefore, Richard Gaffin Jr. flatly contradicts the confessions when he asserts that Romans 2:13 "is best seen as describing what will be true of Christians at the final judg-

37 Heidelberg Catechism A 60, in Schaff, *Creeds of Christendom*, 3:326; emphasis added.

38 Heidelberg Catechism Q&A 61, in ibid., 3:327; emphasis added.

39 Heidelberg Catechism Q&A 62, in ibid.

40 Belgic Confession 22, in ibid., 3:408; emphasis added.

ment."[41] Romans 2:13 reads, "For not the hearers of the law are just before God, but the doers of the law shall be justified." Gaffin's interpretation of the text teaches that God's justification of the sinner at the final judgment will take into account the sinner's own good works, so that the righteousness that finally renders one worthy of eternal life is, in part, his own good works. That Gaffin at once vehemently asserts that the sinner will have performed these good works by the grace of God in him makes absolutely no difference. Gaffin's doctrine is that the righteousness of the justified sinner, in the *final, decisive* justification, consists partly of his own obedience, not wholly and exclusively of the obedience of Christ. This is the characteristic doctrine of the federal vision, as indeed Gaffin's interpretation of Romans 2:13 is the characteristic exegesis of the passage by the federal vision. It might be added that this is the characteristic exegesis of Romans 2:13 by the Roman Catholic Church on behalf of the same doctrine of justification by faith and works.

One thing, and one thing only, needs to be said about Gaffin's interpretation of Romans 2:13: it is condemned by the Reformed and Presbyterian confessions.

> What is justification?
>
> Justification is an act of God's free grace, wherein he pardoneth all our sins, and accepteth us as righteous in his sight, *only for the righteousness of Christ imputed to us, and received by faith alone.*[42]

This is what the righteousness of the justified sinner consists of now. This is what the righteousness of the justified sinner will consist of in the final judgment.

The confessions are clear on justification. They address the

41 Gaffin, *By Faith, not by Sight*, 97.

42 Westminster Shorter Catechism Q&A 33, in Schaff, *Creeds of Christendom*, 3:683; emphasis added.

false doctrines concerning justification that trouble the churches today. They are binding on all Reformed and Presbyterian ministers and elders, regarding both their teaching and their oversight of sound doctrine on the pulpit and in the assemblies.

If the men of the federal vision honored their vows of subscription to the Reformed confessions, their doctrine of justification would never have entered their minds. If it did enter their minds, it could never have escaped their mouths and word processors. If the church assemblies honored their vows of subscription to the Reformed confessions, they would have disciplined Norman Shepherd, Richard Gaffin Jr., John O. Kinnaird, John Barach, Theo Hoekstra, Steve Wilkins, Rich Lusk, and all the other advocates and defenders of the federal vision as soon as they spoke or wrote the first word against justification by faith alone and in favor of justification by works.

That the men of the federal vision *did* promote their doctrine and that the assemblies *failed* (and *still* fail) to discipline these men, regardless of their vows to uphold the confessions, indicate that the toleration, defense, and even approval of the theology of the federal vision in the Reformed churches are a moral issue, as well as a theological one. The officebearers in these churches do not keep their vows. They are dishonorable men.

If the members of the churches where the federal vision is tolerated and even approved honored their own solemn commitments to the authoritative confessions, as members are bound in good conscience to do, one and all, they would protest the doctrine of the federal vision and the decisions of the assemblies protecting and defending the federal vision. They would protest *on the basis of the clear, conclusive testimony of the confessions to justification by faith alone.* They would protest until the assemblies condemned the theology of the federal vision and advised the discipline of the teachers of this heretical theology. Such would be their protest that, if the assemblies defended the federal vision and its teachers, the members would leave the denomination as churches that officially embraced the false gospel of salvation by man's works and will and thus took on the mark of the false church. They would then join churches that demonstrate the main mark of the true church, namely, that "the pure doctrine of the gospel is preached therein."[43]

Inasmuch as the vast majority of members in these churches evidently do not protest or leave, they become responsible for the disobedience and dereliction of their officebearers and for the theology of the federal vision. God will judge them, particularly in their generations.

The Reformed confessions and the vow of subscription to them are important to God.

43 Belgic Confession 29, in ibid., 3:419.

Chapter Eight

JUSTIFICATION AS IMPUTATION

Regarding the truth that was at issue in the sixteenth-century Reformation of the church; the truth that then separated the true churches of Protestantism from the false church of Rome, as it does still today; the truth that Martin Luther described as "the article of a standing and a falling church"; the truth that John Calvin called "the cornerstone of the gospel"; and the truth that the Bible proclaims as the very heart of the gospel of grace, both church and individual Christian must be perfectly clear as to what justification is.

About this truth above all others, there may be no lack of clarity and no confusion. Lack of clarity concerning this truth means lack of clarity concerning the whole of the gospel of holy scripture. Confusion regarding this doctrine must result in confusion regarding all the content of the Bible. Nor do scripture and the confessions leave us in darkness or allow confusion concerning what the saving work of God in Christ known as justification is.

Justification is imputation. It is the divine act of imputing, or reckoning, the righteousness of Jesus Christ to the guilty but elect sinner. To the account of the elect sinner, God imputes the perfect righteousness of Jesus Christ. This righteousness consists of Jesus' lifelong obedience to the will of God and of his atoning suffering and death. The believing sinner experiences this imputation as the forgiveness of his sins—the lifting of sin's guilt, which guilt exposes the sinner to God's punishment of sins—and as the sinner's standing before God the judge as one who has fully accomplished all that the law of God demands of him—the possession of perfect obedience to the ten commandments of the law of God.

Removed is all shame, the deep shame of being a sinner. Bestowed is honor, the genuine honor of being a righteous man or woman.

Gone is fear, the worst of all fears, namely, being an object of the wrath and curse of God and therefore facing the certain punishment of eternal damnation in hell. Present, by justification, is confidence, the all-important confidence of being the object of God's favor, ending in eternal life and glory in body and soul in the day of Jesus Christ.

Legal Act

Justification is a legal act of God. By this act God changes the sinner's standing, or legal position, before himself as judge. The sphere of justification is the heavenly, divine courtroom. Whereas the sinner made his appearance in the courtroom as one who was guilty—guilty of the disobedience of Adam, guilty regarding his totally depraved nature, and guilty on account of all his sinful deeds—justification, as God's act and declaration from the judicial bench, effects the innocence of the sinner, his becoming not guilty, and his position before the judge as one who has perfectly obeyed every demand of the law of God. Justification constitutes the justified sinner *just*.

Such is the state, or legal standing, *before God the judge* of the justified sinner that legally it is with him or her now "as if I had never committed nor had any sin, and had myself accomplished all the obedience which Christ has fulfilled for me." This is the real, unchallengeable state of the justified sinner, "although my conscience accuse me that I have grievously sinned against all the commandments of God, and have never kept any of them, and that I am still prone always to all evil."[1] Justification is a saving act of God not upon good people but upon sinners, indeed upon great sinners. In the parable that is his outstanding proclamation of the gospel of justification, Jesus has the publican confess to God that he is "a sinner." Indeed, the Greek original of the passage has the definite article: "*the* sinner" (Luke 18:13).

God declares the verdict of innocence and changes the legal position of the sinner into one of righteousness in the sinner's own consciousness. It is as if the heavenly courtroom is the sinner's own soul. In any case, the judicial proceedings are carried out in the experience of the sinner. This does not reduce justification to mere subjectivism—how the sinner feels, because of his own thinking or willing. In justification is objective reality. In justification God truly acts. In justification God really speaks. In justification there is awesome divine judgment with blissful effects for time and for eternity.

But the judgment that is justification takes place in the sinner's own experience. This is the implication of the truth that justification is *by faith*. This is also the clear teaching, if not the emphasis, of Jesus in his parable of the Pharisee and the publican in Luke 18:9–14. The occasion of the parable was that some in his audience "trusted in themselves that they were righteous, and despised others" (v. 9). This evil was a matter of their conscious experience. In the event of his justification, the publican "smote upon his breast, saying, God be merciful to me a sinner" (v. 13). He *experienced* his guilt, his liability to the punishing justice of God. He experienced his guilt keenly and deeply.

Regarding his state of righteousness, as one whom God justified, the publican is strikingly described by Jesus as the man who "*went down to his house* justified" (v. 14, emphasis added). Justification sent the publican home (rather than to the gallows)

1 Heidelberg Catechism A 60, in Schaff, *Creeds of Christendom*, 3:326.

with joy on his face, a smile on his lips, laughter in his throat, a spring in his steps, and gratitude in his heart.

Justification is experiential not only in the sense that it consists of the pronouncement of the verdict, "Not guilty!" in the sinner's consciousness. It is also the genuine and most intense joy of the Christian religion. The notion of the charismatic religion that Christian gladness is the experience of their baptism with the Spirit and that the church waited until the twentieth century to learn of and experience heartfelt and hearty gladness is the merest nonsense. The gospel of justification rejoices the believing soul, and the true church has both proclaimed and experienced this joy throughout the ages. In comparison with the Spirit-worked joy of justification, the fraudulent, manufactured exuberance (masquerading as the joy of the gospel) of the charismatic religion is frivolous and shallow. Apart from all else, it does not deliver from the deepest sorrow and most frightful fear: the guilt of sin.

Neither does charismatic exuberance express joy over the one great hope of the Christian, who is a dying human like all the rest of the race. This hope is the expectation of the everlasting glorifying of God in the resurrection body. Justified Christians "rejoice in hope of the glory of God" (Rom. 5:2).

But the experience that is justification is the conscious assurance, and assured consciousness, of the divine deed of *imputation*. Justification is not infusion. It is not God's *making* the sinner righteous as his actual condition, so that one who was formerly a bad man, doing evil things, now begins to be a good man, doing good works. Justification is not the *infusing* of righteousness into the sinner.

There is a saving work of God within sinners that *makes* them obedient, that *imparts* the obedience of Jesus Christ to them so that they begin to be good and to do good, that infuses obedience into them. But this work is not justification. This is the distinct work of sanctification, that is, the divine work that makes the depraved sinner holy. This work always accompanies justification. It invariably follows the act of justification. But it is not justification. Sanctification is a saving work of God that is distinct and different from justification.

The distinction, the difference, and the relationship between God's act of justification (imputing righteousness) and God's work of sanctification (imparting or infusing obedience) are evident in Jesus' word to the woman taken in adultery in John 8:11: "Jesus said unto her, Neither do I condemn thee: go, and sin no more." "Neither do I condemn thee" is Jesus' declaration justifying the guilty woman. This aspect of Jesus' word concerns her legal standing before the judge. It renders her guiltless and therefore righteous before the law.

"Go" sets her free. Hers now is the freedom from condemnation, from punishment, and also, not insignificantly, from shame—the shame of having been an adulteress. But it is also a positive freedom. It is freedom to serve God, freedom from henceforth to obey the seventh commandment of the law of God.

"Sin no more" is Jesus' word that irresistibly calls the sinful woman to be holy. It is the creative word that effectually *makes* the woman obedient; makes her obedient to the ten commandments, including particularly the seventh; makes her holy. This sanctifying word always accompanies the declaration of justification. Whom Christ justifies ("neither do I condemn thee"), he also sanctifies: "Go, and sin no more." But these are two distinct words and works of the Savior. The work of sanctifying *follows* the word of justifying in the grand work of the salvation of the sinner. In the woman's own spiritual experience, sinning no more is her thankful response to Jesus' not condemning her.

Confusion of sanctification with justification, confusion of God's work of *imparting* obedience with his act of *imputing* righteousness, is necessarily corruption of the gospel of grace. This confusion is not harmless. It prevents the publican from going down to his home justified. It is attempted robbery of the people of God of their joy and peace. It detracts from the obedience of Jesus Christ as the complete righteousness of the believing sinner, as though the obedience of the sinner must be added to the obedience of Jesus for the sinner's righteousness with God.

In the saving act of justification, it is all or nothing. Either Jesus' obedient life and atoning death are all of the sinner's righteousness with God (by justification), or if Jesus' obedience must be complemented by so much as one small work of the sinner himself (as an infused righteousness), Jesus' obedience is of no account for the sinner's justification whatsoever. This is the warning of the apostle in the book of Galatians, one of the outstanding passages in scripture on justification: "If ye be circumcised [as a work of the sinner himself on behalf of his justification], Christ shall profit you nothing. Christ is become of no effect unto you, whosoever of you are justified by the law; ye are fallen from grace" (Gal. 5:2, 4).

The outstanding benefit of salvation that justification gives to the justified sinner, according to the Bible, is peace with God: "Therefore being justified by faith, we have peace with God" (Rom. 5:1). The intrinsic and immediate benefit is not goodness of life and behavior, so that a sinner serves and pleases God. This is the benefit of the saving work of sanctification. But the benefit of justification is peace—peace with God. Peace with God is the experience of deliverance from the guilt and punishment of sin. It is the experienced certainty that one is right with God and that God on his part has nothing against the sinner. Peace with God is the blessing of imputation.

That justification is the (legal) *imputation* of righteousness, not the *infusion* or *imparting* of righteousness, is the clear, express testimony of all the Reformed and Presbyterian creeds, as has been shown in a previous chapter. To the condemnation and, one would think, consternation of the Presbyterian theologians and churches that today are proclaiming justification as at least partly the infusion of righteousness in their theology of the federal vision, their creed, the Westminster Confession of Faith, expressly denies that justification is the infusion of righteousness.

> Those whom God effectually calleth he also freely justifieth; *not by infusing righteousness into them*, but by pardoning their sins and by accounting and accepting their persons as righteous: not for any thing wrought in them, or done by them, but for Christ's sake alone.[2]

In thus describing justification as the change of the sinner's legal status before God the judge ("pardoning…accounting and accepting…as righteous") and denying that justification is a change of the sinner's actual, spiritual condition ("not by infusing righteousness"), the creed is biblical. Scripture defines justification in terms of *imputation*, *reckoning*, and *counting* (Ps. 32:2; Rom. 4:9, 3). All of these biblical terms express the divine change of the sinner's standing before the law from that of guilt to that of innocence. They do not describe a change of the sinner's moral condition.

The plea for justification in the fifth petition of the model prayer, "Forgive us our debts as we forgive our debtors," is obviously the request for the cancellation of debts—a legal mercy—not the request for a change of one's spiritual condition—a moral mercy. In keeping with the relationship between justification and sanctification, the request for God's deliverance of the praying sinner from his moral depravity follows the petition for deliverance from guilt in the model prayer: "And lead us not into temptation, but deliver us from evil."

---

2 Westminster Confession of Faith 11.1, in ibid., 3:626; emphasis added. In crassly contradicting their own authoritative creed, by teaching justification as partly the infusion of righteousness, the men of the federal vision show themselves the most lawless of men, despite their presentation of themselves and their theology as defenders and defense of the law.

If any further biblical proof is needed that justification is the change of one's legal standing, by imputation, and not the change of one's moral condition, by infusion, the contrast of opposites in Romans 8:33–34 is conclusive. Having affirmed that "it is God that justifieth," the apostle asks, "Who is he that condemneth?" The contrary of the justifying of the guilty sinner is condemnation. Condemnation is not a work of making one wicked, but the act of pronouncing one guilty. So also justification is not a work of making one righteous, but the act of declaring one to be righteous. Condemnation and justification are legal acts. They establish one's standing regarding the law of God, not one's actual, moral condition.

Inasmuch as justification is the verdict on one of God as judge, consisting of imputing to him a perfect righteousness, justification is importantly a declaration. God imputes righteousness to the sinner by means of a declaration. The righteousness of justification becomes the guilty sinner's own righteousness and his standing before the law becomes that of innocence by way of the declaration, "Not guilty! Righteous!"

This is how the adulterous woman of John 8 became righteous before God. Jesus Christ, her judge on behalf of God, declared, "Neither do I condemn thee" (v. 11). By this declaration of Jesus, the woman was justified.

That justification is the imputation of righteousness to the guilty sinner by declaration of the judge is the teaching of Acts 13:38: "Be it known unto you therefore, men and brethren, that through this man is preached unto you the forgiveness of sins." The forgiveness of sins is justification, as verse 39 makes explicit: "And by him all that believe are justified from all things, from which ye could not be justified by the law of Moses." "Preached" in the translation of verse 38 of the Authorized Version is not the usual Greek word for preaching. It is rather a word that means "announce" or "declare." Through Jesus Christ, forgiveness, or justification, is *declared* unto believers.

The meaning is not merely that justification is taught to an audience, but that justification is bestowed on and realized in believing sinners by declaration. Justification becomes a saving reality in the experience of the elect, believing sinner not by a spiritual work of internal renewal—the infusion of righteousness—but by divine declaration upon the sinner, in his consciousness—a legal verdict from the bench. In justification God speaks to the believing sinner, and he speaks the blessed verdict, "Not guilty! Righteous!"

If one asks where and how God speaks this word that declares sinners righteous, the answer is, in the preaching of the gospel of holy scripture. In every gospel sermon (and there ought not be any other sermon than a gospel sermon), God—not the preacher but God, God himself—declares to the believer, who comes into the courtroom burdened with the guilt of his sins, "Not guilty, for the sake of Jesus Christ and him crucified! Righteous, with the perfect righteousness of Jesus Christ, which by this declaration I impute to you!"[3]

Thus the church forgives sins, as Jesus affirms in John 20:23: "Whose soever sins ye [the apostolic church] remit, they are remitted unto them; and whose soever sins ye [the apostolic church] retain, they are retained." Thus the church opens the kingdom of heaven to sinful humans, as is the teaching of questions 84–85 of the Heidelberg Catechism: "How is the kingdom of heaven opened and shut by the preaching of the holy Gospel?...How is the kingdom of heaven shut and opened by

3 Regarding the truth and reality of justification in particular, and not only the significance of preaching in general, it is of vital importance to recognize that preaching is the living voice of Jesus Christ, not merely the talk, even the orthodox, stirring talk, of a preacher. Preaching is not even only the orthodox talk of a preacher on behalf of God. Only if, as the Second Helvetic Confession (1566) declares, "the preaching of the Word of God is the Word of God," does the preaching of the word justify believers as the very declaration of God himself (*Creeds of the Churches*, ed. John H. Leith [Richmond, VA: John Knox Press, rev. ed. 1973], 133).

Church discipline?"[4] Thus the church looses sinners from their spiritual bondage, as Jesus teaches in Matthew 18:18: "Whatsoever ye shall loose on earth shall be loosed in heaven."

The church forgives, opens, and looses *ministerially*, by preaching the gospel of justification. Preaching justification as the gracious imputation of righteousness, the church forgives, opens, and looses as the minister, or servant, or herald of God himself. God forgives, opens, and looses through the word of the church, his mouth.

The church does not justify sinners on her own authority and by her own judgment, not even if it is acknowledged that she has this authority and right of judgment from God. Only God forgives, opens, and looses on his authority. When Jesus forgave the sinful woman, obviously on his authority, he revealed himself as God in the flesh. Those who witnessed the divine act acknowledged this by their question, "Who is this that forgiveth sins also?" (Luke 7:48–49).

By forgiving sinners, as also by holding sins against sinners, by her own authority and in accordance with her own inherent, lordly judgment, whether in a papal bull or in the confessional, Rome usurps the prerogative of God.

Obedience of Christ

The righteousness that is the content and gift of justification is wholly and exclusively the righteousness of Jesus Christ. It is entirely and only Jesus' obedience to the will of God all his life and his suffering the punishment of the sins of those who are his by election, especially the suffering of the death of the cross under the wrath of God. Just as the disobedience of the one man Adam rendered the entire human race guilty before God, so the "obedience of one [Jesus Christ]" constitutes the "many" who

4 Heidelberg Catechism Q 84–85, in Schaff, *Creeds of Christendom*, 3:337.

make up the elect church "righteous" (Rom. 5:19).[5] The gracious justification of sinners that the apostle proclaims in Romans 3–5 is a reality "through the redemption that is in Christ Jesus." This redemption was bloody "propitiation" that becomes "righteousness for the remission of sins" by God's declaration in the justifying of believing sinners (3:24–25).

According to 1 Corinthians 1:30, Christ Jesus is our righteousness. He alone is our righteousness. We ourselves with our works are not our own righteousness. Christ is all of our righteousness. We ourselves are not any part of our righteousness. *How* Christ is our righteousness, the apostle teaches especially in Romans and Galatians: by justification, which is not the infusion of righteousness but the imputation of righteousness.

The righteousness of justification is wholly and exclusively the doing and dying of Jesus Christ outside the justified sinner, which doing and dying are then imputed to the believing sinner, and not at all a work of Jesus within the sinner that makes him good, so that the righteousness of the sinner is both what Jesus has done for him and what the sinner himself does. The Reformation gospel confessed, and confesses, this by describing the righteousness of justification in the Latin phrase *extra nos*, that is, outside us. It is a righteousness accomplished *for* us by another, not at all a righteousness worked *within* us, taking form as our own efforts. The righteousness of justification is in its totality the obedient work of Jesus Christ in the sinner's stead

5 I use the word "constitutes" advisedly. The Authorized Version has "made": "by the obedience of one shall many be made righteous" (Rom. 5:19). The word in the Greek is not the ordinary word meaning "made." Rather, the word means "constituted" ("shall many be *constituted* righteous"). The subject of the passage is justification, as grounded in the atoning death of Jesus. In justification the sinner is not "made" righteous, in the sense of being changed spiritually and morally from a bad person into a good person. But he or she is *constituted* righteous, by a legal act that changes one's state, or position, in the judgment of the court. The Greek verb is *kathisteemi*.

and on the sinner's behalf, *outside* the sinner's depraved life and disobedient conduct. The Reformed creed is biblical, therefore, when it declares that "only the satisfaction, righteousness, and holiness of Christ is my righteousness before God," denying that "our good works [can] be the whole or part of our righteousness before God."[6]

Since the righteousness of the believer in his justification is not his own natural state or his own production, by virtue of some power for good in himself, but that of another, which is imputed to the believer, Luther described this righteousness as an "alien" righteousness. An "alien" righteousness is contrasted with an intrinsic, or inherent, righteousness. An "alien" righteousness is the righteousness of Jesus Christ in the stead of and on behalf of an unjust sinner, which becomes the sinner's by imputation, in distinction from a righteousness that is the sinner's own by virtue of the sinner's own goodness and obedience to the law.

> A Christian is righteous and holy by an alien or foreign holiness—I call it this for the sake of instruction—that is, he is righteous by the mercy and grace of God...Is not this righteousness an alien righteousness? It consists completely in the indulgence of another and is a pure gift of God.[7]

Every theory of justification that ascribes the righteousness of the sinner to his own works, whether in whole or in part, as is the teaching of Shepherd and the other advocates of the theology of the federal vision, takes issue with Luther's and the Reformation's doctrine of justification by an "alien" righteousness

6 Heidelberg Catechism A 61, Q 62, in Schaff, *Creeds of Christendom*, 3:327.

7 Martin Luther, *What Luther Says* (St. Louis, MO: Concordia, 1959), 2:710–11.

and therefore with the biblical teaching that the complete and perfect righteousness of the justified sinner is the obedience, suffering, and death of Jesus Christ, which becomes the sinner's by imputation.

Here the traditional, Reformed distinction between Christ's passive and active obedience comes to the fore. By Christ's passive obedience is meant his suffering of the punishment, especially the torments of hell, that those for whom he died deserved at the bar of God's justice. By Christ's active obedience is meant his willing performance of all the demands of the law of God—the love of God and the love of the neighbor demanded by the ten commandments. Christ rendered this obedience to God not for his sake personally, but for all those on whose behalf he came into the world as the incarnate Son of God.

The distinction between his active and passive obedience intends to magnify Jesus as the savior of sinners not only by bearing their punishment, but also by perfectly obeying the law on their behalf. By faith in Christ, the guilty and disobedient sinner is righteous not only as having (passively) borne the law's penalty upon him for all his disobedience, but also as having (actively) fulfilled the law's demand for perfect obedience to itself.

Nothing belonging to the righteousness of the law is lacking to the sinner who believes in Jesus the Christ. Everything that the righteous law requires of the human is his or hers who believes in Jesus by means of the faith that he or she has in Jesus. As justified, the believer appears before God the judge as one who has both fully satisfied the law's demand of punishment from a lawbreaker (Christ's passive obedience) and who has perfectly obeyed the law's commandments (Christ's active obedience).

Although the Reformed confessions, the three forms of unity, do not use the terminology passive obedience and active obedience in their statements on justification, the sense of the terminology is found in them. Explaining justification, question

60 of the Heidelberg Catechism teaches that God "imputes" to the believing sinner "the perfect satisfaction, righteousness, and holiness of Christ."[8] The "perfect satisfaction" of Christ is his suffering of the full punishment of the believer's sins according to the justice of God—his passive obedience. The "holiness of Christ," which is also imputed to the believer in justification, is Jesus' perfect consecration of himself to God in love, manifested in his spotless conformity of himself and all his behavior to the law of God—his active obedience.

That by the "holiness of Christ" the Catechism has in view Christ Jesus' conformity to the will of God and obedience to all the commandments of the law, the Catechism puts beyond doubt in what immediately follows: "as if I had never committed nor had any sin, and had myself accomplished all the obedience which Christ has fulfilled for me." Christ's bearing the punishment of the believer's sins has the benefit that it is with the believer as though he "had never committed nor had any sin." This was his passive obedience. In addition, Christ "accomplished all the obedience" to the law that God requires of the believer. This was his active obedience. Both aspects of obedience are imputed to the believer in justification.

The righteousness that comes to the believer by faith, therefore, is not only the satisfaction, or even only the satisfaction and righteousness, of Christ. But it is the "satisfaction, righteousness, *and holiness* of Christ."[9]

The righteousness of God regarding the individual elect child of God is not only the demand for payment in full of the debt he owes God by virtue of the disobedience of Adam, his depraved nature, and all his wicked acts, but also the demand for perfect obedience to all the commandments of the divine law. So also the righteousness of Christ that is imputed to the

8 Heidelberg Catechism A 60, in Schaff, *Creeds of Christendom*, 3:326.

9 Heidelberg Catechism A 61, in ibid.

believing sinner consists both of the satisfaction of God's justice by the enduring of punishment and of the fulfillment of God's justice by the obeying of the law's demand of love for God and the neighbor. Jesus Christ is the righteousness of the believer in justification regarding both of these aspects of the justice of God. "Jesus Christ, imputing to us all his merits, and so many holy works, which he hath done for us and in our stead, is our Righteousness."[10]

When therefore the theologians of the contemporary heresy in Reformed circles of the federal vision limit the obedience of Christ that is imputed to the believer in justification to his suffering the punishment of sin in the believer's stead, contending that the believer must accomplish the righteousness of obedience to the law of God—must accomplish it *for his justification*—they make of Christ only half a savior and burden the conscience of the believer with the impossible, oppressive demand to accomplish the righteousness of perfect conformity to all the commandments of the law of God.

Inasmuch as the obedience and suffering of Jesus Christ on behalf of sinners is the righteousness that God conceived and worked out in Jesus Christ, it is "the righteousness of God": "But now the righteousness of God without the law is manifested…even the righteousness of God which is by faith of Jesus Christ unto all and upon all them that believe" (Rom. 3:21–22). In all his obedient life and especially in his atoning, substitutionary suffering and death, Jesus declared God's righteousness, that God "might be just, and the justifier of him which believeth in Jesus" (vv. 25–26).

He who has the righteousness of Jesus Christ by faith in him possesses the righteousness of God himself. He is secure against the doubts that rise within himself on account of his own inherent wickedness and his own failure to keep the law perfectly;

10 Belgic Confession 22, in ibid., 3:408.

against the challenges to his salvation on the part of Satan and his demons; and with a view to his standing daily in the presence of God the judge, as also in the final judgment.

To despise and reject the righteousness of the justification of the gospel of Christ is to despise and reject the righteousness of God himself. Nothing less than this is the monstrous wickedness and folly of the teaching of justification by the law, that is, the works of the sinner. Such was the charge of the apostle against the Israel of his day, who rejected Jesus as the Messiah of God. "They being ignorant of God's righteousness, and going about to establish their own righteousness, have not submitted themselves unto the righteousness of God." What was the essence of old Israel's ignorance? That "Christ is the end [Greek: *telos*, 'goal'] of the law for righteousness to every one that believeth" (Rom. 10:4).

Exactly this damnable, fatal ignorance in the matter of righteousness is the sin and folly of Rome, of Arminianism, of the cults, and of the contemporary heresy in the sphere of Reformed and Presbyterian Christianity of the federal vision. All share with old Israel the error of proclaiming and embracing "the righteousness which is of the law, that the man which doeth those things shall live by them" (v. 5). All repudiate the gospel of holy scripture that "righteousness…is of faith" (v. 6). "Whosoever believeth on him shall not be ashamed" (v. 11).

Chapter Nine

"BY" AND "OUT OF" FAITH

The urgent question of the guilty but penitent sinner is, how can I be righteous before God my judge?

That every human does not ask this question, and ask it with a fervency that will not be satisfied until it has the answer, is evidence of the sinful foolishness and foolish sinfulness of human nature. The same man who exerts himself with vehement energy and great expense to improve his golf swing and the same woman who is restless until she has lost five pounds show absolutely no interest in a question that concerns their blessedness and peace in this life and their weal or woe in eternity.

Regardless of the disinterest in the question by the majority of mankind, the question is of fundamental importance.

The answer of the gospel of the Bible to this fundamental question is, "by faith" and "out of faith." Although the question and its answer run through the entire scripture, two passages stand out. One is Romans 3:9–5:1. The other is the book of Galatians.

Romans 3:28 answers the question of the possibility of righteousness thus: "A man is justified by faith without the deeds of the law." The answer of Galatians 2:16 is the same: "Knowing that a man is not justified by the works of the law, but by the faith of Jesus Christ." In keeping with this answer, the text adds, "Even we have believed in Jesus Christ, that we might be justified by the faith of Christ, and not by the works of the law: for by the works of the law shall no flesh be justified."

Indicating that this truth is the heart of the gospel of salvation by grace, Christ Jesus made it the power of his reformation of the church in the sixteenth century. Although the children of the Reformation associate the promotion and defense of justification by faith with the reformer Martin Luther, and rightly so, John Calvin was in full agreement with Luther concerning both the meaning and the importance of the truth that justification is by faith, not by works.

Expressing not only the testimony of the Bible but also the full agreement of Calvin with Luther concerning justification by faith, all of the Reformed creeds confess justification by faith, as demonstrated in an earlier chapter. Article 11 of the Thirty-Nine Articles of the Church of England affirms, "That we are justified by Faith only, is a most wholesome Doctrine."[1] Article 23 of the Belgic Confession, a creed of Reformed churches, declares that "the obedience of Christ crucified...becomes ours when we believe in him."[2] Likewise, the Reformed Heidelberg Catechism answers the question, "How art thou righteous before God?" thus: "Only by true faith in Jesus Christ."[3] The Presbyterian Westminster Confession of Faith teaches that God justifies "by imputing the obedience and satisfaction of Christ unto them, they receiving and resting on him and his righteousness by faith."[4]

The relationship of the saving grace of justification to faith makes it necessary that we know what faith is. The necessity of this knowledge is heightened in our day by the presentation of faith as nothing more than a feeling of excitement, an emotional

---

1 Thirty-Nine Articles of the Church of England 11, in Schaff, *Creeds of Christendom*, 3:494.

2 Belgic Confession 23, in ibid., 3:409.

3 Heidelberg Catechism Q&A 60, in ibid., 3:326.

4 Westminster Confession of Faith 11.1, in ibid., 3:626.

high. Faith is not a feeling, an emotion. In truth, faith is the elect sinner's knowledge of Jesus Christ as revealed in the inspired scripture and as preached in the gospel as the Savior from sin, and the sinner's consequent trusting in this Jesus Christ, from the heart, for the forgiveness of sins and righteousness with God. Indeed, faith trusts in Jesus Christ for all of salvation. But our interest now, as it is also an emphasis of scripture, is in faith's trust in Christ for righteousness.

That the faith by which the sinner is justified is both knowledge and trust is the description of faith by the Heidelberg Catechism.

> What is true faith?
>
> It is not only a certain knowledge whereby I hold for truth all that God has revealed to us in his Word, but also a hearty trust which the Holy Ghost works in me by the Gospel, that not only to others, but to me also, forgiveness of sins, everlasting righteousness and salvation, are freely given by God, merely of grace, only for the sake of Christ's merits.[5]

That faith is knowledge of Christ as revealed in scripture is the teaching of John 6:69, Peter's confession of Jesus as the Christ: "We believe and are sure [Greek: *egnookamen*, 'have *known*'] that thou art that Christ, the Son of the living God." Also John 17:3 describes faith as knowledge: "This is life eternal, that they might know thee the only true God, and Jesus Christ, whom thou hast sent."

True faith is also trust in, or depending on, Jesus Christ, according to Ephesians 3:12: "In whom [Christ Jesus our Lord] we have boldness and access with confidence by the faith of him." Faith's trusting in Christ, indeed ultimately in God who promised Christ, is on the foreground in an Old Testament

---

5 Heidelberg Catechism Q&A 21, in ibid., 3:313.

passage that is especially prominent in the debate concerning justification by faith. The passage is Genesis 15:6: "And he [Abraham] believed in the LORD; and he counted it to him for righteousness."

Paul's explanation of Genesis 15:6 emphasizes the trust aspect of Abraham's faith: "He [Abraham] staggered not at the promise of God through unbelief; but was strong in faith, giving glory to God; and being fully persuaded that, what he had promised, he was able also to perform. And therefore it was imputed to him for righteousness" (Rom. 4:20–22). Unbelief is doubt—a staggering at the promise of God. Faith is confidence or trust—full persuasion that God can and will perform what he promises.

Justification "by" Faith

By this faith, by faith that is knowledge of and trust in God as the God and Father of Jesus Christ, the guilty sinner is justified. Faith is the God-ordained *means*, or *instrument*, of his act of justifying sinners. By the means of faith, God justifies the sinner. Faith is the instrument through which God grants to the guilty sinner the righteousness of Christ by imputing it to the account of the sinner. Faith is the means by which the guilty sinner receives from God the righteousness of Christ by imputation. Faith is the means by which God grants, and the sinner receives, the righteousness of Christ by imputation in the sinner's own consciousness, so that the sinner is himself aware and assured of his forgiveness and righteousness.

In the parable of the Pharisee and the publican, Jesus has the publican, who trusted in the mercy of God in Jesus Christ, going home justified, that is, conscious and assured of his righteousness before God the judge (Luke 18:14). The publican's knowledge of and trust in Jesus as the savior was his faith, by which the publican was justified.

What the Heidelberg Catechism calls "a certain knowledge"

and "a hearty trust" are simply the two aspects of the appointed means of justification, namely, faith.[6]

When the elect but guilty sinner believes, God pronounces the verdict, "Not guilty!" into the sinner's soul by means of the sinner's faith, thus changing the sinner's state, or legal standing before the heavenly judge, from guilt to innocence in the sinner's consciousness.

Faith is the appropriate instrument of justification. Faith is the appropriate instrument, first, by virtue of its being essentially the bond of union with Jesus Christ. So the Heidelberg Catechism describes faith when it identifies those humans who are saved by Christ as "only such as by true faith are ingrafted into him, and receive all his benefits."[7] If one is "ingrafted" into Christ by faith, faith is the bond of union with Christ. As the bond of engrafting into Christ, faith in its activity is a knowing and trusting in Christ, who is the sinner's righteousness with God. Faith is the appropriate instrument of justification inasmuch as faith embraces and receives Jesus Christ.

Faith is the appropriate instrument of justification, second, because faith, or believing, is as such the renunciation of all working for righteousness. In all of the Bible's treatment of justification, especially in the New Testament, the contrast between believing for righteousness and working for righteousness is prominent and fundamental.

That justification is "by faith" means that justification is not by or because of works, that is, the works of the sinner himself. Faith as the instrument of justification rules out works as the instrument. This is the implication of "by faith" that the apostle draws out in Galatians 2:16: "Knowing that a man is not justified by the works of the law, but by the faith of Jesus Christ." Likewise, Romans 3:28 presents faith as proscribing

---

6 Heidelberg Catechism Q&A 21, in ibid.
7 Heidelberg Catechism A 20, in ibid., 3:313.

works as the means of the justification of the sinner: "Therefore we conclude that a man is justified by faith without the deeds of the law."

The righteousness of justification does not consist of, is not accomplished by, is not due to, and is not dependent on the sinner's own good works. This is the astounding, heart-melting, comforting message of the gospel of justification by faith. Justification, which is the foundation of all of salvation and itself the saving act of God *par excellence*, is a gracious act of God—"by faith"—not the accomplishment of the sinner himself—"by works of the law." At this crucial point, that of the righteousness of the guilty sinner before God, the Christian gospel differs radically from the message of salvation of all other religions, including the cults. All other religions in one way or another make humans' own works their worthiness for salvation.

By their intrusion of human works into justification, Roman Catholicism, Arminianism, and the contemporary heresy of the federal vision deny the Christian gospel at its heart and plainly show themselves as proclaiming another gospel, which is no gospel.[8]

Works are excluded from justification. Faith as the means, or instrument, of justification excludes works as the means. No work of the sinner himself constitutes his righteousness before

8 See Galatians 1:6–7: "I marvel that ye are so soon removed from him that called you into the grace of Christ unto another gospel: which is not another." The false gospels of Rome, of Arminianism, and of the federal vision are in fact modern versions of the Galatian heresy, as an examination of their doctrines of justification and a comparison of them with the heresy condemned in the book of Galatians clearly show. Like the apostle, the Reformed believer marvels that Rome, the Arminians, and the proponents of the federal vision are removed from him that called the church into the grace of Christ. If the edge of the marvel is taken off by the fact that Rome, Arminianism, and the federal vision removed somewhat later than did the Galatian heretics, it is restored by the fact that these later heretics departed from the gospel of grace in spite of the epistle to the Galatians.

God, whether in whole or in part. Excluded are the Old Testament ceremonial works. Excluded as well are the good works that proceed from true faith and are done according to the law of God of the ten commandments.

In order to maintain their doctrine that the good works of believers constitute at least part of their righteousness with God and contribute to their justification, Rome and the men of the federal vision restrict the "works of the law" in Romans 3 and 4 and in the book of Galatians to obedience to the ceremonial law of the Old Testament. The apostle merely denies, therefore, that works of obedience to the ceremonial law are part of the sinner's justification. The "deeds of the law" that are excluded from the means of justification in Romans 3:28 are only works of obedience to the ceremonial law. Or if these heretics find it difficult to restrict the deeds of the law by which sinners are not justified to obedience to the ceremonial law—a stretch even for these exegetical wizards—they explain the deeds of the law as only evil and outdated *Jewish* works. This bit of exegetical legerdemain allows Rome and the federal vision to explain Romans 3:28 as teaching that a man is justified by faith *and by his deeds of obedience to the moral law of God.* Thus justification is by faith *and by works* after all.

In his foreword to Canadian Reformed theologian Ralph F. Boersema's defense of Shepherd's and the federal vision's theology of justification by works, Shepherd charges that Reformed theologians (and in fact the Reformed *creeds*) have a

> mistaken understanding of what Paul was against when he denied that justification was by "works of the law." These "works of the law" are not any and all good works, leading to the formula...that justification is by the instrumentality of a faith that "stands alone." Paul was against clinging to the old, Mosaic covenant, as though that covenant were still operative...(and) in

> opposition to living according to the requirements of the Mosaic law.[9]

In his contribution to a full-blown explanation and advocacy of the theology of the federal vision by the leading lights, "wandering stars" rather, of this contemporary corruption of the gospel of grace, Shepherd wrote that the "works of the law," which Romans and Galatians exclude from the means and source of justification, "are not simply any and all good works." Rather, "by 'works of the law' Paul is referring to the old covenant, the Mosaic covenant delivered to Israel on Mount Sinai, summarizing the promises and obligations under which Israel lived from the time of the Exodus to the advent of Christ." This explanation of the "deeds of the law," which are excluded as the means of justification, enables Shepherd to conclude: "In Romans 3 Paul is not now teaching...that...*faith without faithfulness* is the real key to justification after all!"[10] That is, the "faithfulness" of faith, which consists of the good works that faith performs, is the "real key to justification." Justification is, decisively, by the genuinely good works of the believer. Justification is by *works.*

The other proponents of the theology of the federal vision similarly gut the biblical rejection of works as the means of justification. "What does Paul mean by 'works of the law' in Galatians?" asks Rich Lusk. His answer:

> Life under the Mosaic covenant as a whole (especially as that form of life took shape in the second temple period) [the time shortly before and during the earthly ministry

---

9 Norman Shepherd, foreword, in Ralph F. Boersema, *Not of Works: Norman Shepherd and His Critics, The Justification Controversy Laid to Rest through Understanding* (Minneapolis, MN: NextStep Resources, 2012), xii.

10 Shepherd, "Faith and Faithfulness," in Sandlin, *A Faith That Is Never Alone*, ed. P. Andrew Sandlin (La Grange, CA: Kerygma Press, 2007), 67–68.

> of Jesus]. Thus, "works of the law" refers to the whole way of life God gave to Israel...The phrase "works of the law" describes Jewish life and culture; the phrase sums up the Jewish mode of life as it existed under the old covenant order.

Lusk's examples are "circumcision, dietary regulations, and calendrical observances."[11]

The practical application of his and the federal vision's interpretation of "deeds of the law" in such a way as to allow for the doctrine that sinners are, in fact, justified by faith *and by (genuine, new testamental) good works* is significant. For Lusk the application is ecumenical. Whereas those who confess justification by faith as excluding all works as the means of justification, including the good works performed by a true and living faith, are "sectarian," by its doctrine of justification by faith and faith's good works the federal vision is "catholic." The federal vision has left the "Reformed ghetto." It "would like to learn from and share with other traditions within Christendom."[12]

What the other traditions toward which the federal vision is moving and has already moved, by its doctrine of justification by faith and by faith's good works, really are can be expressed by changing the lowercase *c* in Lusk's word "catholic" to the upper case. The Bible and the Reformed faith judge this ecumenical movement to be apostasy.

That Romans 3 and 4 and the epistle to the Galatians have the entire law of God, including the moral law of the ten commandments, in view when they deny that justification is by the deeds of the law is evident from these passages. Romans 3:20

---

11 Rich Lusk, "From Birmingham, with Love: 'Federal Vision' Postcards," in *A Faith That Is Never Alone*, 151–52. The book is dedicated to "Norman Shepherd, persevering advocate for a faith that is never alone," by which description is meant "teacher of justification by faith and by the good works that faith performs."

12 Ibid., 154–55.

identifies the law by the deeds of which "there shall no flesh be justified in his sight" as the law "by [which] is the knowledge of sin." It is not only or even especially the ceremonial law that gives the knowledge of sin. On the contrary, it is especially the moral law, the law of the ten commandments, by which God gives the knowledge of sin, as the Heidelberg Catechism authoritatively teaches in question 4. The law of God whence the believer knows his misery is the law that Christ summarized in Matthew 22: "Thou shalt love the Lord thy God with all thy heart, and with all thy soul, and with all thy mind, and with all thy strength…and…thou shalt love thy neighbor as thyself."[13]

Likewise, according to Galatians 3:10–11 the law by which no man is justified in the sight of God is the law that curses every one "that continueth not in all things which are written in the book of the law to do them." The law that curses the disobedient sinner is not only, or even especially, the ceremonial law of the Old Testament. Christ did not exclusively, or even chiefly, redeem us from the curse of the ceremonial law, "being made a curse for us," in accordance with the penalty exacted by the ceremonial law (vv. 13–14). But the law that cursed the lawbreaker in the time of the Old Testament was the whole law of God, civil, ceremonial, and especially moral. The law that curses transgressors today is the moral law of God. Calvin was right when he wrote that "the common mode [by the Roman Catholic theologians] of interpreting all these passages, with reference to the ceremonial law, is mere trifling."[14]

When the Bible denies that justification is by the deeds of the law, it rejects any and all works of the sinner, including the good works of the believing child of God, works done by the

---

13 Heidelberg Catechism Q&A 3–4, in Schaff, *Creeds of Christendom*, 3:308–9.

14 John Calvin, "Articles by the Theological Faculty of Paris with the Antidote," in *Tracts Relating to the Reformation*, trans. Henry Beveridge (Edinburgh: Calvin Translation Society, 1844), 1:81–82.

believer in gratitude for salvation, as the means, or instrument, of justification and as contributing to the righteousness of the sinner before God the judge. A believer's pure and heartfelt worship of the one, true God; a minister's zealous proclamation of the gospel of grace; a husband's faithful love of his wife and devoted rearing of his family; and a martyr's death at the stake are not the means or content of the righteousness that is theirs by justification. Not whatsoever!

All who work for the saving act of justification therefore, that is, all who attempt to merit, or earn, salvation by their good works, are and shall be condemned. This indicates the urgency of the defense of the truth of justification in our day, particularly against the corruption of the truth in Reformed and Presbyterian churches and seminaries by the heresies of the new perspective and of the closely related federal vision.

That justification is by (means of) faith is not the teaching that faith itself is the work of the sinner by which he merits righteousness. Faith itself is not the sinner's worthiness to be justified. The activity of believing on the part of the elect child of God, grand and glorious as it is, is not itself the righteousness of the child of God in justification.

Many nominal "evangelicals" suppose that they confess justification by faith and thus distinguish themselves from the Roman Catholic Church when, in fact, they deny the truth of justification and are one with Rome by their doctrine that faith itself—the act of believing in Jesus—is their righteousness with God. Their belief is that, since sinners are unable to keep the law, God decides to accept faith as the work of the sinner that merits righteousness, or God decides to regard the sinner's faith as the righteousness that satisfies his justice.

In reality this doctrine is simply another, more subtle form of the false doctrine that justification is by the works of the sinner. Now the work is the sinner's faith. Because a work that merits with God, a work that constitutes righteousness in the judgment of God, must always be a contribution on the part of the one who accomplishes the justifying, basic to this view is that faith lies in the natural power of the sinner inasmuch as the sinner is supposed to possess a free will, that is, a will that is able to choose Christ and believe in him. It is to be feared, therefore, that many who suppose themselves evangelical Christians are as guilty of denying the fundamental gospel truth of justification by faith as are the members of the Roman Catholic Church.

That faith—the act of believing—is the sinner's righteousness with God in justification, by virtue of an alleged free will, is the characteristic form of the heresy of justification by works as taught by Arminianism. Often overlooked in the controversy of the Reformed faith with Arminianism is this Arminian heresy regarding justification. The Arminians of the early seventeenth century and the Arminians of the twenty-first century were and are guilty of the false doctrine of justification by works, the work being the sinner's act of believing.

The Synod of Dordt exposed and condemned this aspect of the Arminian false gospel.

> The true doctrine having been explained, the Synod *rejects* the errors of those...who teach that the new covenant of grace, which God the Father, through the mediation of the death of Christ, made with man, does not herein consist that we by faith, inasmuch as it accepts the merits of Christ, are justified before God and saved, but in the fact that God, having revoked the demand of perfect obedience of the law, regards faith itself and the obedience of faith, although imperfect, as the perfect obedience of the law, and does esteem it worthy of the reward of eternal life through grace.

The article in the Canons goes on to charge that, by their heretical doctrine of justification, the Arminians "proclaim, as did the wicked Socinus, a new and strange justification of man before God, against the consensus of the whole church."[15]

That this aspect of the Arminian heresy was no small matter to Reformed orthodoxy is evident from the fact that also the Belgic Confession found it necessary to expose and warn against it. Having confessed that "we are justified by faith alone," the Confession immediately added: "However, to speak more clearly, we do not mean that faith itself justifies us, for it is only an instrument with which we embrace Christ our Righteousness." The Confession then explained the difference between the truth that justification is by faith and the false doctrine that makes faith itself the righteousness of the sinner.

> But Jesus Christ, imputing to us all his merits, and so many holy works, which he hath done for us and in our stead, is our Righteousness. And faith is an instrument that keeps us in communion with him in all his benefits, which, when they become ours, are more than sufficient to acquit us of our sins.[16]

The Arminian doctrine is absurd on the very face of it. Believing is not the righteousness of the sinful human that the justice of God requires. Believing is not the payment in full of the sinner's debt to God. Believing is not the performance of perfect obedience to the law of God that God demands of every human. Were God to accept faith as righteousness with himself, God would be unjust. As the Belgic Confession sharply states, "Jesus Christ...is our Righteousness."

Faith is not the substitute for Jesus Christ. Faith is not the replacement for full satisfaction of the justice of God by the suffering of eternal punishment under the infinite wrath of God. Faith is not in the stead of perfect obedience to the law of God.

---

15 Canons of Dordt 2, error 4, in *Confessions and Church Order*, 164–65.

16 Belgic Confession 22, in Schaff, *Creeds of Christendom*, 3:408–9.

But it is the means, or instrument, by which Jesus Christ in his lifelong obedience and especially in his death of satisfaction becomes the sinner's—by imputation.

Regarding the role of faith in the justification of the sinner, the grammar of the Greek New Testament is important. The language of the New Testament is not that sinners are justified *on account of*, or *because of*, or *on the basis of faith*. This would imply that sinners earn righteousness by their faith, or even that faith is itself the righteousness of these sinners. But the New Testament proclaims that sinners are justified "by" faith, thus teaching that faith is the means by which sinners receive the righteousness that is the obedience to the law and the atoning death of Jesus Christ (see Rom. 3:28; 5:1; Gal. 2:16).

Genesis 15:6 and Romans 4:3 do not contradict the teaching of scripture elsewhere that not faith but the obedience of Jesus Christ is the righteousness of the justified sinner. Genesis 15:6 states that Abraham "believed in the Lord; and he counted it to him for righteousness," where the "it" that was counted for righteousness to Abraham is clearly Abraham's believing, or faith. Romans 4:5 puts this understanding of the Genesis passage beyond all doubt when, on the basis of Genesis 15:6, it declares that the "faith [of the believer] is counted for righteousness."

But the meaning of the two related passages is not that the bare act of believing itself, whether of Abraham in the Old Testament or of the believer in the New Testament, constitutes the righteousness of the sinner. Rather, Genesis 15 and Romans 4 view faith with regard to faith's *object* and *content*. This object of faith is Jesus Christ, who is the righteousness of believers. Faith is counted to Abraham and to every believer for righteousness inasmuch as faith looks to, rests on, and embraces Jesus Christ. By virtue of and with regard to the *object* of faith, faith is counted, or reckoned, by God for righteousness.

The context of both passages supports, indeed requires, this explanation. In Genesis 15, Abraham's believing was faith regarding the promise of an heir, upon whom the whole of the covenant of grace and its salvation, also of Abraham, depended. That heir would be Jesus Christ, and his saving work would be (and already was in the time of the Old Testament) justification. Believing in Jehovah's promise of the coming heir, Abraham believed in Jesus Christ. As knowledge of and trust in the promised Messiah, Abraham's faith was counted to Abraham for righteousness.

Treating the Genesis passage, Romans 4 teaches the same: faith is counted for righteousness in respect of faith's object, namely, Jesus Christ. What follows in Romans 4 bears out this understanding of verse 5. The faith of Abraham that was counted to him for righteousness was embrace of the promise of God concerning Abraham's "seed," which is Jesus Christ (vv. 17–21). The faith that was imputed to Abraham for righteousness and the faith that is imputed to us believers for righteousness is faith whose object is the resurrection of "Jesus our Lord from the dead; who was delivered for our offences, and was raised again for our justification" (vv. 24–25).

Not the worthy, even glorious, nature of the activity of believing is the explanation of faith's being counted for righteousness. But the explanation is faith's object and content, Jesus Christ crucified and risen, the righteousness of God for his chosen people.

Exactly this is the Reformed creed's explanation of justification by faith, both negatively and positively. Here the reader ought to pay special attention not to the Catechism's insistence on faith "only," but to the rejection of the notion that faith itself, as an activity, is reckoned to the believer for righteousness and to the confession's pointing to faith's *object*.

> Why sayest thou that thou art righteous only by faith?
>
> Not that I am acceptable to God on account of the worthiness of my faith; but because only the satisfaction,

> righteousness, and holiness of Christ is my righteousness before God, and I can receive the same and make it my own in no other way than by faith only.[17]

The popular doctrine among Protestants, including Reformed churches, that faith is the *condition* of justification and thus of all salvation in the covenant of grace is not essentially different from the Arminian and Roman Catholic doctrine that faith itself is the sinner's meriting righteousness, or even that God graciously accounts faith itself as the sinner's righteousness. Even though this Protestant doctrine grants that the obedience of Christ is the righteousness of the sinner in justification, it makes the reception and application of Christ's righteousness dependent upon a work of the sinner, namely, believing in Jesus Christ. If faith is a condition on which the efficacy of the justifying act of God depends and that the sinner must perform, the sinner himself accomplishes his own justification. His justification is his work, the work being his faith. It is not without significance that the contemporary heresy of justification by works in the sphere of Reformed and Presbyterian churches calling itself the federal vision insists on viewing faith not as the gift of God, but as a condition.[18]

Justification "out of" Faith

As the Bible teaches justification "by," or "by means of," faith, so also does it teach justification "out of" faith. In this case the Greek preposition is not "*dia*" ("by means of") but "*ek*" ("out of"). The Bible teaches justification "out of" faith in the

---

17 Heidelberg Catechism Q&A 61, in ibid., 3:327.

18 For a thorough critique of the popular presentation of faith as a condition of righteousness and salvation in the interests of a gospel of salvation by works, see David J. Engelsma, *Federal Vision: Heresy at the Root*, and *Battle for Sovereign Grace in the Covenant: The Declaration of Principles* (Jenison, MI: Reformed Free Publishing Association, 2013).

crucially important passage Galatians 2:16. The Authorized Version translates the text as follows: "Knowing that a man is not justified by the works of the law, but by the faith of Jesus Christ, even we have believed in Jesus Christ, that we might be justified by the faith of Christ, and not by the works of the law: for by the works of the law shall no flesh be justified." The Authorized Version translates all the important prepositions in the Greek text with the English preposition "by." However, the Greek original of the text uses two different prepositions to bring out two distinct aspects of justification. One is the preposition "*dia*" ("by means of"); the other is the preposition "*ek*" ("out of").

A literal translation of Galatians 2:16, therefore, reads as follows: "Knowing that a man is not justified *out of* [Greek: *ek*] the works of the law, but *by* [Greek: *dia*] the faith of Jesus Christ, even we have believed in Jesus Christ, that we might be justified *out of* [Greek: *ek*] the faith of Christ, and not *out of* [Greek: *ek*] the works of the law; for *out of* [Greek: *ek*] the works of the law shall no flesh be justified." The text teaches that the sinner is justified both *by* faith and *out of* faith. It also denies that anyone is ever justified *out of* his own works.

The truth that one is justified by faith and the truth that one is justified out of faith are fundamentally the same. But the truth that we are justified out of faith adds something to our understanding of justification. That we are justified out of the faith of Christ describes faith as the source of justification. Just as works of the law are the (supposed) source of justification for those who attempt to be justified by works, so faith is the source of justification for those who believe for justification, rather than work for it.

Faith is the source of justification inasmuch as faith has Christ as its object. In the biblical phrase "out of the faith of Christ," Christ is the object of faith. Faith looks to Christ, trusts in Christ, and embraces Christ. From this Christ, faith receives Christ himself as the believer's righteousness by imputation.

Or to say it differently, from this Christ, to whom faith looks and on whom faith rests and whom faith embraces, the believer receives the righteousness of Christ as his own (by imputation).

Faith is the source of justification inasmuch as faith lays hold of and conveys to the believer the righteousness of Christ (by imputation).

Faith itself, apart from Christ its object, faith considered merely as a human's activity of believing, is not the source of justification and could never be the source of justification. But faith is never alone, by itself, as merely the activity of believing. Faith—*true* faith—always has an object, and this object is the crucified and risen Christ as revealed in the gospel. Thus as the embracing of Christ—in whom is forgiveness, righteousness, and adoption as children of God—is faith the source of justification.

A homely illustration will clarify the Bible's teaching that faith is the source of justification: justification *out of* (Greek: *ek*) faith. The source of drinking water in my home is the kitchen faucet. This is not to say that this piece of plumbing produces water of itself. Nor is anyone so foolish as to suppose so. But the faucet is connected with Lake Michigan, which is the water supply for my home. Only as connected with Lake Michigan and as bringing the water of Lake Michigan to my home is the kitchen faucet the source of water to my home.

As I drink out of the faucet, so I am justified out of faith.

The truth about justification that the phrase "out of the faith of Christ" teaches us is that Christ, and Christ alone, is the source of righteousness, that is, the righteousness that we need and that becomes ours by God's act of justification. God has worked out a righteousness in Christ for penitent, believing sinners, and this righteousness is now in that exalted Christ at the right hand of God in heaven. To grant us and bestow on us this righteousness of Christ (by imputation), God is pleased to use faith. Faith is the bond of union with Christ through which the sinner receives righteousness, just as my kitchen faucet and the other plumbing that connects my home with Lake Michigan are the bond of union with Lake Michigan and thus the source of my drinking water.

Works are not the source of justification. The apostle denies this in so many words, in the Greek of Galatians 2:16: "not out of the works of the law." To any and all of his own works, to his own obedience to the law of God, the sinner looks for justification in vain. His own works of obedience to the law are not the source of justification for the sinner. Righteousness cannot be found in one's works of obedience to the law and therefore in the law itself, regardless whether one's works are performed in the power of the Spirit of Jesus Christ, because righteousness is not in, or from, one's works, that is, in, or from, the law.

To look to one's own good works, that is, to the law, for justification is as foolish as it would be for me to seek drinking water by sticking a faucet into a pile of sand in my backyard. But seeking righteousness in the works of the law is not only foolish. It is also wicked, dreadfully wicked. God has worked out his righteousness for sinners in his incarnate and crucified Son and has clearly revealed that justification is out of faith in him. That is, God has revealed that justification has its source in the faith that unites the sinner with Jesus Christ. As Paul declared about unbelieving Jewry, "They being ignorant of God's righteousness, and going about to establish their own righteousness, have not submitted themselves unto the righteousness of God." Against this folly and wickedness, the apostle proclaimed, "Christ is the end of the law for righteousness to every one that believeth" (Rom. 10:3–4).

Knowing this, namely, that faith is the source of righteousness, we believers do the wise, right, beneficial, Christ-exalting, and God-honoring thing: "Even we have believed in Jesus Christ, that we might be justified out of [Greek: *ek*] the faith of Christ" (Gal. 2:16).

Chapter Ten

THE FAITH "OF JESUS": AN OBJECTION CONSIDERED

Before proceeding to the Protestant and Reformed confession that justification is by faith *alone*, it is necessary to consider a contemporary corruption of the doctrine of justification by faith consisting of an erroneous interpretation of the biblical phrase "the faith of Jesus." This phrase is of fundamental importance for the doctrine of justification by faith. It appears in Galatians 2:16: "Knowing that a man is not justified by the works of the law, but by *the faith of Jesus Christ*, even we have believed in Jesus Christ, that we might be justified by *the faith of Christ*, and not by the works of the law" (emphasis added; see also Rom. 3:22).

The importance of "the faith of Jesus Christ," and of the right understanding of the truth of it, are evident from the fact that, according to Galatians 2:16, it is by this faith that we are justified. The church must rightly know what the faith of Jesus Christ is, so that the members may seek justification where it is to be found as well as to seek justification in the right manner, so that the church herself can preach justification rightly, and indeed so that the children of God can know what justification actually *is*. To err concerning the meaning of the "faith of Jesus Christ" is to falsify the fundamental truth of justification by faith.

The Reformation explained "the faith of Jesus Christ" in

Galatians 2 and elsewhere in the New Testament as the believer's knowledge of and trust in Jesus Christ. In the phrase under consideration, "Jesus Christ" is the *object* of faith. Grammatically, "of Jesus Christ" is the objective genitive. Jesus is not the subject of the believing, that is, the one who does the believing. The faith is not his activity of believing or, as the proponents of the erroneous explanation prefer, intensifying their outrage on the biblical phrase, Jesus' activity of being faithful to God. But Jesus is the object of the believing, that is, the one in whom and upon whom the child of God believes for salvation, particularly for the righteousness that delivers the believer from guilt and constitutes him as having perfectly obeyed the law before the tribunal of God the judge. In the phrase "the faith of Jesus Christ," faith is the activity of the child of God, an activity that looks to and depends on Jesus Christ, particularly, for justification.

The meaning of the phrase "the faith of Jesus Christ" is similar to the meaning of the phrase "the trust of the father," in explaining the trust of a frightened little child in his father's goodness, strength, and willingness to protect the child.

The Dutch expositor S. Greijdanus is right in his explanation of the phrase "the faith of Jesus Christ" in Galatians 2:16:

> The faith exercised by our Savior himself is not meant… but the faith *in* the Lord Jesus (compare also Col. 2:5). Still the apostle speaks now of the faith *of* Jesus Christ, in order to convey that this faith is fulfilled entirely with him, causes one to rest entirely upon him, derives its content entirely from him, and is defined in nature and character entirely by him—in nature, working, and power.[1]

---

1 S. Greijdanus, *Galaten* [Galatians], in the series *Korte Verklaring der Heilige Schrift* [Brief explanation of the holy scripture] (Kampen: Kok, 1922), 51. The translation of the Dutch is mine.

The Reformation explained "the faith of Jesus" in relationship to justification as the believer's faith that has Jesus, his person, and his work as its object. This was the explanation of the important phrase by Martin Luther. In his commentary on Galatians 2:16, Luther wrote, "Faith takes hold of Christ and has Him present, enclosing Him as the ring encloses the gem." Obviously, the "faith of Jesus Christ" is not Jesus' own believing or faithfulness, but the believing of the Christian that has Jesus Christ as its object. Luther continued his explanation of the "faith of Jesus" as taught in Galatians 2:16: "[God says], 'because...your faith takes hold of Christ, whom I have freely given to you as your Justifier and Savior, therefore be righteous.' Thus God accepts you or accounts you righteous only on account of Christ, in whom you believe."[2]

The reformer's interpretation of the "faith of Jesus Christ" in Romans 3:22 is the same: "The faith in Christ by which we are justified is not a matter of believing only in Christ or in the Person of Christ, but in all things which pertain to Christ." The "faith of Jesus Christ" is not Jesus' activity of believing or his active faithfulness, but the believing of the child of God that has Jesus as its object and content.[3]

So also Calvin understood the "faith of Jesus" as the believer's knowledge of and trust in Jesus for righteousness. Explaining Romans 3:22, "the righteousness of God which is by faith of Jesus Christ," Calvin wrote:

> Paul briefly shows what this justification is like, viz. that it is to be found in Christ and apprehended by faith...All men are destitute of righteousness in themselves...It is necessary that Christ should come to our

2 Martin Luther, *Lectures on Galatians 1535*, in *Luther's Works*, ed. Jaroslav Pelikan (St. Louis, MO: Concordia, 1963), 26:132.

3 Luther, *Lectures on Romans*, in *Luther's Works*, ed. Hilton C. Oswald (St. Louis, MO: Concordia, 1972), 25:237.

> aid, for He who alone is just can render us just by transferring to us His own righteousness...Faith is therefore said to justify, because it is the instrument by which we receive Christ, in whom righteousness is communicated to us. When we are made partakers of Christ, we are not only ourselves righteous, but our works also are counted righteous in the sight of God, because any imperfections in them are obliterated by the blood of Christ.[4]

As the interpretation of the text that teaches justification by the "faith of Jesus Christ," Calvin's commentary clearly rejects the novel view that the faith of Jesus in justification is not the believer's faith that has Jesus as its object, but Jesus' own faith or faithfulness.

In a section of his *Institutes* in which the express subject is the relationship between faith and Jesus Christ in the matter of justification, Calvin taught that "by faith in Christ" righteousness is "given to us. Therefore, as soon as you become engrafted into Christ through faith, you are...a partaker in righteousness...All the merits of Christ...are communicated to you."[5]

Throughout the entire, long section of the *Institutes* in which Calvin thoroughly explains the truth of justification and laboriously refutes all the errors concerning this fundamental doctrine that were troubling the church of his time (all of which trouble the church also in our time!), there is not so much as a hint that the "faith of Christ" in justification is Christ's own faith. Everywhere, the "faith of Jesus Christ" in justification is viewed as the believer's faith that has Jesus Christ as its object; the believer's faith that embraces Jesus Christ in his

---

4 John Calvin, commentary on Romans 3:22, in *The Epistles of Paul the Apostle to the Romans and to the Thessalonians*, trans. Ross Mackenzie (Grand Rapids, MI: Eerdmans, 1960), 73.

5 Calvin, *Institutes*, 3.15.6, 1:794.

lifelong obedience and especially in his redemptive death; and the believer's faith by which the believer receives the righteousness of Christ by imputation.[6]

What the Reformed church of the Reformation understood by the "faith of Jesus Christ" in the doctrine of justification is plain from her creeds. Nowhere is the faith of Jesus Christ by which the believer is justified explained as the faith possessed and exercised by Jesus himself. Everywhere, it is rather the knowledge and trust of the believer that have Jesus and his obedience as their object and by which the obedience of Jesus is reckoned to the believer as his own.

According to question 59 of the Heidelberg Catechism, the faith of Jesus is the activity of the believer that "believest all this" concerning the person and work of Jesus Christ, so that by the faith that has Jesus as object the believer is "righteous in Christ before God."[7] In question 60 the Catechism views the faith of Jesus as the believer's "true faith in Jesus Christ," by which the believer embraces the benefit of Christ's "satisfaction, righteousness, and holiness...with a believing heart."[8] According to question 61, the faith of Christ is the means by which the believer receives and makes the righteousness of Christ his own "righteousness before God."[9]

The Belgic Confession expresses the belief of the entire Reformation, Lutheran, Reformed, and Presbyterian, concerning the faith of Jesus Christ in article 22. Faith is that spiritual power in the heart of the child of God that "embraces Jesus Christ with all his merits, appropriates him, and seeks nothing more besides him." Faith is "an instrument with which we embrace Christ our Righteousness." The saving benefit for believers of thus

6 See Calvin, *Institutes*, 3.11–18, 1:738–833.
7 Heidelberg Catechism Q&A 59, in Schaff, *Creeds of Christendom*, 3:326.
8 Heidelberg Catechism A 60, in ibid., 3:326–27.
9 Heidelberg Catechism A 61, in ibid., 3:327.

embracing Christ by their faith is especially that the believers are "acquit[ted]...of our sins."[10]

The novel, exotic interpretation of the phrase "the faith of Jesus Christ" in the statement of justification as Jesus' own faith is part and parcel of the concentrated effort of the men of the new perspective to destroy the biblical and Reformation doctrine of justification by faith alone. If justification is alone by means of our faith in Jesus Christ, there is no place for our works, including our faithfulness to Jesus, as contributing to our justification. But if our justification is by means of Jesus' faith, conceived as Jesus' faithfulness to God and to us, this faith, or faithfulness, on the part of Jesus can very well be construed as consisting in part—indeed, in *decisive* part—of our active faithfulness to God (Jesus, of course, making this his faithfulness available to us, although not sovereignly and irresistibly).

Faith as Faithfulness

The pseudo-evangelical N. T. Wright is a leading figure in the effort to introduce this novel interpretation of the phrase "the faith of Jesus Christ," and thus the old doctrine of justification, into evangelical and Reformed churches today. According to this promoter of the new perspective in evangelical and Reformed circles, "when Paul speaks in Galatians and Romans of *pistis Christou* [faith of Christ], he normally intends to denote the *faithfulness of the Messiah to the purposes of God* rather than the faith by which Jew and Gentile alike believe the gospel."[11]

In keeping with this exegetical decision on behalf of the heretical theology of the new perspective, Wright then offers this translation of the fundamental text on justification in Galatians 2:16: "We know that one is not justified by works of Torah, but

10 Belgic Confession 22, in ibid., 3:408–9.

11 N. T. Wright, *Paul: In Fresh Perspective* (Minneapolis: Fortress Press, 2005), 47. "Fresh" in the title is Wright's beguiling substitution for "new."

through the *faithfulness of Jesus the Messiah*; thus we too have believed in the Messiah, Jesus, so that we might be justified by the *faithfulness of the Messiah* and not by works of Torah, because through works of Torah no flesh will be justified."[12]

Lest anyone miss the radical departure of his understanding of justification by faith in Galatians 2:16 from that of the Reformation and of all Reformed churches hitherto, and thus his departure from the gospel of the Reformation, Wright calls attention to the departure: "I have translated *pistis Christou* [faith of Christ] and similar phrases as a reference, not to human *faith in* the Messiah but to the *faithfulness of* the Messiah, by which I understand...Jesus'...faith*fulness* to the divine plan for Israel... The passage [Gal. 2:16] works far better if we see the meaning of 'justified,' not as a statement about how someone becomes a Christian [that is, by being justified by faith in Christ], but as a statement about *who belongs to the people of God, and how you can tell that in the present.*"[13]

In his book *Justification: God's Plan & Paul's Vision*, Wright expressly draws out the implication of his understanding of the phrase "faith of Christ" as Christ's own faithfulness for the Protestant and Reformed doctrine of salvation by the imputation of Christ's righteousness. The implication is the rejection of an imputed righteousness as fundamental to the salvation of the gospel. Romans 3:21–22 proclaims the "righteousness of God which is by faith of Jesus Christ unto all and upon all them that believe." In Wright's theological thinking, the "faith of Jesus Christ" is the "faithfulness of the Messiah," not the believer's faith in the Messiah. The implication of this translation and understanding of the phrase is that the doctrine of "the imputed righteousness of Christ" is mistaken, indeed misleading.[14]

---

12 Ibid., 111; emphasis added.

13 Ibid., 112. The emphasis is Wright's.

14 Wright, *Justification*, 105.

Wright's and the new perspective's new interpretation of the phrase the "faith of Jesus Christ" in the interests of their new theology of justification as the identification of those who are in the new covenant and are members of the church overturns and subverts the gospel in its entirety. Wright and the new perspective are the contemporary proof of Luther's contention that justification by faith is central to the gospel, so that to go wrong concerning justification is to corrupt the whole of the gospel.

Wright and the new perspective strip righteousness from God's work of salvation in Jesus Christ, a heresy than which a worse can scarcely be conceived. The "righteousness of God" in Galatians and Romans does not refer to God's perfection of justice. Rather, it describes God's faithfulness in the covenant. Accordingly, the "righteousness of Jesus Christ" does not refer to the full satisfaction of the justice of God by Jesus Christ on behalf of and in the place of his elect church. Rather, the "righteousness of Jesus Christ" is Jesus' own faithfulness to the covenant of God.

Regardless of the impressive and soothing message of the covenantal faithfulness of God and his Messiah, the effect of this reinterpretation of the righteousness of God and of his Christ is the stripping of the gospel of salvation of the satisfaction of the justice of God for the believing sinner and the enjoyment of this satisfaction by the one who believes in Jesus. Wright and the new perspective attempt to comfort sinners with a gospel that does not reckon with the justice of God. Theirs is a gospel that not only ignores, but also denies, the satisfying of this awesome, divine justice by the substitutionary death of Jesus Christ under the wrath of God.

The theology of Wright and the new perspective leaves the sinner exposed to the damning wrath of God. This is ultimate terror. There is, there can be, no gospel of divine faithfulness to the covenant by saving guilty sinners *apart from the satisfaction of the justice of God*. There is, there can be, no faithfulness to the covenant on the part of the Messiah apart from satisfying the justice of God on behalf of elect but guilty sinners. There is, there can be, no salvation apart from the satisfaction of the justice of God. As the Heidelberg Catechism, which Wright and the new perspective arrogantly dismiss as outdated and in essential respects erroneous, confesses as an essential truth of the gospel in question 12: "God wills that his justice be satisfied."

God wills that his justice be satisfied!

The Catechism continues: "Therefore must we make full satisfaction to the same, either by ourselves or by another." The righteousness of God is the *requirement* of this full satisfaction, because "the righteous judgment of God" determines that "we deserve temporal and eternal punishment" for our original sin in Adam and for our sinful nature and our actual sins. According to the righteousness of God therefore, the only way to "escape this punishment and be again received into favor" is the way of satisfaction. To the objection of the heretics at the time of the Catechism, that God is merciful, as well as to the similar objection of N. T. Wright and the new perspective today, that God is a God of faithfulness to his covenant, the response of the Catechism is that "God is indeed merciful, but he is likewise just; wherefore his justice requires that sin, which is committed against the most high majesty of God, be also punished with extreme, that is, with everlasting punishment both of body and soul."[15]

This is the righteousness of God in Romans, Galatians, and the entire scripture. It is the perfection of the being of God consisting of the perfect harmony of all his willing and acts with his holiness, or absolute goodness. Regarding the guilty sinner, it is the perfection of God's being that requires and effects the maintenance of God's holy being—his Godhead!—by the infliction

15 Heidelberg Catechism Q&A 11–12, in Schaff, *Creeds of Christendom*, 3:311.

on the sinner of the punishment due the assault on and denial of the holy being of God. Ultimately, this deserved punishment is eternal, awful hell. As the heart, center, and foundation of the gospel of salvation, it is the substitutionary suffering of the punishment for sin by God himself in the human flesh of Jesus, thus executing and satisfying his righteousness, which then is (legally) imputed to the elect but guilty sinner by means of the sinner's faith in Jesus Christ.

This is the righteousness of God proclaimed in the gospel, for example in Romans 1:17: "For therein [in the 'gospel of Christ,' mentioned in v. 16] is the righteousness of God revealed from faith to faith: as it is written, The just shall live by faith." This is the righteousness of God in the background of the apostle's fearful warning in verse 18: "The wrath of God is revealed from heaven against all ungodliness and unrighteousness of men, who hold the truth in unrighteousness."

Ignorant of the righteousness of God, both as a perfection of God and as the fundamental grace of the gospel of Jesus Christ, Wright and the men of the new perspective leave themselves and their followers guilty before a just God, devoid of the imputed righteousness of God in Jesus Christ, and therefore miserable objects of the damning wrath of God. This misery they experience also, regardless of their theological profundity and pious platitudes. The only deliverance from the consciousness of guilt is the imputation of the righteousness of God in Jesus Christ. This righteousness, they reject.

As ignorant as they are of the righteousness of the gospel, so mistaken are they regarding faith. Faith to them is the faithfulness of Jesus. When the gospel preaches justification by the faith of Jesus, Wright and his cohorts explain this faith as Jesus' faithfulness. This exegesis is not innocent, is not merely a mistake in Greek grammar. It is rather part and parcel of the determined effort of these vaunted exegetes to overthrow the heart of the gospel of grace: that by the cross and resurrection of Jesus Christ guilty sinners are justified in the judgment of a just God by believing in Jesus and thus, by means of this faith, having the righteousness of Jesus Christ imputed to their account in their own consciousness.

"Faith" in Galatians 2:16, Romans 3:22, and similar passages is not "faithfulness." In the Bible justification by faith is not justification by the faithfulness of Jesus. Faith in Galatians 2:16, Romans 3:22, and similar passages is believing, that is, knowing and trusting in Jesus Christ. Justification by faith is justification by means of the sinner's believing in Jesus Christ. The evidence for this understanding of faith in its relationship to justification is abundant and incontrovertible.

First, repeatedly the Bible teaches that justification is by faith *in* Jesus. The preposition "in" sets Jesus forth as the object of faith, not the subject. The immediate context, for instance, of Romans 3:22, where is found the phrase "faith of Jesus Christ," describes justifying faith as faith "in" Jesus' blood (v. 25). Verse 26 calls God the "justifier of him which believeth in Jesus." The clear, repeated, express statement of scripture that justification is by the faith of the believer that has Jesus as its object should guide the interpretation of the rarer, less clear statement that justification is by the faith "of Jesus."

Second, one of the main passages in which the phrase "faith of Jesus Christ" occurs, Galatians 2:16, itself explains the phrase as meaning faith that has Jesus as its object. Between the phrase "faith of Jesus Christ" and the phrase "faith of Christ" is the explanatory statement, "Even we have believed in Jesus Christ." The faith *of* Jesus Christ, in the matter of justification, is a believer's faith *in* Jesus Christ, a faith that rests in Jesus Christ for the righteousness of justification. If the exegesis of Wright were correct, the explanatory phrase in Galatians 2:16 should have read: "Even we are confident that Jesus Christ believed and was faithful."

Third, the contrast of ideas in Galatians 2:16 requires explaining the "faith of Jesus Christ" as the believer's faith in Jesus. The contrast in the text is between the "faith of Jesus Christ" and the "works of the law." A man is justified by the faith of Jesus Christ, not by the works of the law. The works of the law are not the works that the law performs, but the works that sinners actively perform in order (illicitly) to be justified. They are works that these sinners perform in compliance with the law. So also regarding the faith of Jesus Christ. It is the sinner's activity of believing, which has Jesus Christ as its end or object.

Fourth, it is simply false that sinners are justified by the "faith" of Jesus. Not by Jesus' faith are sinners justified, but by Jesus' "blood" (Rom. 5:9), by Jesus' "death" (v. 10), and by Jesus' "obedience" (v. 19). The reference is to the cross as substitutionary atonement.

Justification as Church Membership

Mistaken concerning the righteousness of God in Jesus Christ and concerning faith, Wright and the men of the new perspective are grievously in error concerning the saving act of justification. For them justification is not the declaration of God the judge to and upon the believer that his sins are forgiven and that he is righteous before God with the righteousness of Jesus Christ, who obeyed in the sinner's stead, especially by suffering the sinner's punishment in the cross. Justification is not an act of salvation at all. It is merely God's declaration that the sinner is rightfully a member of the church of the New Testament. Salvation may be implied in this declaration, although without any imputation of righteousness, but the divine act of justification is not primarily a saving act of God. It is more of an observation on God's part.

How the new perspective emphasizes this new perspective on justification! "'Justified' [is] not a statement about how someone becomes a Christian [that is, by the forgiveness of sins and the declaration that one is righteous in Christ], but…a statement about *who belongs to the people of God, and how you can tell that in the present.*"[16] "Justification...is not a matter of *how someone enters the community of the true people of God*, but of *how you tell who belongs to that community.*"[17]

That justification is not the saving act of God forgiving the sins of the justified person, but rather God's statement or observation that someone is a member of the church, Wright expresses in a more complete description of his and the new perspective's doctrine of justification in his book *Justification: God's Plan & Paul's Vision.*

> "To be justified" here [in the classic passage in Galatians 2, particularly verse 16] does not mean "to be granted free forgiveness of your sins," "to come into a right relation with God" or some other near-synonym of "to be reckoned 'in the right' before God," but rather, and very specifically, "to be reckoned by God to be a true member of his family, and hence with the right to share table fellowship" [that is, to partake of the Lord's supper].[18]

Nothing is left of the creedal, Reformation gospel of justification by faith. Every element of this gospel, which is the gospel of the Bible, is corrupted: righteousness; faith; and the act of justifying. So much for the truth of justification by faith!

The Cross as ??

Because, as Luther taught, justification is fundamental to all the truths of scripture, Wright and the men of the new perspective necessarily adulterate other biblical doctrines, especially those that bear heavily on the truth of justification. These include the nature of the death of Jesus Christ. Wright never tires of stating in general terms that the death of Jesus was the supreme instance

16 Wright, *Paul*, 112. The emphasis is Wright's.
17 Wright, *What Saint Paul Really Said*, 119. The emphasis is Wright's.
18 Wright, *Justification*, 116.

of God's faithfulness to his covenant; that Jesus' death solved the problem of sin and death; that the cross set things right that had gone horribly wrong by the fall of the human race into sin.

But there is one thing Wright never does. He never clearly and definitely explains *how* and *why* the death of Jesus was God's faithfulness in fulfilling his covenant, solved the problem of sin and death, and set things right. About one thing concerning the cross, the *fundamental thing*, Wright is clear and definite: the explanation of the cross as substitutionary atonement—in that God imputed the guilt of the sins of particular persons to Jesus so that Jesus suffered the wrath and punishment of sinners in their stead, thus satisfying the righteousness of God regarding the guilt of sin—is mistaken.

Such a doctrine of the cross, of course, would expose Wright's rejection of justification as the imputation of Christ's, and thus God's, righteousness to the believing sinner. Inextricably linked with the doctrine of justification as the imputation of Christ's righteousness to the guilty sinner is the doctrine of the cross as God's imputation to Christ Jesus of the guilt of sinners. Rejection of the latter demands rejection also of the former.

This close relationship between the death of Christ as God's numbering of Jesus with the transgressors, reckoning to him the guilt of the sins of others, and justification as God's imputing to the guilty sinners in whose stead Christ died the righteousness of Jesus Christ, the Belgic Confession of Faith declares in articles 21 and 22. The former article concerns the satisfaction of Christ for us. The latter is the confession of the Reformed branch of the Reformation concerning faith in Jesus Christ.

> [In his suffering and death, Jesus the Christ] presented himself in our behalf before his Father, to appease his wrath by his full satisfaction, by offering himself on the tree of the cross, and pouring out his precious blood to purge away our sins...Therefore, he...suffered the just

> for the unjust, as well in his body as in his soul, feeling the terrible punishment which our sins had merited… And hath suffered all this for the remission of our sins.[19]
>
> We justly say with Paul, *that we are justified by faith alone,* or *by faith without works.* However, to speak more clearly, we do not mean that faith itself justifies us, for it is only an instrument with which we embrace Christ our Righteousness. But Jesus Christ, imputing to us all his merits, and so many holy works, which he hath done for us and in our stead, is our Righteousness. And faith is an instrument that keeps us in communion with him in all his benefits, which, when they become ours, are more than sufficient to acquit us of our sins.[20]

This confession makes plain that justification by faith as the imputation of the righteousness of Christ to the believer depends on the cross as God's imputation of the guilt of the elect sinner to Jesus Christ. Rejection of justification by faith, as is the case with Wright and the new perspective, necessarily involves denial of the cross. The student of the theology of Wright and of the new perspective must not therefore be deceived by the fine-sounding generalities with which Wright and the others seemingly extol the work of the Messiah, particularly his death.

> This [the cross and resurrection of Jesus] is how the problem within the existing creation, namely sin and death, has been dealt with through the Messiah, more specifically through the way in which the Messiah has been the means of fulfilling the promises of great victory through which evil would be overthrown.[21]

---

19 Belgic Confession 21, in Schaff, *Creeds of Christendom,* 3:406–7

20 Belgic Confession 22, in ibid., 3:407–9.

21 Wright, *Paul,* 28–29.

Similarly, in his big book on justification, Wright can proclaim that "the Messiah's faithful death is the basis of everything that he [Paul] says about justification, about the covenant family, about God's purposes for the world."[22]

Never does Wright clearly and definitely explain exactly how and why the cross of Christ solved the problem of sin and death. That is, Wright does not clearly set forth his doctrine of the cross as atonement. Also he is at pains clearly and definitely to reject the truth of the death of Christ as substitutionary atonement, in that God imputed to Christ the guilt of others so that Christ suffered the infinite wrath of God against their sins in their stead.

In the same paragraph in which he proclaims the death of the Messiah as the "basis" of all of Paul's gospel, Wright damns the doctrine of the cross as substitutionary atonement with faint praise: "The Messiah's death under the curse of the law (Galatians 3:13) is much, much more than a simplistic exchange ('We were under the curse; he took it; we go free')."[23]

Later, Wright damns the doctrine with louder and more forthright condemnation. "The 'obedience' of Christ [especially Christ's death] is not designed to amass a treasury of merit which can then be 'reckoned' to the believer, as in some Reformed schemes of thought" [including the Reformed and Presbyterian creeds]."[24]

> *It is...a straightforward category mistake, however venerable within some Reformed traditions...to suppose that Jesus "obeyed the law" and so obtained "righteousness" which could be reckoned to those who believe in him.*[25]

---

22 Wright, *Justification*, 136.
23 Ibid., 135–36.
24 Ibid., 228.
25 Ibid., 232. The emphasis is Wright's.

Whatever a "category" mistake may be, it is a *mistake.*

In the "lawcourt scene" that the biblical teaching of justification portrays, "the judge has not clothed the defendant with his own 'righteousness.' That doesn't come into it. Nor has he given the defendant something called 'the righteousness of the Messiah'—or, if he has, Paul has not even hinted at it."[26] To suppose this about the death of Jesus, as the Reformed and Presbyterians have believed and confessed for some five hundred years, would, according to Wright, be "to concede, after all, that 'legalism' was true after all—with Jesus as the ultimate legalist."[27]

It is never enough for an opponent of justification by faith simply to reject the doctrine as a mistake. Always he must attack it as heresy, in this case the horrendous heresy of legalism. What the attack amounts to is the charge that the God who is righteous and who maintains his righteousness is a legalist. Indeed, the God who must maintain his righteousness, as much as he must maintain his holy Godhead, and who therefore, in order still to redeem and save sinners, gives his Son for the satisfying of his justice is a legalist. By this attack on God, particularly his perfection of righteousness, Wright identifies himself—and the new perspective—with the old liberalism, which blasphemed the orthodox Christian doctrine of the atonement as "butcher-shop theology."

Wright identifies Calvinism as a preeminent exponent of this legalistic theology of the cross of Christ, adding the explicit explanatory (and inflammatory) charge of "works-righteousness." He condemns the "Calvinist scheme whereby the law is a good thing which Christ obeyed and thus procured 'righteousness' (works-righteousness, we note) to be then 'imputed' to those who believe."[28]

---

26 Ibid., 206.
27 Ibid., 232.
28 Ibid., 244.

The charge against the Reformed faith that it is legalism and a doctrine of works-righteousness is not only blatant falsehood. It is also ironic. With the theologians of the new perspective, Wright absolves the Jewish foes of Jesus Christ and of the gospel preached by Paul of the charge of works-righteousness. Reading the teaching of Jesus in the gospels and the controversy of Paul in the book of Galatians as the exposure of legalism and works-righteousness was a gigantic mistake on the part of the Reformation, as of the churches that are the heirs of the gospel of the Reformation. The Jewish enemies of Jesus and of Paul ("second temple Judaism," in the vernacular of the new perspective) were not legalists, as the Reformation supposed. Those Jews were, on the contrary, theologians and believers of salvation by grace alone. Nor was the Roman Catholic Church at the time of the Reformation guilty of legalism and works-righteousness. In its conviction that Rome's gospel is the quintessential heresy of salvation by works of obedience to the law, the Reformation was, at the very least, a gigantic mistake.

Who, in fact, were and are the legalists and proponents of works-righteousness?

Why, they were Luther, Calvin, the entire Reformation, and the authors of the Heidelberg Catechism and of the Westminster Confession of Faith. Today, they are the Reformed churches that hold the Heidelberg Catechism, the Belgic Confession, and the Westminster Confession of Faith. These churches are legalists by virtue of confessing that in the cross God reckoned the iniquity of his people to his Son in human flesh so that he might reckon the righteousness of his Son to his people by means of their faith.

Either Wright is theologically ignorant in this matter, which is unlikely, or what is worse, he demeans himself by conducting theological controversy by slanderous name-calling. Legalism, as every first-year seminarian, indeed every Reformed Christian, knows, is not a theology that has God upholding his law and its claims, and thus his own righteousness. Legalism is not a theology that has God upholding his law to the last jot and tittle. Legalism is not a gospel that honors the law of God.

Legalism is a theology that teaches salvation by the sinner's own obedience to the law. Legalism is a theology especially that conditions God's justification of the sinner upon something in the sinner himself, or upon something that the sinner himself performs. Legalism is the teaching of salvation by the works of the sinner. Legalism is the false gospel of justification by works of the law.

No confessing Reformed Christian with even a modicum of theological knowledge can read the three forms of unity and then blaspheme the theology of these creeds as the religion of legalism. Only an enemy of the gospel of grace is able to make such an outrageous charge. This is N. T. Wright.

The last step that the inveterate enemy of the gospel invariably takes is that of ridiculing the truth of the gospel of grace. Wright does not hesitate to take this step. The historic Protestant doctrine of justification leaves us "with God as a distant bank manager, scrutinizing credit and debit sheets."[29] Criticizing the Reformation's doctrine of justification being the imputation of righteousness as a "legal transaction," he judges the doctrine as a "cold piece of business, almost a trick of thought performed by a God who is logical and correct but hardly one we would want to worship."[30]

Time and again Wright and his disciples ridicule even more crudely the biblical and Reformation doctrine of justification as the imputation of righteousness. One of Wright's federal visionist disciples dismisses the biblical and creedal doctrine of justification as the imputation to the believing sinner of the righteousness of Christ as "God doing mental tricks or shuffling

---

29 Ibid., 188.

30 Wright, *What Saint Paul Really Said*, 110.

righteousness around heavenly ledgers."[31] This, let it be noted, is Wright's and the men of the federal vision's judgment upon the sixteenth-century Reformation: the reformers devoted their lives to, and often gave up their lives on behalf of, the silly, if not blasphemous, notion of God as the supreme trickster. N. T. Wright amuses himself by representing the orthodox doctrine of justification as the scatological teaching that someone—God—"passes gas" across a courtroom.[32] The Roman Catholic Church was not so vile in its opposition to the heart of the gospel at the time of the Reformation.

All this rejection and ridicule do not remove the responsibility of Wright positively to set forth his doctrine of the death of Christ. He makes one of his best attempts in *The Climax of the Covenant.* In a section that purports to give the biblical "view of Jesus' death," specifically in Romans 8:1–11, Wright explains that condemnation "has been meted out on the real culprit, namely, sin…It is therefore true to Paul to speak of the punishment which all have deserved being enacted, instead, on the cross." Lest anyone conclude that Wright has in mind the orthodox Reformed doctrine of Christ as the substitute of sinners, he immediately adds, "Paul has here nuanced this view in two ways which distance it from the cruder theories made familiar in some branches of theology" (read: Reformed, creedal orthodoxy). Wright continues:

> First, he [Paul, Romans 8] is careful to say that on the cross God punished (not Jesus, but) "sin," just as in ch. 7 he was careful to distinguish "sin" as the real culprit, rather than "I." Second, his argument functions within the whole matrix of thought according to which the death of Jesus can be interpreted in this way because he represents Israel and Israel represents humankind as a whole.

---

31 Rich Lusk, "From Birmingham, with Love," in Sandlin, *A Faith That Is Never Alone*, 132.

32 Wright, *What Saint Paul Really Said*, 98.

This explanation of the cross is supposed to comport with the Reformed and evangelical doctrine of "vicarious representative suffering."[33]

The attempt by Wright to smuggle his doctrine of the cross into the Reformed churches as a form, indeed the reality, of the orthodox doctrine of "vicarious representative suffering" is deceit, falsehood, and sheer nonsense. Wright's theory of the cross is simply not that of substitution. God did not, according to Wright, punish Jesus in the stead of sinners. But God punished "sin." Whatever substitution there may have been at Calvary was the substitution of sin for sinners.

The notion is absurd. Sin *is* no substitute for sinners. A thing is not a substitute for persons. Much less is the very thing on account of which sinners need a substitute a possible substitute in the just judgment of God. To propose the notion as the orthodox doctrine of "vicarious representative suffering" is as foolish on its very face as it would be to suggest that the state punish murderers by tormenting and then hanging homicide.

Sin *cannot function* as the substitute for sinners. Only a human, a child of Adam, who is therefore one with those in whose stead he is the substitute, and then a child of Adam who is himself sinless can function as the substitute for sinners. If Wright would subject himself to the creeds of the churches of the Reformation, including his own Thirty-Nine Articles of the Church of England, he would know the basic truth of substitution regarding the cross of Jesus Christ, which truth is fundamental to the doctrine of justification by faith. The Heidelberg Catechism is as simple and sound an explanation as any of the Reformation creeds. It has taught hundreds of thousands of children and youths this truth of the "vicarious representative suffering" of Jesus Christ, to their comfort in time and to their eternal salvation.

---

33 Wright, *Climax of the Covenant*, 212–13.

Can any mere creature make satisfaction for us?

None [much less Wright's proposed vile entity, sin]; for, first, God will not punish, in any other creature, that of which man has made himself guilty; and, further, no mere creature can sustain the burden of God's eternal wrath against sin, and redeem others therefrom [much less can Wright's vile entity, sin].[34]

What manner of mediator and redeemer, then, must we seek?

One who is a true and sinless man, and yet more powerful than all creatures; that is, one who is at the same time true God.[35]

Why must he be a true and sinless man?

Because the justice of God requires that the same human nature which has sinned should make satisfaction for sin; but no man, being himself a sinner, could satisfy for others.[36]

Why must he be at the same time true God?

That by the power of his Godhead he might bear, in his manhood, the burden of God's wrath, and so obtain for and restore to us righteousness and life.[37]

But who, now, is that mediator, who is at the same time true God and a true, sinless man?

Our Lord *Jesus Christ*, who is freely given unto us for complete redemption and righteousness.[38]

---

34 Heidelberg Catechism Q&A 14, in Schaff, *Creeds of Christendom*, 3:311–12.

35 Heidelberg Catechism Q&A 15, in ibid., 3:312.

36 Heidelberg Catechism Q&A 16, in ibid., 3:312.

37 Heidelberg Catechism Q&A 17, in ibid., 3:312.

38 Heidelberg Catechism Q&A 18, in ibid., 3:312–13.

God did not hang sin on the cross, except as Jesus himself bore the mass of all the sins of all those in whose stead he died by the imputation to him of all these sins. God hanged *Jesus* on the cross. God cursed *Jesus*, so that Jesus himself, not some impersonal entity, sin, became "a curse for us: for it is written, Cursed is every one [not sin] that hangeth on a tree" (Gal. 3:13). *Jesus*, not sin, cried out in the pain of his punishment in the stead of others, "My God, my God, why hast thou forsaken me?" *Jesus*, not sin, died under the wrath of God about three o'clock on Good Friday afternoon.

Without Jesus as their substitute in his death, Wright and his followers, and all the adherents of the new perspective, have no substitute, no "vicarious representative suffering." They must therefore suffer the punishing wrath of God against their sins themselves. This is their experience in this life, and this must be their terror regarding their eternal future. Living and dying without a substitute, they live and die under the punitive wrath and dreadful curse of the God who is, despite their denial, just. If Jesus was not punished in their stead, they are and will be punished in their own persons, body and soul.

The gospel of Wright and the new perspective is a message of unmitigated wrath, unborne curse, and unending damnation. This is the only message of their gospel. This is the message of their gospel for everyone. Some gospel!

But this is the gospel that prominent, influential theologians and ministers are defending and promoting in reputedly conservative Reformed and Presbyterian churches and seminaries, including the Orthodox Presbyterian Church, the Presbyterian Church in America, and the United Reformed Church, in the theology of the federal vision.

The second heretical feature of Wright's doctrine of the cross of Christ, as set forth in the quotation above, is that it presents the death of Christ as universal atonement (ignoring for the moment that it was not, according to Wright, atonement at all, for anyone). Christ died as the representative of Israel, "and Israel represents humankind as a whole." Whatever he was, and was doing, on the cross, Christ was, and was doing, for all of humankind without exception.

This doctrine of the cross the Reformed faith has condemned as the teaching of universal atonement.[39] Inasmuch as Wright, like most purveyors of the false doctrine, acknowledges that not all humans, however, will be saved, this theory of the cross denies the efficacy of the death of Christ—many perish for whom Christ died—and necessarily makes the saving power of the cross depend on the will and works of the sinner. The reason the cross saves one and not the other is that the one believes in Christ, whereas the other does not.

Implied is the heresy of free will. In their natural, sinful condition, sinners nevertheless have the spiritual power to believe in Christ by a decision of their will. If Wright would not embrace the heresy of free will outright, he holds it in the form of teaching a universal grace of God that enables all sinners to believe and be saved, which grace, however, is not efficacious but dependent on every sinner's assent to this grace.

The theology of Wright and the new perspective is Arminian and Pelagian, the only alternative to the theology of salvation by sovereign grace, as confessed by Augustine, Luther, Calvin, and the Reformed creeds, which theology of sovereign grace Wright bluntly repudiates.

Rejection of justification by faith, entailing repudiation of the doctrines of grace as confessed by the Canons of Dordt and the Westminster Confession of Faith, necessarily demands, if it does not proceed from, rejection of the truth of predestination. Although I reserve critique of Wright's open rejection of the eternal decree of election and reprobation for a later chapter in

---

39 See the Canons of Dordt 2, in ibid., 3:586–87.

this book, I note here the fact of Wright's contemptuous rejection of predestination.

Offering his explanation of Romans 9–11 at the end of *The Climax of the Covenant*, Wright at once dismisses the view that regards the passage as a "doctrinal section dealing with the abstract doctrine of predestination." Romans 9–11 is not "'about' predestination or election." Nowhere, not even in Romans 9:19–24, does this section of the book of Romans teach that "the creator decides, arbitrarily, to save some and condemn others."[40]

Wright's rejection of predestination is related to his heretical doctrine of justification in at least two important respects. First, justification for Wright is not a saving act of God, but merely a badge that identifies one as a member of the people of God. If justification is not salvation from sin, there need not be, and is not, an eternal source of justification unto salvation in a decree of election, or an explanation of the absence of justifying faith in others in a decree of reprobation.

Second, inasmuch as justification out of faith, as a badge of membership in the covenant and church, is, according to Wright, intended by God for all of humankind; and since the death of Christ that is somehow the basis of this membership was for all humans without exception; the Reformed doctrine of predestination, as taught in reality in Romans 9–11, has absolutely no place in the theology of N. T. Wright. Predestination is the deathblow to Wright's and the new perspective's universalism.

One notes with astonishment that this blatantly heretical theology, openly falsifying the fundamental gospel truth of justification and equally as openly denying the doctrines of grace confessed by the Reformed Canons of Dordt and the Presbyterian Westminster Confession of Faith, has made, and is

---

40 Wright, *Climax of the Covenant*, 231–57.

making, huge inroads into Reformed and Presbyterian churches, chiefly through the theology that calls itself the federal vision; has not been clearly and forcefully condemned by the Orthodox Presbyterian Church, the Presbyterian Church in America, and the United Reformed Churches (and in some cases has been approved); and is not refuted by addressing its main error and the powerful engine of its popularity in Reformed circles, namely, its doctrine of a covenant of grace that is universal and conditional, that is, a doctrine that divorces covenant and election.[41]

The New Perspective as Ecumenicity

Yet one more doctrinal deviation, which is at the same time intensely practical, of N. T. Wright demands to be exposed. This too is an implication of his theory of justification. The error is an antichristian ecumenicity. His doctrine of justification not only makes possible but also requires the union of all Protestant churches and especially the reunion of Protestant churches and the Roman Catholic Church. If justification is not a doctrine of salvation, indeed the fundamental doctrine of salvation, but only an identifying mark of membership in the church, the doctrine of justification by the faith of Christ Jesus unites all those who claim to have this faith. All belong in one and the same church or in churches united by close ecumenical relations.

If justification by faith is not, as the Reformation supposed, the fundamental truth of the gospel of saving grace that divides the true (Protestant) church from the false (Roman Catholic) church, the Reformation was a sinful division of the church of Christ and should be undone as quickly as possible by the return

---

41 For the exposure of the federal vision, and of the new perspective of which the federal vision is an expression, regarding specifically the relationship of election and covenant, see David J. Engelsma, *Covenant and Election in the Reformed Tradition* (Jenison, MI: Reformed Free Publishing Association, 2011) and *Federal Vision.*

of Protestants to Rome—on bended knee in supplication before the pope.

If justification is not the central truth of the gospel of gracious salvation, with its implications for the doctrines of grace, as Dordt judged, all divisions of the church due to the controversies of Calvinism with Arminianism are an unfortunate mistake. The theology of Wright demands and enables reconciliation of the hitherto warring churches. Whatever confession of fault might be appropriate would fall to Calvinism. For Calvinism mistakenly thought that justification by faith, and Calvinism's five points, are essential doctrines of salvation and the marks of a true church.

Wright makes no secret of these ecumenical implications, indeed of the very ecumenical *nature*, of his theology of justification. At the very least, its ecumenical implications are, in Wright's thinking, commendations of his theology of justification. Now and again, the British theologian suggests that ecumenicity was the purpose of his espousal and development of the new perspective. This ecumenicity is by no means limited to the divided Protestant churches. It is an ecumenicity that has the reunion of Protestant churches with the Roman Catholic Church mainly in view.

> Paul's doctrine of justification by faith [as explained by Wright] impels the churches, in their current fragmented state, into the ecumenical task. It cannot be right that the very doctrine which declares that all who believe in Jesus belong at the same table (Galatians 2) should be used as a way of saying that some, who define the doctrine of justification differently, belong at a different table. The doctrine of justification, in other words, is not merely a doctrine which Catholic and Protestant might just be able to agree on, as a result of hard ecumenical endeavour. It is itself the ecumenical doctrine,

> the doctrine that rebukes all our petty and often culture-bound church groupings, and which declares that all who believe in Jesus belong together in the one family... The doctrine of justification is in fact the great *ecumenical* doctrine...Because what matters is believing in Jesus, detailed agreement on justification itself, properly conceived, isn't the thing which should determine eucharistic fellowship.[42]

Himself drawing out the practical, ecumenical implication of his doctrine of justification as a badge of membership in the church of Jesus Christ, rather than as the fundamental saving work of God in Jesus Christ, Wright proclaims that there is "neither Catholic nor Protestant."[43] In the *Reformation & Revival Journal,* it is acknowledged freely that Wright's doctrine of justification is vitally important for ecumenicity with Rome and that this ecumenicity is a chief purpose of the new perspective.[44] By their doctrine of justification and their insistence on this doctrine as fundamental to the gospel of grace, the churches of the Reformation were, and are, and so long as they maintain the doctrine remain "fissiparous Protestantism."[45]

Norman Shepherd carries this ecumenical project into the conservative Presbyterian and Reformed churches on the wings

---

42 Wright, *What Saint Paul Really Said*, 158–59. The emphasis is Wright's.

43 N. T. Wright, "The Letter to the Romans," in *The New Interpreter's Bible: A Commentary in Twelve Volumes* (Nashville, TN: Abingdon Press, 2002), 10:485.

44 Travis Tamerius, "Sounding the Alarm: N. T. Wright and Evangelical Theology," *Reformation & Reviva. Journal* 11, no. 2 (Spring 2002): 28. How complicit much of the Reformed and Presbyterian community of theologians is in the spread of the heresy of Wright and the new perspective, we learn from this magazine's mention that recently S. Ferguson and D. Wright allowed Wright to define justification in their dictionary of theology. Wright's definition explicitly *bases* justification on the sinner's faith (see 48–49).

45 Wright, *Justification*, 131.

of his theology of the federal vision. He laments that there are "unresolved questions" (having to do with justification by faith in particular and with salvation in general) remaining in the Protestant churches "that are really the legacy of the Protestant Reformation." The Reformed creeds evidently do not resolve the issue of justification as it separates Reformed churches from the Roman Catholic Church. Shepherd supposes that his, the federal vision's, and the new perspective's doctrine of justification offers "hope for a common understanding between Roman Catholicism and evangelical Protestantism regarding the way of salvation."[46]

In this ecumenical proposal, Shepherd is right. His doctrine of justification unites all the Protestant churches that are deceived by it with the Roman Catholic Church, for it is the Roman Catholic doctrine of justification by faith and by faith's good works. When he and his disciples return to Rome, however, as they already have spiritually and as they certainly will physically, they must confess several egregious sins. First, by its gospel of grace alone through faith alone on the basis of the cross of Christ alone, the Reformation corrupted the true gospel of grace and merit, by faith and good works, on the basis of the cross and the sinner's will. Second, the Reformation was grievous sin on the part of the reformers in wickedly instigating schism in the holy body of Christ, headquartered at Rome. Third, by preaching as the gospel the doctrine of justification by faith alone, Luther, Calvin, the other reformers, and the Reformed churches to the present day are responsible for the perishing of multitudes who lived and died trusting for salvation in the grace of God alone, rather than in their own will and works.

46 Shepherd, *Call of Grace*, 4, 59.

Chapter Eleven

JUSTIFIED BY FAITH *ONLY*

In the controversy over the doctrine of justification, it has always been the word *only* that has expressed and defended the truth, exposed heresy concerning justification, and distinguished the true church from the false church.

Only or *alone* in the confession of justification divided Protestantism, both Lutheran and Reformed, from the Roman Catholic Church at the time of the Reformation. In his sermons on Galatians, John Calvin preached to his congregation in Geneva:

> For the Papists will well enough confess that we be justified by faith, howbeit they add that it is but partly. But that gloss marreth all. For here it is proved that we cannot be found righteous before God, but by the means of our Lord Jesus Christ, and by resting upon the salvation which he hath purchased for us. The Papists see this well enough: and therefore for fashion sake they say we be justified by faith, but not by faith alone: they will none of that. That is the thing that they fight against: and it is the chief point that is in controversy between them and us.[1]

1 John Calvin, *Sermons on Galatians* (Audubon, NJ: Old Paths Publications, 1995), 246. Calvin was preaching on Galatians 2:16.

In light of the crucial importance of *only* or *alone* in the confession of the gospel truth of justification, of which importance both the Roman Catholic Church and Protestantism have always been well aware, it was highly significant that the basic document of the ecumenical movement and organization Evangelicals and Catholics Together confessed justification by faith and omitted *only*: "We affirm together that we are justified by grace through faith because of Christ."[2] Glaringly evident is that the faith the evangelicals and Roman Catholics "affirm together" omits *only*: "by grace *only* through faith *only* because of Christ *only*." The omission was deliberate. Thus the Roman Catholic doctrine of justification was promoted by deceptive evangelical leaders and will be accepted by gullible Protestant church members. As Calvin remarked in the above quotation from his *Sermons on Galatians*, the papists know only too well the fundamental importance of *only* in the confession of justification.

Also the men of the federal vision within Reformed and Presbyterian churches gladly confess justification by faith. But they repudiate *only*. According to this contemporary heresy, sinners are justified by faith, but they are not justified by faith *only*. Leading federal vision theologian Norman Shepherd rejects both *alone* in Romans 3:28 and the doctrine that Luther's use of the word in his translation of the text was intended to highlight. In defense of his Romanist denial of justification by faith *alone*, Shepherd, like the Roman Catholic opponents of justification by faith alone, calls attention to the fact that "Romans 3:28 does not use the word 'alone,' when it speaks of justification by faith." "Luther *inserted* this word into the translation of his German Bible." By this insertion the reformer "tweak[ed] the inspired word of God," which is no small error of translation *of*

2 "ECT Statement," in Colson and Neuhaus, *Evangelicals & Catholics Together*, xviii.

the Bible and no minor corruption of fundamental doctrine—justification. *Alone* in the biblical statement of justification, and in the Protestant confession of justification based on this biblical statement, is nothing but a "Lutheran gloss."[3] A "gloss," as Shepherd here intends is according to *Webster's New Collegiate Dictionary*, "a false and often willfully misleading interpretation (as of a text)."

Shepherd's condemnation of Luther's "insertion" of "alone" into Romans 3:28 becomes even stronger, and his objection to the doctrine of justification that the word teaches becomes even clearer: "[Luther's] insertion [of 'alone'] actually distorts Paul's meaning."[4] Now the "insertion" of "alone" into Romans 3:28 is not merely a tweaking of the text. It is a distortion of the doctrine of the apostle of Christ, a distortion of the fundamental doctrine of justification.

In this harangue against Luther's translation of Romans 3:28, which translation clearly reveals the gospel of grace of the Reformation and Shepherd's hostility to the Reformation's gospel of grace, Shepherd takes issue with Luther's use of the German word *allein* (*only*) in his translation of the Greek text into the German language. The Greek text is correctly translated into English by the Authorized Version: "Therefore we conclude that a man is justified by faith without the deeds of the law." Luther's translation of the Greek into the German has the last part of text as: "*ohne des Gesetzes Werke,* allein *durch den Glauben*" ("without the works of the law, *only* by faith"). What enraged Rome about Luther's translation of the text at the time his translation appeared, and what angers Shepherd about the translation today, is that there is no word in the Greek text that corresponds to Luther's "*allein.*"

3 Norman Shepherd, "Faith and Faithfulness," in Sandlin, *A Faith That Is Never Alone*, 65; emphasis added.

4 Shepherd, "Justification by Faith Alone," 87.

Compelled to recognize Calvin's defense of the "Lutheran gloss" in Romans 3:28, Shepherd attributes this defense to the reformer's "misunderstanding" of the text. Both Luther's gloss and Calvin's misunderstanding are deadly serious doctrinal error, in the thinking of Shepherd and the federal vision. The error is denial that justification is by faith and by faith's good works.[5] Shrewdly, Shepherd here couches his defense of the heresy of justification by works in language that will pass orthodox Reformed muster: "Justifying faith is a living and active, penitent and obedient faith."[6] In the context of his rejection of *alone* in Romans 3:28, Shepherd's meaning is that justification is by faith *and by faith's activity, penitence, and obedience*, that is, by faith's *works*.

Shepherd and all the representatives of the federal vision do not object merely to the insertion of a word into Romans 3:28 that is not found in the Greek original of the text. They object to Luther's, Calvin's, and the entire Reformation's understanding of the gospel message of the text as this message is made explicit by the implied word *only*. Objecting to *only*, they necessarily approve the Pharisaic and Roman Catholic doctrine of justification as a becoming and continuing righteous before God by faith—*and by works*.

To deny *only* in the doctrine of justification by faith is to commit oneself to *and—and by works*. Deny that Romans 3:28 teaches justification by faith *only*, regardless whether the word has been inserted into the translation or is understood as the clear implication of the text, and one necessarily explains the text as teaching justification by faith and by good works.

In the days of the apostle, the Judaizing heretics taught what amounted to justification by faith and thus by grace. The

---

5 Shepherd, "Faith and Faithfulness," in Sandlin, *A Faith That Is Never Alone*, 65.

6 Ibid.

Pharisee of Jesus' parable, after all, thanked God for his righteousness: "God, I thank thee, that I am not as other men are" (Luke 18:11). Those other men were unrighteous. But the Judaizing heretics with whom the apostle contends in the book of Galatians did not believe, teach, or practice justification by faith *alone*, any more than did the Pharisee of the parable. Therefore, the Galatian heretics, like the Pharisee, remained unjustified (v. 14). The issue for the Pharisee of Jesus' parable and regarding the heresy combatted by the book of Galatians was, and still is, the word *only* in the matter of justification.

To *only* or *alone* therefore, in the orthodox Protestant confession of justification, we must attend closely. Now the word *alone* is our concern. What does this word establish about justification? What does this word rule out in the saving act of justification? How does this word necessarily safeguard not only the truth of justification, but also the gospel of grace in its entirety?

The Reformed confessions teach justification by faith *alone*. Question 60 of the Heidelberg Catechism asks, "How art thou righteous before God?" The answer is, "Only by true faith in Jesus Christ."[7] The Belgic Confession states, "Therefore we justly say with Paul, *that we are justified by faith alone,*" adding in explanation, "or *by faith without works*."[8] The Westminster Confession of Faith declares that "faith, thus receiving and resting on Christ and his righteousness, is the alone instrument of justification."[9]

As for the Thirty-Nine Articles of the Church of England, by which N. T. Wright is bound and against which he rebels, this creed has believing Anglicans confess the following concerning the justification of man:

---

7 Heidelberg Catechism Q&A 60, in Schaff, *Creeds of Christendom*, 3:326.

8 Belgic Confession 22, in ibid., 3:408.

9 Westminster Confession of Faith 11.2, in ibid., 3:626.

> We are accounted righteous before God, only for the merit of our Lord and Saviour Jesus Christ by Faith, and not for our own works or deservings. Wherefore, that we are justified by Faith only, is a most wholesome Doctrine, and very full of comfort.[10]

"That we are justified by Faith *only* is a most wholesome Doctrine." This is the official, binding doctrine of the Anglican Church. This doctrine, particularly the doctrine expressed by "only," Wright does not believe and opposes in all his writings. To him the truth of justification by faith *only* is not "wholesome" but noxious.

The "Big Lie"

The Reformed creeds, which officially express the Reformed faith and which in their confession that justification is by faith *only* accurately reflect the doctrine of Calvin, expose the "big lie" that advocates of the federal vision are now foisting on Reformed and Presbyterian churches. The phrase "big lie" I deliberately borrow from the lexicon of Nazi Germany. Josef Goebbels, cynical head of the propaganda ministry, practiced the tactic of convincing Germans of whatever falsehood Hitler wanted them to believe by trumpeting the obvious lie boldly, without embarrassment, often, and by every means. It is the nature of the tactic of the big lie, whether in politics or in theology, that it overpowers the truth, which is evident, simply by the loudness, boldness, and repetition of the utterance of the outrageous falsehood contradicting the truth.

The big lie of the federal vision is the proclamation that Calvin differed from Luther on justification in that, whereas Luther taught justification by faith *only*, Calvin taught justification by faith *and by good works*. According to the men of the federal

---

10 Thirty-Nine Articles of the Church of England 11, in ibid., 3:494.

vision, a staunch, uncompromising confession of justification by faith *only* is Lutheran, not Reformed. It is Calvinistic and Reformed to preach and teach justification by faith *and works*.

Merely to state the big lie in plain language is sufficient to expose it: "It is Calvinistic and Reformed to preach and teach justification by faith *and works*."

Inasmuch as this charge of the alleged difference between Luther and Calvin on justification by faith *alone* is a form of the big lie, the men of the federal vision are big liars. What Goebbels practiced in the political arena in Germany, the men of the federal vision practice in the doctrinal and ecclesiastical sphere in North America.

One of the most influential practitioners of the big lie on behalf of the federal vision is the Presbyterian theologian Peter A. Lillback. In a recent book on the covenantal doctrine of John Calvin, Lillback argued that Calvin differed from Luther on justification. Lillback argued this utterly wretched case from what he presented as Calvin's doctrine of the covenant. Since Calvin (according to the [mis]reading of Lillback) taught a conditional, gracious covenant with all the children of believers alike, Esau as well as Jacob (in complete disregard of the gracious election of Jacob and the sovereign reprobation of Esau taught in Romans 9:6–24), a covenant dependent on the faith and works of the children, Calvin also taught justification by faith *and by the good works that faith performs*, that is, justification by faith *and works*. According to Lillback, confession of justification by faith *alone* is a Lutheran doctrine, not a Reformed doctrine.

In a section of his book headed, "Calvin's Disagreement with Luther Regarding God's Acceptance of the Believer's Good Works," Lillback wrote:

> Luther's understanding of justification by faith alone had no room for inherent righteousness, while Calvin's view required it as an inseparable but subordinate

> righteousness...Calvin is insistent that works have a proper place in the discussion of justification by faith alone...The law had no place in Luther's discussion of justification. But in Calvin's mind, the believer's obedience was an "inseparable accident" to the justification doctrine.[11]

Lillback became bold (as is the nature and effectual power of the big lie) in his assertion of utter and obvious falsehood. He aligned Calvin with the Roman Catholic theologians, and opposed him to Luther, in the matter of the confession of justification by faith *alone.*

> Calvin occupies a middle ground between the Schoolmen [Roman Catholic theologians] and Luther on the issue of the acceptance of good works in relationship to justification...Calvin, in agreement with the Schoolmen and contrary to Luther, accepts the fact that God can by covenant receive the works of man. Calvin's doctrine of the acceptance of men's works by God is therefore an intermediate position between Luther and the medieval tradition.[12]

For his efforts on behalf of the Roman Catholicizing and Judaizing of orthodox Presbyterians in the fundamental matter of justification by faith, whether by faith *alone* or by faith *and works*, Lillback was rewarded with the presidency of Westminster Theological Seminary in Philadelphia.

Differing fundamentally from Luther, Calvin and the Reformed faith are said to confess justification by faith and by works: the big lie on the part of the new perspective, the federal

---

11 Lillback, *The Binding of God*, 192–93. The heading of the section in which the quotation is found, concerning Calvin's disagreement with Luther over Justification by faith *alone*, appears on page 185.

12 Ibid., 308.

vision, and their disciples within Reformed churches and institutions today.

Characteristic of the big lie, with the boldness of its utterance, is its obvious falsity. That the Reformed faith does not differ from Luther in holding and proclaiming justification by faith *alone* and that the Reformed faith uncompromisingly rejects as heresy every form of the teaching that justification is by faith *and works* are clearly evident from the Reformed creeds, some of which have been quoted.

To dullards and against the big lie, it must be expressly stated that the Reformed creeds teach the official Reformed faith, under the dominant influence of John Calvin. In view of the tactic of the big lie to bury the truth by loud repetition of the lie, it is probably wise, if not necessary, to repeat that all the Reformed creeds express concerning justification what the Heidelberg Catechism confesses:

> How art thou righteous before God?
>
> *Only* by true faith in Jesus Christ...[13]

> But why can not our good works be the whole or part of our righteousness before God?
>
> Because the righteousness which can stand before the judgment-seat of God must be perfect throughout, and wholly conformable to the divine law; whereas even our best works in this life are all imperfect and defiled with sin.[14]

To dare to posit against the Reformed creeds that Calvin and the Reformed faith reject justification by faith alone, differing

13 Heidelberg Catechism Q&A 60, in Schaff, *Creeds of Christendom*, 3:326–27; emphasis added.

14 Heidelberg Catechism Q&A 62, in ibid. 3:327.

from Luther and compromising with the Schoolmen, is not only a lie. It is the big lie.

Then there is the plain teaching of Calvin in his authoritative *Institutes of the Christian Religion.* In that section of his *Institutes* in which Calvin treats of the doctrinal subject of justification and distinguishes his and the Bible's doctrine from that of the Sophists, Schoolmen, and Roman Catholic Church, Calvin teaches the following concerning justification by faith *alone,* excluding all the works of the believing sinner.

> A great part of mankind imagine that righteousness is composed of faith and works. Let us also, to begin with, show that faith righteousness so differs from works righteousness that when one is established the other has to be overthrown...If faith excludes all boasting [which Calvin has just shown from scripture to be the case], works righteousness can in no way be associated with faith righteousness...Farewell, then, to the dream of those who think up a righteousness flowing together out of faith and works.[15]

> Faith is said to justify because it receives and embraces the righteousness offered in the gospel. Moreover, because righteousness is said to be offered through the gospel, all consideration of works is excluded...The gospel...bestows free righteousness apart from the help of works.[16]

> Works...are not required for faith righteousness...Faith rests entirely upon God's mercy without the assistance of works.[17]

---

15 Calvin, *Institutes*, 3.11.13, 1:743–44.
16 Ibid., 3.11.17, 1:746–47.
17 Ibid., 3.11.18, 1:747–48.

> We say that man is justified by faith alone...[With reference to the word *alone*], not only by a false but by an obviously ridiculous shift they [Roman Catholic theologians in Calvin's day, Shepherd and the men of the federal vision today] insist upon excluding this adjective. Does not he who takes everything from works firmly enough ascribe everything to faith alone?[18]

In his commentary on Romans 3:28, Calvin understands the text as refuting those who "allow indeed that man is justified by faith, but not by faith alone." Thus it should be noted in passing, Calvin expresses that he agrees with Luther's explanation of the text as teaching justification by faith *alone*. The project of Shepherd and his federal visionist allies to pit Calvin against Luther in the doctrine of justification by faith alone, and that regarding the very text on which Luther is charged with having performed an outrage of exegesis and of translation, is exploded by Calvin. Calvin adds that "Paul affirms in this passage that justification is free in such a way as to make it quite evident that no merit of works can at all be associated with it."[19] By "merit of works," Calvin means not only the distinctively Roman Catholic doctrine that works earn salvation with God, but also the teaching that works contribute in any way to the divine act of justifying the sinner. According to Calvin, justification is by faith *alone*; no justifying power or influence of works "can at all be associated with it."

Although it is not the worst sin of the big lie, one of its offensive characteristics is its assumption that its enemies—the defenders of the truth—are too lazy or too dumb to read

---

18 Ibid., 3.11.19, 1:748–49. Here Calvin deliberately approves and makes his own Luther's "insertion" into, and the "Lutheran gloss" upon, Romans 3:28 consisting of the word *alone*: "a man is justified by faith alone."

19 John Calvin, *The Epistle of Paul the Apostle to the Romans*, trans. Ross Mackenzie (Grand Rapids, MI: Eerdmans, 1961), 79.

the documents that disprove the big lie, or if they do read the documents, too stupid to understand them. We have read the Reformed creeds on justification by faith alone and understand them. We have read Calvin on justification by faith alone and understand him. Calvin and the Reformed creeds confess justification by faith *alone.* They confess justification by faith *alone—in so many words.* They confess justification by faith *alone—by the sense of their theology of justification.*

Denial that Calvin and the Reformed creeds teach justification by faith *alone* and insistence that Calvin and the creeds teach, or allow for, justification by faith *and works* are a lie—the big lie.

Since even practitioners of the big lie must reckon with the possibility that someone might oppose to the big lie these statements of Calvin confessing justification by faith *alone,* and since these statements so plainly and emphatically contradict the big lie that Calvin taught justification by faith and works, those theologians who are contending that Calvin taught justification by faith and by works are forced to supplement their loud noise with a semblance of argument. Their argument is that the works repudiated by Calvin in the matter of justification are only ceremonial, Jewish works, or works performed by unsaved people. The argument is that the works Calvin rejects are not the truly good works that a believer performs by the power of the sanctifying Spirit.

Thus Calvin is made to support the doctrine of the men of the federal vision (as also of the Roman Catholic Church): the works that Paul excludes from justification in Romans and Galatians are not the truly good works of the believer but only the ceremonial works of the Jews of the Old Testament, for example circumcision, or works performed by unregenerated persons. Justification then *is* by faith *and by works,* the works being the genuinely good works of the believing child of God, works done in love for God according to the moral law.

Calvin calls this attempt to circumvent the doctrine of justification by faith alone in Romans 3 and 4 and to save the heresy of justification by faith and works sophism, a corrupting of scripture, and "empty caviling."

> The Sophists, who make game and sport in their corrupting of Scripture and their empty caviling, think they have a subtle evasion [to escape the teaching of Romans 3 and 4 that justification is by faith *alone*]. For they explain "works" as meaning those which men not yet reborn do only according to the letter by the effort of their own free will, apart from Christ's grace. But they deny that these refer to spiritual works. For, according to them, man is justified by both faith and works provided they are not his own works but the gifts of Christ and the fruit of regeneration. For they say that Paul so spoke for no other reason than to convince the Jews, who were relying upon their own strength, that they were foolish to arrogate righteousness to themselves, since the Spirit of Christ alone bestows it upon us not through any effort arising from our own nature.

Calvin rejects this "corrupting of Scripture" and "empty caviling."

> In the contrast between the righteousness of the law and of the gospel, which Paul elsewhere introduces, *all works are excluded*, whatever title may grace them [Gal. 3:11–12]. For he teaches that this is the righteousness of the law, that he who has fulfilled what the law commands should obtain salvation; but this is the righteousness of faith, to believe that Christ died and rose again [Rom. 10:5, 9]...Not even spiritual works come into account when the power of justifying is ascribed to faith.[20]

20 Calvin, *Institutes*, 3.11.14, 1:744; emphasis added.

Herman Bavinck therefore was correct in judging that "there is no material difference between Lutheran and Reformed theology with respect to the doctrine of justification."[21]

In teaching justification by faith *alone*, Calvin and the Reformed creeds, like Luther before them, are biblical. Not only does the Bible teach that justification is by faith, but it teaches also that justification is by faith *alone*. The Bible teaches justification by faith alone not by using the word *alone*, but by contrasting faith as the means of justification with the only alternative, namely, the works of the sinner. When in its great passages on justification the Bible affirms that justification is by faith and immediately adds that justification is not by works, the Bible teaches not only that justification is by faith, but also that justification is by faith *alone*. So clearly, purposely, and decisively does the Bible thus teach justification by faith *alone* that *alone* is, in fact, *in the text*. It is in the text implicitly.

Luther did not "insert" "only" in Romans 3:28. By translating the text with "only," he made *explicit* what the Holy Spirit inspired *implicitly*. Roman Catholic and federal vision fury are not, in reality, directed against the "insertion" of a word into Romans 3:28 by Luther the translator. Roman Catholicism and the federal vision are not opposed merely to a "Lutheran gloss." In reality their fury rages against the Holy Spirit's gospel in Romans 3:28 that a man is justified by faith alone—by faith and not by works.

There are two, and only two, conceivable ways of being justified: by faith or by works. By affirming faith and denying works, by affirming faith and denying works in the same sentence and breath, by affirming faith in contrast to and negation of works, scripture teaches that justification is by faith *alone*.

---

21 Herman Bavinck, *Reformed Dogmatics*, ed. John Bolt, trans. John Vriend, vol 4., *Holy Spirit, Church, and New Creation* (Grand Rapids, MI: Baker Academic, 2008), 200.

This is the teaching of the crucial text, Romans 3:28. Summing up all that he has written about justification in the chapter, the apostle concludes that "a man is justified by faith without the deeds of the law." That the "deeds of the law" in Romans 3:28 are any and all works demanded by the law, including especially the ten commandments of the moral law, and not merely ceremonial works required of Old Testament Israel, has already been demonstrated.

By his ringing, conclusive affirmation in verse 28, the apostle proclaims a justification manifesting "the righteousness of God without the law" (v. 21). He proclaims the good news of "the righteousness of God which," in contrast to an imaginary righteousness consisting of the sinner's own obedience to the law, "is by faith of Jesus Christ." This is a righteousness that the sinner receives not by working, but "by faith of Jesus Christ unto all and upon all them that believe" (v. 22). "Justified by faith without the deeds of the law," the sinner is "justified freely by his grace through the redemption that is in Christ Jesus" (v. 24), rather than being justified as a matter of God's paying the sinner what he owes him by virtue of the sinner's having performed works that indebt God to the sinner. Such justification, that is, justification by faith *alone*, forever shuts the boasting mouth of the justified sinner, opening his mouth to thank and praise God alone for justification and all of salvation, whereas justification by works would be warrant for boasting. "Where is boasting then? It is excluded...by the law of faith," in explicit contrast to the law of works (v. 27).

Romans 4 continues the apostle's grand sermon of justification by faith alone, apart from, or without, works. When verse 5 states, "To him that worketh not, but believeth on him that justifieth the ungodly, his faith is counted for righteousness," it utterly and decisively rules out working as the way to be justified. Not working but believing is the way to be righteous with God. Not appearing before God the judge as a good man with a fistful of good works, but as an ungodly man without one good work of one's own *for justification*, is the way to appear before God in the judgment, if there is to be the happy outcome of justification.

Romans 4:5, indeed the entire chapter, clearly and emphatically teaches justification by faith alone. Not only justification by faith, against sheer legalists, against Pharisees who out-Pharisee the Pharisees of Jesus' day. But justification by faith *alone*, against legalists who would befool the saints by teaching justification by faith *and works*, against Roman Catholicism, against the new perspective, against the federal vision.

The epistle to the Galatians likewise teaches justification by faith *alone*, defending this gospel truth against its adversaries. Galatians 2:16 affirms justification "by the faith of Christ," contrasting justification by faith with the spurious justification "by the works of the law." The sharp warning is given that "by the works of the law shall no flesh be justified." The warning indicates the seriousness of one's trusting for righteousness in one's own good works: he is not, and will not be, justified. Worse still, the heretical doctrine of justification by faith and by good works, as is the teaching of Rome, of the new perspective, and of the federal vision, frustrates the grace of God and proclaims that "Christ is dead in vain" (v. 21). The doctrine of justification by works is the denial of the gospel of the cross of Christ.

Similarly, Galatians 3 sharply contrasts justification by faith with justification by the law, justification by believing with justification by doing. "That no man is justified by the law in the sight of God, it is evident: for, The just shall live by faith" (v. 11). Working for righteousness and believing for righteousness are mutually exclusive. If one believes for righteousness, he does not, and does not need to, work for righteousness. However, if one works for righteousness, works for righteousness *at all*, he does not in fact believe. It is either/or: either one works, not believing, or one believes, without working. "The law [demanding working] is not of faith: but, The man that doeth them shall live in them" (v. 12).

God did not give his Jewish people the law, whether ceremonial, civil, or moral, as the means by which they might be justified. But the law was "our schoolmaster to bring us unto Christ, that we might be justified by faith" (v. 24). Only the willfully blind fail to see that the apostle here teaches justification by faith *alone*.

Foreseeing what Calvin described as the sophistry, corrupting of scripture, and empty caviling of Rome and of the federal vision, the apostle identifies the law, the works of which do not justify, as the law that curses the disobedient (v. 10) and the law from whose curse Christ has redeemed us (v. 13). The law that curses the disobedient and from whose curse Christ redeemed his people is the entire law of God, especially the moral law of the ten commandments. It is not merely the ceremonial law of the Old Testament. It is the law requiring obedience out of love to God for his gracious redemption of Israel or the church. Galatians 3 therefore makes plain that justification is not by the good works of obedience to the moral law of God.

Confessing justification by faith *alone*, sound Reformed churches today, with the reformer Martin Luther, proclaim that faith in Jesus Christ, that is, the elect sinner's believing in Jesus Christ as presented in the gospel, is the one and only way of becoming righteous with God. Faith is the one and only means, or instrument, by which the guilty and condemnable sinner is reckoned, or accounted, righteous before God the judge—reckoned righteous by a verdict of God in the sinner's own consciousness.

By the word *alone* the Reformed faith decisively rejects, warns against, and wards off the false teaching that the way to be righteous is by working, whether to earn righteousness, or to make oneself worthy of righteousness (which is the same as earning), or to obtain righteousness in a non-meritorious way (if this were possible). The working of the sinner himself is not the way to become righteous before God. Works of the sinner himself are excluded in the matter of becoming righteous. *All* works of the sinner himself are excluded, whether works done before conversion or works done after conversion, whether ceremonial works such as the Jews performed or truly good works of obedience to the moral law such as regenerated and thankful saints perform in the power of the Holy Spirit, whether works done with the motive of earning or works done with the motive of thanking God for gracious salvation.

By the word *alone* the Reformed faith denies that works are the way to be righteous, whether in whole or in the very smallest part. Just as it is false doctrine to respond to the question, "How can a sinner be right with God?" by saying, "Only and entirely by his own works," so is it false, *equally* false, doctrine to answer the question by saying, "*Partly* by his own works," even though the sinner's own works are minute in comparison with the work of Jesus Christ.

The consequences of the teaching of justification *partly* by one's own works are as grave as are the consequences of the doctrine of justification *wholly* by the sinner's own works. The consequences are the working sinner's damnation. This is the warning of the apostle in Galatians 5. To add one, even small, work of the sinner himself to the redeeming work of Christ for justification is to forfeit the work of Christ entirely. "If ye be circumcised, Christ shall profit you nothing" (v. 2).

The explanation is the either/or, all or nothing, nature of believing and working in the matter of justification. Regarding the saving grace of justification, either justification is by faith *alone*, or there is no justification at all. If the working of the sinner himself plays a part in his justification (and it is invariably the decisive part), the working and works of Jesus Christ are forfeited entirely. The apostle testifies to every man that one who performs any work at all, even the least significant, for his justification "is a debtor to do the whole law" (v. 3). To posit one small work of one's own as necessary for one's justification is in reality to seek to be "justified by the law." In this case, "Christ is become of no effect unto you," whatever; "ye are fallen from grace," entirely (v. 4).

The working of the sinner contributes nothing to the accomplishing of his justification. The works of the sinner himself do not constitute any part of his righteousness with God.

The truth is that the faith by which alone the elect sinner is justified is a knowing and trusting that renounce works and working for righteousness. This is an important aspect of the doctrine of Romans 4:5: "But to him that worketh not, but believeth on him that justifieth the ungodly, his faith is counted for righteousness." The faith that is counted for righteousness is a faith that consciously and deliberately "worketh not." It is as if the sinner whom God has awakened to his guilt and burdened with the weight of deserved punishment cries out, "How shall I seek and find forgiveness and righteousness with the God whom I have offended?" Hearing the word of the gospel of grace, the sinner then responds to his cry, "I will not work; I will believe only." The faith that renounces working and works for justification is true faith. Whatever supposed "faith" insists on working for righteousness is thereby exposed as a false faith. No one is justified by a false faith.

The sinner's working and works do not accomplish his justification now, that is, his personal justification in the private forum of his consciousness in this life. The sinner's working and works will not effect or contribute to his public justification at the final judgment. Justification is by faith alone always and in every forum of the divine judgment of the believing sinner. To this I will return, in detail and with proof, in a subsequent chapter. But I note the truth here in light of the concerted effort by many, including theologians and churches that are regarded as conservative and confessional, to make the decisive justification of the final judgment a justification by faith *and works*.

To construe the justification at the final judgment as a justification by faith and works is to nullify whatever one might have taught about justification by faith alone in the sinner's own lifetime, within history; is to terrorize the believing sinner; and is to render Christ of no effect unto those who teach and believe the false doctrine.

How is a guilty sinner righteous before the just God, now and in eternity, in the forum of his own consciousness and at the public bar of justice on the world's last day?

By believing on Jesus Christ!

Only by believing on Jesus Christ!

By believing, without working!

By believing with a faith that renounces working!

That is, by grace, not by the law!

This is amazing. The truth of justification by faith alone is contrary to depraved human nature, which always supposes and insists that the way to be righteous is by exerting oneself to attain this status, since righteousness makes one worthy of salvation and of every blessing. The truth of justification is truly amazing since faith itself is not a work that makes one worthy of righteousness but merely a means, an instrument, by which God gives—by imputation—and the sinner passively receives righteousness as a gift. Indeed, the faith itself by which the sinner is justified is God's gift to the sinner.

It is this doctrine that makes the Christian gospel and religion unique. All other religions require men's works and working for righteousness and for the salvation that depends upon righteousness.

It is this doctrine that makes the Christian gospel the only way of escape from God's condemnation and damnation. All other religions, teaching the guilty sinner to trust in his own sinful, imperfect works as the ground of righteousness and salvation, shut up to the sinner the way of escape, which is God's grace in the work of Jesus Christ.

In the truth of justification by faith alone, the gospel of Jesus Christ reveals itself as the gospel of grace. At stake therefore in the contemporary controversy within Reformed and Presbyterian churches over justification by faith alone is the gospel of grace. Nothing less!

There is still another aspect to the significance of *alone* in the Reformed faith's proclamation and confession of justification by faith. *Alone* maintains that the content of the sinner's righteousness with God is exclusively the obedience of Jesus Christ—his working and works on behalf of elect sinners. *Alone* not only delimits the way to be righteous: faith in Jesus Christ. *Alone* also defines the righteousness itself with which the sinner is righteous before God. If faith in Christ is the only way to be righteous, to the exclusion of all the works of the sinner himself, then the sinner's righteousness with God consists exclusively of the works of Christ in his stead and on his behalf. In the saving work of God of justification the sinner's righteousness is solely the obedience of Christ—his lifelong, perfect obedience to all the commandments of the law in our stead and his obedience in our place to the demand of the law that we be cursed for our transgressions. "By the obedience of one shall many be [constituted] righteous" (Rom. 5:19).

In justification by faith alone, the work of Christ alone is imputed to the account of the believing sinner, thus becoming the sinner's own.

In contrast (and here the gross wickedness of the heresy of justification by faith and works is exposed), the false doctrine of justification by faith and by works teaches that the righteousness of the justified sinner is partly Christ's obedience and partly the sinner's own obedience. According to this false doctrine, that which renders the sinner acceptable to God, that which atones for the sinner's guilt, that which is the basis of God's favorable verdict, that which makes the sinner worthy of the blessings of salvation, and that upon which entrance into heaven will depend is something the sinner himself has done. Indeed, what the sinner himself has done or must do is fundamental to his salvation. Without the doing of the sinner himself, the obedience of Christ is of no avail. Christ's work may be the greater part of the sinner's righteousness, but the sinner's own work is necessary, indeed is decisive for his salvation.

Justification by faith alone answers the question, how can a sinner be right with God? Justification by faith alone also answers the question, whose are the works that constitute the sinner's righteousness with God? The answer to this question by the doctrine of justification by faith alone is, not the sinner's own works. His good works add nothing to his righteousness. His evil works do not detract from his righteousness of justification. Only the works of Jesus Christ are the sinner's righteousness in justification.

The gospel truth of justification honors Jesus Christ and his glorious work of salvation. What a dishonoring of him and his work to propose that sinners must contribute something to the work of Jesus for their justification! What folly to suppose that what the Son of God in sinless human flesh did was not enough for complete righteousness with God! What arrogance to propose that we sinful people add a little something to the righteousness that God has worked out in Jesus Christ!

What a slap in the face of the God of grace in Jesus Christ that the sinner says to God, as the sinner does indeed say in the doctrine of justification by faith and works, "Now I will complete what you have begun in the ministry of Jesus Christ and make what you have begun effectual, by doing my good deed."

The gospel truth of justification by faith alone glorifies God. He himself became our righteousness in the person and work of his incarnate Son. As the prophet foresaw and foretold, Jehovah God "saw that there was no man…therefore his arm brought salvation unto him; and his righteousness, it sustained him" (Isa. 59:16). His own perfect work in Jesus Christ satisfies God. The one who believes only, declining to work for righteousness, comes to God lacking all justifying works, only guilty, wholly ungodly in the matter of righteousness, supplicating and magnifying the grace of God.

The truth of justification by faith alone is a message of comfort and hope to the sinner who knows the greatness of the misery of his sinfulness and sins. This is the only message of comfort and hope. Every message that sets the sinner to work for righteousness and that causes him to depend upon his own works for righteousness with God is a message of despair. Who can work his way into the favor of God? How can our tainted works satisfy the holy God? How can one ever know that he has done enough?

Only the message of justification by faith alone gives peace with God. "Therefore being justified by faith, we have peace with God through our Lord Jesus Christ" (Rom. 5:1). Clearly implied is that we have peace with God being justified *only* by faith.

In light of the fundamental importance of justification by faith alone for the gospel of grace, for the glory of God, for the honor of Christ Jesus, and for the peace of the believing people of God, to say nothing of the well-known importance of this truth for the Reformation of the church in the sixteenth century, the bold appearance of the heresy of justification by faith and works in reputedly conservative Reformed and Presbyterian churches is clear evidence of the appalling apostasy of these churches.

Some of these churches have taken official decisions exonerating the heretics and approving the heresy. These include the Orthodox Presbyterian Church and the Presbyterian Church in America. These decisions are the taking on of the mark of the false church, according to the testimony of the Belgic Confession that the marks of a true church include that a true church preaches "the pure doctrine of the gospel" and that a true church exercises "church discipline...in punishing of sin," which sin certainly includes false doctrine.[22]

22 Belgic Confession 29, in Schaff, *Creeds of Christendom*, 3:419.

That other Reformed and Presbyterian synods and general assemblies have responded to the presence of the heresy of justification by works within the Reformed community today or even within their own denomination by taking decisions affirming justification by faith alone, commendable in itself as such action is, by no means indicates that these churches regard the heresy with the hatred that the heresy calls for or even that these churches have taken the action necessary to root the heresy out of their fellowships and to safeguard the churches against the heresy.

One weakness is the obvious reluctance of some of these churches to add a negative, condemnatory declaration to their positive statement of justification by faith alone. But defense of the truth always requires a sharp, pointed condemnation of the error that opposes the truth in addition to the positive statement of the truth that is under attack. Another weakness on the part of some of the churches that make a show of defending justification by faith alone is their failure to advise discipline of those theologians in their fellowships who are teaching justification by faith and works and their failure to investigate the seminaries where the heresy is being taught to aspiring ministers.

Yet another weakness of these churches is that, despite their orthodox confession of justification by faith alone, they evidently are able to have good fellowship with those churches that have exonerated the heretics who have taught justification by works and approved the heresy. This good fellowship, this ecumenical oneness, regardless of the denial of and attack on justification by faith alone, is found in such an ecumenical organization as NAPARC.

Source of the Big Lie

The most serious weakness is that even the churches that publicly denounce the heresy of justification by faith and works and that go on synodical record as confessing justification by faith alone refuse to take hold of the doctrine that is, by admission of the heretics, the root and source of the heresy of justification by faith and works. The contemporary expression of the heresy of justification by faith and works within the Reformed and Presbyterian churches is rooted in an erroneous doctrine of the covenant. This is the teaching that God graciously makes his covenant of salvation with all baptized persons alike, particularly all baptized children of believing parents. In fact, he begins the work of salvation in them all alike. But the covenant and its salvation are conditional. They depend for their continuance and fulfillment in the eternal salvation of the children on works the child must perform, including faith, which is regarded as a work of the child rather than as the gift of God.[23]

It is this doctrine of a conditional covenant of grace and salvation with all baptized children alike that implies and produces the heresy of justification by faith and works. The heretics openly confess this inasmuch as they call their theology, which includes justification by faith and works, the federal vision. *Federal* means "covenant." Theirs is a distinctive *covenantal* vision. This distinctive covenantal vision sees justification as a sinful child's becoming and remaining righteous not by faith alone, but by faith and works. If the covenant is conditional, covenantal

23 For the statement by the men of the federal vision themselves that their doctrine of justification by works is the implication of the theology of a conditional covenant, see Shepherd, *Call of Grace*; Wilkins and Garner, *The Federal Vision*; and Beisner, *The Auburn Avenue Theology*. The doctrine of a conditional covenant, as the fountain and foundation of the federal vision, is pervasive in these and in all other federal vision writings. The refusal of the purported foes of the federal vision to recognize this reminds one of the refusals of officials in the United States government publicly to recognize that the motivation of the terrorists now troubling the United States is Islamic ideology, even though the terrorists themselves *declare* that this is their motivation. In both cases it embarrasses the critics to admit the basic issue, and in both cases the result is the advance and victory of the enemies on the one hand of Reformed orthodoxy and on the other hand of Western civilization. To both stubborn deniers of reality, the urgent call comes, "Tell the truth; simply tell the truth!"

salvation is conditional. And if covenantal salvation is conditional, justification is conditional, that is, dependent upon the works of the sinner who is justified.

The theology of a gracious, conditional covenant with all baptized persons alike, particularly all baptized children of believers alike, necessarily implies justification by faith and works. That is, the theology of a gracious covenant and covenantal salvation that are divorced from eternal election necessarily corrupts the fundamental gospel truth of justification by faith alone.[24]

That the denial of justification by faith alone in the theology that calls itself the federal vision is rooted in the doctrine of a conditional covenant is plainly, even bluntly, acknowledged, indeed vigorously advanced, in a recent book by a proponent of the conditional covenant. The book is *Not of Works: Norman Shepherd and His Critics*. The sub-subtitle is *The Justification Controversy Laid to Rest through Understanding*. The author is a Canadian Reformed theologian, Ralph F. Boersema.[25] The Canadian Reformed Churches, like their parent churches in the Netherlands, the Reformed Churches in the Netherlands (liberated), are known for their theology of a conditional covenant of grace with all the baptized children of believers alike, the Esaus as well as the Jacobs. As the title indicates, the book is a defense of the theology of Norman Shepherd and of the federal vision. It is therefore also a defense of justification by faith and works.

Shepherd writes the foreword. In it he bluntly describes the gist of his covenantal theology: "The New Testament as well as the Old makes our eternal welfare contingent in some way and

24 For a thorough demonstration of the origin of the contemporary teaching of justification by faith and works in the covenantal doctrine of the men of the federal vision, see David J. Engelsma, *Federal Vision*; *The Covenant of God and the Children of Believers*; and *Covenant and Election in the Reformed Tradition*.

25 Boersema, *Not of Works*.

to some extent on what we do."[26] Contingency is dependency or conditionality. This blunt statement by the theologian who is most responsible for the contemporary theology of the federal vision exposes the heretical nature of the theology and condemns it out of hand: Our salvation depends on what we do. Inasmuch as justification is an important part of our salvation, indeed the foundation of it in the justice of God, our justification depends upon what we do—upon what we *do*; upon what *we* do.

Shepherd continues by insisting that justification is by an "obedient faith."[27] This language is cautious—Shepherd does not explicitly state that justification is by faith *and by faith's obedience*. But his subsequent insistence that "works of the law" in Romans and Galatians (excluded from God's justifying act) "are not any and all good works"[28] and his explanation elsewhere of James 2 as teaching justification in the same saving sense that the doctrine has in Romans and Galatians[29] make indisputably evident that by "an obedient faith" Shepherd means the obedience of faith. For him justification is by faith and by faith's obedience, that is, by faith and works.

---

26 Norman Shepherd, foreword, in ibid., ix.

27 Ibid., x–xiv.

28 Ibid., xii.

29 Shepherd maintains that justification in James 2, which teaches that "by works a man is justified, and not by faith only" (v. 24), has the very same forensic, saving sense that justification has in Romans 3 and in Galatians 2–3. See Shepherd, "Justification by Faith Alone." According to Shepherd, the verses in James 2 that teach justification by works have the same "forensic, soteric sense" that justification has in Romans and Galatians. Shepherd thinks that "James is talking about faith and justification in the same sense that Paul uses these terms" in Romans and Galatians (80). Shepherd's staunch defender Ian A. Hewitson is correct in his analysis that Shepherd "believes both Paul and James are speaking of justification in the declarative sense" (Ian A. Hewitson, *Trust and Obey: Norman Shepherd & the Justification Controversy at Westminster Theological Seminary* [Minneapolis, MN: NextStep Resources, 2011], 119). Thus Shepherd commits himself to a doctrine of forensic, saving justification by faith and by works.

As Shepherd suggests in his foreword to the book by Boersema and explicitly states elsewhere, his denial of justification by faith alone and affirmation of justification by faith and by faith's good works are rooted in his doctrine of the covenant as conditional, that is, dependent for its continuance with a baptized child and for its bringing of the child to eternal salvation upon the child's work of believing—faith as a condition—and the child's works of obedience to the law of God.

In the foreword to the book by Boersema, Shepherd indicates, briefly but unmistakably, the nature of his covenantal doctrine, out of which his denial of justification by faith alone arises: "The new covenant in the blood of Jesus...[has] two sides, promise and obligation."[30] The covenant is God's gracious promise of salvation to every baptized child, if not to every human who ever comes under the preaching of the gospel. But the realization of the promise, as of the salvation that is promised, depends upon the child's performance of his "obligation," that is, the child's work of believing and obeying.

The covenant is "promise and obligation," with promise depending upon obligation—a conditional covenant. This covenantal doctrine is the root of the teaching of justification by faith and works by the men of the federal vision, as it is also the root of the new perspective, at least regarding the theology of N. T. Wright.[31]

---

30 Shepherd, foreword, in Boersema, *Not of Works*, xvii.

31 For Shepherd's own more complete, and blunt, description of the conditionality of the covenant of grace out of which flows his doctrine of justification by faith and works, see his *Call of Grace*. Regarding the covenant with Abraham, "Conditions were, indeed, attached to the fulfillment of the promises made to Abraham" (14). Specifically regarding the new covenant in Jesus Christ, "Faith, repentance, obedience, and perseverance...are conditions" to the enjoyment of the blessings of salvation that are promised in the new covenant (50). Shepherd thinks to avoid the blatant denial of gracious salvation that this teaching of a conditional covenant propounds by denying that the conditions of the covenant are

The ardent defender of Shepherd and his theology against his critics in the conservative Reformed community, Ralph F. Boersema, rightly finds the origin of Shepherd's doctrine of justification by faith and works in Shepherd's doctrine of the covenant, to which Boersema as a Canadian Reformed, liberated theologian is himself committed. Boersema defends Shepherd's doctrine of justification as the implication of a conditional covenant of grace.

> [God] has a covenant with believers and all their children. It is not only with the elect. The covenant is not unconditional. In it God gives his promises and also his people have their obligations and must make their commitments. The promises are addressed to all…It is this solution that Shepherd has adopted.[32]

As bold and heretical as any Pelagian, Roman Catholic, or Arminian, Boersema defends Shepherd by affirming that "Scripture conditions eternal weal and woe on our works in this life."

"meritorious." Regardless whether the works of the sinner upon which the covenant depends are meritorious or non-meritorious, such a doctrine of a conditional covenant is the denial of the biblical gospel of covenantal salvation by grace alone. The covenant does not depend upon the works of the sinner, but solely upon the grace of God in Jesus Christ. When Shepherd later states that "grace is not without conditions," he is explaining what he means by asserting that there are "two parts of the covenant: grace and faith, promise and obligation" (63). The fundamental point is that Shepherd's and the federal vision's doctrine of justification by faith and works is, by their own testimony, rooted in their doctrine of a conditional covenant. There can be no successful opposition to their doctrine of justification without examination—and refutation—of their covenantal doctrine. All the noisy opposition to Shepherd and the federal vision regarding the denial of justification by faith alone by supposedly conservative Presbyterian and Reformed theologians that does not take up the issue of the conditionality of the covenant, whence the federal vision's corruption of justification springs, is mere empty, impotent, fruitless, deceptive show.

32 Boersema, *Not of Works*, 85.

Immediately, he echoes Shepherd in declaring that "James 2... uses justification in the same forensic sense as Paul."[33] What this means, beyond any misunderstanding or dispute, is that the doctrine of a conditional covenant teaches that, in the forensic sense that justification has in Romans 3 and 4 and in Galatians 2 and 3, sinners are justified by God by faith and by good works.

Justification by faith and works! As the necessary implication of a conditional covenant! If the covenant is conditional, justification is by faith and works. And the eternal salvation (weal) of believers depends upon their works in this life!

Almost none of the conservative Reformed and Presbyterian churches that profess to maintain the Reformation's doctrine of justification by faith alone repudiates the doctrine of the covenant out of which the contemporary heresy of justification by faith and works arises. For all the noisy proclamation of holding still the doctrine of justification by faith alone, none takes hold of the root whence the bitter fruit grows. None emphatically confesses that the covenant and its saving grace are unconditional, due to and dependent upon the sovereign, electing grace of God in Jesus Christ alone.

It is as if one, aware of a cancerous growth on his body, would insist on the superficial removal of the growth from his arm or chest but would refuse to have the surgeon cut to the malignant source of the growth deep within his body. Such a person would not be taking the cancer seriously, as it deserved to be taken. He would also be consigning himself to certain death from the cancer that he tolerates within himself.

Churches that tolerate the theology of a gracious but conditional covenant with all baptized children alike do not take the heresy of justification by faith and works, which is implied by the theology of a conditional covenant, seriously. They may by their synodical pronouncements lop off an excrescence of

33 Ibid., 42.

false doctrine here and there. They may take pompous issue with some egregiously heretical statement or other. But they deliberately allow the source and power of the cancer to remain within the body of the church. Therefore, they make themselves responsible for the eventual death of the church body by the open, prevailing teaching of justification by faith and works.

Regarding the contemporary attack on justification by faith alone by Shepherd, the federal vision, Wright, and others, it remains to expose and refute what is undoubtedly the subtlest argument against the truth of justification. It is at the same time the most powerful argument promoting their heresy of justification by faith and faith's works. The argument is simply that, since the Bible teaches that true faith is always a working faith—a faith that loves God and the neighbor and therefore performs the works of love—justification is a work of God by means of a working faith.

How the men of the federal vision and their defenders in the sphere of the Reformed and Presbyterian churches emphasize that justification is by a *working* faith!

To this emphatic declaration, they usually add the warning that, if the faith that claims to be the means of justification is not a working faith, it is no true faith at all. And there can be no justification by means of a false faith. The charge raised against those who challenge their doctrine of justification is that, contending for justification apart from works, we are opposed to the truth of justification by a true, working faith and therefore are promoting the false doctrine of justification by a false, dead faith, which shows itself in a life of disobedience to the law of God—the heresy of antinomianism.

Shepherd likes to leave the impression that his contested doctrine of justification amounts to nothing more than this, "that justifying faith must be a living and obedient faith."[34]

---

34 Shepherd, foreword, in Boersema, *Not of Works*, xv.

Boersema begins his spirited defense of Shepherd's doctrine of justification with appeal to the truth that true faith is a working faith, as though this were all that Shepherd were teaching. "Faith without works is dead. A dead faith cannot justify...Believing works...are the manifestation of faith and faith without such works is dead (Jas 2:26). Dead faith cannot possibly justify. This is the point that...Shepherd make[s] and no other."[35]

That Shepherd, however, is indeed making quite another point, and that Boersema, for all his protestations, recognizes the other point, Boersema himself makes plain when he correctly explains Shepherd's doctrine of justification as teaching that "works are required for justification."[36] It is one thing to affirm that the faith that justifies, as a living faith, is a faith that works. Obviously, it is an entirely different thing to affirm that works are required for justification. In the language of Galatians, it is one thing to affirm that true faith, the faith by which alone a sinner is justified, is a faith that "worketh by love" (5:6). It is a radically different thing to conclude that justification is both by faith and by faith's loving, that is, both by faith and by faith's working.

Against this subtlest of all forms of the heresy of justification by faith and works stands the biblical and Reformation doctrine of justification by faith alone. Justification by faith alone means that, although genuine faith is always a working faith, in the divine work of justifying the sinner the working of faith is excluded by God. In justification the works that faith always performs, for example, loving God, are excluded as much as a self-righteous Jew's circumcision of himself. Faith's working and works are not the instrument, or means, of the justification of the believing sinner. The working of faith, that is, faith's love of God

35 Boersema, *Not of Works*, 20, 28.

36 Ibid., 22.

and the neighbor, is not even a part of the righteousness of the justified sinner in the judgment of God. Regarding the means of justification and regarding the righteousness that is the content of justification, such is the exclusion of faith's working and works that it makes no difference whether faith works or does not work, whether faith has its works or does not have its works.

That justification is by faith alone means that God justifies the elect, believing sinner apart from the working and works of faith. Faith is the sole means, or instrument, of justification strictly inasmuch as faith rests on and receives (by imputation) the working and works of Jesus Christ that are outside the sinner. As the sole means of justification, faith renounces its own working, its own works, its repenting, its loving God, its loving the neighbor, its confession of the truth, its membership in a true church, its all—everything except Jesus Christ, his working, and his works *outside* the sinner.

If this seems strong, it is still not as strong as the biblical statement that justification is always and only God's declaring righteous one who is "ungodly" (Rom. 4:5). This is how the justified sinner appears in the judgment of God, this is truly the state of the justified sinner when God justifies him: He is only, wholly, and truly "ungodly," not only devoid of any working of faith, of any works of faith, of any love of God and of the neighbor, but also guilty of unbelief, of the working of unbelief, of hatred of God, and of hatred of the neighbor. He is only, wholly, and truly "ungodly" regarding the means of his justification and regarding his righteousness before God that is the content of his justification.

The explanation is that all his working and works of faith, his love of God, and his love of the neighbor are imperfect, defiled by sin, worthy of condemnation, and therefore incapable of being the means of his justification or the content of the righteousness of justification. Works that justify must be perfect. Works that make up a sinner's righteousness with the thrice-holy

God must be perfect. The explanation is that even his faith is tainted and corrupted by unbelief. "Lord, I believe," confesses every believing child of God to the day of his death; "help thou mine unbelief" (Mark 9:24).

Regardless of the subtle formulation of the heresy—"justified by a working faith"—the federal vision is a form of the teaching of justification by faith and works that is condemned by scripture and the Reformed creeds. According to the federal vision, the sinner's own working and works are, in part, the means of justification. Faith, apart from its working and works, is not the sole means. According to the federal vision, when God justifies a sinner, he does not have regard solely to the working and works of Christ, *outside the sinner*, but also to the sinner's own working and works. According to the federal vision, the righteousness of the sinner in his justification is not wholly and exclusively the obedience of Jesus Christ, both in observing God's law and in suffering the curse of the law upon his disobedient people, but also the obedience of the sinner himself.

Does the faith that alone justifies always work? Yes!

Does this faith work in the matter of justification, so as to contribute to the divine act of justifying the sinner? No!

Is true faith always a working, obedient faith? Yes!

Is this working of faith either the instrumentality of justification or the content of the righteousness of justification, even in part? No!

The reformers responded to the subtle argument of Rome that, because faith is a working faith, justification is by faith and works with a pithy Latin saying: "*Sola fides justificat, sed fides non est sola*" ("Only faith justifies, but faith is not alone"). The sense of the saying is that even though faith is never alone, without its works, faith alone, without its works, justifies. This is the contradiction beforehand of the contemporary, fallacious argument of the federal vision that, because faith is never alone (without its works), faith alone does not justify.

Subtle as the argument of the federal vision on behalf of justification by faith and works is, it is nothing but the traditional argument of Rome in defense of its denial of justification by faith alone. The only difference between Rome and the federal vision is that the federal vision illogically and insignificantly denies that the works of the sinner that justify are meritorious. The ablest apologist for the Roman doctrine of justification by faith and works at the time of the Reformation was Robert Bellarmine. Bellarmine argued on the basis of Galatians 5:6 that since faith works by love, sinners are justified by faith and by faith's works of love. Faith, contended the Roman Catholic theologian, is "informed" by charity, or love. Only a faith that is "informed" by love justifies. And it justifies because it is "informed" by love. Faith is a working, loving faith. This working and loving of faith belong to the instrumentality of faith as the means of justification. This working and loving of faith are part of the righteousness of the sinner with God in justification. The conclusion is that justification is by faith and works.

Indeed, Rome has made this subtle argument on behalf of justification by works its official dogma in the Canons and Decrees of the Council of Trent. In chapter 7 of the Sixth Session (on justification), Rome confesses:

> In the said justification of the impious, when by the merit of that same most holy Passion, *the charity of God is poured forth*, by the Holy Spirit, *in the hearts* of those that are justified, and is inherent therein: whence, man, through Jesus Christ, in whom he is ingrafted, receives, in the said justification, together with the remission of sins, all these [gifts] infused at once, faith, hope, and charity. For faith, unless hope and charity be added thereto, neither unites man perfectly with Christ, nor makes him a living member of his body. For which reason it is most truly said, that *Faith without works is*

> *dead and profitless*; and, *In Christ Jesus neither circumcision availeth any thing nor uncircumcision, but faith which worketh by charity.*[37]

This charity, the article goes on to say, one should "bear... before the judgment-seat of our Lord Jesus Christ" in order to "have life eternal."[38]

Making plain that Rome understands full well that its ascription of justifying power to the charity, or love, by which faith works is the rejection of the Bible's and Reformation's doctrine of justification by faith *alone*, Rome states:

> If any one saith, that men are justified, either by the sole imputation of the justice of Christ, or by the sole remission of sins, to the exclusion of the grace and *the charity which is poured forth in their hearts by the Holy Ghost*, and is inherent in them; or even that the grace, whereby we are justified, is only the favor of God: let him be anathema.[39]

It is the shame of Norman Shepherd, the other men of the federal vision, N. T. Wright, and the Reformed and Presbyterian churches that have approved the federal vision that this anathema does not fall on them. It is the glory of those churches that yet preach and confess justification by faith alone that they are the object of Rome's (vain) curse. "Blessed are ye when Rome curses you, for so cursed she the prophets that were before you." One might well add: "Cursed are ye when Rome

---

37 Canons and Decrees of the Council of Trent, Sixth Session, Decree on Justification 7, in Schaff, *Creeds of Christendom*, 2:95–96.

38 Canons and Decrees of the Council of Trent, Sixth Session, Decree on Justification 7, in ibid., 2:97.

39 Canons and Decrees of the Council of Trent, Sixth Session, [Canons] on Justification 11, in ibid., 2:112–13. The emphasis is Trent's.

blesses you, for so blessed she the enemies of the gospel that were before you."

To the subtle argument of Rome, specifically the argument of Rome at the Council of Trent, on behalf of justification by faith and works on the ground that faith always works by charity, or love, Calvin replied: "When we say a man is justified by faith alone, we do not fancy a faith devoid of charity, but we mean that faith alone is the cause of justification."[40]

A practical benefit of the repudiation of the working and works of faith in the great matter of justification is that the guilty sinner is not driven to despair by the weakness of his faith and by the imperfection of his works of faith. The strength or weakness of his faith and the purity or impurity of the works of faith have nothing to do with his justification. Those who teach justification by the works of faith direct the sinner to his own faith and its works for righteousness with God and for peace with God. This must rob a believer of the consciousness of his justification and of assurance of salvation.

But the truth of justification by faith alone, that is, justification apart from faith's own intrinsic worth and from faith's works, directs the sinner to Christ alone and to the work of Christ alone for righteousness with God and for the peace of assurance of salvation. In justification the sinner must not look to his faith, much less to faith's works, but to Christ as presented in the gospel. Like the physical eye, faith, in the matter of justification, sees not itself but only the object outside itself, namely, Jesus Christ.

---

40 John Calvin, "Antidote to the Canons of the Council of Trent," in *Calvin's Tracts*, trans. Henry Beveridge (Edinburgh: Calvin Translation Society, 1851), 3:151. Are the learned scholars of the federal vision and those Presbyterians and Reformed who are swayed by the subtle argument that, because faith works, justification is by works ignorant of Calvin's demolition of the argument four hundred odd years ago? Or do they suppose that the orthodox are ignorant of the heretical argument and of the Reformed refutation of the argument?

Still less does justifying faith depend upon itself or anything pertaining to itself. *Only* upon Jesus Christ!

Thus faith, faith *alone,* justifies. And thus, thus *only,* does faith give peace with God.

The Reformation preached, confessed, and defended the truth of justification by faith alone, even though the visible church was rent asunder, even though nations went to war, and even though the result for the orthodox was persecution and death. Where is this zeal on behalf of the orthodox doctrine of justification today? Where is this defense of the truth of justification today? Where is such love for justification by faith alone today? Where is such commitment to the gospel of grace today? Where is such hatred of the lie of self-salvation today?

The trouble with many of the reputedly conservative Reformed churches today, which is apparent in their refusal to root God-dishonoring and soul-destroying heresy out of their fellowships, is not that they do not *know* the truth, but that they do not *love* the truth. Theirs is the sin that explains the perishing of many in these last days, according to 2 Thessalonians 2:10: "because they received not the love of the truth, that they might be saved."

"The *love* of the truth." Not the *knowledge* of the truth, but the *love* of the truth. The love of the truth of justification by faith alone, which justification is rooted in the unconditional covenant of particular, sovereign grace.

That is, the love of the gospel of salvation by grace alone.

Chapter Twelve

ASSURANCE OF JUSTIFICATION

An aspect of justification that is often overlooked is the assurance of its righteousness and therefore of salvation.[1] The reality of justification includes that the Spirit of the justifying Father of Jesus Christ assures everyone whom the Spirit justifies that he is justified. This assurance is an essential element of the act of justification itself. Not only is the elect, believing sinner justified, but he also knows that he is justified. In fact, the conjunction "but" in the preceding sentence is misleading. It can leave the impression that justification is one thing and assurance of justification another. The truth is that justification *is*, *essentially* is, the assurance of justification by faith alone. If the believing sinner is not sure of his righteousness with God, he has not been justified by faith. Christ has died for him. The Spirit has regenerated him. God has elected him. But he has not been justified by faith.

It is false doctrine, a denial of the biblical truth of justification, to teach that Christ justifies many through faith in himself who nevertheless remain in doubt whether they are justified and therefore remain in doubt whether they are saved. It is false doctrine, a denial of the biblical truth of justification,

1 This chapter borrows heavily from a section of my article in the April 2009 issue of the *Protestant Reformed Theological Journal*, "The Gift of Assurance: The Spirit of Christ and Assurance of Salvation" (3–46).

to teach that assurance of justification comes much later in time than justification itself and that this assurance is the possession only of a few, usually old, believers in this life. It is false doctrine, a denial of the biblical truth of justification, to teach that, whereas justification is a gift of God to his people, assurance of justification is something that only a few believers obtain by their strenuous spiritual work, usually over a long period of time. It is false doctrine, a denial of justification by faith, to teach that, whereas justification is a gift to the elect, obtaining assurance is a matter of the believer's quest for it over many years and by dint of arduous struggle. It is false doctrine, a denial of justification by faith alone, to teach that, whereas justification is by faith alone, assurance of justification, really justification's assurance, is by faith and by good works or by faith and by a mystical experience.

A Doctrine of Doubt

This error concerning justification and its assurance is real and widespread in the Reformed and Presbyterian churches. Prominent theologians teach the false doctrine. Persuasive preachers proclaim it. It seriously troubles many confessing Reformed and Presbyterian Christians. The effect of this false doctrine is to cast many confessing Reformed Christians into doubt of their salvation for many years, some as long as they live.

An aspect of the erroneous doctrine is that it casts believers upon a special, extraordinary, mystical "experience," or upon their own works, for assurance of justification and salvation. For many the experience never comes, despite their ardent prayer for it or their ardent work for it. These die in terror that their death will usher them into perdition. Others suppose that they have had the experience and rely on it, or that they have worked sufficiently and rely on their work. This is worse than the honest doubt of those who lack the experience or of those who are dubious about the sufficiency of their working.

This doctrine of doubt afflicts some in the Dutch Reformed tradition. These tormented souls and the preachers who torment them identify themselves as belonging to a movement that calls itself the *nadere reformatie*. This Dutch phrase should be translated and understood as further reformation. The phrase expresses the movement's false and foolish charge that the sixteenth-century Reformation of the church did not do justice to piety and experience. This is to charge that Luther's, the Reformation's, the Reformed creeds', and the Bible's gospel message of justification by faith alone is not sufficiently pious and experiential for their exotic, exalted, and esoteric taste.

This movement boasts that with its theology and practice of pietism and experientialism it furthers the Reformation. To this the Reformed response is that their movement "furthers" the Reformation by depriving thousands of believers of the assurance of justification and salvation. Under the influence of the *nadere reformatie,* thousands of Reformed believers languish under the same doubt of salvation that plagued, and still plagues, members of the Roman Catholic Church. From this doubt it was the practical, pastoral purpose of Luther and the Reformation to deliver the people of God.

The further reformation accomplishes this ambitious program of furthering the Reformation (which reflects badly on the Reformation of the sixteenth century) by imposing on the Reformed faith the theology of English Puritanism. Arie de Reuver, a reliable student of the further reformation, notes that the name of the movement in the Netherlands was the importation of a distinctively English, Puritan term: "Teellinck...the father of the Further Reformation introduced the Puritan term 'further reformation' from England to the Netherlands." De Reuver goes on to describe the nature of the purpose and theology of the men of the further reformation:

> The Further Reformation developed a comprehensive pastoral psychology by which it intended to provide guidance on the manner in which the applied work of the Holy Spirit brought people to certainty of faith [that is, assurance of justification and salvation].[2]

De Reuver frankly acknowledges that the spirituality and experientialism of the further reformation are derived from the medieval (Roman Catholic) mystics.

The characteristic Puritan doctrine of assurance—of *doubt* really—denied that assurance is an essential element of faith. The Puritan Thomas Brooks, of whom J. I. Packer asserted that he was "one of the greatest of the later Puritans" and one of the "finest Puritan minds," described the Puritan theology of doubt this way:

> Now though this full assurance is earnestly desired, and highly prized, and the want of it much lamented, and the enjoyment of it much endeavoured after by all saints, yet it is only obtained by a few. Assurance is a mercy too good for most men's hearts, it is a crown too weighty for most men's heads. Assurance is *optimum maximum* [greatest good], the best and greatest mercy; and therefore God will only give it to his best and dearest friends.
>
> Augustus in his solemn feasts, gave trifles to some, but gold to others. Honours and riches, &c., are trifles that God gives to the worst of men; but assurance is that "tried gold," Rev. 3:18, that God only gives to tried friends. Among those few that have a share or portion in the special love and favour of God, there are but a very few that have an assurance of his love.

2 Arie de Reuver, *Sweet Communion: Trajectories of Spirituality from the Middle Ages through the Further Reformation*, trans. James A. De Jong (Grand Rapids, MI: Baker, 2007), 15–24.

> It is one mercy for God to love the soul, and another mercy for God to assure the soul of his love.[3]

The Puritan and further reformation denial that assurance is of the essence of salvation necessarily implies, indeed consists of, the denial that assurance is of the essence of justification—of the essence of justification *by faith alone*. If one does not have assurance of salvation, he certainly does not have the assurance that his sins are forgiven and that he is right with God. However, if one is assured of his righteousness with God on the basis of the death of Christ for him, he surely knows with certainty that he is saved. But the Puritans expressly denied that justification brings with it, indeed consists of, assurance.

> The first conclusion we will begin with and premise as a foundation to what follows, is, that that act of faith

---

3 Thomas Brooks, "Heaven on Earth: A Serious Discourse, Touching a Well-Grounded Assurance," in *The Works of Thomas Brooks* (Edinburgh: Banner of Truth, repr. 1980), 2:335. The quotations of J. I. Packer are taken from his *A Quest for Godliness: The Puritan Vision of the Christian Life* (Wheaton, IL: Crossway, 1990), 179–80. Noteworthy in Packer's title is the fittingly chosen "Quest." Puritan theology exhorts to a "quest" for assurance of salvation. Inasmuch as assurance is an essential element of faith, Puritan theology is a quest for faith. Reformed theology proclaims the *gift* of faith and through faith of justification and salvation. It is also worthy of note that multitudes of confessing believers, under the influence of Puritan theology, engage in a quest for assurance their lives long and never find. They die as they have lived: in doubt of their salvation. But the Puritan theology of assurance reflects badly not only on Puritan theologians. It reflects badly also on God. What kind of merciful God loves a soul but refuses to assure the miserable soul of his love? Year after year? Even as long as the soul lives its earthly life? What is the fatherhood of a God who withholds from the majority of his children the certainty of his love for them? What would one think of an earthly father who behaved himself in this way, allowing only a select few of his numerous children to arrive at confidence of his love for them, and even in their case only by virtue of their strenuous "quest" for this confidence, while withholding this confidence from the majority of his children?

> which justifies a sinner, is distinct from knowing he hath eternal life, and may therefore be without it, because it doth not necessarily contain prevailing assurance in it. By prevailing assurance, I mean such an assurance as overpowereth doubts and sense to the contrary, so as, in the believer's knowledge, he is able to say, Christ is mine, and my sins are forgiven; such an assurance whereby a man is a conqueror, as Paul speaks, Rom. 8:37, when he expresseth such strong assurance.[4]

According to Goodwin and the Puritans, it is possible that the justified sinner lacks the assurance that his sins are forgiven and that God judges him righteous with the righteousness of Christ. There can be justification without assurance of justification.

In denying that the justified sinner has assurance of forgiveness and righteousness, the Puritans and their disciples of the *nadere reformatie* today press their theology of doubt to the point of absurdity. Justification by faith alone *is* God's declaration of forgiveness and righteousness *in the consciousness of the sinner.* Rightly, the Reformation proclaimed justification by faith alone as justification "in the forum of the conscience" [Latin: *in foro conscientiae*], which refers to the sinner's consciousness.

Justification as Assurance

Justification as taught in Romans and Galatians is not a declaration of God upon a believing sinner away in the heavenly heights, out of the hearing and apart from the experience of the justified sinner. It is the divine declaration in the soul of the believer, so that he *knows* his justification. It is justification *by faith*. It is justification *experienced.* It is justification that gives the justified sinner "peace with God" (Rom. 5:1). It is

---

4 Thomas Goodwin, *The Objects and Acts of Justifying Faith* (Marshallton, DE: National Foundation for Christian Education, n.d.), 338.

justification that effects the justified sinner's rejoicing in hope of the glory of God (v. 2). To teach that God justifies sinners but that most of them remain unsure whether they are justified is as foolish as to suppose that a man would hear the judge pronounce him innocent in the courtroom and go from the jail cell and the courtroom acquitted and free, but still doubt whether the judge had really declared him not guilty.

In the act of justification, God the judge declares in the soul, in the consciousness, of the believing sinner, "I cancel the debt of the guilt of your sins and sinfulness! I reckon to your account the obedience of my Son, Jesus Christ!" This judge has a loud, clear voice in the gospel. He does not whisper or mumble. Besides, the divine justifying judge speaks his divine verdict not only in the ears of the justified believer. He also speaks it in the believer's *heart*, where faith resides. The justified sinner knows his righteousness and salvation.

Fundamental to this convincing, convicting verdict from the heavenly bench is the judicial ground, which the verdict includes: "My Son, your redeemer, obeyed in your stead his life long and died as your substitute, under my wrath, on the cross." There is no justification, regarding particularly its assurance, except on the basis of the obedience of Christ in the forgiven sinner's stead, and the obedience of Christ only. Any intrusion here of the sinner's own good works makes justification impossible, with respect particularly to assurance. The Belgic Confession defines justification as "the remission of our sins *for Jesus Christ's sake*."[5] Every true believer *seeks* justification on the basis not of his own good works, but of the death of Christ for him. This the Heidelberg Catechism teaches in its explanation of the fifth petition of the model prayer, "Forgive us our debts": "Be pleased, *for the sake of Christ's blood,* not to

5 Belgic Confession 23, in Schaff, *Creeds of Christendom*, 3:409; emphasis added.

impute to us, miserable sinners, our manifold transgressions," and so on.[6]

Having forgiven the sinful woman, Christ dismisses her with the words, "Go in peace" (Luke 7:48, 50). This word of Christ is radically different from, "Go on a lifelong quest for peace." Forgiveness is justification, and justification is—even for the most wretched, lowly sinner and not only for a few aristocratic Puritan divines trusting in their mystical experiences rather than in Christ crucified—assurance of a right standing with God and therefore of salvation.

Likewise, the parable of the Pharisee and the publican has the publican going to his home justified (Luke 18:9–14). He did not go home from God's justification of him wondering whether he was justified. He did not go home on a years-long, or even lifelong, quest for the assurance and experience of justification. Justification for him was the assurance of forgiveness and righteousness with God. Just as he experienced his guilt before he was justified, so also going home justified meant, indeed emphasized, the publican's assurance and experience of justification. The publican goes home leaping and dancing, with joy in his soul and gladness on his face.

The Reformed confessions, to which the contemporary disciples of the Puritans subscribe, plainly teach justification as the assurance—the *personal* assurance—of forgiveness and righteousness. Those who strip assurance from justification but are bound to the Heidelberg Catechism must perform interpretative gymnastics in explaining this confession's explanation of justification. First, the Catechism's definition of faith, the faith by which one is justified, makes the personal assurance of justification an element of faith's essence: "a hearty trust which the Holy Ghost works in me by the Gospel, that not only to others, but to me also, forgiveness of sins, everlasting righteousness and

6 Heidelberg Catechism A 126, in ibid., 3.353–54; emphasis added.

salvation, are freely given by God, merely of grace, only for the sake of Christ's merits."[7] The giving of forgiveness of sins and everlasting righteousness is justification. This justification consists of personal assurance of justification: "to me also."

Second, regarding the Heidelberg Catechism's explicit treatment of justification, the help, or profit, of the believer's believing the truths of the Apostles' Creed is that "I am righteous in Christ before God, and an heir of eternal life."[8] This is justification. This justification, which is assurance of righteousness before God and therefore certainty that one is heir of eternal life, is contemporary with believing, indeed is an essential element of believing. The benefit of believing the truths of the gospel is not that the believer engages on a quest for the certainty that he is righteous before God and an heir of eternal life.

Similarly, the plain sense of answer 60 of the Catechism is that true faith in Jesus Christ consists of the assurance that to the believer God "grants and imputes…the perfect satisfaction, righteousness, and holiness of Christ." This is the assurance of every one "if [and when] I accept such benefit with a believing heart."[9] Assurance of justification does not come later, after one believes the truths of the gospel and in the Christ revealed in the gospel, when one has a mystical experience.

The Belgic Confession is, if possible, even clearer that justification *is* the experience and assurance of righteousness before God. Article 23 confesses that God's imputation of righteousness to the believing sinner, expressly and emphatically an imputation "*without works*," is "the happiness of man." Who will deny that "happiness" is experience, the experience of assurance? The article goes on to assert that justification, expressly and emphatically a justification that relies and rests upon "the obedience of

---

7 Heidelberg Catechism A 21, in ibid., 3:313.

8 Heidelberg Catechism Q&A 59, in ibid., 3:326.

9 Heidelberg Catechism A 60, in ibid., 3:326–27.

Christ crucified alone," "give[s] us confidence in approaching to God" and "[frees] the conscience of fear, terror, and dread."[10]

To teach justification by faith alone but then to deny that those who are thus justified know and are certain that they are justified is as much a denial of justification as Rome's teaching of justification by faith and works or the doctrine of the federal vision that one can lose his justification. The effect is the same: doubt of salvation! The terrifying, paralyzing, God-dishonoring doubt of salvation!

Since the contemporary disciples of the Puritans and proponents of the doubt of the *nadere reformatie* claim to be Reformed, it is in order to appeal to the teaching of John Calvin against them. Although he was combating the Roman Catholic doctrine of doubt, what he wrote plainly refutes the Puritan doctrine, as well as all other doctrines that strip assurance of righteousness and salvation from justification by faith alone. Calvin was responding specifically to the false doctrine of Rome concerning assurance as declared by Rome at its Council of Trent. Calvin observed that Trent "inveigh[ed] against what they call The Vain Confidence of Heretics. This consists, according to their definition, in our holding it as certain that our sins are forgiven, and resting in this certainty."[11]

Trent condemned the certainty of forgiveness, that is, justification, as the vain confidence of heretics. Puritanism and the further reformation do the same. Indeed, their error is worse. Puritanism and the further reformation condemn as vain confidence the certainty of forgiveness of *elect believers who are believing the gospel.*

With appeal to Psalm 32, Romans 5:1–5, Ephesians 3:12, Romans 8:37, and James 1:6, Calvin declared that certainty,

---

10 Belgic Confession 23, in ibid., 3:409–10.

11 John Calvin, "Acts of the Council of Trent with Antidote," in *Calvin's Tracts*, 3:125. Calvin wrote this "Antidote" in 1547.

indeed a *bold* certainty of forgiveness, is the gift of God to all believers and that it is the gift of God with forgiveness, as an element of the forgiveness itself. Charging the Roman Catholic theologians with "rob[bing] all consciences of calm placid confidence" by their "leaving it in suspense to whom and when they are forgiven," Calvin asked rhetorically,

> Where, then, is that boldness of which Paul elsewhere speaks, (Eph. 3:12) that access with confidence to the Father through faith in Christ? Not contented with the term confidence, he furnishes us with boldness, which is certainly something more than certainty.[12]

Calvin exposed a fundamental error of Rome, as of Puritanism and the further reformation, concerning faith when he added, "Faith is destroyed as soon as certainty is taken away."[13]

Rome, the further reformation, and the Puritans contend that Paul's claims of assurance of justification and salvation apply only to himself and to a few other specially favored saints (mostly Puritan and further reformation theologians), and that they had their assurance by "special revelation" or by a mystical experience. Calvin denied this contention as a "frivolous quibble": "[Paul] claims nothing so special for himself as not to share it with all believers, when in their name as much as his own, he boldly exults over death and life, the present and the future [in Romans 8:35–39]."[14]

At Trent Rome declared as the authoritative doctrine of the Roman Catholic Church: "Neither is it to be asserted that it becomes those who are truly justified to determine with themselves, without any kind of doubt, that they are truly justified."[15]

---

12 Ibid.

13 Ibid.

14 Ibid., 3:137.

15 Quoted in ibid., 3:97.

Puritanism and the further reformation agree with the Roman Catholic Church, as the quotation of Thomas Goodwin above indicates. Calvin responded: "Paul makes it [full assurance] the perpetual attendant of faith."[16]

Calvin took note of Rome's "ingenious" ploy of seeming to do justice to the Bible's teaching of faith's certainty, all the while maintaining its false doctrine that individual believers live in doubt of their own forgiveness and salvation: "They think... that they ingeniously obviate all objections when they recommend a general persuasion of the grace of Christ...[while] they allow none to apply grace to themselves with the firm assurance of faith."[17] The Puritans and their contemporary disciples of the further reformation employ the same subterfuge when they maintain that believers are certain that Christ forgives sins, but themselves remain uncertain whether Christ forgives *their* sins.

Calvin scoffed at this worthless certainty. Those who teach it put both certainty and the efficacy of the death of Christ "in the air, so as to be only in confused imagination." Calvin continued: "Christ is not set before me and others, merely that we may believe him to have been the Redeemer of Abraham, but that every one may appropriate the salvation which he procured."[18]

The gravity of the false doctrine concerning assurance of justification as essential to justification by faith alone is indicated by Calvin's blunt statement: "Paul and John recognise none as the children of God but those who know it," that is, those who are righteous with God in their own consciousness.[19]

In another of his writings, Calvin might have been directly addressing the miserable theology of the Puritans and the further

16 Ibid., 3:126.
17 Ibid., 3:127.
18 Ibid., 3:127.
19 Ibid.

reformation, although in fact he had the theology of Rome in view and was demonstrating the necessity of the Reformation.

> Lastly, there was another most pestilential error, which not only occupied the minds of men, but was regarded as one of the principal articles of faith, of which it was impious to doubt, viz., that believers ought to be perpetually in suspense and uncertainty as to their interest in the divine favor. By this suggestion of the devil, the power of faith was completely extinguished, the benefits of Christ's purchase destroyed, and the salvation of men overthrown. For, as Paul declares, that faith only is Christian faith which inspires our hearts with confidence, and emboldens us to appear in the presence of God (Rom. 5:2). On no other view could his doctrine in another passage be maintained, viz., that "we have received the Spirit of adoption, whereby we cry, Abba, Father" (Rom. 8:15).[20]

According to the great reformer, the Puritan, further reformation, and other forms of the message that one can have true faith, with the justification that true faith always embraces, without being certain of one's righteousness and salvation is not "further reformation." On the contrary, this message of doubt is a suggestion of the devil, the extinguishing of the power of faith, the destruction of the benefits of Christ's redeeming death, and the overthrowing of the salvation of men.

One may say that Calvin was wrong about faith, justification, and certainty of forgiveness, righteousness, and eternal life. One may not say that Puritanism, the further reformation, or anyone else who denies that justification by faith alone is assurance of righteousness with God is faithful to Calvin and the entire Reformation on these great issues.

---

20 John Calvin, "The Necessity of Reforming the Church, Presented to the Imperial Diet at Spires, A.D. 1544, in the Name of All Who Wish Christ to Reign," in *Tracts relating to the Reformation*, 1:136.

Whoever charges Calvin and the Reformation with error on this doctrine, taking his stand with Puritanism and the further reformation, finds himself in agreement with Rome on one of the most fundamental issues of the sixteenth-century Reformation of the church, as this issue is authoritatively settled in all the Reformed, indeed Protestant, creeds. His error is nothing less than a denial of justification by faith alone, the very heart of the gospel of grace.

This is not to say that a believer is never tempted to doubt his righteousness and therefore his salvation. The Heidelberg Catechism recognizes the possibility of such temptation in its treatment of the phrase in the Apostles' Creed, "He descended into hell." The practical benefit of this part of the Christian's confession is "that in my greatest temptations I may be assured that Christ, my Lord, by his inexpressible anguish, pains, and terrors which he suffered in his soul on the cross and before, has redeemed me from the anguish and torment of hell."[21]

This is doubt of one's righteousness with God. Thus it is the fearful doubt that one is liable to perish forever in the torments of eternal hell. To such doubt, a believer is liable. But this fear is not the normal spiritual condition of believers or of any believer. It is not a fear to which any believer is taught to succumb, even for a long time, until he has a special revelation from God that his fear is unfounded. Rather, this fear is a "temptation"—a temptation to sin the sin of doubt; a temptation against which he must strive; a temptation to which he may not yield, no not for an hour; and a temptation over which he is called and enabled to conquer by believing that Jesus descended into hell for him, as for everyone who believes on Jesus (which is not the same as having Puritanism's mystical experience).

A temptation to sin is one thing. Accepting the condition of doubt, as proclaiming it, is quite another.

21 Heidelberg Catechism A 44, in Schaff, *Creeds of Christendom*, 3:321.

Chapter Thirteen

JUSTIFIED, WHEN?

In one respect, the question, when is the elect sinner justified? is easily answered: When he or she believes on Jesus Christ preached in the gospel.

In other important respects, the question is difficult, even controversial, and perhaps for this reason often ignored. The controversial aspects of the question include the issue of eternal justification. Does God's saving act of justifying the guilty but elect sinner occur only in time—by means of the sinner's faith—or does the justifying of the sinner by faith in time and history originate in and realize a justifying decree of God in eternity? Over this question of eternal justification, Reformed theologians and churches have fought vigorously. Still today there is controversy over the issue of eternal justification among those who are one in confessing justification by faith alone.

But even the truth of justification by faith in time has its difficulties regarding the question when this saving act takes place. These difficulties are sometimes overlooked or ignored in the treatment of the doctrine of justification. Frankly raising the difficulties in some detail in order to solve them rightly has its benefit in the daily experience and assurance of justification by the believing child of God.

Regarding the time of justification in the life of the elect, believing child of God, the question is whether one is justified once, and once only, in his or her life or repeatedly. If one is justified once, exactly what is the moment when this justification takes place?

The issue is not whether justification is the declaration by God of a moment, perfectly forgiving the guilt of sin and perfectly imputing to the sinner the righteousness of Jesus Christ, or the lifelong, ongoing, gradually improving work of God actually making the sinner more and more righteous in the sense of increasing holiness. As has already been demonstrated, justification is not the continuing work of God that progressively conforms the elect sinner to the image of God in Christ. This is rather the work of sanctification, which is distinct from, though not separated from, justification.

Justification is the divine declaration, the judicial verdict, that instantaneously and perfectly acquits the sinner of guilt before the tribunal of God and constitutes him perfectly righteous. Upon the instantaneous verdict of justification, there is nothing imperfect about the justified sinner regarding righteousness with God, nothing to improve and nothing to increase. It is with the justified sinner as though he never had had nor committed any sin, as though he were as guiltless as the perfect Jesus Christ, as though he had fully atoned for all his sins and perfectly obeyed all the commandments of God, and as though he had completely satisfied the justice of God.

But the issue concerning the time of justification is whether this verdict of God is sounded upon and within the sinner once, and once only, in his life or repeatedly, even daily. Does justification reoccur, or is it a once-for-all-time act of God, in the life and experience of the believer? Is justification limited to the moment I first believed, or ought I to seek, and should I experience, justification again and again throughout my life?

There are statements in the Presbyterian and Reformed creeds that might be construed as teaching that justification occurs but once in the life of every elect believer. The Westminster

Confession of Faith assures believers that "they can never fall from the state of justification."[1] Similar is the language of the Canons of Dordt. With reference specifically to the "melancholy falls" of the elect into sins, the Canons deny that elect, regenerated believers ever "forfeit the state of justification."[2] One might understand these statements to imply that the initial act of justification establishes a permanent state of justification, so that a repetition of the act is neither necessary nor possible.

This seems to be the view of the Presbyterian theologian Robert L. Dabney. The view that justification is a single saving act in the life of the believer, taking place at the moment of conversion, forces Dabney to consider "the relation which justification bears to the believer's future sins." If justification takes place once, how can the believer be justified regarding sins committed after this act of justification? Dabney acknowledges that his problem is an "intricate subject." On the one hand, Dabney supposes that a continuing state of justification means that the act of justification is not repeated. On the other hand, he recognizes that "it is illogical to speak of sin as pardoned before it is committed," that is, he recognizes that an initial act of justification cannot forgive sins that are committed later in life.

Nevertheless, his solution of the problem, although stated quite unclearly and therefore unsatisfactorily, amounts to adopting the view that the initial justification early in the believer's life applies to all the sins that will follow: "Justification from future sins is not so much a pardoning of them before they are committed, as an unfailing provision by God both of the meritorious and instrumental causes of their pardon, as they are committed."[3] "Not so much" is an admission that an initial justification

1 Westminster Confession of Faith 11.5, in Schaff, *Creeds of Christendom*, 3:627.

2 Canons of Dordt 5.6, in ibid., 3:593.

3 Robert L. Dabney, *Lectures in Systematic Theology* (Grand Rapids, MI: Zondervan, 1972), 644–45.

is in fact the pardoning of sins before they are committed. What follows does not mitigate the admission in the slightest. The teaching of one, and one only, act of justification in one's life necessarily implies "justification from future sins," or the provision in that act for the pardon of future sins "as they are committed."

It is evident also from Dabney's defense of justification as a once-for-all-time act of God in the consciousness of the elect believer that justification is essentially forgiveness or pardon. Dabney virtually defines justification as pardon, and this is right. But this truth should have directed Dabney away from the view that justification is a single act in the life of the believer, for the act of forgiveness on the part of God is repeated over and over in the life of every child of God and needs to be repeated many times.

What the Westminster Confession of Faith and the Canons of Dordt deny when they state that one who has been justified cannot lose the state of justification is the falling away of saints. One who has been forgiven by God and had imputed to him the righteousness of Jesus Christ cannot lose his standing as righteous before God the judge, so as to come under God's damning condemnation. The Canons' statement is part of the chapter of the creed that affirms the preservation of saints. If a justified believer were to lose the state of justification, he would become the object of God's condemning wrath. It would then be conceivable that, although once justified on the basis of Christ's death for him, he might perish under the sentence of condemnation. This would mean the falling away of the saints.

When God (initially) justifies one of his chosen people by faith in Jesus Christ, he gives that justified person the standing, the legal status, with God of righteousness—the righteousness of God himself as worked out for the elect sinner by Jesus Christ. This status or standing is firm, permanent, everlasting. It is as sure as is all the saving work of God in Jesus, indeed as sure and steadfast as is God himself. Its sure source is God's eternal election. Its solid ground is the perfect obedience of Jesus Christ in the sinner's place and on the sinner's behalf. Its certain accomplishment is the unfailing word of God, spoken at the (initial) justification of the sinner by means of faith. Concerning this last, God's "Not guilty! Innocent!" stands as the decisive, final word upon the sinner.

Nothing can undo or change this state, or legal position, before God of the justified sinner. His subsequent sins cannot undo or change it. Not even the gross sins of a David of adultery and murder, or of a Peter of denying Jesus, can change God's gracious, justifying verdict into a verdict of condemnation. This state, or legal standing, abides even when the justified child of God is not conscious of it or doubts it because of a deep fall into sin. His abiding state of justification is the basis of God's bringing him to repentance, thus saving him, both by renewing in him the peace of pardon and by delivering him from the power of sin. When God brings his straying child to repentance—a David, or a Peter, or any one of us—the legal ground for doing so is the righteousness of the sinner: his abiding state of justification. Apart from this state of justification, the sinner would have no right to be brought to repentance.

The reason that the state of justification cannot be lost is that, like all the rest of salvation, justification is gracious, that is, unconditional. It does not depend on the sinner, but on the free mercy of God in Jesus Christ. This is exactly the explanation given by the Canons for its confession that God does not allow his justified people to "forfeit the state of justification": "But God, who is rich in mercy, according to his unchangeable purpose of election..."[4]

Because they proclaim conditional justification and salvation, justification and salvation that depend not on the grace of God but on the sinner, the Roman Catholic Church, all Arminian churches and theologians, the federal vision, and the

4 Canons of Dordt 5.6, in Schaff, *Creeds of Christendom*, 3:593.

spiritual, theological, and ecclesiastical mother of the federal vision, the Reformed Churches in the Netherlands (liberated), do teach the possibility of the forfeiting of the state of justification by the sinner who has once been justified by God.

The Roman Catholic Church confesses a conditional and therefore losable justification in its creed The Canons and Decrees of the Council of Trent. In its treatment of justification, Rome warns of the possibility of the loss of justification when it declares that "God forsakes not those who have been once justified by his grace, unless he be first forsaken by them."[5] Asserting the real possibility of the loss of justification, the creed adds, "No one, moreover…ought so far to *presume*…as to determine for certain…that he that is justified…if he do sin…ought to promise himself an assured repentance."[6] The Roman Catholic creed speaks of "those who, by sin, have fallen from the received grace of Justification."[7] "The received grace of Justification is lost…by any…mortal sin whatever."[8] "If any one saith, that a man once justified [cannot]… lose grace [the grace of justification]…let him be anathema."[9]

The loss of justification is included in Rome's denial of the perseverance of (justified) saints, which denial is an element of Rome's treatment of justification: "If any one saith, that he will for certain, of an absolute and infallible certainty, have that great gift of perseverance unto the end…let him be anathema."[10]

---

5 Canons and Decrees of the Council of Trent, Sixth Session, Decree on Justification 11, in ibid., 2:101.

6 Canons and Decrees of the Council of Trent, Sixth Session, Decree on Justification 12, in ibid., 2:103; emphasis added.

7 Canons and Decrees of the Council of Trent, Sixth Session, Decree on Justification 14, in ibid., 2:104.

8 Canons and Decrees of the Council of Trent, Sixth Session, Decree on Justification 15, in ibid., 2:106.

9 Canons and Decrees of the Council of Trent, Sixth Session, [Canons] on Justification 23, in ibid., 2:115.

10 Canons and Decrees of the Council of Trent, Sixth Session, [Canons] on Justification 16, in ibid., 2:113–14.

For the Roman Catholic Church, one can be justified today, condemned tomorrow, and lost under condemnation forever.

But this is also the theology of the Arminian doctrine of salvation by the sinner's free will. As by the sinner's free will he is justified and saved by believing, so by his free will he is able again to refuse to believe and thus lose the justification and salvation that once he enjoyed. The Canons expose and condemn this aspect of the Arminian heresy:

> The Synod *rejects* the errors of those…who teach that the true believers and regenerate not only can fall from justifying faith…wholly and to the end, but indeed often do fall from this and are lost forever.
>
> Rejection: For this conception makes powerless the… justification…by Christ…contrary to the express words of the apostle Paul:…*being justified by his blood, shall we be saved from the wrath of God through him* (Rom. 5:8–9).[11]

Also the theology of the federal vision, which is essentially the ugly Arminian whore beautified in covenantal dress for contemporary seduction of Reformed churches, denies the teaching of Dordt and Westminster that the state of justification cannot be forfeited or lost. The denial is blunt. According to a quasi-official federal vision statement of belief, all baptized children, those who perish as well as those who are finally saved, receive "the same initial covenant grace."[12] This "initial covenant grace," which all baptized children alike receive, brings all the children "into union with Christ" and causes all to "share in His [Christ's] blessings."[13] These "blessings of the covenant"

11 Canons of Dordt 5, error 3, in *Confessions and Church Order*, 177. The emphasis is in the original.

12 Summary Statement of [Auburn Avenue Presbyterian Church's] Position on the Covenant, Baptism, and Salvation, cited in R. Fowler White, "Covenant and Apostasy," in Beisner, *The Auburn Avenue Theology*, 214.

13 John Barach, "Covenant and Election," in Wilkins and Garner, *The Federal Vision*, 37.

include "the forgiveness of sins, adoption, possession of the kingdom, sanctification, etc., and yet [some of these children] apostatize and fall short of the grace of God."[14] Forgiveness of sins certainly, and likely adoption as well, are basic elements of justification. According to the federal vision therefore, many baptized children of believers forfeit and lose the grace of justification. They forfeit and lose the state of justification finally and eternally. Thus this theology contradicts and is condemned by the Reformed creeds, creeds to which the vast majority of federal vision theologians subscribe—with crossed fingers.

The source of the federal vision's rejection of the creedal denial that the state of justification can be lost is the covenantal theology of the Reformed Churches in the Netherlands (liberated). Their leading theologians, including Klaas Schilder, taught that at the baptism of the infants of believers God establishes a legal relationship that is saving in nature with all the children alike. This is supposed to be the meaning of the phrase in the first question of the Reformed baptism form, that our infant children "are sanctified in Christ."[15] According to liberated covenantal theology, this phrase is not qualified by eternal election. That is, it applies to all the children, those who

---

14 Steve Wilkins, "Covenant, Baptism and Salvation," in ibid., 62. Lest anyone misunderstand or lovingly mitigate this bold declaration of the forfeiting and losing the state of justification by those who were once graciously placed by God in this state—and therefore the defiant contradiction of the Westminster Confession and the Canons of Dordt by a Presbyterian pastor—Wilkins adds, in italics for emphasis (by Wilkins), "*The apostate doesn't forfeit 'apparent blessings' that were never his in reality, but real blessings that were his in covenant with God*" (62). No Reformed or Presbyterian theologian or church member may overlook that this denial, particularly of justification as an enduring state, is, by the testimony of the men of the federal vision themselves, the necessary implication of their doctrine of a conditional covenant with all the baptized babies of believers alike, that is, of a doctrine of the covenant that is divorced from election.

15 Form for the Administration of Baptism, in *Confessions and Church Order*, 260.

ultimately perish in unbelief as well as those who finally are saved.

But the meaning of sanctification in the phrase (according to the liberated) is not the cleansing work of the Holy Ghost on the hearts of the baptized children, delivering them from the bondage of sin and devoting them to God in love for him. Rather, the sanctification of all the baptized children alike is God's establishment of a legal relationship with all the children. They are now the objects of his covenantal grace in Jesus Christ. In this grace God desires their salvation, indeed graciously promises this salvation to them, but on condition that they, when come to years, will fulfill the condition upon which the realization of the promise depends, namely, their believing on Jesus Christ.

Nevertheless, this legal relationship is saving in nature. To this saving nature of the relationship established by baptism belongs God's preliminary (legal) justification of all the infants alike. This is implied by the first question of the baptism form. The phrase "sanctified in Christ" is contrasted with the preceding declaration that the children are subject to "condemnation itself."[16] If all alike are sanctified at and by their baptism, all alike are by this sanctification delivered from condemnation, and deliverance from condemnation is justification. All are justified. But all can forfeit this state by failing to fulfill the condition of believing. And some do forfeit their state of justification.

This forfeiture, which is essentially the doctrine of the falling away of saints, is the unavoidable implication of a theology of covenant that divorces covenant from election and rather makes the covenant conditional upon works of the baptized children.

Leading liberated theologian Klaas Schilder described the covenant that is signified and sealed in baptism as a "legal relationship" between God and every baptized child. In the baptism of a child, God gives a promise to every child. He also makes a

16 Form for the Administration of Baptism, in ibid.

demand upon the child, on which the promise depends, but the interest now is the promise. The promise bestows covenantal, saving grace on every child: "A baptized child has that [covenantal] grace [of the right to Christ and salvation]." "Through the promise of the washing through the blood of Christ they [all the baptized children without exception] have the right to righteousness, and now the Spirit wishes to continuously sanctify them."[17] Strange as the phrase "right to righteousness" is, the "righteousness" that is the benefit of "washing through the blood of Christ" and the "grace" that gives the right to Christ and salvation are justification. Nevertheless, this grace of justification, supposedly given by grace at baptism to every child, is conditional and therefore forfeitable and losable by every child.

Even clearer is the testimony of Schilder's liberated colleague Cornelis Veenhof:

> In his wonderful love, the Lord gives his *promise* to *all* the children of believers...He says to all those children, head for head...I establish my covenant with you. I wash you from all sins in the blood of our Lord Jesus Christ...I promise you the complete forgiveness of sins and eternal life...Therefore, when God baptizes a child, that child thus receives, in that baptism, in that sealed promise, the entire salvation that God wills to bestow upon sinners.[18]

---

17 Klaas Schilder, "The Main Points of the Doctrine of the Covenant: A Speech Given by Professor Dr. K. Schilder in the Waalsche Kerk in Delft, the Netherlands on August 31, 1944," trans. T. van Laar (Canada: n.p., 1992), 3–14.

18 C. Veenhof, "*De zaak waar het om gaat*" [The real issue (in the controversy over the covenant in the Reformed Churches in the Netherlands, resulting in the formation of the Reformed Churches in the Netherlands liberated)], in *Appel!* [Appeal!], 5–12. The booklet has no publishing data. Internal evidence indicates that the piece was published in or soon after 1948. The translation of the Dutch is mine. For a more complete account of the teaching by the federal vision of the loss of justification, of the

Washing from all sins in the blood of Jesus Christ and complete forgiveness of sins are justification. In the promise, according to Veenhof, every baptized child "thus receives" justification. But many lose their justification by failing to fulfill the condition of believing. Many lose their justification in such a full and final way that they are condemned eternally.

Against all these related affirmations—related in that all teach a *conditional justification and salvation*—that the grace of justification can be lost stands the Reformed confession of the Canons of Dordt that God does not suffer any of his elect people "to lose the grace of adoption and forfeit the state of justification."[19]

Repeated Justification

That the state of justification cannot be forfeited or lost does not, however, imply that the act of justification is not repeated throughout the life of the elect child of God or that there is no need of this repetition. On the contrary, God maintains the state of justification by repeatedly, even daily, justifying his beloved, elect child.

Justification is fundamentally the forgiveness of sins. It is God's declaration in the consciousness of the believer, "I pardon the guilt of your sins for the sake of the atoning death of Jesus Christ." At the same time, justification is the imputation to the guilty sinner of the righteousness of Jesus Christ—through the believer's faith and in his own experience. Daily every believer needs this divine, saving act of God. Daily he receives this gracious gift. Whenever the believer repents, confesses, and cries out to God, "Forgive my sins and sinful nature," he is justified.

---

dependency of the federal vision in this heresy upon the covenantal theology of the liberated churches, and of the conditionality of covenantal salvation, including justification, in liberated theology, see my *Covenant and Election in the Reformed Tradition.*

19 Canons of Dordt 5.6, in Schaff, *Creeds of Christendom*, 3:593.

There is a real verdict from heaven in the soul of the penitent believer, "Righteous, for the sake of the cross of Christ." By this verdict the believing, penitent child of God is delivered from the conscious burden of his guilt and damnworthiness. By this judicial declaration he becomes, in his own experience, just in the judgment of God.

Because he sins repeatedly, he needs justification repeatedly. Because he sins daily, he needs justification daily. Because his sins render him guilty before God in his consciousness—a grievous reality—again and again, he needs the gracious lifting of his guilt and the gracious gift by imputation of the righteousness of Jesus Christ in his consciousness—a blessed reality—again and again.

Indeed, it is exactly this repeated justification by faith that constitutes the most blessed, ineffable experience of salvation of the child of God. The child of God who has been justified and who lives in the consciousness of his justification does not need the vaunted, mystical experiences of the charismatic movement. For him, "Blessed is he whose transgression is forgiven, whose sin is covered. Blessed is the man unto whom the Lord imputeth not iniquity" (Ps. 32:1–2). Justification and with it the restoration in his consciousness of fellowship with God, which his sins have troubled, are the best and highest and most satisfying experience one could possibly enjoy. Having this, he needs nothing more. Having this, he is, and feels himself to be, "blessed."

Jesus taught us that justification is a divine, saving act that is often repeated—not progressively continuing but repeated—by instructing us to pray the fifth petition of the model prayer: "Forgive us our debts as we forgive our debtors." This petition is not to be prayed only once, any more than are the other petitions. But the prayer for forgiveness is the request for justification, as the Heidelberg Catechism makes plain in its explanation of this petition, using "impute," the word most closely associated with justification. "Be pleased, for the sake of Christ's blood, not to impute to us, miserable sinners, our manifold transgressions, nor the evil which still always cleaves to us."[20]

The Heidelberg Catechism's main explanation of justification clearly expresses that justification is a repeated act of God. In answer to the question, "How art thou righteous before God?" the Catechism teaches that God "imputes to me the perfect satisfaction, righteousness, and holiness of Christ…*if only I accept such benefit with a believing heart.*" The German original of the word translated in the English version as "if" is "*wenn*": "wenn *ich allein solche Wohlthat mit glaubigem herzen annehme*" ("*when* I only accept such benefit with a believing heart"). "*Wenn*" in the first instance means "when" and has this meaning in this question of the Catechism. Indeed, the thought is that God imputes to the believer the righteousness of Christ *whenever* one accepts such benefit with a believing heart.[21]

The reality and necessity of the repetition of justification are shown in Psalm 32, which passage Paul quotes in Romans 4:6–8: "Even as David also describeth the blessedness of the man, unto whom God imputeth righteousness without works, Saying, Blessed are they whose iniquities are forgiven, and whose sins are covered. Blessed is the man to whom the Lord will not impute sin." In Psalm 32, David extols the blessedness of the man unto whom the Lord does not impute iniquity in the specific case of the child of God's having fallen into enormous sins after he first believed in God. David extols his own blessedness in exactly such a case. David had been justified prior to his melancholy fall into adultery and murder. But there was blessed justification, or non-imputation of guilt, upon his repentance and by means of his trusting in the Lord for forgiveness after his fall.

Our own misery throughout our lives of repeatedly and consciously incurring a burden of guilt and being afflicted with a

---

20 Heidelberg Catechism A 126, in ibid., 3:353–54.

21 Heidelberg Catechism Q&A 60, in ibid., 3:326–27; emphasis added.

sense of shame necessitates daily justification, indeed, more frequent justification.

Justification, this grand act of a gracious God, is as real to every believing child of God as the forgiveness of sins, *today*. *Today* we stood in the divine courtroom. There on his seat of judgment sat the holy God in the exalted Jesus Christ. All our sins and our sinful natures as we came to experience them anew *this day* were laid out before the divine judge. Through our faith in Jesus, a faith that renounced all our works for justification, including the activity of believing, and that appealed only to the perfect work of Jesus, we received the verdict from the bench, *today*: "Not guilty! Righteous as though you never did one sin, as though you kept the whole law perfectly, and as though your natures were as spotlessly pure and holy as the nature of the Son of God in human flesh! Heir, therefore, of every blessing of God in this life, and one day of the eternal life and glory of the new world that is coming!"

Away we went, out of the courtroom, at peace with God, rejoicing in the greatest benefit that ever any man or woman could enjoy, and eager to work, indeed to outwork all those who work merely to earn salvation or to pay for their sins. Especially on the Lord's day, *every* Lord's day, from the services of public worship, at the center of which is the divine gospel word of justification by faith alone, we publicans go home justified.

Justification is not progressive and in this life imperfect, as is the saving work of sanctification. But the perfect verdict is sounded from the heavenly bench again and again, even as our consciences accuse us again and again.

Speaking personally (though on behalf of most covenantal children, who have been regenerated, justified, and sanctified from earliest childhood), if justification is a onetime act when one first believes on Jesus, and if daily forgiveness is merely assurance of (past) justification, present assurance of past justification (regarding *present* sins and sinfulness, let it be noted) is far more important and precious to me than that original, onetime justification. I cannot even remember when first I consciously and actively believed in Jesus and was justified. But I do remember distinct times in later childhood and in young manhood, particularly when first I was to partake of the Lord's supper, that my sinfulness and sins deeply troubled me, and I was forgiven in my own consciousness. Those acts of God the gracious judge to forgive and to declare me righteous were precious to me.

Similarly, today in my old age, when I am more grieved by my depraved nature and my sins than ever before, daily forgiveness with imputed righteousness by the verdict of God in the gospel, that is, justification, is dearer to me than ever it was. This includes my early childhood, when according to Dabney and others, I was justified in the onetime act of God. It seems strange to me that "assurance of past justification" in the present should be more precious to me than justification itself in the distant past, on the view now of those who insist that justification is a onetime act of God when one first believes on Jesus Christ.

Or to refer yet again to David's experience of justification in later life, as celebrated in Psalm 32, it seems strange that "assurance of past justification," when David first believed, should have been more precious to him than God's justifying him in later life upon his sin with Bathsheba. David does not rejoice over the blessedness of the man unto whom the Lord did not impute iniquity in the distant past, but over the blessedness of the man unto whom the Lord "*imputeth* not iniquity" in the present (Ps. 32:2, emphasis added).

Even those who contend that justification is a onetime act of God, so that subsequent forgiveness and constituting the sinner righteous before God are only "assurance of justification once for all time in the distant past," must acknowledge that there are more divine acts of justification of the elect sinner than one only. There is that onetime act in the consciousness of the elect sinner at the moment he first believes. But there will also be the public justification of the believer at the final judgment. The final judgment will be justification, and that justification will be public. It will be a verdict that resounds in the soul and experience of the believer: "Not guilty! Righteous with the righteousness of Jesus Christ!"

Therefore, there can be no fundamental objection to the teaching that justification is a repeated verdict of God the judge.

The repeating of the verdict of justification by the divine judge to the sinner in the time of her earthly life is dramatically and undeniably evident in the earthly ministry of Jesus. Jesus explained the presence and loving behavior of a sinful woman as her response to his earlier justification of her. In the parable of the two debtors that Jesus spoke to Simon the Pharisee on the occasion of a sinful woman's standing at his feet weeping, washing his feet with her tears, kissing his feet, and anointing him with ointment, Jesus explained her actions as the response to his earlier justification of her. She loved him because he had freely forgiven her the enormous debt of the guilt of her sin (Luke 7:36–50). He had justified her in the past.

Nevertheless, upon her courageous appearance in the house of the Pharisee, to express her thankful love to Jesus for his earlier justification of her, Jesus "said unto her, Thy sins are forgiven" (Luke 7:48). He justified her once again. He did not merely remind and assure her that he had justified her once in the past. But he justified her. He justified her once again. She needed this repetition of the verdict for the peace of soul with which he sent her away (v. 50).

That justification is a repeated declaration of God upon the guilty but believing sinner was the view of *the* theologian of justification, Martin Luther. According to renowned Luther scholar Karl Holl,

> For Luther, "justification" was not something that works itself out automatically once it has been experienced. It

> was rather an ever-recurring event that receives its special meaning and increasing profundity from the particular impressions of the respective moment. Paradoxical as it may at first seem, Luther saw in these continual "new starts" the indispensable method for genuine inner progress.[22]

This defense of the repetition of justification having been argued against those who hold that justification is a once-for-all-time, never-to-be-repeated act of God, I deny that the difference between the two doctrinal positions is fundamental. Those who most vehemently defend the position that justification occurs only once in a sinner's believing consciousness virtually acknowledge that, in fact, in the daily forgiveness of sins justification is repeated after all. And those who hold that justification is repeated whenever God forgives sins can, with some effort, find themselves in the explanation given by the defenders of a one-time justification.

Outstanding Reformed theologian Francis Turretin insisted that God justifies the believing sinner only once. Turretin taught that justification "take[s] place in this life in the moment of effectual calling, by which the sinner is transferred from a state of sin to a state of grace and is united to Christ, his head, by faith. For hence it is that the righteousness of Christ is imputed to him by God, by whose merit apprehended by faith he is absolved from his sins and obtains a right to life."[23]

Turretin contends that "justification is one numerically in individuals." Although his explanation confuses the issue by comparing a repeated justification with a continuing

---

22 Karl Holl, *What Did Luther Understand by Religion?* (Philadelphia, PA: Fortress Press, 1977), 95.

23 Francis Turretin, *Institutes of Elenctic Theology*, ed. James T. Dennison Jr., trans. George Musgrave Giger (Phillipsburg, NJ: P&R Publishing, 1994), 2:684.

sanctification, Turretin explains that by justification's being "one numerically" he means that justification is a one-time act of God for each believer: "It [justification] is not promoted successively after the manner of sanctification by repeated acts, but is finished in one judicial act and brings to the believer the remission of all sins."[24]

Defending his contention that justification is a onetime act of God, however, Turretin comes so close to acknowledging that justification is, in fact, a repeated act of God in the believing consciousness of the elect child of God as to negate the difference between his avowed position and the position that God repeats the perfect act of justification as often as he forgives the guilty sinner.

> It is one thing to apply justification often and to extend it to sins of daily occurrence (in which sense we are commanded to seek remission of sins every day); another to

24 Ibid., 2:686. Here Turretin admits the inescapable implication of his position that justification is a onetime act of God in the life and consciousness of the elect believing sinner: this onetime act "brings to the believer the remission of all sins," that is, the sins that he has not yet committed but will commit in the future. In his consciousness the believer then enjoys forgiveness regarding the sins he will commit tomorrow and next year. As David contemplates adultery with Bathsheba, as he is in the very act of adultery with her, and as he is ordering the murder of her husband, he is justified. That is, before he repents and flies to God in Jesus Christ in faith, sorrowing over and confessing his sins, indeed while he is plotting and committing his sins, David enjoys in his consciousness justification—forgiveness of the sins he plans to commit and is in the process of committing and the imputation to himself of the righteousness of Jesus Christ regarding these sins. Consisting as justification does of the *consciousness* of forgiveness, being right with God in one's *experience*, it is foolish, dangerous, and indeed the affirmation of an impossibility to speak of justification regarding sins yet to be committed. As the saving declaration of God in the consciousness of the penitent believer, justification is the forgiveness of past sins and the declaration of righteousness to the sinner who has made himself, and feels himself to be, guilty by the committing of sins in the past.

> repeat and renew justification often. The former we grant, but not the latter. Nor is there need that a new justification should take place as often as the believer falls into a new sin. It is sufficient that the justification once made (which if not formally, virtually and generically contains the remission of all sins) be applied and extended specifically and determinatively to this or that sin by an intimation of the Holy Spirit and the apprehension of faith.[25]

The distinction between repeating the act of justification and, in Turretin's terminology, applying justification often and extending it to sins of daily occurrence is a distinction without a difference.

On his part a defender of the truth that God repeats the act of justification whenever he forgives the iniquities of the penitent, believing sinner could accept Turretin's doctrine of the repeated application and extension of justification to sins of daily occurrence. As he left the conference at which this matter had been discussed, however, he would be heard muttering to himself, "Nevertheless, the repeated application and extension of justification to sins of daily occurrence *is repeated justification.*"

Eternal Justification

More divisive, however, regarding the time of justification is the controversy between those Reformed theologians who confess eternal justification and those Reformed theologians who deny eternal justification.

Rightly to understand the controversy, it is necessary clearly to apprehend the issue. The issue is not whether God has eternally decreed to justify the elect in time and history. No Reformed theologian denies that God eternally decreed to justify the elect. Herman Hoeksema is mistaken, therefore, when

25 Ibid., 2:687.

he appeals to the Westminster Confession in support of eternal justification.

> It is worthy of note that in this same confession, that is, the Westminster Confession of Faith, we read for the first time of eternal justification. For thus we read in Article 4, under Chapter 11: 'God did, from all eternity, decree to justify all the elect, and Christ did, in the fulness of time, die for their sins, and rise again for their justification: nevertheless, they are not justified until the Holy Spirit doth, in due time, actually apply Christ unto them.' From this article it is plain that, according to the Westminster Confession, justification is eternal.[26]

Westminster does not confess that God justified the elect from all eternity. Rather, it confesses that God from all eternity did decree *to* justify the elect, that is, in eternity God decreed to justify the elect in time and history. No more than the eternal decree to create implies an eternal creation does an eternal decree to justify necessarily imply an eternal justification.

Eternal justification, or justification in eternity, if a reality, is the decree in God's eternal counsel imputing the righteousness of Christ to the elect, forgiving all their sins, and adopting them as his children for the sake of Christ's death. It is not a decree that God would, in time and history, reckon Christ's righteousness to their account. But it is a decree actually reckoning the righteousness of Christ to their account. According to eternal justification, by virtue of the decree the elect are righteous with the righteousness of Jesus Christ before they are born, indeed before the creation of the world.

---

26 Herman Hoeksema, *Reformed Dogmatics* (Grand Rapids, MI: Reformed Free Publishing Association, 1966), 499. For the statement in the Westminster Confession 11.4 of an eternal decree to justify the elect, see Schaff, *Creeds of Christendom*, 3:627.

Notable Calvinist and Reformed theologians have taught and vigorously defended eternal justification. The so-called Calvinistic Baptists in Great Britain, John Gill, Tobias Crisp, and John Brine, taught eternal justification. Brine is typical. "I have reason to believe Justification from Eternity to be a scriptural doctrine."[27] The grounds given by Brine for this belief make plain that Brine taught eternal justification as God's act of justifying the elect in eternity, not merely as a decree to justify the elect in time by means of their faith:

> The elect were blest with all spiritual blessings in Christ before the foundation of the world; and therefore with Justification, for that is a spiritual blessing. "This grace by which we are justified, was given us in Christ from eternity, because from eternity God loved us in Christ, and made us accepted in him."[28]

> When Christ, as a surety, engaged for the elect, they were justified. "At the same time in which Christ became a surety for us, and our sins were imputed to him, we were absolved from guilt, and reputed just; that is, actively justified:" Which was from everlasting, or before the foundation of the world.[29]

Lest there be any misunderstanding that for him and his English Calvinistic Baptist cohorts eternal justification is the decree of God forgiving sins and imputing the righteousness of

---

27 John Brine, "A Defence of the Doctrine of Eternal Justification" (London: A. Ward, 1732; repr., Columbus, MS: Pinehaven Baptist Church, 1979), 4. In this and subsequent quotations of Brine, I have modernized the old English spelling of the work but retained the eccentric capitalization of words, as well as the old spelling of certain words.

28 Ibid., 16. The quotation within the quotation is from Girolamo Zanchi, *De natura Dei.*

29 Ibid., 16–17. The quotation within the quotation is from the Dutch Reformed theologian Maccovius.

Jesus Christ, that is, a justifying decree and not merely a decree *to* justify in history, Brine wrote: "Justification, as it is an act in God, or as it is taken for his non-imputation of sin, and imputation of righteousness, ought not to be considered as the birth of time, but is eternal...a personal Justification from eternity."[30]

Among contemporary Reformed theologians, Herman Hoeksema strongly advocated eternal justification.

> We certainly may speak of our justification from eternity. We are justified in the decree of election from before the foundation of the world...Some, evidently afraid to over-emphasize the counsel of God, maintained that one could speak only of justification by faith. They denied eternal justification. But it is very evident that this is not correct...God knew the elect in Christ as justified from all eternity. The elect do not become righteous before God in time by faith, but they are righteous in the tribunal of God from before the foundation of the earth. God beholds them in eternity not as sinners, but as perfectly righteous, as redeemed, as justified in Christ. Confer Numbers 23:21: "He hath not beheld iniquity in Jacob, neither hath he seen perverseness in Israel."[31]

But other Reformed theologians, including some of great stature, have rejected the doctrine of eternal justification, insisting that the only justification that scripture knows and teaches is justification through faith, that is, justification in time and history. Of those who deny eternal justification, Turretin may serve as the representative: "But although we do not deny that our justification was decreed even from eternity...still we do not think (speaking accurately) justification itself can be called eternal...

30 Ibid., 37–38.
31 Hoeksema, *Reformed Dogmatics*, 502.

Actual justification takes place in time and follows faith."[32] Turretin argues that the Bible everywhere teaches justification "through and by faith" and that "this could not be said if justification was done from eternity." Also, since justification is a blessing, it can "pass to us and be actually bestowed upon us" only "in time."[33]

Despite his emphatic rejection of eternal justification, Turretin does not charge the doctrine with being heretical—the heresy alleged always being antinomianism—as do some contemporary opponents of eternal justification. On the contrary, Turretin is willing to view eternal justification as an "aspect" of justification, with justification by faith in time being another "aspect": "Justification can be viewed in a twofold aspect…: either as to the 'eternal destination' in the decree…or as to its execution in time."[34] This insight points the way to the right resolution of the longstanding controversy between the confession and denial of eternal justification in Reformed churches.

In the late nineteenth and early twentieth centuries, the controversy over eternal justification threatened to undo the recent union of two Reformed denominations in the Netherlands. In 1892 the Christian Reformed Church in the Netherlands, the denomination that seceded from the state church in 1834 under the lead of Hendrik de Cock, merged with the Reformed churches that had seceded from the state church in 1886, in the reformatory movement known as the *Doleantie*. The leading theologian of the Christian Reformed Church was Herman Bavinck. The leading theologian of the Reformed Churches of the *Doleantie* was Abraham Kuyper.

Kuyper was a vehement advocate of eternal justification. "Justification does not occur when we become conscious of it, but…on the contrary, our justification was decided from

32 Turretin, *Institutes of Elenctic Theology*, 2:683.
33 Ibid.
34 Ibid., 685.

eternity in the holy judgment-seat of our God."[35] Kuyper taught the same in his dogmatics, thus influencing not only his many ministerial students and disciples but also the entire Reformed denomination in which he was the leading theologian.

According to Kuyper, the first step, or stage, of justification is "justification from eternity." "Justification from eternity is… an immanent work" of God that will be realized outside God's being. It is a "decree" that is preceded in God's counsel by "election and the constituting of the Mediator."[36]

But the leading theologian in the denomination that had recently merged with Kuyper's churches, a theologian of nearly the stature and influence of Kuyper, Herman Bavinck, outrightly denied that justification is eternal. In his magisterial dogmatics, Bavinck, though recognizing the worthy intention of such defenders of eternal justification as Kuyper, concluded that it is not

> advisable to speak of an eternal justification or of a justification from eternity. For Scripture nowhere models this usage. Reformed theologians almost unanimously opposed it and distinguished between the eternal decree of justification and its execution in time.[37]

Controversy over the issue of eternal justification in the Reformed Churches in the Netherlands became so heated as to threaten the newly won unity of the churches. Therefore, a synod of the Reformed Churches in the Netherlands—the Synod of Utrecht of 1905 (both Kuyper and Bavinck yet being alive and very much involved in the decisions of the synod)—found it

---

35 Abraham Kuyper, *The Work of the Holy Spirit*, trans. Henri De Vries (Grand Rapids, MI: Eerdmans, repr. 1973), 370.

36 Abraham Kuyper, *Dictaten Dogmatiek* (Grand Rapids: J. B. Hulst, n.d.), 4:61. Translation of the Dutch is mine.

37 Bavinck, *Reformed Dogmatics*, 4:216.

necessary to pronounce on the issue, thus putting an end to the controversy and forestalling schism.

> In regard to…eternal justification, Synod declares:
>
> that the term itself does not occur in our Confessional Standards but that it is not for this reason to be disapproved, any more than we would be justified in disapproving…similar terms which have been adopted through theological usage;
>
> that it is incorrect to say that our Confessional Standards know only of a justification by and through faith, since both God's Word (Rom. 4:25) and our [Belgic] Confession (Article XX) speak explicitly of an objective justification sealed by the resurrection of Christ, which in point of time precedes the subjective justification;
>
> that, moreover, as far as the matter itself is concerned, all our churches sincerely believe and confess that Christ from eternity in the Counsel of Peace undertook to be the Surety of His people; taking their guilt upon Himself as also that afterward He by His suffering and death on Calvary actually paid the ransom for us, reconciling us to God while we were yet enemies; but that on the basis of God's Word and in harmony with our Confession it must be maintained with equal firmness that we personally become partakers of this benefit only by a sincere faith.
>
> Wherefore Synod earnestly warns against any view that would do violence either to Christ's eternal suretyship for His elect, or to the requirement of a sincere faith to be justified before God in the tribunal of conscience.[38]

38 J. L. Schaver, *The Polity of the Churches*, 4th ed. (Grand Rapids, MI: Kregel, 1958), 2:35. This and the other decisions taken by the Synod of Utrecht to settle the doctrinal controversies in the Dutch Reformed Churches at that time are known as the Conclusions of Utrecht.

Evident, and outstanding, in the Utrecht decision is that the Reformed synod both affirmed the doctrine of eternal justification and did justice to the concern of the opponents of eternal justification that the teaching of eternal justification minimizes, if it does not deny, the emphatic doctrine of scripture that justification is by faith. Some are critical of the Conclusions of Utrecht as compromising. If the decision on eternal justification is a compromise, it is the kind of compromise that Reformed churches must learn to appreciate and practice. Certain issues of difference of doctrine, although important, may not become divisive. Another such issue, which also occupied the attention of the Synod of Utrecht, is that of the order of the eternal decrees, the issue of supra- or infralapsarianism.

It is worthy of note that Herman Hoeksema, as strong an advocate of eternal justification as the Reformed churches have produced, quoted the Utrecht decision on eternal justification approvingly.[39]

Churches and theologians committed to justification by faith will not even give a defense of eternal justification a hearing unless they recognize the fundamental theological concern that drives the defense. Eternal justification is not merely an expression of an exaggerated fascination with God's eternal counsel on the part of such Reformed theologians as Kuyper and Hoeksema, although one may take issue with the contemporary dismissal in Reformed circles of the importance of the eternal counsel.

The concern that underlies the defense of eternal justification is the recognition that the righteousness of justification is fundamental to the divine blessing of the elect sinner with the benefits of salvation. The justice of God requires that one upon whom he bestows the benefits of salvation be righteous.

---

39 Hoeksema, *Reformed Dogmatics*, 502. Having quoted the decision, Hoeksema added, "This...is what we mean by justification from eternity."

He must have the right to these benefits. God will not, God may not bless the unrighteous. The elect sinner must have the right to union with Christ by the establishment of the bond of true faith, must have the right to the new life of Christ that he receives in regeneration, must have the right to the effectual, saving call that brings him consciously to Christ Jesus as his savior, must have the right to the gift of faith itself. But all of these gifts of salvation precede the righteousness that comes to the elect sinner through faith. There must therefore be a justifying declaration of God on the elect sinner prior to that declaration that God sounds in his consciousness by means of faith. There must be an act of God imputing the righteousness of Christ to the elect sinner prior to the act that occurs by means of the sinner's faith. Hence, eternal justification.

Struggling with this theological problem, Kuyper not only proposed eternal justification, but also put justification first in the *ordo salutis*, the order of the saving acts of God upon the elect sinner in the time of his life. Kuyper emphatically affirmed eternal justification.

> It should therefore openly be confessed, and without any abbreviation, that justification does not occur when we become conscious of it, but that, on the contrary, our justification was decided from eternity in the holy judgment-seat of our God.[40]

Kuyper was not speaking merely of a decree *to* justify, but of a justifying decree: "He [God] has justified us in His own judgment-seat *from eternity*."[41]

A reason for this affirmation of eternal justification is that "faith itself is fruit and effect of our justification," that is, the guilty sinner has a right to the faith by which he is justified in

40 Kuyper, *The Work of the Holy Spirit*, 370.
41 Ibid., 371. The emphasis is Kuyper's.

his own consciousness only because he has been justified eternally.[42] Only one who is already righteous has the right to the benefit of faith, the faith by which he will be justified in time.

So convicted was Kuyper of the necessity of the sinner's being righteous by justification in order to receive from God the other blessings of salvation that in his doctrine of salvation Kuyper put justification first in the order of salvation. Justification precedes regeneration, calling, faith, and the other benefits of salvation.[43]

Although recognizing Kuyper's sound intentions and in full agreement with Kuyper's doctrine of eternal justification, Hoeksema rightly criticizes Kuyper's ordering of the saving works of God upon the elect sinner and indicates the proper understanding of the harmony of justification by faith and eternal justification. According to Hoeksema, in making justification first in the order of salvation Kuyper

> confuse[d] the objective with the subjective. In soteriology we face the question in which order the different benefits of salvation come into the active possession of the elect sinner. And although it is true that in the objective sense justification is also the juridical ground for regeneration, fact is that justification is not the first blessing of salvation which is subjectively bestowed upon the sinner.[44]

Reformed theologian G. H. Kersten excellently sets forth the basic issue in the controversy over eternal justification.

> Faith is a gift of God. But how can God bestow faith upon a sinner who is an object of His wrath, if the immutably righteous God did not actually account this

---

42 Ibid.

43 Kuyper, *Dictaten Dogmatiek*, 4:45ff. The work has not been translated.

44 Hoeksema, *Reformed Dogmatics*, 450.

> sinner in Christ, and look upon him in His righteousness; in other words, if there were not a justification before faith?

Answering his question, Kersten emphatically affirms eternal justification: "Not one who is Reformed can deny *justification before faith*. That is from eternity in the decree of God." He adds, "The elect were ordained and justified from eternity."[45]

Yet another practical aspect of the defense of eternal justification, an aspect of no little importance to Reformed, covenantal theology, is the justification of elect infants who die in infancy. These elect children of God must be justified. Without justification is no salvation of guilty sinners, and also infant children of believing parents are guilty from conception. But elect infants who die are not (experientially) justified by the faith that knows and trusts in Jesus Christ. Elect infants who die are not justified in their own consciousness. That is, elect infants who die are not justified with the justification by faith that those who deny eternal justification have in mind when they contend that justification by faith is the only justification there is.

In fact, the justification of elect infants who die is one of the lesser grounds that Kuyper adduces on behalf of eternal justification.[46] "Even an elect infant which dies in the cradle is declared

---

45 G. H. Kersten, *Reformed Dogmatics*, trans. J. R. Beeke and J. C. Westrate (Grand Rapids, MI: Eerdmans, 1983), 2:415–21.

46 "Lesser" in Kuyper's own argumentation on behalf of eternal justification. Other defenders of justification from eternity, however, have emphasized the salvation of infants of believers who die in infancy as an important ground of justification from eternity. The Dutch Reformed theologian J. C. De Moor made the salvation of elect infants who die a prominent ground of the doctrine of justification from eternity. Such infants are saved. But no human can be saved without being justified. Infants are not justified by conscious faith, as is the significance of the doctrine of justification by faith. Therefore, children of believers who die in infancy are justified by an eternal decree of God: justification from eternity. "If now really only justification by faith constitutes us righteous, how shall it then

just, tho the knowledge or consciousness of its justification never penetrated its soul."[47] It is creedal with Reformed churches that elect children of believers who die in infancy are saved.[48] But there can be no salvation without justification.

Contrary to the protestations of those who reject eternal justification, there are biblical grounds for the doctrine. But these grounds are not first of all grounds expressly for justification in eternity. Rather, they are grounds for an objective, historical justification of the elect in the crucifixion and resurrection of Jesus Christ. These grounds bear on the controversy between those who affirm and those who deny eternal justification in two respects. First, those who deny eternal justification argue that the only justification that scripture teaches is justification by faith in the life and experience of the believing sinner. But this argument, which is of the greatest importance to those who make it, is patently false. Scripture clearly teaches a justification of sinners outside their own experience, a justification that does not take place by means of their faith, a justification that is a reality prior to the life and faith of New Testament Christians.

Second, a justification at the cross establishes justification in eternity inasmuch as the Bible teaches a reality of the cross of Jesus Christ in eternity, in God's counsel.

Romans 4:25 teaches God's act amounting to his declaration of the righteousness of all for whom Christ died in the cross and death of the Savior: "Who [Jesus our Lord] was delivered for our offences, and was raised again for our justification." It is a mistake to understand the second part of the text as teaching that Jesus was raised again in order that in the future he might justify

go with the children [who die in infancy], who cannot possibly possess this [conscious] faith?" J. C. De Moor, *De Rechtvaardigmaking van Eeuwigheid* [Justification from eternity] (Kampen: J. H. Kok, 1905), 33. The translation of the Dutch is mine.

47 Kuyper, *Work of the Holy Spirit*, 370.

48 Canons of Dordt 1.17, in Schaff, *Creeds of Christendom,* 3:585.

us. In the Greek original of the passage, the word translated as "for" is the same in both instances. The word means "for" in the sense of "on account of." Therefore, the right understanding of the text is that Jesus was delivered *on account of* our offences and was raised again *on account of* our justification. Just as our offences were the reason for, or explanation of, the deliverance of Jesus to the cross, that is, the reason for his death, so our justification was the reason for, or explanation of, his resurrection. Because we were sinners, Jesus died. Because we were justified (by his expiatory, satisfactory, atoning death), Jesus was raised.

The death of Jesus in the distant past justified us New Testament Christians. Had the death of Jesus not been our justification, God would not have raised him from the dead. The cross and death of Jesus were our justification, then and there. Those who restrict a real justification to that which occurs by the faith of the elect child of God are mistaken. Romans 4:25 contradicts their doctrinal position regarding justification.

This truth of the justification of the elect by the cross helps to clarify the otherwise puzzling statement of 1 Timothy 3:16: "Great is the mystery of godliness: God was manifest in the flesh, *justified in the Spirit.*" The subject is Jesus. He is God manifest in the flesh. About him the text states that he was justified. Whether the reference is to his death, his resurrection, or both his death and resurrection, the teaching of the text is that Jesus was justified, not for himself but as the head of a guilty, condemnable people. As their head he was justified by his own saving work during his earthly ministry. In their head all the members of the body were justified objectively in the saving work of Jesus on their behalf during his earthly ministry. The head was justified with respect to the body; the members of the body were justified in the justification of their head.

Similarly, Romans 5:9 teaches that the shedding of the blood of Jesus on the cross justified all in whose stead he suffered and died: "Being now justified by his blood." The precise grammar of the Greek text puts beyond all doubt that the apostle teaches that the blood of Jesus justified those for whom Christ died, *when that blood was being shed.* A literal translation of the text would read: "*Having been* justified by his blood." Calvin explains correctly: "If Christ has attained righteousness for sinners by His death, He will now much more protect them from destruction when they are justified."[49]

Verse 10 continues in the same line: "When we were enemies, we were reconciled to God by the death of his Son." The death of Christ reconciled us to God, and it did so not when we were believers, but when we were yet enemies. Although verse 10 speaks of reconciliation rather than of justification, justification is implied, inasmuch as there neither can nor may be peace with God (reconciliation) apart from justification.

In addition, scripture teaches everywhere that the cross satisfied divine justice, so that it delivered the elect from their guilt, that is, justified the elect. According to Romans 5:12–21, just as Adam's disobedience rendered all guilty before and apart from all actual unbelief and any consciousness of guilt on the part of the rest of the human race, so Christ's obedience rendered all the elect of the New Testament righteous before they believed and apart from their experience of this righteousness. This objective justification at and by the cross really settles the controversy over eternal justification, since those opposed to eternal justification contend that there is no justification other than that which takes place by faith and since scripture explicitly teaches that the cross, which justified, is eternal in the counsel of God.

Revelation 13:8 teaches the death of Christ in eternity, that is, in the decree of the cross in the counsel of God: "the Lamb slain from the foundation of the world." Jesus was not slain only in history. He was slain also "from the foundation of the world," which is a way of describing eternity. The Lamb was also slain in

49 Calvin, *The Epistle of Paul the Apostle to the Romans*, 109.

the eternal counsel of God. Since the slaying of the Lamb was the justification of the elect, according to Romans 4 and 5, the elect were also justified "from the foundation of the world," or eternally.

Eternal justification therefore is the profoundest truth of the grand gospel message concerning God's Israel in Numbers 23:21: "He hath not beheld iniquity in Jacob, neither hath he seen perverseness in Israel." The explanation is that "the Lord his God is [eternally] with him, and the shout of a king is among them [in the shout of the crucified Jesus, 'It is finished,' from 'the foundation of the world']."

Eternal justification having been defended as a creedal, biblical, Reformed truth, certain warnings concerning the doctrine must be sounded in light of the history of controversy over the doctrine. First, the issue is not one of a necessary doctrine, as though the Reformed theologian or church member who denies it thereby shows himself heretical or as though the Reformed theologian or church member who affirms it thereby shows himself a radical or an extremist. This was the gist of the wise decision of the Synod of Utrecht in 1905, quoted above.

Second, the doctrine of eternal justification is no more antinomian than is the doctrine of eternal election. "Antinomian" is the charge that is commonly raised against the doctrine of eternal justification. Not only are the force and intention of the charge false, but also the charge itself is absurd. "Antinomian" expresses that a doctrine intends or tends toward a carefree life of lawlessness. The antinomian despises the law of God as the guide or rule of the thankful Christian life. Eternal justification has nothing to do with rejecting the law as a guide of the Christian life. Eternal justification confesses the grace of God in justifying the guilty sinner apart from anything in the sinner himself that is the ground or reason for the divine act of justifying. The thinking that regards eternal justification as antinomian must also regard justification by faith alone as antinomian. It is thinking that is offended by grace. The doctrine of eternal justification is not routed by the illicit charge of antinomianism.

Third, eternal justification does not, and may not be allowed to, detract from the reality and saving importance of justification by faith. This was certainly the error of the "Calvinistic Baptist" John Brine. He denied that justification by faith is real justification but said it is merely one's consciousness of the real justification. The real justification for Brine is eternal justification.

Kuyper also leaves this impression. He distinguishes eternal justification from justification by faith in this way, that eternal justification is the reality, whereas justification by faith is the consciousness of this (eternal) reality.

> Justification does not occur when we become conscious of it, but…on the contrary, our justification was decided from eternity in the holy judgment-seat of our God. There is undoubtedly a moment in our life when for the first time justification is *published* to our consciousness; but let us be careful to distinguish justification itself from its publication…The justification of God's children take[s] effect, not on the day when for the first time it is *published to their consciousness*, but at the moment that God in His holy judgment-seat declares them just [that is, in eternity].[50]

Kuyper's mistake is not that he grounds the justifying judgment of God in the believer's consciousness by faith in an eternal decree of justification, or even that he makes eternal justification an aspect of the reality of justification. But his mistake is that he leaves the impression that the eternal decree that declares the elect sinner righteous is the *reality* of justification, whereas the declaration by the gospel in the soul of the guilty but elect

50 Kuyper, *Work of the Holy Spirit*, 370.

sinner, through the sinner's faith, is merely the *consciousness* of the eternal reality.

Any explanation of justification that fails to do justice to the reality of justification as God's word of the sinner's forgiveness and righteousness in the sinner's consciousness (knowledge) by means of the sinner's faith in Jesus Christ comes seriously short of the Bible's teaching about justification.

Paul does not teach justification as merely the sinner's being made aware of a justification that "really" took place in eternity. The apostle proclaims justification as the very real act of God in time and history that declares the guilty but believing sinner righteous on the basis of the lifelong obedience and atoning death of Jesus Christ. The justifying word that God speaks through the preaching of the gospel very really changes the believing sinner's state, or legal standing before God the judge, from guilt to innocence in the sinner's experience. The sinner goes to church guilty. He leaves church righteous. The sinner falls on his knees damnworthy before God the judge. He arises, having prayed, "Forgive us our debts, as we forgive our debtors," justified and deserving of the divine blessing of salvation and eternal life.

It is worthy of note that the Conclusions of Utrecht concerning eternal justification do not present the relationship of eternal justification and of justification by faith as the relationship between "real" justification and merely the "consciousness" of that real justification. Even though the main purpose was to defend the doctrine of eternal justification, that synodical decision of the Reformed churches in the Netherlands declared "with…firmness that we personally become partakers of this benefit [of justification] only by a sincere faith." The synod concluded with a warning "against any view that would do violence…to the requirement of a sincere faith to be justified before God in the tribunal of conscience." "Sincere faith" is required, not merely to become conscious of a "real" justification that occurred in eternity. But it is required very really "to be justified before God." This real justification by faith takes place "in the tribunal of conscience."[51]

Justification by faith is "real" justification. It is the "reality" of justification. This does not imply the unreality of eternal justification. But it does justice to the truth that biblical justification is a declaration of God by the gospel through faith in the believer's consciousness. This is what justification *is*. Justification in eternity is a full reality, according to God's own decision, only when it realizes itself in the word of the gospel in the consciousness of the elect but guilty sinner, by the operation of the justifying Spirit of Jesus Christ. God himself graciously conceived and willed justification as the divine verdict sounded, in the words of the Conclusions of Utrecht, "in the tribunal of conscience."

Implied by the reality of justification in time by means of faith is that it is a mistake for a Reformed preacher or teacher, when treating of justification, to put eternal justification first and foremost in his sermon or lesson. Reformed preaching and teaching must follow scripture and the creeds, not only regarding truths themselves, but also regarding what is emphasized, what is central, what is the main thing. The main message and issue is not eternal justification, but justification by faith—justification by faith alone.

Important as the doctrine of eternal justification is, therefore, it is not, and should not be allowed to become, a *necessary* doctrine, as though hesitancy regarding it may become occasion for charges of heresy or for schism in the church. This was the force of the decision of the Synod of Utrecht in its Conclusions in 1905. Although fierce opposition to eternal justification might indicate serious weaknesses of a church or theologian regarding the eternal counsel of God as the sovereign, gracious

---

51 Conclusions of Utrecht, in Schaver, *Polity of the Churches*, 2:35.

source of Jesus Christ and all of salvation, difference regarding eternal justification in itself belongs to the category of differing usages referred to in article 85 of the Church Order of Dordt: "Churches whose usages differ from ours merely in nonessentials shall not be rejected."[52]

---

52 Church Order 85, in *Confessions and Church Order*, 403.

Chapter Fourteen

THE GROUND OF JUSTIFICATION

The aspect of justification that consists of the ground, or basis, of the justifying of the sinner is fundamental because the justifying God is, must be, and cannot but be just, or righteous. The burning question that necessarily arises in the mind of the God-fearing man or woman when the truth of justification is rightly preached or taught is, "How can God be just when he freely cancels the debt of sin of one who has assailed the most high majesty of God, and when he declares righteous one who is, in fact, guilty and depraved? How can God be the righteous God when he justifies one who is not only undeserving of the state of righteousness in the presence of God, but who is also deserving of the opposite—condemnation, curse, and damnation?"

The wonder of the grace of justification—freely acquitting the guilty and declaring righteous the unrighteous—underscores the greatness of the difficulty: how can the justifying God himself be just in this saving act?

There is no difficulty for the theological liberal, whose god is only love, an idol devoid of righteousness. The god of the liberal, like the liberal himself in whose image the god of the liberal has been made, can wink at and excuse sin (which is not the same as forgiving sin).

But for the believer, whose God is the true God revealed in

scripture, matters are different. God is not only love, but also righteousness, perfect, awesome righteousness. His righteousness "requires that sin, which is committed against the most high majesty of God, be also punished with extreme, that is, with everlasting punishment both of body and soul."[1] As righteous, or just, "God wills that his justice be satisfied; therefore must we make full satisfaction to the same."[2] For God to wink at sin, that is, to allow it to go unpunished or to justify the sinner by waiving the punishment due the sinner, would be for God to deny himself. It would be for him to concede that sins' attacks on him were, if not justifiable, then tolerable. Thus he would deny his goodness and Godhead.

Precious as justification is to the genuine Christian, this "ungodding" of God would be too high a price to pay for the blessing of the imputation of righteousness. Hence with urgency the believing child of God, hearing the gospel's message of God's justifying sinners by faith alone, asks, "What is the ground of this gracious justification of guilty sinners?" God must be and remain God in this work of salvation.

In addition, there is a note of concern in the question. Such is the believer's conviction of God's righteousness that if the saving work of justification lacks a ground, or basis, the reality of justification is dubious. God cannot deny himself, that is, set aside his justice in the interests of his mercy.

For earthly judges in his kingdom, God-ordained righteousness is that they "justify the righteous, and condemn the wicked" (Deut. 25:1). That this righteousness in his servants reflects God's justice in judging is indicated by Solomon's prayer in 1 Kings 8:32, where Solomon asks God to condemn the wicked, "to bring his way upon his head," and to justify the righteous, giving him "according to his righteousness."

---

1 Heidelberg Catechism A 11, in Schaff, *Creeds of Christendom*, 3:311.
2 Heidelberg Catechism A 12, in ibid.

The righteousness of God in justifying the wicked and ungodly, freely—apart from any righteousness in the one who is justified, indeed without any mitigating goodness whatever in the one who is justified—is astounding, is unheard of apart from the wonderful gospel. Such is the wonder of justification that the believer asks in amazement, "How is God just in this astounding revelation of his righteousness?"

Eye has not seen, ear has not heard, and it has never entered into the heart of man to imagine the things God has prepared for those who love him. Specifically, eye has not seen, ear has not heard, and the heart of man has not imagined the righteousness of God in justification, particularly his righteousness in the matter of the fundamental and necessary *ground* of the justification.

God is just in our justification in that he has himself satisfied his own justice regarding our guilt, has himself obeyed his own law perfectly for us, and has himself earned for us the right to be acquitted from the sentence of death and to receive the verdict of innocence. The justice of God in our justification is the lifelong obedience, the lifelong suffering, and especially the hellish death of the cross of Jesus Christ, the eternal Son of God in our flesh and thus the representative head of the elect church in the covenant of grace.

There is a divinely realized basis of justification—a *judicial* basis: Jesus' lifelong, perfect obedience to the law and Jesus' cross. There is a divinely established ground of justification—a *legal* ground: the lifelong, perfect obedience of Jesus to the law and the cross of Jesus. Concerning the cross—Jesus' "blood"—the apostle proclaims that the effectual purpose of God with it was that "he [God] might be just, and the justifier of him which believeth in Jesus" (Rom. 3:26). On the (legal) basis of the cross of Jesus Christ, God is just when he justifies the ungodly, inasmuch as Jesus has paid in full the debt of suffering for the one who is justified and earned for him the right to be righteous with God. On the (legal) ground of the cross, God may be the justifier of the one who believes in Christ, inasmuch as Christ has taken away this sinner's guilt.

The wondrous legal transaction that is the ground of justification is that the innocent Jesus "was numbered with the transgressors," as was the case in his crucifixion (Mark 15:28). Because Jesus was numbered with the transgressors in the place of the sinner who is justified, the sinner who is to be justified may be numbered, or reckoned, with Jesus as one who has fully satisfied the justice of God for his sins. Or as Paul expresses this legal transaction in 2 Corinthians 5:21: "[God] hath made him [Christ] to be sin for us, who knew no sin; that we might be made the righteousness of God in him." In the divine act of justification, the guilty sinner becomes the righteousness of God on the ground of Christ's having been made sin, that is, the guilt of sin, in the stead of the guilty sinner.

The justice of God requires that the sins of the elect, believing sinner be paid for in full by the suffering of the punishment that those sins deserve, to the upholding and honoring of the goodness and holiness of God. The justice of God does not require the sinner to suffer this punishment himself personally. On the contrary, because God is merciful as well as just, he not only allows that another, who is willing and able, may make the requisite payment in the sinner's place, but also himself becomes that other who provides the ground of justification by satisfying divine justice.

Because the death of Christ Jesus was the (legal) basis of the (legal) justification of the believing sinner, Romans 4:25 refers to the death of Christ as itself the justification of sinners. Literally, the text reads: "Who [the Lord Jesus] was delivered on account of our offences, and was raised again on account of our justification." The apostle teaches that God raised Jesus from the dead *because of* our justification (by Jesus' death), just as Jesus' death was *because of* our offenses. Because Jesus accomplished our justification by his deliverance unto death, God raised him from the dead on the third day. Jesus' death therefore, as the full satisfaction of the justice of God for all in whose place Jesus died, was the (legal) ground, or basis, of the justification of all for whom he died.

Confessed by the Reformed Faith

That there is a judicial ground of justification and that this ground is the substitutionary, obedient life and substitutionary death of Jesus Christ is the teaching of the Reformed confessions. The Heidelberg Catechism is representative. In its explanation of justification by faith, the Catechism affirms that God "imputes to me the perfect satisfaction, righteousness, and holiness of Christ, as if I had never committed nor had any sin, and had myself accomplished all the obedience which Christ has fulfilled for me."[3] Justification is not a lawless, if gracious, act of ignoring the sinner's guilt. Required on behalf of the sinner who is justified are perfect satisfaction for sins committed and sinfulness inhering; perfect righteousness regarding both guilt and the unmitigated demand of God on his human creature that he perfectly conform to the law; and perfect consecration to God in love for God and the neighbor. Noteworthy in view of the contemporary denial in Reformed circles that justification includes the imputation to the believing sinner of Christ's obedience to the law—the *active obedience* of Christ—is that the Catechism expressly includes active obedience in the righteousness of Christ imputed to the sinner in justification: the "holiness of Christ."

The Catechism clearly teaches that the imputation of perfect obedience to the believing sinner is due to, based on, and grounded in "the obedience which Christ has fulfilled for me." Justification has its solid and unassailable ground with respect to the justice of God. This ground is the lifelong obedience of Jesus Christ to the God of righteousness, which obedience culminated in his obedient death.

---

3 Heidelberg Catechism A 60, in ibid., 3:326–27.

Likewise, the Catechism's explanation of the fifth petition of the model prayer, "Forgive us our debts as we forgive our debtors"—the petition for justification—grounds the verdict of forgiveness in the atoning, satisfying death of Christ: "Be pleased, *for the sake of Christ's blood,* not to impute to us, miserable sinners, our manifold transgressions, nor the evil which still always cleaves to us."[4] The justifying act of God, though gracious, is not groundless. The ground is "Christ's blood."

This ground is an integral element of the gospel truth of justification. Apart from the obedience and death of Christ in the stead of elect sinners, God may not justify guilty sinners. Apart from the cross of Christ, God would show himself unrighteous were he to justify the ungodly. The Christian gospel is not simply that God justifies the sinner who believes in Jesus Christ. The Christian gospel is that God justifies the sinner who believes in Jesus Christ, *on the ground of Christ's substitutionary obedience,* especially the obedience of his suffering and death.

The ground of justification must be an element of justification that lives in the consciousness of the believing sinner when God speaks his justifying verdict upon him. When the guilty but believing sinner hears the Savior's blessed verdict, "Neither do I condemn you; go in peace," it is a temptation that the sinner responds, in his weakness, "But I have offended grievously! My debt is huge! Oh how I have sinned against the most high majesty of God! Oh how I have injured my neighbor! For me, justification is impossible!"

If with the verdict "Your sins are forgiven; you are right with God," we do not hear the *ground* of the verdict, "on the basis of what I myself have done to remove your guilt by suffering the full penalty that was your due and on the basis of what I have done to earn for you the standing before the divine Judge of one who has perfectly obeyed the law of God

---

4 Heidelberg Catechism A 126, in ibid., 3:353–54; emphasis added.

regarding you,"—if, I say, we do not hear, as an aspect of the justifying verdict, the word of the cross as the ground of justification, we must live still in fearful uncertainty, if not in mortal terror.

Sin cannot merely be ignored, or winked at, or excused, not only regarding the holy God, but also regarding the experience of the sinner. Despite all their claims to the contrary, this holds true also for the theological liberal, for the professed secular humanist, and for the avowed atheist. They know God; they know God as righteous; they know that his righteousness must and will be satisfied with respect to their sinfulness and sins. This is the secret terror of their lives.

The gospel includes the ground of justification with the justifying verdict: "for the sake of Christ's blood." This element of the justifying verdict alleviates all fears and establishes assurance. In God's justifying of one who believes in Jesus, the justifying God is himself just (see Rom. 3:26).

Such is the tight, important relationship between the act of justification and the ground of justification, between the justifying word, "Your sins are forgiven," and the justifying ground of this word, the cross of Christ, that to deny or corrupt the one is to deny or corrupt the other. Concretely, to find the ground, or basis, of justification in the sinner himself is necessarily to diminish the cross as the judicial ground of justification. This is denial of the cross.

By the same token, to deny that the cross was substitutionary satisfaction in the place of and on behalf of elect mankind is to make justification impossible, since in this case there is no ground, or basis, for it. Or denial that the cross was satisfaction of the justice of God is to declare that God is unrighteous in forgiving sinners. In this case forgiveness takes place at the cost of God's perfection of justice.

Martin Luther called attention to the essential relationship between justification and its ground, the death of Jesus Christ:

> This article,—namely, that faith alone, without works, justifies us before God,—can never be overthrown, for…Christ alone, the Son of God, died for our sins; but if He alone takes away our sins, then men, with all their works, are to be excluded from all concurrence in procuring the pardon of sin and justification. Nor can I embrace Christ otherwise than by faith *alone*; He cannot be apprehended by works. But if faith, before works follow, apprehends the Redeemer, it is undoubtedly true, that faith *alone*, before works, and without works, appropriates the benefit of redemption, which is no other than justification, or deliverance from sin. This is our doctrine; so the Holy Spirit teaches, and the whole Christian Church. In this, by the grace of God, will we stand fast, Amen![5]

Undermined by Arminianism

Because the Arminian heresy corrupts and thus denies the truth of the cross, it also corrupts and denies the truth of justification. Arminianism denies the cross by teaching that, in his love for and desire to save all humans without exception, God sent Christ to die for all humans without exception. Since all humans are not saved, the clear and necessary implication of the Arminian doctrine of the cross, according to Arminianism's own admission, is that Christ's death was not substitutionary satisfaction.

What the cross was, in Arminian theology, varies from heretic to heretic. The main Arminian explanation of the cross at the time of the Synod of Dordt (1618–19) was that the death of Christ merely made known to all humans what God could

---

5 Martin Luther, quoted in James Buchanan, *The Doctrine of Justification* (Edinburgh: T. and T. Clark, 1867; repr., Grand Rapids, MI: Baker, 1977), 129.

do to them in his justice, if he willed to do so. This terrifying illustration in Jesus Christ of what God could justly do to all is supposed to move sinners to repent and believe. This theory of the death of Christ is known as the governmental theory. Its father was the Arminian theologian Hugo Grotius. Most of the Arminians at the time of Dordt held this view of the cross.

Obvious concerning this explanation of the death of Christ is that on this view the death of Jesus Christ was not a matter of justice, but a deed of gross injustice. If Jesus died only to illustrate what God might do to guilty sinners (of whom Jesus was not one), it was gross injustice on God's part so to punish the holy Jesus. In addition, even if sinners are moved by the terrifying example of the crucified Jesus to repent and believe, their salvation is unjust, for neither Jesus nor they themselves have satisfied the justice of God.

Denying that the cross of Christ was satisfaction of the justice of God in the place of the guilty sinners for whom Christ died, Arminianism in reality denies the cross. Denying the cross, Arminianism necessarily also denies justification. That the denial of justification is an important element of the Arminian heresy is not known as well as are other aspects of the Arminian doctrine. The reason is that Dordt did not devote an entire chapter to the exposure and condemnation of this aspect of the heresy. The explanation is not the unimportance of justification but rather that Dordt responded to the five points of doctrine that the Arminians proposed and defended at Dordt, and these five points did not include justification.

Nevertheless, the Canons of Dordt do include a distinct, clear exposure of the Arminian error concerning justification and a strong rejection and condemnation of the error. Significantly, Dordt's reference to the Arminian error concerning justification occurs in the chapter that treats of the death of Christ. Error concerning Christ's death—the ground of justification—necessarily involves error concerning the justifying verdict.

Error 4 of the second head of doctrine of the Canons of Dordt exposes and condemns the Arminian heresy regarding justification:

> The true doctrine (of the death of Christ) having been explained, the Synod *rejects* the errors of those...who teach that the new covenant of grace, which God the Father, through the mediation of the death of Christ, made with man, does not herein consist that we by faith, inasmuch as it accepts the merits of Christ, are justified before God and saved, but in the fact that God, having revoked the demand of perfect obedience of the law, regards faith itself and the obedience of faith, although imperfect, as the perfect obedience of the law, and does esteem it worthy of the reward of eternal life through grace.[6]

The error of Arminianism regarding justification is monstrous. Not the obedience of Christ, including his suffering and death, is the righteousness of the sinner in justification, but the sinner's own act of believing and the good works that accompany his believing are his righteousness with God: "faith itself and the obedience of faith." Not the "merits of Christ" but the works of the sinner in believing and obeying are the sinner's righteousness with God, making him worthy of eternal life. In justification therefore, according to Arminianism, God does not impute the righteousness of Christ to the sinner. Rather, God merely recognizes the righteousness of the sinner—his believing and his obeying.

The fathers at Dordt noted the unrighteousness of God in the Arminian doctrine of justification. First, it has God revoking the demand of perfect obedience of the law. This is the same as having God revoke his righteousness. Second, the Arminian

6 Canons of Dordt 2, error 4, in *Confessions and Church Order*, 165.

doctrine of justification has God regarding what is actually "imperfect" as the "perfect obedience of the law."

Especially significant for Reformed churches and Christians in the twenty-first century is Dordt's observation that this heretical doctrine of justification came into the Reformed churches in the sixteenth and seventeenth centuries on the wings of a false teaching about "the new covenant of grace."[7] Today also, false doctrine concerning justification, namely, that justification is by faith and by works, makes inroads into Reformed churches as an aspect of a heretical teaching about the covenant. This is the heresy that calls itself the federal, that is, covenantal, vision.

The heretical doctrine of justification condemned by Dordt was the necessary implication of Arminianism's heretical doctrine of the cross—Arminianism's refusal to explain the cross as substitutionary satisfaction of the justice of God on behalf of all the elect.

Dordt rejected this Arminian doctrine of justification with appeal to one of the grand passages on justification in holy scripture. The Canons continue:

> For these contradict the Scriptures: *Being justified freely by his grace through the redemption that is in Christ Jesus: whom God hath set forth to be a propitiation through faith in his blood* (Rom. 3:24–25). And these proclaim, as did the wicked Socinus, a new and strange justification of man before God, against the consensus of the whole church.[8]

The ground of justification, according to Romans 3:24–25, is not the sinner's act of faith and good works, but the redemption of the cross of Christ. This cross was not an example of what God might justly do to sinners but propitiation, the

7 Canons of Dordt 2, error 4, in ibid.
8 Canons of Dordt 2, error 4, in ibid.

satisfying of the justice of God regarding all the guilty sinners for whom Christ died. Justification, accordingly, is not God's recognizing the worthiness of the sinner to be declared righteous on account of his faith, as God supposedly is bound to do. But justification is free and gracious. It is the imputing to the guilty sinner of the (perfect) obedience of Another who satisfied for the sinner. Faith is not the justified sinner's righteousness. But it is the *means by which* the sinner receives the righteousness of Christ Jesus: *through* faith, not *on account of* faith.

Well may the entire Protestant church world today hear Dordt's testimony: denial of the cross of Jesus Christ, by denying that the cross was satisfaction of the justice of God in the stead of every sinner for whom Christ died (and this is the denial that is inherent in the theory of universal atonement), is the corruption and denial of justification. It is such a corruption of the gospel truth of justification as renders all those who believe the corruption unrighteous in the judgment of God and therefore exposed to condemnation and damnation.

The close relationship between the death of Christ, which is the ground of justification, and the justifying verdict means also that error regarding justification necessarily involves error regarding the death of Christ. If, as many are teaching today, justification is conditioned on the faith and obedience of the sinner, so that his righteousness with God is at least in part the sinner's own good, meritorious deeds, necessarily implied is that the death of Christ was not substitutionary satisfaction of the justice of God on behalf of all in whose stead Jesus died. Rather, on this view of justification, the death of Christ was a death for all humans that merely made salvation possible for all, on condition of their doing something to earn that salvation or to make the death of Christ effectual in their own case.

Whatever the salvation that the death of Christ made possible for all humans may be, according to those who are committed to this theory of the death of Christ by their heretical doctrine of justification, the death of Christ was definitely not substitutionary satisfaction of the justice of God on behalf of those for whom Christ died. If the death of Christ were satisfaction, all for whom Christ died must be saved. God's justice does not require double satisfaction—one made by the crucified Christ and another made by the sinner.

This denial of the truth of the death of Christ by means of a false doctrine of justification is a grievous error that is today being introduced into evangelical and even conservative Reformed and Presbyterian churches. I refer, first, to the theological movement of the new perspective on Paul, with its most influential proponent, N. T. Wright. He denies that justification in Galatians and Romans is God's forgiveness of sins and imputation of righteousness by faith alone. One aspect of this denial is the denial that justification, as Wright explains justification, is by faith *alone*. The necessary implication of Wright's view of justification is that Wright criticizes the doctrine of the death of Christ that understands his death as God's punishment of Christ in the stead of sinners—satisfaction of divine justice—as a "crude theory." Openly he teaches that Christ died for all humans without exception—universal, ineffectual atonement.

> It is therefore true to Paul to speak of the punishment which all have deserved being enacted, instead, on the cross. But Paul has here nuanced this view in two ways which distance it from the *cruder theories* made familiar in some branches of theology. First, he is careful to say that on the cross God punished (not Jesus, but) "sin", just as in ch. 7 he was careful to distinguish "sin" as the real culprit, rather than "I." Second, his argument functions within the whole matrix of thought according to which the death of Jesus can be interpreted in this way

> because he represents Israel and Israel represents *humankind as a whole.*[9]

The "cruder theories" of the cross that Wright here rejects are the doctrine that Christ satisfied the justice of God by a substitutionary atonement. On the less crude theory of the death of Christ proposed by Wright, Jesus died as the representative of "humankind as a whole," that is, in Wright-speak, all humans without exception. Wright's heretical doctrine of justification necessarily implies a heretical doctrine of the death of Christ.

It is worth noting, in passing, that the doctrine of the cross that Wright dismisses as a crude theory is, in fact, the authoritative doctrine of the cross of Wright's own creed, the Thirty-Nine Articles of the Church of England, binding upon Wright as the very truth of scripture: "The Offering of Christ once made is that perfect redemption, propitiation, and satisfaction, for all the sins of the whole world...and there is none other satisfaction for sin but that alone."[10]

So far from, and contrary to, the orthodox doctrine of the death of Christ does Wright's heresy of justification take him that he must deny that the death of Jesus Christ was God's punishment of Jesus in the stead of guilty sinners. In the theology of Wright, the cross was not God's punishment of Jesus but his punishment of sin. As though sin were crucified, but not Jesus. As though not Jesus but sin cried out, "My God, my God, why hast thou forsaken me?" As though sin, not the man Jesus, died on the cross.

In its proclamation of the death of Christ as satisfaction of divine justice, Isaiah 53:4 declares that Christ's bearing our griefs and carrying our sorrows meant for him that he was "stricken, smitten of God, and afflicted." Verse 10 adds that "it pleased the LORD to bruise him"—not sin but "him," the suffering servant

---

9 Wright, *Climax of the Covenant*, 213; emphasis added.

10 Thirty-Nine Articles of the Church of England 31, in Schaff, *Creeds of Christendom*, 3:507.

of Jehovah, who is Jesus the Messiah. Galatians 3 teaches concerning the death of Jesus Christ that God made Jesus, not sin, "a curse for us," as was evident in Jesus' hanging on a tree (v. 13).

So egregious is the false doctrine of justification of Wright and the new perspective that they must deny that the death of Jesus was his bearing the punishment due to the sins of those for whom he died, at the hands of the just God. To err concerning the great benefit of the cross—justification by faith alone—is necessarily also to err concerning the ground of justification—the death of Jesus Christ.

Is any corruption worse than the corruption of the truth of the death of Jesus Christ? If this truth is corrupted, can anything of the gospel of grace remain? If, as Wright contends, the cross of Christ was not the bearing of the punishment that sin deserves by a human substitute, the grim fact is that all sinners suffer, must suffer, and will eternally suffer this punishment themselves. Such is the message of the new perspective rooted in its error concerning justification.

Also federal vision theology corrupts the truth of the death of Christ by virtue of its false doctrine of justification. The federal vision denies the gospel truth of justification by faith alone, as confessed by the Reformed and Presbyterian creeds. It teaches, rather, justification by faith and by the good works that faith performs. Denying thus the divine, saving work of God's justifying the sinner (which divine, saving work is justification *by faith alone*), the federal vision necessarily denies also the ground of justification, that is, the death of Jesus Christ. For the federal vision, the death of Christ was a universal, ineffectual atonement—a death that did not effectually satisfy the justice of God on behalf of all for whom Christ died, but only made salvation possible for those sinners who fulfill the condition of faith. Even in the case of those who do fulfill the condition and are somehow saved by the death of Christ, the death itself was not satisfaction of the justice of God. If it were, all for whom Christ died would be saved.

The leading spokesman for the federal vision is the Presbyterian theologian Norman Shepherd, longtime professor of theology at Westminster Theological Seminary in Philadelphia, Pennsylvania. Shepherd contends that the "Calvinist" is mistaken in restricting the "saving love of God revealed in the atonement...only for the elect." This is to affirm that the saving love of God in the cross of Christ is for all humans without exception. Jesus Christ died for all humans without exception, as the expression of the saving love of God for all without exception. This is the right understanding of John 3:16, according to Shepherd: "The Reformed evangelist can and must preach to everyone on the basis of John 3:16, 'Christ died to save you.'"[11]

The cross of Jesus Christ, the ground of justification, is as universal, conditional, and ineffectual as is the justification that supposedly rests upon the cross.

Covenantal Heresy

Of the greatest significance for Reformed and Presbyterian churches in the twenty-first century is that the contemporary heresy of the federal vision makes known that both the false doctrine of justification by faith and good works and the false doctrine of justification's ground in a universal, conditional, ineffectual cross have their unholy source in an erroneous

11 Shepherd, *Call of Grace*, 84–85. Shepherd blames the "Calvinist" for what Shepherd regards as the error of limited, or particular, atonement. What he is careful not to divulge to the reader is that both the Westminster Confession of Faith, by which he was bound for many years as a professor at Westminster Theological Seminary in Philadelphia, and the Canons of Dordt, the creed by which he was bound later as a minister in the Christian Reformed Church, both confess limited, or definite, atonement and condemn the theory of universal atonement as heresy. In accordance with the doctrine of predestination, both creeds forbid an evangelist to say to all his hearers, "Christ died to save you." Therefore, in charging the doctrine of limited atonement to be an error, Shepherd does not merely differ with the Calvinist, no small matter in itself, but violates his oath of subscription to the Reformed confessions.

theology of the covenant. As the subtitle of his little book that advocates justification by faith *as the good deed of the sinner* and by the good works of faith indicates, Shepherd's and the federal vision's doctrine of justification by faith and works is the implication of a certain theology of the covenant: *The Call of Grace: How the* Covenant *Illuminates Salvation and Evangelism.*

Justification is conditional, that is, dependent on the sinner's own works, especially his work of believing, because, according to Shepherd and the federal vision, the covenant is conditional, depending not only on (gracious) promise, but also on "obligation."[12] The "obligation" is a "condition" that the sinner must fulfill and on which the covenant and its salvation depend: "Faith, repentance, obedience, and perseverance are indispensable to the enjoyment of these blessings [of the new covenant]. They are conditions."[13] Faith and its works are the condition fulfilled by the sinner in order to receive and retain his justification, because faith and its good works are the "condition to be met for the fulfillment of [the] promise [of the covenant]." Lest anyone miss the essential relationship between this theology of a conditional covenant and his and the federal vision's teaching of justification by faith and works, Shepherd immediately adds, "Abraham's faith [required in the Abrahamic covenant] was so significant that it was credited to him as righteousness! If so, then righteousness [the righteousness of justification] was a condition to be met, and faith met that condition."[14]

No less explicit are Shepherd and the federal vision in spelling out that their doctrine of universal atonement is rooted in their theology of the covenant. It is "from the perspective of the covenant" that the words of John 3:16 mean that God loves every human with a saving love that expressed itself in the death

12 Ibid., 45–50.
13 Ibid., 50.
14 Ibid., 15.

of Christ for every human and that "the Reformed evangelist can and must preach to everyone on the basis of John 3:16, 'Christ died to save you.'" John 3:16, understood as teaching universal atonement in a universal love of God, "is covenant truth."[15]

The theology of the covenant that the federal vision is thus boldly developing into a doctrine of universal atonement and a doctrine of justification by faith and works is that of the Dutch theologians Klaas Schilder, Benne Holwerda, and Cornelis Veenhof; of the Reformed Churches in the Netherlands (liberated); and of the Canadian Reformed Churches in North America. A gracious but conditional covenant of God in Jesus Christ with all the baptized children of believers alike implies justification by faith and works, grounded on a death of Christ that is universal at least regarding all the children of believers, the profane Esaus as well as the spiritual Jacobs.

This theology of the covenant is therefore the complete overthrow of the entire system of Reformed doctrine as confessed in the Reformed and Presbyterian creeds. This is to say, it is the overthrow of the gospel of grace alone.

The gospel truth is justification by faith alone, grounded on the death of Christ as substitutionary satisfaction of the justice of God for the elect alone, as the realization of the covenant of grace with elect believers and their elect children.

That the ground, or basis, of the justification of elect sinners is the lifelong obedience and atoning death of Jesus Christ in their stead refutes the railing accusation against justification by faith, especially on the part of the Roman Catholic Church, that the Protestant doctrine of justification is a legal fiction.

---

15 Ibid., 84–85. Shepherd goes on to argue that his and the federal vision's distinctive view of the covenant is as destructive of the gospel of grace regarding the preservation of saints as it is regarding the efficacious atonement of Christ and justification by faith alone. Shepherd explains John 15:1–8 as teaching the falling away from Christ into perdition of men and women who once were truly, savingly united to Jesus Christ (88–91).

Chapter Fifteen

THE CHARGE OF LEGAL FICTION

In the ground of justification, that is, the death of Christ as the substitute of his elect people, is the refutation of the charge against the Protestant doctrine of justification that it is nothing but a legal fiction. This charge has always been the favorite attack on the Reformation's doctrine of justification by the Roman Catholic Church and her theologians. Rome's charge has been picked up by other enemies of the Reformation's doctrine of justification by faith, apart from the sinner's own works and worth.

By the charge Rome accuses the Reformation doctrine of justification of teaching that God declares a man or a woman to be innocent and perfectly righteous when, in fact, he or she is not innocent and perfectly righteous, but sinful and guilty. The doctrine of the Reformation amounts to having an earthly judge find a defendant not guilty when, in fact, the man is guilty as Beelzebub of the crimes that have been lodged against him and is still possessed of a murderous nature besides.

In support of its charge of legal fiction, Rome appeals to the acknowledgment by the Reformation that when he appears before the tribunal of God in the matter of justification, the sinner is certainly guilty of all the damning charges of the law of God concerning his disobedience and is, in addition, actually depraved. In fact, according to Reformation orthodoxy, the justified sinner retains his depraved nature after the verdict of justification is sounded in the divine courtroom.

Gleefully, in support of its charge of legal fiction Rome points to the Reformation's explanation of justification by means of the phrase "as if": It is with the justified sinner *as if* he had never committed any sin; It is with the justified sinner *as if* he had perfectly obeyed the law of God and suffered the punishment of all his sins. This is, to be sure, the language of the Reformed faith concerning justification. In justification, according to the Heidelberg Catechism, God imputes to the believing sinner the righteousness of Christ, so that the state of the justified sinner before God is "*as if* I had never committed nor had any sin, and had myself accomplished all the obedience which Christ has fulfilled for me."[1] The same "as if" language occurs in the Reformed Form for the Administration of the Lord's Supper. The supper assures the believer of his justification, that is, that "the perfect righteousness of Christ is imputed and freely given him as his own, yea, so perfectly *as if* he had satisfied in his own person for all his sins and fulfilled all righteousness."[2]

"As if"!

But not *in reality*, charge Rome and all other opponents of the Reformed doctrine of justification by faith alone. The righteousness of the justified sinner, according to the Reformation and the Reformed faith, is only an *as if* righteousness, not a *real* righteousness. The justification of the Reformed faith is a legal *fiction*.

The charge, if sound, would be a devastating indictment of the Reformed doctrine of justification. According to the charge, the Reformed faith leaves the believing sinner unrighteous, though he supposes himself to be justified. The justifying verdict

---

1 Heidelberg Catechism A 60, in Schaff, *Creeds of Christendom*, 3:326–27; emphasis added.

2 Form for the Administration of the Lord's Supper, in *Confessions and Church Order*, 268; emphasis added.

is a fiction. The assurance of righteousness is fraudulent. The Protestant and Reformed believer remains in a state of unrighteousness. The verdict of God on him is condemnation. The outcome of the judgment will be damnation.

How does the Reformed faith respond to the charge of legal fiction against its doctrine of justification? Harsh language aside—fiction—does the Reformed faith perhaps admit the truth of the charge? Does the Reformed faith respond by proclaiming that such is the grace of God in the saving work of justification that he pronounces a fiction? Does the Reformed faith counsel believers to comfort themselves concerning the guilt of their sins and their legal standing before God the judge in a fiction, albeit, if this were possible, a divine fiction? Does the phrase "as if," in the Reformed explanation of justification by faith alone, express and admit that the righteousness of the justified believer is not a reality?

Rome's understanding of "as if" in the Reformed explanation of the truth of justification is mistaken. Rome's charge of a legal fiction is utterly false. In the divine act of justification, according to the Reformed faith, one who is in himself guilty becomes righteous, not fictitiously but really. The Protestant and Reformed doctrine of justification does not amount, disturbingly, to a legal fiction but, assuringly, to a legal reality. The justified sinner is no longer guilty. There is no sin or sinfulness that God the righteous judge can find to charge to the sinner's account. The just and truthful God, who can neither weaken his righteous demands upon the human creature nor lie, declares concerning the believing sinner, who in himself is certainly guilty, that he has perfectly met every demand of God's law.

Righteous in Reality

God's verdict in justification is truth and reality.

The state of the justified sinner is real righteousness. To have no guilt in the judgment of God and to possess perfect obedience to the law of God, in the judgment of God, is not a state of fictitious righteousness but reality.

In passing, I note that by its charge of legal fiction, Rome exposes itself most fully. Rome intends to expose the Protestant and Reformed faith; in fact, it exposes itself. It exposes itself as self-righteous. It exposes itself as despising the righteousness of God and going about to establish its own righteousness, as Paul describes the heresy in Romans 10:3. For what underlies Rome's charge is that the Protestant doctrine of justification is not based upon, nor does its righteousness consist of, the inherent righteousness of the good works of the sinner himself. The Reformed doctrine is purportedly a fiction because the righteousness of the justified sinner is not his own works but entirely the works of another, even Jesus Christ.

Rome refuses to recognize as real and genuine a righteousness of the sinner that is not the sinner's own deeds of obedience to the law of God. If the righteousness of a sinner before God is not at all the sinner's own good works, granted that he performs them with the help of grace; if his righteousness is nothing whatsoever of himself, including his believing; if his righteousness is not some love he has for God; if, that is to say, his righteousness is wholly and exclusively the obedience of Christ *for* the sinner, *in the stead of* the sinner, and *on behalf of* the sinner, "Well then," concludes the Roman Catholic Church, "the whole business of justification is nothing but a legal fiction."

This is the great sin of Rome, far outstripping all her other enormous sins, including her challenge to the headship of Christ over the church in the papacy and her persecution of multitudes of God's dear children for their confessions of the gospel of grace. The great sin of Rome is the Roman teaching that the righteousness of sinners before God is in part, in *decisive* part, what they themselves actually are and what they themselves do, although with the assistance of grace.

The dreadful implication for Rome and for every deluded

soul who presents himself for justification before God as deserving by virtue of his own works is that Rome's justification is, in reality, a fiction. "For by the works of the law shall no flesh be justified" (Gal. 2:16). Whoever takes his stand before God in the judgment without the "wedding garment" of the obedience of Christ, received and put on by (legal) imputation through faith alone, is and will be cast away by God into the outer darkness (Matt. 22:11–14). Only the sinful man or woman who pleads in the judgment, whether daily in this life or finally at the last judgment, "God, be merciful to me the sinner" (merciful by imputing freely the obedience and works of Jesus Christ) goes down to his house "justified" (Luke 18:9–14).

A righteousness in the matter of justification that consists of one's own works and goodness is no reality. It is a spurious righteousness, because even our best works are defiled with sin and therefore not acceptable by God the judge in the great matter of justification. A righteousness consisting of imperfect works performed by an imperfect human is not the reality of justification, because God, who determines reality, has revealed that only the perfect work of the incarnate Son of God in human flesh for sinners and in the place of sinners will be accepted by him as the righteousness of guilty men and women. "Whom God hath set forth to be a propitiation through faith in his blood, to declare his righteousness for the remission of sins that are past…to declare, I say, at this time his righteousness" (Rom. 3:25–26).

Like self-righteous Israel, "going about to establish their own righteousness," Roman Catholics and all who share their heretical doctrine of justification by works "have not submitted themselves unto the righteousness of God. For Christ is the end of the law for righteousness to every one that believeth" (Rom. 10:3–4). The message that "the man which doeth those things shall live by them" is not the message of genuine justification. Rather, it is the message of "righteousness which is of the law." The message of attaining righteousness by one's own obedience to the law is a fiction. It is worse. It is heresy. The gospel message of "righteousness which is of faith" is the truth. This is the message that "with the heart man believeth unto righteousness" (vv. 5–10). One is righteous by believing, not by working. True righteousness consists of the works of Jesus Christ, not of one's own works, not even in part.

In justification by faith, therefore, the believing sinner becomes righteous, truly and really righteous. He becomes righteous by imputation. The perfect obedience of Jesus Christ is made over by God to the sinner. It is made over to the sinner's account *legally*. Thus it is made over to the sinner so that now the obedience of Christ is the sinner's own—truly and really his own. It is the sinner's righteousness as much as it is Christ's.

"As if," in the Reformed explanation of justification, does not at all suggest unreality, as though the sinner is merely *said* to be righteous when in fact he is not. On the contrary, "as if" intends to emphasize the reality of the justified sinner's righteousness. There are two important aspects to the meaning of the phrase "as if" in the Reformed confession of the effect of justification upon the justified sinner: "God…imputes to me the…righteousness…of Christ, *as if* I had never committed nor had any sin, and had myself accomplished all the obedience which Christ has fulfilled for me."[3] First, the phrase affirms the completeness, the absolute perfection, of the justified sinner's righteousness. He is so completely, fully, and perfectly righteous *as if* he had never committed one sin, *as if* he had perfectly fulfilled all the demands of the law, and *as if* he had a perfectly sinless nature. *This*, and nothing less, is the righteousness of the justified sinner. Is not this some (real) righteousness?

Second, "as if" insists that the justified sinner is himself personally, truly righteous by imputation. Imputation does not

3 Heidelberg Catechism A 60, in Schaff, *Creeds of Christendom*, 3:326–27; emphasis added.

leave righteousness hanging somewhere in the air over the sinner's head but makes righteousness the sinner's own personally. Being righteous by imputation does not suffer in comparison with being righteous by one's own accomplishing of his righteousness through paying the penalty of sin himself and perfectly obeying the law himself. "As if" intends exactly to ward off the charge that righteousness by imputation cannot be a genuine righteousness for the sinner, as well as to guard against the justified sinner's own fear that because his righteousness before God the judge is not his own obedience, it cannot be a real righteousness for him.

The sinner justified by faith is truly righteous with the righteousness of Jesus Christ. So much is this the case that it is with the justified sinner as if he himself never sinned, as if he himself perfectly obeyed the law of God, as if he himself had a sinless, perfectly holy nature, and as if he himself hung on the cross under the wrath of God, atoning for his sins. Righteousness could not be his own more personally, more truly, more really, if he himself *did* live a sinless life, *did* have a holy nature, and *did* hang on the tree of Golgotha for six hours of eternal, satisfactory suffering.

"As if" does not cleverly or foolishly disguise a sad "not really." "As if" celebrates an amazing, triumphant "in reality."

"As if" does not unwittingly acknowledge a legal fiction. But "as if" proclaims God's legal realizing of the wonder of justifying the ungodly—the wonder of salvation.

This is because of who he was who obeyed in the stead of and on behalf of the elect human race and therefore because of the nature of his obedience.

How is it that in justification the righteousness of another—Jesus Christ—becomes the righteousness of the believing sinner, personally and truly? The explanation is, first, the nature of imputation, or reckoning, in the divine act of justification. It is simply the nature of the divine act of reckoning the obedience of Christ to the account of the believing sinner by means of the sinner's God-given faith that this reckoning *constitutes* the sinner righteous before God. The righteousness of Jesus Christ is now legally the sinner's own. Having fully satisfied for all his sins and sinfulness by suffering the complete punishment demanded by the justice of God, *in the satisfaction rendered in his stead by Jesus Christ*, and having fully met all the demands of the law of God on him for a holy life of obedience to the law of God, *in the obedience offered to God on his behalf by Jesus Christ*, the justified sinner stands before God the judge as one who is exempt from all punishment due to the guilt of sin and as one who is worthy of the blessings of eternal life.

That justification, as the imputation of the obedience of Jesus Christ, effects this real, personal change in the legal standing of the justified sinner is the clear teaching of the apostle in Romans 5:18–19: "By the righteousness of one the free gift came upon all men unto justification of life...by the obedience of one shall many be made righteous." As the context, which sets forth the truth of justification, shows, the apostle teaches what happens when one is justified by Christ's obedience: he is "made" righteous. Thus, according to verse 21, he has the right to and receives "eternal life."

It is necessary, once again, to note that the translation of verse 19 by the Authorized Version is unfortunate. The word translated as "made" is, in the Greek original, the word that means "constituted," referring to one's legal standing before the judge. Verse 18, with its use of the words "condemnation" and "justification," indicates this. "Made" can leave the impression that the apostle is teaching a change in the sinner's actual, spiritual condition, so that now he loves God and performs good works. The justified sinner will certainly love God and perform good works, but this is not the subject in the concluding verses of Romans 5, as the question with which Romans 6 begins makes plain: "What shall we say then [in response to what has just been taught about justification in chapter 5]? Shall we continue in sin, that grace may abound?" The subject at the end of Romans 5 is the real change in the sinner's legal position before God the judge. Justified, he is now righteous—personally and truly righteous. Justification has "constituted" him righteous. Nothing less than this is the unique saving efficacy of the divine work of imputation.

Whoever charges against this act of God that it is merely a legal fiction, leaving the sinner in his guilt and shame, is guilty of denying one of God's grand works of salvation in Christ Jesus and of contradicting the clear revelation of the word of God.

So also am I, a believer, guilty of unbelief and fighting against God if I persist in doubting whether my sins are forgiven and whether I have the right to salvation with all its blessings, ultimately communion with God in heaven, "because I am so sinful." Some theologians, influenced by the Puritans, not only have great sympathy for this doubt of their salvation by many believers, but also actually encourage this doubt and leave the impression that it is quite spiritual to succumb to this doubt in uncertainty of salvation and therefore abstain from the Lord's table. Scripture and the Reformed confessions do not share this thinking, much less encourage it. This thinking is not praiseworthy on account of its lively knowledge of sin. Rather, it is blameworthy on account of its weakness of faith.

Against the determined foes of the gospel truth of justification and against the sinfully doubting believer stands the mighty, glorious word of Romans 8:33–34: "Who shall lay anything to the charge of God's elect? It is God that justifieth. Who is he that condemneth?" Immediately the apostle adds, "It is Christ that died."

Substitutionary Death

The explanation of how it is that the righteousness of another becomes the righteousness of the believing sinner, personally and truly, in justification is, first, the gospel truth of imputation.

But the explanation also importantly includes the truth of the death of Jesus Christ, including the office that he exercised in dying the accursed death of the cross. Christ died in the stead of the sinners, who under the gospel have Christ's obedience imputed to them, as also Christ obeyed the precepts of the law ("love God perfectly, and love your neighbor as yourself") in their place and for them all his life.

Christ lived and died as the substitute for others. His lifelong obedience and his death were substitutionary. An essential aspect of this truth of the nature of Christ's living and dying is that he was the substitute for the church of the elect human race. Necessarily implied is that his death was not a substitutionary death on behalf of all humans without exception. But our concern now is that Christ was the substitute for others. He took their place.

Only because he was the substitute for others—those to whom his obedience was imputed in the time of the Old Testament and those to whom his righteousness would be imputed in the time of the New Testament—may his obedience be imputed to them, so that his righteousness truly becomes theirs. If Christ was not the substitute for others, his obedience may not, and cannot, be imputed to others as their own. This is the seriousness, in part, of the denial that Christ died for the elect alone. Those who teach that Christ died for all humans without exception but that many perish nevertheless are necessarily denying that Christ was the substitute, for if he was the substitute of all and died for all, all are and must be saved. Denying substitution, these theologians and churches deny justification, for justification rests on the truth that Christ was the substitute for sinners.

As the substitute, Christ represented all those for whom he died. He represented them before God the judge. To Christ, justly as the representative of the others, was imputed by God the judge the guilt of the others. This is the explanation of the cross in Mark 15:28. As soon as the Holy Spirit had inspired the account of Christ's being crucified between the two evildoers, the Holy Spirit explained: "And the scripture was fulfilled, which saith, And he was numbered with the transgressors." "Numbered" is the Authorized Version's translation of the Greek word for "imputation," "accounted," and "reckoned" in Romans 3–5 and in Galatians 2 and 3. The Greek word is *logizomai*. (The critical Greek text of Nestle-Aland omits this crucial text at its crucial place in Mark 15:28 because the two newly discovered Greek manuscripts, Sinaiticus and Vaticanus, omit it. This is another reason to reject the critical text for the Traditional Text, used by the Authorized Version. Following the critical text, the New International Version of the Bible also omits this text, which is yet another reason to reject this version for the faithful, reliable Authorized Version.)

God the judge "numbered," or reckoned, Jesus Christ with the transgressors. The numbering of Jesus with wicked men—charging him with sin, condemning him to death, and then crucifying him between two evildoers—by *human* accusers and judges is of little interest to us. This numbering has no saving worth. It only reveals the desperate wickedness of the whole world, religious as well as political. But the numbering of Christ with transgressors by *God* himself, who decreed and arranged the cross, interests us greatly. In this numbering lies our salvation, very much including the reality of God's imputing Christ's suffering and death to us in the saving work of justification.

Reckoning the crucified Christ with the transgressors, God imputed to Christ the disobedience of all those for whom Christ was the substitute on the hill outside Jerusalem. That imputation was no legal fiction. Christ became guilty, as if he had eaten the forbidden fruit in paradise, as if he had been conceived and born with the totally depraved nature of the innumerable host in whose stead he suffered and died, and as if he had broken all the commandments of God and kept none of them, hating God and the neighbor.

As our representative, Christ became a guilty, shameful, damnworthy man—*legally*! by *imputation*! regarding his *standing before God the judge*! There was nothing make-believe about Jesus' guilt and damnworthiness, nothing unreal, nothing fictitious. To describe the cross as a legal fiction is to deny the cross, stopping one's ears to the cry of dereliction, "My God, my God, why hast thou forsaken me?"

The truth of the crucifixion is that "he [God] hath made him [Jesus] to be sin for us, who knew no sin" (2 Cor. 5:21). "Christ hath redeemed us from the curse of the law, having become the curse on our behalf" (Gal. 3:13; my translation of the Greek). God dealt with Christ Jesus as the guilty one, representationally and legally: God punished Jesus with the suffering that his guilt as the substitute required. This suffering was the eternal torment in body and soul inflicted by the infinite wrath of the offended God—God-forsakenness, hell.

Because he removed our guilt by taking it upon himself and paying the penalty that his own justice demanded, in his incarnate Son, God may and does forgive our sins in the act of justification. The explanation is not only that the penalty of our sins has been paid, but also, and more importantly regarding our present concern, that our *representative* paid the penalty. We ourselves paid the penalty, *in our representative, our substitute.*

Because, in our stead and on our behalf, he perfectly obeyed all the commandments of his law regarding us and our behavior, in his incarnate Son, God may and does reckon complete and perfect righteousness to us in the act of justification. The explanation is not only that the obedience required by the law has been performed by a real human, but also, and more importantly regarding our present concern, that our *representative* performed this obedience. We ourselves rendered perfect obedience to the law of God, *in our representative, our substitute.*

In light of the official position of Jesus in all his life's work, and especially in his dying, as the substitute of others, who can lay anything to the charge of those whom God justifies for Christ's sake? Who can possibly condemn those whom God declares innocent? Who can challenge the justifying verdict of God upon those for whom Jesus the Christ was the substitute?

Does one—the old accuser—object, "You may not forgive the sinner, because his sins demand payment according to your own justice"? Comes back the answer from the just God: "His debt has been paid to me in full." Does the calumniator of God and his people insist, "But the man in fact is and remains guilty as one who continually thinks evil thoughts, entertains vile desires, is subject to ungodly passions, utters unholy words, performs wicked deeds, and fails often to do the right"? God denies the charge: "His guilt was transferred to another, so that no guilt remains to him; he is guiltless." Does the objector persist, "But *he himself* has not paid the penalty, and your justice demands that *he* pay the penalty"? God replies, "Ah, but he himself *did* pay the penalty—*in his representative, in the one who was his substitute.*"

Exactly this is the controversy that rages, and not infrequently, in the soul of the believing child of God, as he struggles with the guilt and shame of his sinfulness and sins. God has the last word: real justification on the basis of the work of Jesus Christ as the believing sinner's substitute. Similarly, every attempt to challenge the justice of justification by charging that the justified sinner has not positively obeyed all the commandments of the law perfectly is rebuffed by the response that the justified sinner has, in fact, truly fulfilled the law's demands *in his representative, in his substitute.*

Precisely at this point, all earthly analogies of justification halt. An earthly judge may forgive a guilty criminal and find that the guilty criminal stands before the law of the land as one who has complied with all the law's demands, but never on the basis of the judge's enduring the punishment that the criminal deserved and on the basis of the judge's obeying the law in the criminal's place. No earthly judge presents himself as the criminal's representative before the law, as the criminal's substitute. For an earthly judge to declare a guilty criminal innocent and to free him from all penalty for his crimes is not justice but injustice.

Divine justification very much belongs to the realities of salvation that never entered into the heart of man (1 Cor. 2:9). It is a wonder. It is an outstanding wonder. It is the wonder of God's grace in Jesus Christ. "God was in Christ, reconciling the world unto himself…[making] him to be sin for us, who knew no sin; that we might be made the righteousness of God in him" (2 Cor. 5:19–21).

That at the foundation of justification is the truth of Christ's being the substitutionary representative of his elect people requires further theological exploration. This exploration will take us deeply into covenantal theology—covenantal theology that is widely disparaged by those who claim to be evangelical Christians and that is corrupted by many who profess to be covenantal theologians. This further exploration of the truth that Christ lived and died as the substitute of his people will be the subject of the next chapter.

But let us not close this chapter without exalting over the reality—the comforting reality—of biblical justification. Believing on the crucified and risen Jesus Christ, as presented in the gospel of scripture and confessed in the creeds of the Reformation, I, the believing sinner, am justified. I am justified *in reality*. For I was crucified with Christ. I obeyed in the Christ. I paid for all my sins in the Christ. I earned the right to heaven in the Christ.

In this bold confidence, I live my sinful (although also sanctified) life.

In this boldness, I intend one day to die.

In this boldness, I am resolved to come before God the judge in the great, public, final judgment, when eternity depends on the verdict pronounced over me. When the question is put to me, "How do you plead?" I fully intend to respond with a claim that will resound throughout the courtroom: "Not guilty!"

About this boldness, there will be nothing whatsoever unseemly. God wills it! Otherwise, why does he justify me? Otherwise, why did he become my representative in Jesus Christ at Golgotha?

The Spirit of Jesus Christ gives the believer this bold confidence of justification through the cross of Christ, as the cross of our *representative*.

Chapter Sixteen

THE COUNSEL OF THE COVENANT

In the divine act of justification, the believing sinner becomes righteous in his own experience—personally, truly righteous. This is due simply to the nature of the act of justification. The righteousness of another, Jesus Christ, is imputed to the account of the believer so that the righteousness of Christ is now the sinner's own—his own personally, his own truly, as truly as if he himself had died under the punishing wrath of God in payment of his sins and as truly as if by his own lifelong obedience of perfect love for God and the neighbor he had fulfilled all the demands of the law.

But this is and can be the nature of the divine act of justification only because of the basis, or ground, of justification: Christ's death satisfying the justice of God in the stead of and on behalf of all those who by the work of the Spirit believe in Jesus Christ. Christ died (and lived) as the representative, the legal representative, of others. These others are the elect out of all nations. To Jesus Christ, to his account, as the one now responsible for the sins of those in whose stead he died, God imputed our sins. Although personally the man Jesus was sinless, the guilt of the others became his own on the cross, indeed throughout all his life of suffering, by God's imputation of this guilt to him. God held Jesus responsible for the sins and sinfulness of all the elect, for whom Jesus was the divinely appointed substitute. God dealt with Jesus accordingly, cursing and damning him.

In proof of the substitutionary nature of the suffering of Jesus as the basis of justification by faith, especially at the end of his life, more particularly when he was crucified, I appealed in the preceding chapter to 2 Corinthians 5:21: "He [God] hath made him [Jesus the Christ] to be sin for us, who knew no sin; that we might be made the righteousness of God in him." John Calvin's commentary on the text explains both what the cross was—God's imputation of our sins to Christ—and that the cross, so explained, was the basis, or ground, of God's justification of us. The text, according to Calvin, declares the wonder of grace of the great, legal "exchange":

> Do you observe, that, according to Paul, there is no return to favor with God, except what is founded on the sacrifice of Christ alone?...How are we righteous in the sight of God? It is assuredly in the same respect in which Christ was a sinner. For he assumed…our place, that he might be a criminal in our room, and might be dealt with as a sinner, not for his own offences, but for those of others…and might endure the punishment that was due to us—not to himself. It is in the same manner, assuredly, that we are now *righteous in him*—not in respect of our rendering satisfaction to the justice of God by our own works, but because we are judged of in connection with Christ's righteousness, which we have put on by faith, that it might become ours.[1]

Calvin makes the strong statement that "Christ was a sinner." Strong as it is, the statement is correct. Christ was a sinner. He was, in fact, the greatest and worst sinner who ever lived. The evidence is that God punished him with the worst punishment

1 John Calvin, *Commentary on the Epistles of Paul the Apostle to the Corinthians*, trans. John Pringle (Grand Rapids, MI: Eerdmans, 1948), 2:241–42. The emphasis is Calvin's.

that any sinner ever endured. Nothing less than the worst punishment could have pressed from the eternal Son of God in human flesh, who had come into the world exactly to drink the cup of God's wrath against the sinful elect, the pathetic plea in Gethsemane, "Let this cup pass from me." To be sure, in the vehemence of his love of his heavenly Father and of us his people, he added, "Nevertheless not as I will, but as thou wilt." Still, he prayed, "If it be possible, *let this cup pass from me*" (Matt. 26:39, emphasis added). He was the worst sinner, not actually, by virtue of his own developed depravity and his own evil deeds, but legally, by virtue of representing a countless throng of vile sinners—and thus *truly*.

Now we are ready to penetrate more deeply into the wondrous mystery, and mysterious wonder, of justification. The basis of justification is Christ's death as the substitute of others. He died (and lived) as the representative of others. We have seen that this is the refutation of Rome's charge against the Protestant doctrine of justification that it is nothing but a legal fiction. In the cross Christ truly became guilty with the guilt of others inasmuch as he was their representative before God the judge.

Christ could be and was the representative of others because he was their covenantal head. Covenantal headship, in the end, is the rock-bottom justification of justification by faith alone.

I demonstrate the truth of this assertion by playing the devil's advocate against one who confesses to be justified by faith alone.

"I challenge your justification on the ground that you are a guilty sinner."

You explain, "God imputes to me the righteousness of Jesus Christ."

I challenge the justice of any such action on God's part: "Who ever heard of such a thing, that a just God would account a guilty sinner righteous with the obedience of another person?"

You respond, "Jesus was my substitute."

I challenge such substitution: "What gives another person the right to be your substitute?"

You respond, "Christ Jesus was and is my representative."

I challenge the justice of such representation. I challenge it, of course, by appeal to God himself, who is justice and the criterion of justice—the only appeal that can possibly carry the day. "Granted the love of Christ Jesus for you, that he was willing to be the representative of such a worthless creature as you, God cannot allow another to be your representative. Suppose that I had a dear child, who committed a capital offense, and who was justly sentenced to death. Were I to appear in court offering to die in the place of my child, the judge would disallow my offer, even though I pleaded one of the closest human bonds, that of father and child. If he were a Christian judge and dared to mention the name of God in the judicial proceedings, he would kindly inform me, 'God himself, who appointed me judge, does not permit me to sentence a father to die for the crime of his child. To do so would not be just. The sinner shall die for his own iniquity. God demands it.'"

Covenantal Headship

Responding to this challenge, we come to the deepest ground, and therefore to the decisive justification, of the gospel truth of justification by faith alone. To this ground the faith that justifies, instrumentally, must finally come in believing in Jesus Christ for justification. Upon this ground the faith by which the sinner is justified must finally settle.

Jesus had the right to be the representative of others, of guilty sinners, of the entire host of elect, guilty sinners, because he was and is the head of the elect church in the covenant of grace. More simply, the deepest ground and profoundest truth of justification by faith alone is that Jesus lived and died as the covenantal head of the new human race of the elect from all nations.

Not anyone at all could be the representative, and therefore the substitute, of the elect with respect to the justice of God. Not even Jesus himself, although a perfectly sinless human and the second person of the Godhead, could have been the representative of others, *apart from his covenantal headship*. As a sinless man and God himself in one person, he would have had the *ability* to live a perfect life and to die a substitutionary death for others. But apart from being our covenantal head, he would not have had the *right* to live and die as our representative, that is, to accomplish our justification. And justification is very much a matter of *right*.

In his eternal counsel the triune God—Father, Son, and Holy Ghost—appointed the incarnate Son of God, Jesus the Christ, as covenantal (federal) head of the elect church. This appointment established Jesus' right to be the representative of the church in his lifelong obedience to the law and especially in his death. His covenantal headship is the reason our guilt could become his, by imputation, and why his righteousness can become ours, by imputation. The head may and does act representatively for the body, and the body may and does receive the benefit of this action of the head on its behalf as its own. This substitution is right in the judgment of the just God and according to his righteous will.

To my final challenge to the defender of justification by faith, against his appeal to Christ's being his representative, the defender's reply must be, "Christ was rightly my representative *because he was and is my head in the covenant of grace, according to God's eternal, gracious, but also righteous decree.*"

This is the end of all challenge to justification by faith alone.

Elect believers obeyed the law of God perfectly, truly and personally obeyed, *in their covenantal head*! Elect believers suffered and died for their sins, truly and personally died, under the infinite wrath of God, in the cross of Christ, *in their covenantal head*! The justice of God is fully satisfied regarding elect believers both with respect to their deserved punishment (hell) and with respect to their meriting eternal life (heaven) *in their covenantal head*! By means of faith in this covenantal head, *only* by faith in him who is the head of the covenant of grace, all his obedience becomes ours, truly and personally, in our consciousness by imputation, just as all our disobedience became his at the cross by virtue of his identifying himself with us legally as our covenantal head.

The covenantal headship of Jesus Christ is set forth prominently, in the midst of the apostle's teaching of the truth of justification by faith alone, in Romans 5. The passage treats of the ground of the grand reality of justification. Romans 5! No discussion of justification may overlook Romans 5. The subject is the death of Jesus Christ. The subject is the death of Jesus Christ as the substitute for others. The subject is the death of Christ as the basis of justification by faith alone. By no means, however, is this all of the subject of Romans 5. The subject of Romans 5 is the death of Christ as the *covenantal head* of the "all" who are justified by Christ's death, as Adam was the covenantal head of the "all" who were condemned by Adam's disobedience.

Even though the word *covenant* does not occur in Romans 5, the headship—the representative, legal headship—in the chapter is covenantal headship both regarding Adam and regarding Christ.

This reminds us that there is another divine judgment similar to that of justification. This is the condemnation of all humans without exception by God the judge by way of imputing to all humans the disobedient deed of another. According to Romans 5:12–21, God imputes to the account of all humans the disobedience of Adam in paradise, as that disobedience is made known in Genesis 3. "By the offence of one [man] judgment came upon all men to condemnation" (Rom. 5:18). The reason for the condemnation of all humans on account of the sin of Adam is that "all have sinned" in the disobedience of that one man, Adam (v. 12).

The explanation is that Adam too was a covenantal head of the human race by virtue of God's appointment. As a covenantal head, Adam represented us all. Because he represented us all, as head of the covenant of creation, I, as well as every other human, personally and truly disobeyed legally in his disobedience. Therefore, God is just in imputing Adam's deed with the forbidden fruit to the account of every human. This is what the Christian religion means by original sin, specifically original guilt.

This imputation to me of Adam's disobedience is no legal fiction. It is rather a legal reality, as my being a dying man proves: "death by sin, and so death passed upon all men, for that all [truly and personally] have sinned" (Rom. 5:12).

In light of Romans 5 and the comparison the chapter draws between Adam and Christ, the Roman Catholic Church is compelled to maintain that also the doctrine of the imputation of Adam's disobedience to the entire human race—God's declaring the entire race guilty on account of Adam's sin—is a legal fiction. Not only does this pit Rome against the clear, powerful testimony of the gospel in Romans 5, but it also renders Rome incapable of explaining why, to use the language of Romans 5:14, "death reigned…even over them that had not sinned after the similitude of Adam's transgression." Why should death, which is the punishment of sin, reign even over infants newly born, indeed yet in their mothers' wombs?

There are in history two, and only two, covenantal headships: Adam's and Christ's. As the covenantal head of the entire human race, Adam disobeyed not for himself alone, but involving all humans. God imputed his disobedience to all the members of the covenant God made with Adam, that is, the entire human race, Christ Jesus only excepted. All are guilty of Adam's act of disobedience. "By one man's disobedience many were made [constituted, according to the Greek] sinners." Therefore, from birth every human is justly subject to sin's punishment, which is death. "By one man's offence death reigned by one" (v. 17).

First Corinthians 15:21–22 teaches the same: "For since by man came death, by man came also the resurrection of the dead. For as in Adam all die, even so in Christ shall all be made alive." The dying of all humans is due to their relationship to Adam. Men do not die on their own; they die in Adam. Since death is the divine punishment of the guilty sinner, not merely a natural phenomenon, men die because Adam rendered them all guilty before God. Adam did this, and could only do this, inasmuch as he was the covenantal, or federal, head of the race.

So it is, according to 1 Corinthians 15, with the "all" who shall be made alive. Their living does not happen because of them themselves. It is entirely due to their being "in Christ." Since life (which in 1 Corinthians 15 is the heavenly, immortal, resurrection, eternal life of the risen Christ) must be merited for these sinners, who deserve the opposite of this life, Christ must have rendered the "all" who shall be made alive righteous before God. Christ did this as their covenantal head.

If Adam had not been our covenantal head in the covenant of creation, he could not have represented us in his disobedience, and God could not then reckon his disobedience to our account. If Christ were not our covenantal head in the covenant of grace, he could not have represented us in his obedience, and God could not impute his obedience to our account through faith.

The headship of Christ in the covenant of grace, as the ultimate source of the gospel of justification by faith alone, is also the teaching of Galatians 3:16, 29. Regarding the covenantal promise God made to Abraham in Genesis 17:7 and other passages of scripture, the apostle says in Galatians 3:16 that "to Abraham and his seed were the promises made. He saith not, And to seeds, as of many; but as of one, And to thy seed, which is Christ." The "seed" of Abraham to whom the promise of the covenant was made and with whom therefore the covenant of grace was established was Jesus Christ. The "seed" was not all the physical children of Abraham, just as the word used in Genesis 17:7 is not the plural "seeds" but the singular "seed." The covenantal promise was not directed to many but to one. This one is Christ. To him was the covenantal promise made. Galatians 3:19 reaffirms this: "till the seed should come to whom the promise was made." Thus by promise to Christ, God established his covenant with Jesus Christ, inasmuch as God had appointed him *head* of the covenant.

Galatians 3:29 reveals that the Christ to whom the covenantal promise was made and with whom the covenant of grace was thus established includes all those men and women who are "Christ's": "And if ye be Christ's, then are ye Abraham's seed, and heirs according to the promise." These humans are those, and those only, who believe, as Galatians 3:22, 26 make plain. The covenantal promise to Abraham, that "in thee shall all nations be blessed" (v. 8), is "given to them that believe" (v. 22). Men and women are "the children of God"—the fullness of Abraham's seed—"by faith in Christ Jesus" (v. 26). Elsewhere scripture teaches that faith is the gift of God to the elect (Acts 13:48). The full reality of the Christ with whom the covenant of grace is established by promise is therefore Christ himself and all the elect, whom the Father has given him in eternity to be his own (John 6:37, 39; 17:2, 6, 9, 11, 24). The head of the covenant of grace is never without his body and all its members.

In Galatians 3 the apostle of Christ affirms and explains the headship of Christ in the covenant of grace on behalf of the gospel truth of justification by faith alone. Justification by faith alone is the theme of the chapter, as it is the central truth of the entire epistle. The chapter makes clear that the truth of Christ's covenantal headship serves the apostle's defense of justification by faith against the Galatian error of justification by faith and works. The great concern of the apostle in the chapter, as in the entire epistle, was to convince the Galatian churches that "God would justify the heathen through faith" (v. 8). He reminded them of the Old Testament passage that declared that "Abraham believed God, and it [faith] was accounted to him for righteousness" (v. 6). The law was never intended to function as the means of righteousness. Rather, "the law was our schoolmaster to bring us unto Christ, that we might be justified by faith" (v. 24). "The just shall live by faith" (v. 11).

The deepest foundation and decisive defense of the gospel of justification by faith, according to Galatians 3, is the covenantal headship of Jesus Christ. Because he is the covenantal head of elect believers, he may be and is their righteousness with God by faith alone in him. Because he is the covenantal head of elect believers, the obedience of these believers need not be, may not be, and is not their righteousness with God. For their obedience to be their righteousness with God would be to dispossess, displace, disregard, and disgrace the head of the covenant, who is Jesus the Christ. It is the precise purpose of Galatians 3 to establish that the precious but contested truth of justification by faith alone in Jesus Christ has its ground in the covenantal headship of Jesus Christ.

Implied is that denial of the federal, or covenantal, headship of Jesus Christ imperils the gospel truth of justification by faith. This the Reformed and Presbyterian community of churches sees happening at the beginning of the twenty-first century within this community. The federal vision rejects the Reformation doctrine of justification by faith alone. It boldly teaches the Arminian and Roman Catholic heresy of justification by faith *and works*. It teaches this gross heresy because the theology of the federal vision denies that Jesus Christ is the federal, or covenantal head of his (elect) people. The fundamental issue of Reformed, Protestant orthodoxy with this contemporary heresy, therefore, is not the right doctrine of justification, important as this issue is. But the fundamental issue is the doctrine of the covenant, specifically the covenantal headship of Jesus Christ.

Scripture's teaching of the covenantal headship of Jesus Christ, particularly in Romans 5, 1 Corinthians 15, and Galatians 3, is confessional for all Reformed and Presbyterian Christians. The headship of Jesus Christ in, of, and over the covenant of grace is implied wherever the creeds teach the accomplishment of the salvation of the church of the elect by the work of Jesus Christ as the legal representative and substitute of the elect, regardless that *covenant* is not used in the teaching. Only one who is the covenantal head of others may redeem them as their substitute, even as only one who was covenantal head of the race could have rendered the race guilty in the beginning and plunged those of whom he was the head into death.

There are passages in the Reformed confessions that explicitly teach the federal headship of Jesus Christ. Even though the Canons of Dordt do not emphasize or develop the truth of the covenant, this creed teaches that Christ is head of the covenant. It teaches this headship of Christ at the critically important place in the creed: the leading article on the death of Christ as particular, limited, effectual atonement.

> For this was the sovereign counsel and most gracious will and purpose of God the Father, that the quickening and saving efficacy of the most precious death of his Son should extend to all the elect, for bestowing upon them alone the gift of justifying faith, thereby to bring them infallibly to salvation: that is, it was the will of God, that Christ by the blood of the cross, *whereby he confirmed the new covenant*, should effectually redeem out of every people, tribe, nation, and language, all those, and those only, who were from eternity chosen to salvation, and given to him by the Father; that he should confer upon them faith, which, together with all the other saving gifts of the Holy Spirit, he purchased for them by his

> death; should purge them from all sin, both original and actual, whether committed before or after believing; and having faithfully preserved them even to the end, should at last bring them free from every spot and blemish to the enjoyment of glory in his own presence forever.[2]

The article teaches not only that Christ died for the elect, for the elect alone, but it teaches also that the death of Christ as the redemption of the elect and thus as the purchase for them of "justifying faith" was Christ's *confirmation of the new covenant.* Confirmation of the covenant was, and could only be, the saving act of the *head* of the new covenant. The article of the Reformed creed identifies Christ as the head of the covenant. Likely, the fathers of Dordt had their eye on Daniel 9:27, where the great messianic prophecy of the seventy weeks promised that the Messiah would "confirm the covenant."

Noteworthy also is the insistence of the creed on the close relationship between Christ's death as the confirmation of the new covenant by the federal head and justification by faith. The creed is at pains to emphasize that the death of Christ as the confirmation of the new covenant had particularly in view "bestowing upon [the elect for whom he died] the gift of justifying faith." Federal headship and justification by faith alone are, to use a contemporary colloquialism, "joined at the hip."

Dordt had good reason for affirming that Christ confirmed the new covenant with the elect, thus clearly teaching that Christ died as head of the covenant. This reason was not simply that the Canons intended to deny the Arminian heresy that Christ died for all humans without exception, although they certainly intended to deny this. The reason was also that the Canons intended to reject the Arminian doctrine of the covenant.

---

2 Canons of Dordt 2.8, in Schaff, *Creeds of Christendom*, 3:587; emphasis added.

There is a distinctively Arminian doctrine of the covenant, just as there is a distinctively Arminian doctrine of the atonement. The Canons of Dordt accurately describe this doctrine:

> [The Arminian doctrine of the covenant is] that it was not the purpose of the death of Christ that He should confirm the new covenant of grace through His blood, but only that He should acquire for the Father the mere right to establish with man such a covenant as He might please, whether of grace or of works [and]...that the new covenant of grace, which God the Father, through the mediation of the death of Christ, made with man, does not herein consist that we by faith, inasmuch as it accepts the merits of Christ, are justified before God and saved, but in the fact that God, having revoked the demand of perfect obedience of the law, regards faith itself and the obedience of faith, although imperfect, as the perfect obedience of the law, and does esteem it worthy of the reward of eternal life through grace.[3]

Obvious yet again is the intimate relationship between the doctrine of the covenant and the doctrine of justification. Because Arminianism errs concerning the covenant, particularly the headship of Christ in the covenant, Arminianism errs also concerning justification. Denying that Christ is covenantal head, Arminianism holds that God regards the believer's faith itself and the believer's obedience of faith as the believing sinner's righteousness. Denying the federal headship of Christ, Arminianism necessarily plunges itself into the heresy of justification by faith (as the work of the sinner) and the good works of the sinner.

The Arminian conception of the covenant, which now is prominent in Reformed and Presbyterian churches, denies that

3 Canons of Dordt 2, errors 2 and 4, in *Confessions and Church Order*, 164–65.

Christ confirmed the covenant—denies that the death of Christ confirmed the covenant with or for anyone at all. What the death of Christ did was to acquire for God the right to deal with all humans in such a way as to require of them faith as a condition unto membership in the covenant and unto the enjoyment of covenantal blessings. Christ did not die as covenantal head of a definite number of humans—God's elect. By his death therefore, he did not make the covenant sure, absolutely sure, and its salvation certain, absolutely certain, for himself as the head of the covenant and for a definite number of others, the elect members of his body.

The Reformed Form for the Administration of Baptism refers to the source and foundation of the covenant in the federal headship of Jesus Christ when it describes the covenant of grace as eternal: "Baptism is a seal and undoubted testimony that we have an *eternal covenant of grace with God*."[4] The form does not merely state that there is an eternal decree of God to establish the covenant in time and history. But it confesses, and has every Reformed believer who has his or her child baptized confess, that the covenant itself is eternal. The covenant of grace is eternal in its establishment by the triune God with Jesus Christ as head of the covenant in the eternal decree.

Presbyterianism also has its creedal statement of the covenantal headship of Jesus Christ. This statement is sharper and clearer than the teaching of the Canons and of the Reformed baptism form. I refer to question and answer 31 of the Westminster Larger Catechism. Having affirmed in question 30 that God delivers "his elect" out of "the estate of sin and misery into which they fell by the breach of the first covenant...and bringeth them into an estate of salvation by the second covenant, commonly called the Covenant of Grace," the Larger Catechism

4 Form for the Administration of Baptism, in ibid., 258; emphasis added.

asks: "With whom was the covenant of grace made?" The answer of the Presbyterian Catechism is, "The covenant of grace was made with Christ as the second Adam, and in him with all the elect as his seed."[5]

Covenantal Headship Opposed

There is nothing humorous about the spreading heresy of the federal vision. Nevertheless, I confess to amusement when I observe the theologians of the Canadian Reformed Churches, in their ecumenical contacts with the Orthodox Presbyterian Church, assuring themselves and others, on behalf of the covenantal doctrine that is the root of the federal vision, that question 31 of the Larger Catechism does *not*, in fact, teach that Christ is head of the covenant of grace and does *not*, in fact, teach that God establishes the covenant of grace with the elect children of believing parents and with them only. The Canadian Reformed, of course, are bound to defend the doctrine of the Reformed Churches in the Netherlands (liberated) that Christ Jesus is not the head of the covenant (lest the covenant and its grace be particular with and to the elect alone); that the gracious covenantal promise, the covenant itself, and the covenantal blessings, including justification, are for all the children of believers alike, those who perish as well as those who are saved, Esau as well as Jacob; and that this denial of the federal headship of Jesus Christ and this universalizing of the covenant of grace and its blessings among the children of believers are in harmony with question 31 of the Larger Catechism.

Canadian Reformed, liberated theologian Jelle Faber bluntly acknowledged the liberated Reformed rejection of the doctrine that Christ is the head of the covenant: "It is certainly good

---

5 Westminster Larger Catechism Q 31, in *The Subordinate Standards... of the Free Church of Scotland* (repr. Edinburgh: William Blackwood & Sons, 1973), 57.

to abandon the concept of Christ as Head of the covenant of grace…Although Christ is Mediator *in* the covenant, he is not the Head *of* the covenant."[6] Faber immediately added the underlying reason for this rejection of the headship of Christ of the covenant: there may be no "identification of covenant and eternal election."[7] "Identification" of covenant and election for Faber and all liberated theologians is their misleading way of denying that election governs the covenant and its salvation. The federal headship of Christ imperils, indeed demolishes, the liberated severance of covenant and election. Faber goes on to observe that this denial of the federal headship of Christ by the Reformed Churches in the Netherlands (liberated) and by the Canadian Reformed Churches finds its immediate source in the founding father of the liberated churches, Klaas Schilder. "[Schilder] denies that Christ is Head *of* the covenant of grace."[8]

Schilder and the other leading theologians of the Reformed Churches in the Netherlands (liberated) certainly denied that Jesus Christ is the head of the covenant. Writing in 1939, at the time of the controversy in the Reformed Churches in the Netherlands over the covenant, Schilder denied that "the Covenant of grace was established 'with' Christ." Immediately, he indicated what was both the implication of his denial and the reason for it: the doctrine that the covenant was made in eternity with Christ would mean that "the Covenant of grace…was established with the elect." Schilder's problem with Christ's headship in the covenant was election.

A few years later Schilder again inveighed against the teaching that "Christ is the Head of the Covenant." According to Schilder, the federal headship of Christ is "a wrong view." What

6 Jelle Faber, *American Secession Theologians on Covenant and Baptism* (Neerlandia, Alberta, Canada: Inheritance Publications, 1996), 37.

7 Ibid.

8 Ibid., 46.

was troublesome to Schilder about the federal headship of Christ is that headship involves the confession that "the Covenant is established with the elect." For Schilder and the other leading theologians of the churches that separated from the Reformed Churches in the Netherlands, the covenant was made by God with "believers and their seed," that is, with all the offspring originally of Abraham, with Esau as well and as much as with Jacob, and today with all the physical children of believers, that is, with those who perish in unbelief as well and as much as with those who are saved by faith.[9]

Rejecting the federal headship of Christ enabled Schilder to deny that the covenant "touches only the elect." What he meant by "touches," he made clear by immediately denying that "the covenant depends on election" and that God gives the covenant promise only "to the elect." On the contrary, Schilder insisted that "the covenant is established with the believers and their children." "All believers with their children are real covenant children." By "their children," Schilder meant all the physical offspring of believers without exception, all to whom the sacrament of baptism was administered.[10]

What the establishment of the covenant with all the children alike, those who ultimately perish and those who ultimately are saved, means for all the children, Schilder suggested, albeit cautiously in view of the doctrine of the Canons of Dordt, to which he subscribed and by which he was bound: Every "baptized child has that grace and that demand which he is allowed to have, which have been promised." All the baptized children, those who eventually perish as well as those who finally are saved, "are sanctified in Christ, the Holy Spirit will sanctify

---

9 The quotations are taken from J. Kamphuis, *An Everlasting Covenant* (Launceston [TAS], Australia: Publication Organization of the Free Reformed Churches of Australia, 1985), 70–73.

10 Schilder, "The Main Points of the Doctrine of the Covenant," 11–12.

them. Through the promise of the washing through the blood of Christ *they have the right to righteousness, and now the Spirit wishes to continuously sanctify them.*"[11]

The reason some of the children, nevertheless, are not saved by the grace of their baptism, come short of the righteousness to which they were given the "right" in their baptism, and perish in unholiness despite the Spirit's wish to sanctify them is the conditionality of the covenant, its promise, and its blessings. "We must speak of conditions: I will not receive it [covenantal salvation] if I do not comply with the demand...God does not say 'I promise you' as a special decree, but He speaks to me with a concrete condition:...the demand of faith."[12]

This rejection of the federal headship of Christ plainly makes for difficulty in ecumenical relations of the Schilderian

---

11 Schilder, "The Main Points of the Doctrine of the Covenant," 13–14; emphasis added. The content of the booklet is a speech that Schilder gave in the Netherlands in 1944, at the height of the controversy in the Reformed Churches in the Netherlands over the doctrine of the covenant. Particularly worthy of note is that Schilder's "liberation" of the covenant and its salvation from the eternal decree of election made it impossible for him to do justice to the language and doctrine of the Reformed baptism form. The first question in the form to the parents at the baptism of their children has them confess that the as-yet-unbaptized children are "sanctified in Christ." The children's sanctification in Christ is the ground of their being baptized. Schilder was forced to explain the phrase as teaching that "the Holy Spirit *will* sanctify them" and "*wishes* to continuously sanctify them." As Schilder's following explanation indicates, this futurity of the children's sanctification and this wish of the Spirit regarding the children's sanctification depend on the children's performing the condition of faith. But the form does not speak of a possible future sanctification by the Spirit. Nor does it lamely teach an impotent wish of the Spirit to perform this work. Much less does it make the sanctification of the children conditional on some act they must perform. The form has the parents (and the Reformed church) "acknowledge" concerning the children of believers, as-yet-unbaptized infants in their mother's arms, that they "*are* sanctified in Christ, and therefore, as members of His church [already prior to baptism] ought to be baptized."

12 Ibid., 13.

Canadian Reformed Churches with Presbyterians, whose Larger Catechism confesses that God made his covenant with Christ, that is, that Christ is head of the covenant. But learned theologians are evidently able to convince themselves that when the Larger Catechism answers the question, "With whom was the covenant of grace made?" by declaring, "The covenant of grace was made with Christ as the second Adam," the Catechism does not, in fact, mean that God made the covenant with Christ as the second Adam. *Mirabile dictu,* the Catechism rather is allowing for the doctrine of the liberated Reformed, including the Canadian Reformed, that Christ is not the federal head of the covenant.

The covenant therefore is not made by God with humans only as they are in Christ, as members of a body of which he is head. Rather, the Catechism teaches that God makes the covenant with humans individually, apart from Christ and any relationship to Christ. When the Catechism goes on to declare that "in him," that is, in Christ as the second Adam, God made the covenant of grace "with all the elect as his [Christ's] seed," the Catechism does not, in fact, mean that God made the covenant with the elect. The Catechism rather allows for the liberated Reformed doctrine that God makes the covenant with all the physical offspring of believing parents alike, reprobate as well as elect, those who eternally perish as well as those who are saved, the Esaus as well as the Jacobs.[13]

Such interpretation of the clear language of the creed is as ridiculous as it is reprehensible. It is not even an intelligible misinterpretation of the creed. It is the deliberate explaining *away* of the clear creedal language, and thus the rejection of the confession of the creed, in the interests of maintaining the theological error that denies that Christ is head of the covenant of grace.

---

13 Westminster Larger Catechism Q 31, in *The Subordinate Standards...of the Free Church of Scotland*, 57.

The deepest motivation of this inexcusable rejection of the creed (for rejection is what this misinterpretation really is) is the liberated Reformed's determination that election shall not govern the covenant of grace and its salvation.

Covenantal Ground of Justification

But justification by faith alone in Jesus Christ is founded on the federal (covenantal) headship of Jesus Christ, and all the Reformed creeds confess this. To reject the federal headship of Christ is to contradict the creeds and to put the gospel truth of justification by faith alone at risk.

The federal headship of Jesus Christ has its source in the eternal decree of the triune God appointing the man Jesus, as the incarnate Son of God, as head of the covenant. About this source of the covenantal headship of Jesus, and therefore also about the ultimate source of the gospel truth of justification by faith alone, there have been and are still today serious confusion and controversy in the Reformed churches. This confusion and controversy contribute to the appearance in Reformed churches of the heresy of justification by faith and works, particularly in the form of the federal vision. The root of the federal vision is the doctrine of God's establishing the covenant of grace conditionally with all the physical offspring of believing parents alike. This root is uprooted by the right understanding of the source of the covenant in the federal headship of Jesus the Christ.

Herman Bavinck spoke on behalf of all orthodox Reformed theology when he said that the covenant of grace has "a stable, eternal foundation in the counsel of God."[14] He added that "the covenant of grace revealed in time does not hang in the air but rests on an eternal, unchanging foundation...the covenant of

---

14 Herman Bavinck, *Reformed Dogmatics*, vol. 3: *Sin and Salvation in Christ*, ed. John Bolt, trans. John Vriend (Grand Rapids, MI: Baker Academic, 2006), 212–13.

grace was ready-made from all eternity in the pact of salvation of the three persons."[15]

The confusion and controversy concern the explanation of this foundation, or source, of the covenant of grace in God's eternity. Many Reformed and Presbyterian theologians explained the source of the covenant as a conditional "pact," or "agreement," or even "bargain," between the first and second persons of the Trinity, the eternal Father and the eternal Son. According to this conception of the source of the covenant, the Father promised to save a church from the fallen human race on condition that the Son would redeem this people by his atoning death. The Son on his part agreed to fulfill the condition. This "pact," concluded in eternity, is the foundation and source of all the saving work of God in Jesus Christ in time and history that is comprehended in the realization and fulfillment of the covenant of grace.

Louis Berkhof taught this view of the eternal source of the covenant. He described this source, which he called the "covenant of redemption," as "the agreement between the Father, giving the Son as Head and Redeemer of the elect, and the Son, voluntarily taking the place of those whom the Father had given Him."[16]

Similarly, the Presbyterian "Sum of Saving Knowledge" describes the source of the covenant in eternity (which it names "the covenant of redemption") as an agreement between "God the Father and God the Son." This statement, although not one of the official, authoritative creeds of the Presbyterian churches, is nevertheless often included in the books containing the Presbyterian creeds, so that it is influential in forming Presbyterian thinking about the covenant. The Sum goes on to explain:

> God having freely chosen unto life a certain number of

15 Ibid., 3:215.

16 Louis Berkhof, *Systematic Theology*, 4th Revised and Enlarged Edition (Grand Rapids, MI: Eerdmans, 1965), 271.

> lost mankind...did give them, before the world began, unto God the Son, appointed Redeemer, that, upon condition he would humble himself so far as to assume the human nature...and submit himself to the law, as surety for them, and satisfy justice for them...he should ransom and redeem them all from sin and death...This condition the Son of God...did accept before the world began.[17]

Even the Reformed theologians who almost instinctively shied away from this cold, commercial conception of the origin of the covenant, who saw clearly that the main biblical proof of this conception was mistaken, and whose theology of the covenant of grace as a whole repudiated the notion of a conditional "bargain" between contracting parties did not entirely shake themselves free from the idea of the source of the covenant as an agreement. Although he never explicitly described the foundation of the covenant in the counsel of God as an agreement between the Father and the Son and although, on the contrary, he did describe it in terms of God's "counsel" and "decree," Bavinck persisted in referring to the source of the covenant as a "pact," indeed "the pact of salvation."[18]

It is now time for Reformed and Presbyterian theology thoroughly to purge from its doctrine of the covenant the notion and terminology that suggest that the source and foundation of the covenant of grace is a pact or agreement or bargain between two persons of the Trinity, or even among all three persons of the Godhead. First, there is absolutely no biblical warrant for

17 "The Sum of Saving Knowledge," in *The Subordinate Standards...of the Free Church of Scotland*, 191. The Sum does not hesitate to call this agreement between the Father and the Son a "bargain": "By virtue of the foresaid bargain made before the world began," etc. (191).

18 Bavinck, *Reformed Dogmatics*, 3:215. For a thorough examination of Bavinck's doctrine of the covenant, see the chapter "Bavinck on Covenant and Election," in my *Covenant and Election in the Reformed Tradition*, 163–76.

such a conception of the source of the covenant. The main biblical passage adduced on behalf of the conception of a pact or agreement has been Zechariah 6:13: "and the counsel of peace shall be between them both." From this passage one of the names traditionally describing the source of the covenant has been derived: counsel of peace.

But the passage has nothing whatever to do with the source, or foundation, of the covenant in eternity, as though it were speaking of an agreement between the Father and the Son. The passage rather refers to the relationship between the priestly and kingly offices of the Mediator of the covenant (who is called "The BRANCH" in verse 12), which accomplishes the peace of the people of God. In "the man whose name is The BRANCH" and who "shall build the temple of the LORD," the office of priest and the office of king are united (vv. 12–15).

Bavinck called attention to this gross misunderstanding of verse 13 on the part of Reformed theologians who saw the source of the covenant in an agreement between the first and second persons of the Trinity. Accusing this theory of "scholastic subtlety," Bavinck declared, "The classic text (Zech. 6:13) cited in support of this doctrine [namely, that the foundation of the covenant of grace is a pact between God the Father and God the Son] does not prove anything and only states that the Messiah, who unites in his person both the kingship and the priesthood, will consider and promote the peace of his people."[19] So important has the Zechariah text been for the theory of the source of the covenant's being a pact between the Father and the Son that it is no exaggeration to judge that with the loss of this text as proof the theory itself falls away.

A second reason for Reformed theology's abandonment, once and for all, of the notion that the source of the covenant is an agreement between two persons of the Trinity is the obvious

---

19 Bavinck, *Reformed Dogmatics*, 3:213.

fact that the biblical passages that do reveal the source of the covenant and that are often also adduced on behalf of the theory of an agreement describe the source of the covenant as a divine *decree*—not an *agreement* but a *decree.* Psalm 2:7 "declare[s] the decree" concerning the source of the covenantal Messiah and the foundation of all his covenantal work. Isaiah 42:1 calls the Messiah "mine," that is, Jehovah God's elect. The source of the Messiah and all his saving work on behalf of God's covenant (verse 6 has God giving the Messiah "for a covenant of the people") is not an agreement but an eternal, electing decree.

Psalm 89 is clear and decisive concerning the source and foundation of the covenant of grace. How anyone can read this eminently covenantal psalm and come away with the notion either that Christ is not the head of the covenant or that the source of the covenant is an agreement between two persons of the Trinity defies understanding. Verse 3 states that God has made his covenant with "my chosen," by promise "unto David my servant." David in the psalm is the type of the Messiah, who is Jesus, as the psalm reveals. The Messiah is the one who "shall cry unto me, Thou art my father, my God, and the rock of my salvation" (v. 26). God made his covenant not with a number, even a large number, of disparate individuals all on their own, but with the Messiah as the head of the covenant. "With him," God's "covenant shall stand fast" (v. 28). Only because the elect are "his seed" will they "endure for ever" (v. 29).

Equally clearly, the psalm locates the source of the covenant with Messiah and his seed in Jehovah God's decree electing, or choosing, the Messiah, the incarnate Son. One person of the Trinity does not conclude the covenant by a pact with another person, but Jehovah God "made" his covenant by the decree of electing David/Messiah (v. 3). The source of the covenant with Israel/church is not an agreement in the Godhead between two, or even all three, persons. Rather, Jehovah God, the triune God—Father, Son, and Holy Ghost—"exalted one chosen out of the people," that is, chosen, or decreed, as head of the covenant by Jehovah God (v. 19). This object of the electing decree is "David my servant" (v. 20).

The related passages describing the coming into the world of Jesus the Christ as God's *sending* of him teach the same about the source and foundation of the covenant. In John 6:38–39 Jesus describes his coming into the world as God's sending of him. His sending has its origin in God's will: "This is the Father's will which hath sent me" (v. 39). As often in the New Testament, "Father" refers to the one being of God, who is father of the man Jesus, as he is also father of all those humans who belong to Jesus. The source of the covenant is not a divine bargaining session but the will, or counsel, or decree of God.

In light of the determination of those who deny the federal headship of Jesus to escape the biblical teaching that the covenant and its salvation are governed by election—election of a definite number of humans, in distinction from others who are reprobated—it is worth noting that Jesus continues in John 6:39, "that of all which he hath given me I should lose nothing, but should raise it up again at the last day." The source of the covenant of grace is God's eternal will: the election of Jesus the Christ as federal head of a certain, definite number of elect humans, whom he is to save from sin and glorify in their resurrection.

Because kingdom and covenant in the New Testament are not essentially different realities, Luke 22:29 is applicable to the truths that the source of the covenant is God's decree appointing Christ as head of the covenant and that this source is, indeed, a divine appointment, not an agreement. Said Jesus Christ to his disciples on the eve of his crucifixion: "I appoint unto you a kingdom, as my Father hath appointed unto me."

A third reason Reformed theologians ought to renounce the explanation of the source and foundation of the covenant as an eternal bargaining of the first and second persons of the Trinity is brought home to them in the twenty-first century by the heresy of the federal vision. The federal vision denies the cardinal gospel truth of justification by faith alone. It boldly teaches justification by faith and works. It promotes this heresy in conservative Reformed and Presbyterian churches and seminaries. The heresy itself advertises that its teaching of justification by faith and works is part and parcel of its covenantal theology. This theology holds that the covenant and its salvation are conditional; they depend on actions that the sinner performs. This doctrine of a conditional covenant, with its conditional justification, is embedded in the view of the very source of the covenant as a conditional agreement between God the Father and God the Son.

The erroneous conception of the covenant as a conditional contract or pact infects the source and foundation of the covenant in God's eternity. Louis Berkhof expressed the intimate relationship between viewing the source of the covenant as an agreement between the Father and the Son and viewing the covenant of grace similarly as a pact or compact: "The former [the *pactum salutis*] is a compact between the Father and the Son... while the latter [the covenant of grace] is a compact between the triune God and the elect."[20]

At the very beginning of the Reformation, which was the rediscovery of the gospel of grace, Luther cried out, "Away with that profane, impious notion of merit!" Today, at the similarly critical moment, when the Reformation with its gospel of grace will either be preserved and rightly developed or fatally compromised and lost, let Reformed theology cry out, "Away with that profane, impious notion of a conditional, contractual covenant!"

---

20 Berkhof, *Systematic Theology*, 270. The reason for this agreement between the source of the covenant in eternity and the covenant of grace itself as conditional pacts, according to Berkhof, is that "the counsel of redemption [Berkhof's name for the source of the covenant in the Godhead] is the eternal prototype of the historical covenant of grace" (270).

More than one hundred years ago, the Scottish theologian C. G. M'Crie denounced the view of the covenant as a conditional agreement or pact, including the *pactum salutis.*

> Detailed descriptions of redemption as a bargain entered into between the First and the Second Persons of the Trinity, in which conditions were laid down, promises held out, and pledges given; the reducing of salvation to a mercantile arrangement between God and the sinner, in which the latter signifies contentment to enter into covenant, and the former intimates agreement to entertain a relation of grace, so that ever after the contented, contracting party can say, "Lord, let it be a bargain,"—such presentations have obviously a tendency to reduce the gospel of the grace of God to the level of a legal compact entered into between two independent and, so far as right or status is concerned, two equal parties. The blessedness of the mercy-seat is in danger of being lost sight of in the bargaining of the market-place; the simple story of salvation is thrown into the crucible of the logic of the schools and it emerges in the form of a syllogism.[21]

Apparently, no one listened.

The same deafness has prevailed in the Reformed community of theologians regarding Herman Hoeksema's objection to the presentation of the covenant as a conditional contract, beginning with the source and foundation of the covenant in what Reformed theology has traditionally referred to as the *pactum salutis.*[22]

---

21 C. G. M'Crie, *The Confessions of the Church of Scotland* (Edinburgh: Macniven & Wallace, 1907), 72–73.

22 See Hoeksema's superb critique of the "traditional" explanation of the source of the covenant, "The *Pactum Salutis*," in *Reformed Dogmatics*, 285–336. I acknowledge my indebtedness to Hoeksema for my exposition of the source and foundation of the covenant in this chapter.

The gospel truth of the covenant is that it is the divinely established and maintained relationship of friendship in love between the triune God in Jesus Christ and the elect church. Its origin and foundation are the wholly gracious and sovereign divine decree choosing the man Jesus Christ, who is the incarnate Son of God, as covenantal head of the elect human race.

Renouncing what admittedly has been a prominent strain in the Reformed tradition, namely, viewing the source of the covenant as an agreement or pact, Reformed theology should also settle on the proper name of the source. It is not "*pactum salutis*," or "counsel of peace," or "covenant of redemption," or "bargain between the Father and the Son." The proper name of this important aspect of the covenant, expressing what in fact it is and derived from the biblical revelation, is "counsel of the covenant."

To the question, "Whence does the covenant of grace originate?" the answer is, the counsel of the covenant. The counsel of the covenant is the sovereign, eternal, unconditional decree of the triune God ordaining the incarnate Son as head of the covenant of grace and in him electing a great host out of all nations of the human race as his body, to be saved from sin and death and to be brought into covenantal fellowship with God by him.

Chapter Seventeen

GRACIOUS JUSTIFICATION

From what has been taught so far concerning justification, especially that justification is by *faith* and by faith *alone*, the important conclusion follows: justification is gracious—wholly gracious. In view of the centrality of the truth of justification to the entirety of the Christian gospel of salvation, the doctrine of justification by faith alone affirms and secures that salvation in its entirety is by grace alone.

That justification by faith alone is gracious justification is not only a theological implication. Scripture and the Reformed confessions explicitly teach that justification is God's gracious act, that is, that justification is "by grace." Because justification is by faith alone, apart from any works of the sinner, justification is by grace. This is the teaching of the apostle in one of the outstanding passages on justification: Romans 3 and 4. Romans 3:24 reads: "Being justified freely by his grace." The Greek word translated as "freely" is a word that means "as a gift," that is, "without cost or price or deserving." One might read the text this way: "Being justified by his grace, gratuitously."

The relationship between faith and grace in justification as in all of salvation is indicated in Romans 4:16: "It is of faith, that it might be by grace." As the means of justification, faith reveals and secures that justification is a gracious act of God. Indeed, God determined faith as the means of justification in order that justification and all of salvation might be according to grace.

Also the Reformed confessions describe justification as gracious. The Heidelberg Catechism explains that being "righteous before God...only by true faith in Jesus Christ" means that "God, without any merit of mine, *of mere grace*, grants and imputes to me the perfect satisfaction, righteousness, and holiness of Christ."[1] Contending that faith is the "alone instrument of justification," the Westminster Confession of Faith explains that God "freely justifieth."[2] Westminster adds that "justification is only of free grace."[3]

The doctrine of justification by faith alone is the gospel of *gracious* justification and, in view of the fundamental significance of justification for all of salvation, the gospel of gracious *salvation*. The heresy of justification by faith and works is the denial of gracious justification and of gracious salvation.

At Stake Is the Gospel

What is at stake in the controversy over justification both regarding Reformed Protestantism's conflict with Rome and regarding the struggle of the orthodox Reformed faith against the new perspective on Paul and against the federal vision is the gospel of grace. Justification by faith and works is ungracious justification, that is, the sinner's justification of himself by his own efforts. Justification by faith and works is the overthrow of the whole gospel of salvation by the grace of God. As the repudiation of the sixteenth-century Reformation of the church, the contemporary attacks within Protestantism and even within conservative Presbyterian and Reformed churches on justification by faith

1 Heidelberg Catechism Q&A 60, in Schaff, *Creeds of Christendom*, 3:326; emphasis added.

2 Westminster Confession of Faith 11.1, in ibid., 3:626.

3 Westminster Confession of Faith 11.3, in ibid., 3:627.

alone are assaults on the biblical gospel of grace. Plainly, no more damning charge could be leveled against the doctrine of justification by works.

That justification by faith alone is the bedrock of the gospel of salvation by grace, so that the lie of justification by faith and works is the corruption and loss of the entire gospel of grace, ought to be demonstrated. First, the justification of the sinner is by means of faith, not by means of the sinner's own works. Second, faith is only the instrument of justification, not the ground, or basis, of justification.

Third, the righteousness with which the believing sinner is justified is exclusively the obedience of Christ in his stead and on his behalf, not the sinner's own obedience. In addition, this righteousness is outside the sinner, in Jesus Christ in heaven, not within the sinner as a spiritual power making the sinner actually a just man, worthy of God's favorable verdict upon him. The righteousness of justification is, as the reformers described it, an "alien" righteousness, not an inherent righteousness. It is a righteousness *imputed* to the guilty sinner, not *infused* into him.

The final defense of grace in the doctrine of justification by faith alone is the truth that faith itself, by which the sinner is justified, is not the sinner's own work, is not his own contribution to his justification. Rather, faith is the gift of God to the elect sinner. Not only is the faith that justifies only the means of justification, not the basis or condition of justification, but also faith is the gracious gift of God to the sinner, not the sinner's own meritorious contribution to his justification. His believing is the gracious operation of the Spirit of Jesus Christ within him.

Faith as a gracious gift is the teaching of Ephesians 2:8: "For by grace are ye saved through faith; and that [faith] not of yourselves: it is the gift of God." Philippians 1:29 proclaims, "It is given [to those who do believe in Christ]...to believe on him." Gracious salvation is a reality only inasmuch as salvation, particularly and centrally justification, is "through faith." This requires that the faith through which the sinner is saved be the "gift of God."

The necessity of confessing that the faith by which sinners are justified is the gift of God cannot be emphasized strongly enough. The last-ditch effort of the enemies of gracious justification, and thus of gracious salvation, to accomplish the overthrow of the gospel of grace is the assertion that the faith that justifies is the work of the sinner himself, a condition upon which his justification and salvation depend, the sinner's own contribution to the act of justification, and a contribution that makes the sinner worthy of God's declaring him righteous. Faith is taught as the *basis* of justification, rather than the *means*; the sinner is said to be justified *on account of* faith, rather than *by means of* faith. The activity of believing becomes the sinner's righteousness with God, rather than the obedience of Christ that faith only embraces and receives.

In the end this question decides the struggle of the orthodox Reformed faith with Rome, Arminianism, and the federal vision: Is faith the gift of God to the (elect) sinner who is justified? Then, as the Canons of Dordt press the issue, is faith the gift of God, not only as his bestowal of the ability to believe, but also regarding the activity itself of faith—the knowing of Christ alone and the trusting in Christ alone for righteousness?

The orthodox Reformed faith confesses that faith is the gift of God, and thus safeguards the gospel of grace, in the Canons of Dordt:

> Faith is therefore to be considered as the gift of God, not on account of its being offered by God to man, to be accepted or rejected at his pleasure, but because it is in reality conferred, breathed, and infused into him; nor even because God bestows the power or ability to believe, and then expects that man should, by the exercise of his own free will, consent to the terms of

> salvation, and actually believe in Christ; but because he who works in man both to will and to do, and indeed all things in all, produces both the will to believe and the act of believing also.[4]

The Scottish Presbyterian George Smeaton expressed the importance for the gospel of justification of the truth that faith is the gift of God:

> The Reformers connected faith as the receptive organ or hand by which men receive the imputed righteousness which justifies us in the closest possible way with the operation of the Holy Spirit as its author or producing cause. While they asserted the first point, that justification before God proceeds only from faith, they asserted not less strongly the second point, *that faith in the heart proceeds only from God's Spirit.* And on all occasions they declared that if there be allowed in man any natural power or natural capacity for believing without the operation of the Holy Spirit, this inevitably overthrows at the second stage the very doctrine of grace which had been laid as the foundation of all.[5]

Justification is the wholly gracious verdict of God upon certain sinners. The righteousness imputed in justification is a gift—a *free* gift. The basis of justification is a gift: the lifelong obedience and the death of Jesus Christ. The content of justification is a gift: the righteousness of the substitutionary obedience in life and in death of Jesus Christ. The divine act in the sinner's consciousness is a gift: declaring the sinner righteous. The faith by which the sinner receives the righteousness

---

4 Canons of Dordt 3–4.14, in ibid., 3:591.

5 George Smeaton, *The Doctrine of the Holy Spirit* (London: Banner of Truth, 1958), 308.

of God in Jesus Christ is a gift. All is a gift, according to grace, gratuitously given.

And what a gift! Jesus Christ, the incarnate Son of God, with all his saving life and work, as the believer's righteousness with God. Since righteousness with God is the ground of all the blessings of salvation, the gift of righteousness implies the gift of eternal life, or to say it differently, eternal life as a gift—a *free* gift; a gift unmerited; a gift of which the recipients are unworthy; a gift that those who receive it have not themselves by their efforts obtained; a gift for the reception of which those who receive it did not distinguish themselves in any way from those to whom God does not give it.

In justification absolutely nothing is man's own contribution, work, fulfilled condition, merit, or worth.

As the cornerstone of the gospel, the truth of gracious justification reveals and defends all the doctrines of grace, all the so-called five points of Calvinism. I demonstrate this regarding two of these essential doctrines of the gospel of grace.

First, regarding gracious (unconditional) election, the source of salvation, inasmuch as the justification of the sinner is gracious there is only one possible answer to the question, why does God justify certain sinners rather than others? More personally, why does God justify me and not my neighbor, or even sometimes not my blood brother or sister? The answer cannot be, because I believed, whereas my neighbor, or even my brother or sister, did not believe. This cannot be the answer because faith is not the cause of justification but only the means and, decisively, because my faith is God's gift to me. The answer can be only God's gracious, sovereign election of me in eternity, to the praise of the glory of his grace, whereas he eternally and sovereignly reprobated the neighbor, or even my brother or sister, unto damnation in his or her unrighteousness.

Noteworthy in this regard is how closely the apostle relates justification and election in the book of Romans. The justification that is proclaimed in chapters 3–5 and developed regarding its fruit in sanctification in chapters 6 and 7 and the first part of 8 has its source in the election taught in the second part of chapter 8 through chapter 11. Romans 8:33 expresses the close connection between gracious justification and election: "Who shall lay any thing to the charge of God's elect? It is God that justifieth."

Second, justification as the verdict of God imputing the righteousness especially of the death of Christ to particular sinners, which imputation is gracious and the basis of which imputation is the substitutionary death of the head of the covenant, implies the doctrine of limited, or definite, atonement. If, however, the atonement of the cross was universal, either all humans in the end will be justified and saved; or the cross fails to accomplish the purpose of God to justify all humans without exception; or the cross is not after all the basis of the forgiveness of sins and righteousness. A church's theology of justification has inescapable implications concerning that church's doctrine of the atoning death of Christ.

What is true regarding the doctrine of the atonement of the cross of Christ is also the case regarding the gospel of grace in its entirety. A heretical doctrine of justification, which in one form or another is always the error of justification by faith *and by the works of the sinner*, spells the perversion and denial of all the gospel of grace. Rome not only denies justification by faith alone; Rome denies the whole of the gospel of grace, teaching the false gospel of salvation by man's own works and working. Arminianism not only has what the Canons of Dordt refer to as a "new and strange justification of man before God,"[6] but also, and because of its doctrine of justification, a new and strange gospel—a gospel of salvation founded on and effectual by man's own will.

Today, in reputedly conservative Reformed and Presbyterian churches, the heresy of the federal vision openly rejects not only

6 Canons of Dordt 2, error 4, in *Confessions and Church Order*, 165.

the Reformation's doctrine of justification by faith alone, that is, gracious justification, but it also openly denies all the doctrines of grace *with specific regard to salvation in the covenant.*[7] Necessarily so! For gracious justification is the heart of the gospel, including the gospel of covenantal salvation.

Today, as in the sixteenth century, the true church is called by God to proclaim the gospel of justification by faith alone, contending vigorously against the false gospel of justification by the works and will of the sinner. The true church must do this for the salvation of God's elect people. By their own works, will, and worth shall no sinner be justified in the judgment of God.

Still more importantly, the true church is called to proclaim the gospel of justification by faith alone, contending vigorously against the false gospel of justification by the works and will of the sinner, for the sake of the glory of God. The false doctrine of justification by the works and will of the sinner does not end in the doxology, "For of him, and through him, and to him, are all things: to whom be glory for ever. Amen" (Rom. 11:36).

Away with That Impious and Profane Word "Merit"

Martin Luther vehemently expressed one of the important implications of his, and the Bible's, gospel of justification by faith alone, and thus of salvation by grace alone, when he exclaimed, "Away with that impious and profane word 'merit.'"[8]

7 For thorough demonstration of this observation about the contemporary theology that calls itself the federal (covenantal) vision, see my *Federal Vision*. For the bold, open advocacy of the rejection of the doctrines of grace regarding covenantal salvation, rooted in the false doctrine of justification by faith and works, see Shepherd, *Call of Grace*.

8 His own explanation of his abomination of human merit was revelatory of the deepest wellsprings of the faith of the reformer: "If I were to see heaven standing open and could earn it by picking up a piece of straw, I still would not want to do so; for I would not want to be in a position to say: Behold, I have earned it. No, no! Not to my merit but to God be the glory, to God who has sacrificed His Son for me and destroyed my sin

The implication of the doctrine of justification by faith alone is the rejection of merely human merit. Justification by faith alone denies that the justified sinner's relationship with God is established by the sinner's own merit. In accordance with the thought of Romans 11:6, if justification is by faith alone, and thus by grace, then is it no more of merit: otherwise "grace is no more grace." But if righteousness with God is even partly by the sinner's own works (including the work of willing), then justification and salvation are by merit.

Merit is some work of the sinner that deserves righteousness with God. Since righteousness with God is the basis of God's blessing the sinner with eternal life, merit is a work of the sinner that deserves salvation and eternal life. Merit makes God a debtor to the sinner: he owes the sinner something, and this something is salvation. According to merit, when God bestows eternal life on a sinner, he is in reality not *giving* the sinner salvation but *paying* the sinner what he *owes* him. Salvation then is payment earned, not a gift graciously given.

Because mere man owes God perfect obedience by virtue of being God's creature, merit implies a work on the part of mere man above and beyond this perfect obedience (as though this were conceivable). In the matter of meriting, there ought to be definite agreement between the worth of the meritorious work and the value of the good that is earned by the work. One does not pay the surgeon who has performed a successful heart transplant with a bushel of tomatoes. If a human merits righteousness and eternal life, he must be able to pay God with a work deserving of the payment. This establishes the utter folly of the notion of merit on the part of mere man. What does mere, finite, sinful man have with which to repay God for deliverance from eternal death and for the bestowal of eternal life?

---

and hell." Martin Luther, in *What Luther Says*, comp. Ewald M. Plass (St. Louis, MO: Concordia, 1959), 2:923.

In addition, the human who merits is not thankful to God for the good thing he has earned, that is, eternal life, nor should he be. He has this good thing coming to him. He deserves eternal life. God owes it to him. Eternal life is payment of a debt owed. The justified sinner, in this case, may legitimately boast of having obtained the great good by his own (meritorious) work. Everlastingly, the song of the sinner who has justified himself by meritorious works (if this were a possibility) may and will be, "Mine is the glory!"

Nothing would be as jarring a line in the heavenly song of men and angels as this. Nothing would be as obnoxious to God, the saints, and the angels as this disruption of the heavenly chorale. Nothing, not even impenitent idolatry or sodomy, would so defile the heavenly choir as this attribution of the glory of salvation to the saved sinner. To the redeemed in heaven forever, as to the saints now on earth, comes the effectual call, "Praise our God, all ye his servants, and ye that fear him" (Rev. 19:5). From the great multitude in heaven, as from the true church in the world today, comes back the response, "Let us…give honour to him" (v. 7).

Two things are necessary if a sinner is to merit with God. First, he must have something of his own to offer to God, something that he did not receive from God. Second, he must be able to do something more than is strictly required of him by God, something more than he owes God.

As the champion of justification by faith and works, the Roman Catholic Church is also the vocal proponent of merit. According to Rome, the sinner's merit establishes the relationship between himself and God. By his own good works (admittedly done with the help of grace, but emphatically his own good works), which good works are part of the sinner's righteousness with God, the sinner has a legal claim on God. The claim is that God repay his good works with eternal life. The sinner deserves eternal life.

Two aspects of the well-worked-out and consistent Roman doctrine of merit are fundamental to the doctrine. First, according to Rome, fallen man does indeed have something of his own to offer to God in order to make the good work meritorious. This something is man's free will. On Roman doctrine, remaining to every sinner after the fall of Adam is the ability of the fallen sinner to choose for God. Even though this free will must be helped by divine grace if the sinner is to perform a meritorious work, the sinner's contribution of the good choice of his free will makes the good work truly meritorious.

Fundamental to every aspect of Rome's false gospel is the heresy of free will! Likewise, basic to the gospel of the grace of God, which the Spirit of Jesus Christ restored to the church in the Reformation of the sixteenth century, is the truth expressed in the title of Martin Luther's great, insightful, and decisive work *The Bondage of the Will.*

Second, Rome's doctrine of merit includes the notion that especially some sinners are able to perform good works that exceed what God requires of them. These are the works of supererogation. Rome describes them as works done beyond the normal measure of ordinary duty. All Christians should strive to perform such works and are able to do so. But certain outstanding saints have performed many such works, which are now in a treasury of merits available to the ordinary church members. These merits are at the disposal of the pope and can be bought or otherwise obtained by prayers and by masses on behalf of the living and the dead. Here, of course, indulgences and purgatory come into the fantastic picture.

It is evident that the simple, biblical gospel truth of justification by faith alone did away with indulgences and annihilated purgatory. It is also evident how threatening the doctrine of justification by faith alone was, and still is, to the Roman Catholic Church. Not only does the doctrine condemn the very heart of Roman teaching, namely, justification and eternal life by the will and works of the sinner, but it also destroys practical Roman piety, as well as drying up one of the main fountains of Roman income.

Rome officially confesses her doctrine of merit in her Canons and Decrees of the Council of Trent, the authoritative response of Rome to the Reformation and the Reformation's condemnation of merit by its doctrine of justification by faith alone. In chapter 16, the heading of which is "...on the merit of good works, and on the nature of that merit," Rome declares:

> Life eternal is to be proposed to those working well *unto the end*, and hoping in God, both as a grace mercifully promised to the sons of God through Jesus Christ, and as a reward which is according to the promise of God himself, to be faithfully rendered to their good works and merits...We must believe that nothing further is wanting to the justified, to prevent their being accounted to have, by those very works which have been done in God...truly merited eternal life.[9]

Adding her anathema to the Reformed rejection of merit, Rome becomes even clearer and stronger in her commitment to merit:

> If any one saith, that the good works of one that is justified are in such manner the gifts of God, that they are not also the good merits of him that is justified; or, that the said justified, by the good works which he performs through the grace of God and the merit of Jesus Christ, whose living member he is, does not truly merit increase of grace, eternal life, and the attainment of that eternal life,—if so be, however, that he depart in grace,—and also an increase of glory: let him be anathema.[10]

---

9 Canons and Decrees of the Council of Trent, Sixth Session, Decree on Justification 16, in Schaff, *Creeds of Christendom*, 2:107–8. The emphasis is Rome's.

10 Canons and Decrees of the Council of Trent, Sixth Session, [Canons] on Justification 32, in ibid., 2:117–18.

Significantly, these affirmations of meritorious good works are part of Trent's doctrine of justification. The Second Vatican Council of the 1960s did not retract, or even mitigate, this confession of merit.

Under the pressure of the Bible's clear and emphatic teaching that salvation and eternal life are gifts in God's grace, the Roman Catholic Church has found it necessary to befool the people by resorting to a distinction between two kinds of merit: a condign merit and a congruous merit. The former is supposed to refer to works that merit by their intrinsic worthiness; the latter refers to works that merit because they please God, even though, strictly speaking, they do not deserve the payment God makes for them.

We may ignore the distinction. The main significance of Rome's moderating "congruous merit" is that it testifies to the guilty consciences of the Roman theologians who invented it. They themselves were uneasy with the Roman doctrine of meritorious good works, earning the sinner's justification and salvation. The distinction also serves to deceive gullible people.

The distinction between two kinds of merit in Roman Catholic theology is a distinction without a difference. Merit is merit is merit. Whether condign or congruous, merit is condemned by the gospel of grace, particularly by the truth of justification by faith alone.

The Reformation opposed any and all merit on the part of the sinner, that is, any and all deserving of righteousness and eternal life by the sinner's own working. The Heidelberg Catechism expresses this flat condemnation and absolute rejection of merit:

> How art thou righteous before God?
>
> Only by true faith in Jesus Christ; that is, although my conscience accuse me that I have grievously sinned against all the commandments of God, and have never kept any of them, and that I am still prone always to all

> evil, yet God, *without any merit of mine*, of mere grace, grants and imputes to me the perfect satisfaction, righteousness, and holiness of Christ.[11]

The Belgic Confession of Faith likewise condemns the teaching of merit. Significantly, this condemnation occurs in the article that confesses the Reformed doctrine of sanctification, the believer's performance of good works.

> Therefore we do good works, *but not to merit by them (for what can we merit?)—nay, we are beholden to God for the good works we do, and not he to us, since it is he that worketh in us both to will and to do of his good plea*sure. Let us therefore attend to what is written: *When ye shall have done all those things which are commanded you, say we are unprofitable servants: we have done that which was our duty to do.*[12]

This creedal condemnation of merit accurately expresses the biblical condemnation of merit. Scripture condemns merit in Romans and Galatians. If the sinner's own works are not his righteousness with God or the basis of God's declaration that the sinner is just and worthy of eternal life, the sinner's own works do not merit eternal life. Since faith receives the obedience of Christ as the sole righteousness of the justified sinner, only the obedience of Christ in the sinner's stead and on the sinner's behalf merits eternal life for the elect sinner.

Wherever the Bible teaches salvation by grace alone, it condemns the heresy of human merit. Ephesians 2:8–9 is such a passage: "For by grace are ye saved through faith…not of works,

---

11 Heidelberg Catechism Q&A 60, in ibid., 3:326; emphasis added.

12 Belgic Confession 24, in ibid., 3:411–12; some emphasis added. To be noted is that this rejection of merit incorporates in the expression of that rejection two biblical passages on which the rejection is founded, Philippians 2:13 and Luke 17:10.

lest any man should boast." Grace rules out works as the cause or reason or basis of salvation. Grace rules out works as a cause or basis of salvation altogether. But merit makes works a cause or reason or basis of salvation. Therefore, grace rules out merit. Salvation is God's free, gracious gift to the elect sinner. Salvation is not the payment that the sinner deserves and that God owes him.

The parable of the laborers in the vineyard, in Matthew 20:1–16, teaches that the reward God gives to the works of his people is pure grace, not the payment of a debt. If the reward were the payment of a debt, those who worked longer and in more difficult circumstances—the heat of the day—would have a claim on God for payment exceeding the payment given to those who worked only a short while, under less strenuous circumstances.

The parable of the prodigal son, in Luke 15:11–32, plainly teaches that God's warm reception of and lavish bestowal of all kinds of blessings on the wayward son is due to grace, not to the son's merit.

Luke 17:10 strikes the deathblow to the doctrine of merit. Expressly, it denies one of the two teachings that are fundamental to the theory of merit, namely, that one can do more than his duty, in order thus to earn with God. The text has Jesus declaring that when his disciples have done all that God commands them to do they are unprofitable servants, for they have only done their duty. God's demand on humans, including saved humans, is that they love God and the neighbor perfectly. No one, though she be the mother of Jesus, or he, the apostle Paul or the godly Augustine, can do more than this.

Other passages of scripture deny the other basic element to Rome's doctrine of merit: man has something of his own to offer to God, that is, the decision of his free will to believe in Jesus and to love God. The fallen sinner has no free will. He is dead in sin (Eph. 2:1); unable to will the good (Rom. 8:7–8); and incapable of choosing Christ (John 6:44). Everything good that the child of God is or possesses and that results in the performance of good works, including the will that desires God, is God's gift to him and gracious work in him. The fallen sinner has nothing of his own to give to God with which to merit anything, much less eternal life. He is an utter, spiritual bankrupt.

Also bearing on the issue of merit is the reality that all the good works of even the most holy saint are tainted and defiled with sin. As imperfect, even the best works of the saint not only cannot merit with God, but also in strict justice (and the justice of God is strict) deserve punishment, rather than eternal life. In its total war against the Roman Catholic compromising of grace, the Catechism does not overlook this aspect of the utter impossibility of merit.

> But why can not our good works be the whole or part of our righteousness before God?
>
> Because the righteousness which can stand before the judgment-seat of God must be perfect throughout, and wholly conformable to the divine law; whereas even our best works in this life are all imperfect and defiled with sin.[13]

What the rejection of merit by the gospel truth of justification by faith alone *denies* is that the sinner himself ever puts God in his debt; that God ever owes the sinner anything, specifically eternal life, because of the sinner himself or because of what the sinner has done; and that salvation is payment due, rather than grace gratuitously given. What justification by faith alone *affirms* is that the believing sinner's standing with God is on the foundation of grace. Who wants to stand before the awesomely holy and terribly just God on any other footing?

Who can?

Justification by faith alone admonishes Christians not to work with the motive of meriting. All such works, although they may

---

13 Heidelberg Catechism Q&A 62, in ibid., 3:327.

accomplish great things in the estimation of men and although they gain the applause of the church and of the world, are sinful and damnable in the judgment of God. Such works oppose grace; they challenge the sufficiency of the merits of Jesus Christ; they glorify the sinner. Works done with the motive of earning salvation are the very worst of sins. Genuine good works are performed with the motive of thanking God for a wholly gracious salvation. Indeed, the saved sinner ought to be grateful to God for the good works themselves that he performs. "God hath before ordained" these good works "that we should walk in them" (Eph. 2:10).

What a deliverance, what a blessed consciousness of salvation, is the truth of justification by faith alone! How dreadful, how terrifying, it must be to live and work under the burden of merit! No one can be sure that he is doing enough and that he is doing enough *well* enough to deserve and earn salvation.

Away with the Impious Notion of Adamic Merit

The controversy of the Reformed faith with Rome over merit exposes a serious error that establishes itself in Reformed and Presbyterian churches today. This is the teaching that Adam in paradise might have merited a higher, better, heavenly, and eternal life by obeying the "probationary command" of refraining from eating of the fruit of the tree of the knowledge of good and evil. Reformed theologians defend the doctrine that Adam could very really have earned for himself and for the entire human race the eternal life that Christ has merited for the elect church by his (Adam's) obedience to God's prohibition in Genesis 2:17.

The defense of this doctrine is essentially the same as Rome's doctrine of congruous merit. It is admitted that in strict justice Adam could not earn with God, certainly not eternal life. But, it is argued, Adam could have merited by virtue of his freely willing to do what God had revealed pleased him, or by virtue of his willing not to do what God had revealed displeased him. God himself permitted Adam to merit. Between this explanation of

Adam's meriting in paradise and Rome's doctrine of congruous merit, there is no essential difference. Both teachings have man meriting with God. Both ascribe the possibility of meriting to God's good pleasure. Both find the possibility of meriting in the free will of man. Both, in fact, have mere man earning the same thing: eternal life.

About this doctrine concerning Adam in paradise, commonly (and ominously) referred to as the "covenant of works," I do not comment here in any detail.[14] My concern is the impossibility and illegitimacy of any and all merit on the part of mere man. Adam, a mere man, could not have merited anything with God, certainly not that high, glorious, eternal life that the Son of God in human flesh merited for himself and his people by his lifelong, strenuous obedience and by his accursed death. Luke 17:10 applies also to Adam in paradise. If he had done what God commanded him to do and refrained from doing what God forbade him to do, he would have been an unprofitable servant. He would only have been doing his duty. Nor did Adam have anything of his own to contribute to God. God made him in his own image, including a will that was able to choose the good.

In the way of obedience, Adam would have merited nothing, absolutely nothing. He would only have continued to live the earthly life of paradise. Obedience to the prohibition against eating of the tree of the knowledge of good and evil would not have earned for Adam and the race the higher, better, eternal life that Jesus Christ has merited for the elect church. Adam's obedience would only have been the way in which he and the race would have continued to live the blissful but earthly life into which God created him originally.

---

14 For a thorough critique of the theory in Reformed circles of the covenant with Adam as a covenant of works by which Adam might have merited eternal life, see my "The Covenant of Creation with Adam" in the *Protestant Reformed Theological Journal* 40, no. 1 (November 2006): 3–42.

"The first man Adam was made a living soul…natural…[and] of the earth, earthy" (1 Cor. 15:45–47). All he was capable of passing on to his progeny was earthiness. Only the "second man…the Lord from heaven," who is a "quickening spirit," could obtain for himself and his body, the elect church, and create the life that is "heavenly" (vv. 45–49).

God could not have put himself in a position in which he was indebted to Adam—to a mere man, indeed to the entire human race. God could no more have done this than he could have denied himself. For God to permit mere man to merit would be for God to "ungod" himself. Always, and necessarily, mere man is indebted to God. Never is God indebted to mere man.

The seriousness of the popular notion in Reformed and Presbyterian circles that Adam might have merited eternal life by his obedience in the garden is nothing less than its introduction into Reformed theology of the Roman Catholic heresy of (congruous) merit. Theologians who espouse and defend the doctrine make plain that they have no fundamental objection to the wickedness that lies at the heart of merit: man indebting God; God owing man; man receiving eternal life itself not as a gracious gift, but as payment. For them it is objectionable to teach that sinful man can by the help of grace merit salvation, but they have no objection to Adam's meriting, of course by the grace of God. To them, it is not offensive that mere man merits with God, indeed merits the highest and most glorious life. To them it is not objectionable to suppose that Adam, merely by not eating a piece of fruit, might have brought the entire human race into the heavenly life and glory that Jesus won for the elect church by his incarnation, lifelong obedience, atoning death, and resurrection.

According to them, the first man Adam, who was of the earth, earthy, might very well have done all that the last Adam, who is the Lord from heaven, has done (see 1 Cor. 15:45–49). No matter how loudly these Reformed theologians may oppose the Roman Catholic heresy of merit, essentially they have no objection to the Roman doctrine: mere man might have merited eternal life, in the person of Adam.

That Adam could not have merited and that the depraved sinner cannot merit do not imply, however, that Jesus Christ did not merit. If the Reformed faith in the twenty-first century is troubled by the error that attributes the possibility of meriting to unfallen Adam, it is also troubled by a recent denial that the saving work of Jesus Christ was meritorious. This is the important subject of the next chapter.

Chapter Eighteen

THE MERITORIOUS WORK OF CHRIST

The contemporary heresy that the saving work of Jesus Christ was not, and did not need to be, meritorious is that of the theological movement known as the new perspective on Paul. The new perspective theologian who is most influential on Reformed and Presbyterian theologians and churches is N. T. Wright. Wright is widely recognized as an evangelical in the Church of England.

One with the new perspective within the Reformed and Presbyterian churches is the theology of the federal vision—federal because the root of its heretical views is an aberrant doctrine of the covenant of grace. *Federal* derives from the Latin *foedus*, which means "bond" or "covenant." The federal vision's doctrine of the covenant is that the covenant of grace in scripture is a conditional contract between God and everyone who has been baptized, especially all the children of believing parents. Leading advocates of the federal vision include Norman Shepherd, James B. Jordan, Rich Lusk, Peter Leithart, John Barach, and Douglas Wilson. There is reason to believe that the men of the federal vision are influenced by the proponents of the new perspective, especially Wright. Regardless of the influence, the federal vision, like the new perspective, rejects the meritorious nature of the saving work of Jesus Christ. The federal vision advocates and argues this rejection within the sphere of Reformed and Presbyterian churches, apparently without restraint.

Wright is bold in his denial that the saving work of Jesus Christ was meritorious. "The 'obedience' of Christ [Wright has reference especially to Jesus' death] is not designed to amass a treasury of merit which can then be 'reckoned' to the believer, as in some Reformed schemes of thought."[1] Important to note in this rejection of the meritorious nature of the work of Christ are, first, that the rejection is closely related to a denial of justification (reckoning Christ's obedience to the believer) and, second, that Wright advertises his rejection of Christ's meritorious work as his departure from the confessions of the Reformed faith ("some Reformed schemes of thought").[2]

Worthy of note is Wright's disdain for the Reformed and Presbyterian confessions, indeed for his own creed, the Thirty-Nine Articles of the Church of England. They are not authoritative, binding documents expressing the Christian faith of holy scripture. They are merely "some Reformed schemes of thought" that Wright may contradict at his pleasure.

So vehement is Wright's objection to explaining Jesus' saving work as meritorious, which merit is imputed to the account of the believer, that he condemns this doctrine as a "category mistake":

> *It is therefore a straightforward category mistake, however venerable within some Reformed traditions including part of my own, to suppose that Jesus "obeyed the law" and so obtained "righteousness" which could be reckoned to those who believe in him.*[3]

A "category mistake" is a total and dreadfully serious mistake. In this case it is nothing less than a gospel-denying heresy, as

1 Wright, *Justification*, 228.

2 Ibid.

3 Ibid., 232. Italics are Wright's, indicating the importance to him of this rejection of the biblical and, as he acknowledges, of the Reformed creeds' doctrine of justification.

Wright goes on to make plain when he charges that such a view of the work of Christ amounts to the concession "that 'legalism' was true after all—with Jesus as the ultimate legalist."[4] What it is that Wright charges with being a "category mistake," it must be kept in mind, is the Reformation's and all the Reformed creeds' doctrine of justification. This doctrine is "legalism" and proclaims Jesus as the "ultimate legalist." No heavier charge against the gospel of the Reformation can be imagined.

Wright's god is a god only of love and mercy—a love and mercy that negate justice. Wright's gospel is the news of God's love nullifying the demands of justice. Having dismissed the "logic of merit," Wright extols, in the place of merit, "the logic of love."[5] Wright ridicules the gospel of the meritorious nature of the saving work of Christ, that is, the gospel that confesses the justice of God. Such a gospel presents God "as a distant bank manager, scrutinizing credit and debit sheets."[6]

Rejection of the Merit of Christ's "Active Obedience"

The men of the federal vision likewise deny that the saving work of Jesus was, or needed to be, meritorious. Because these heretics advocate their false doctrine within Reformed and Presbyterian churches, which are all creedally committed to the meritorious nature of the work of Jesus, the men of the federal vision cannot be as outspoken and bold as Wright and the other proponents of the new perspective. Especially do the men of the federal vision attempt to disguise their rejection of the meritorious nature of Christ's work under the cloak of a rejection of what Reformed theology calls the "active obedience" of Christ. The "active" obedience of Christ, in distinction from his "passive" obedience, is

---

4 Ibid.

5 Ibid., 188.

6 Ibid.

his lifelong obedience to all the law of God, in distinction from his suffering the wrath of God against the sins of his people, especially by his death on the cross.

The federal vision is forthright and vehement in its repudiation of the teaching that Jesus' active obedience merited eternal life for his people and that the merit of this active obedience is an aspect of the righteousness of Christ that God imputes to the believer. Norman Shepherd denies that "the lifelong, perfect and perpetual obedience of Jesus Christ" was meritorious on behalf of and in the stead of his people. The only necessity of this active obedience on the part of the Savior was that it enabled him to offer the sacrifice of himself as without blemish.[7] The doctrine of Jesus' active obedience meriting eternal life for sinners "has no Biblical warrant."[8] In fact, Shepherd rejects the doctrine that Christ's work in its totality was meritorious, "including both his active and passive obedience": "my rejection of 'merit' [regarding the saving work of Christ in its entirety]."[9]

Similarly, Rich Lusk emphasizes that "it is not Christ's lifelong obedience per se [his active obedience] that is credited to us." Significant for indicating both the doctrinal source and the theological purpose for the federal visionists of this denial of the imputation of Christ's active obedience is what Lusk immediately adds, "God's righteousness is his own righteousness, not something imputed...God's righteousness is simply his covenant trustworthiness."[10]

At issue in the controversy of Reformed orthodoxy with the federal vision's avowed rejection of the active obedience of

---

7 Norman Shepherd, "The Imputation of Active Obedience," in Sandlin, *A Faith That Is Never Alone*, 267.

8 Ibid., 275.

9 Ibid., 277.

10 Rich Lusk, "A Response to 'The Biblical Plan of Salvation,'" in Beisner, *The Auburn Avenue Theology*, 141.

Christ is justification as the imputation to the believing sinner of the righteousness of God worked out in the ministry of Jesus Christ—the *entire* ministry of Jesus Christ—nothing other and nothing less. For all the deceptive emphasis on the active obedience of Christ, what is intended—and achieved—by the federal vision by the rejection of the active obedience is the rejection of justification itself, as the imputation to the sinner of the merit of Jesus Christ as the sinner's own.

Explicitly defending Shepherd and the theology of the federal vision, liberated Reformed theologian Ralph F. Boersema also labors to leave the impression that his objection is against the teaching of the meritorious nature of Christ's lifelong obedience—his active obedience.

> The point of discussion then, is whether, for justification, there is a twofold imputation of Christ's obedience, that of his atonement plus the merits of his law-keeping, or only the imputation of his priestly obedience in offering the sacrifice and shedding his blood for the atonement of sin...His [Christ's] active obedience was not imputed to us for righteousness.[11]

This emphasis by the federal vision on the active obedience of Christ, as though the objection is only against the merit of his active obedience, is misleading, if not deliberately deceptive. In fact, the federal vision objects to the doctrine of the meritorious nature of the saving work of Jesus Christ *as such* and regarding the *totality* of that saving work, whether active or passive. Whatever the work of Christ may have been, according to the federal vision, it was not the *earning* with God of deliverance from damnation and of the right to eternal life.

The rejection of the meritorious nature of the work of Christ is required by the federal vision's denial of justification by faith

11 Boersema, *Not of Works*, 110, 121.

alone. For the federal vision the heart of the saving work of Jesus Christ is not the legal imputation of the righteousness of God in Jesus Christ to the account of the guilty but believing sinner. If the fundamental saving work of Jesus Christ is the legal imputation of a righteousness that is alien to the sinner, the life and death of Jesus were meritorious on behalf of the elect people of God. The merit of Jesus' lifelong obedience, especially his obedient suffering and death, becomes the elect sinner's own by imputation.

At bottom the denial of the meritorious nature of Christ's saving work is the denial of the justice of God in salvation. Divine justice requires that deliverance from the guilt of sin be *earned*, and earned by the suffering of the punishment that sin deserves. Divine justice requires that the enjoyment of eternal life be *merited*, merited by an obedience to the will of God that deserves eternal life.

Denial of merit regarding the saving work of Jesus Christ is the denial of the justice, or righteousness, of God in salvation. It is the proclamation of the possibility of salvation from sin unto eternal life apart from the satisfaction of divine justice, indeed at the *expense* of God's righteousness.

The denial of merit regarding the saving work of Jesus by Wright and by his closet disciples, the men of the federal vision, is nothing but a new form of the old modernism. The old modernism blasphemed as butcher-shop theology the orthodox Christian doctrine of salvation as the legal imputation of righteousness to guilty sinners on the basis of the cross of Christ as the satisfaction of divine justice. Obscure it as they make every effort to do, under the cloak of opposing only the meritorious nature of the active obedience of Christ, the men of the federal vision make plain that their real objection is against merit theology *as such*, regarding God's work of salvation in the life and especially in the death of Jesus Christ.

The heresy of the men of the federal vision is their denial of the truth confessed in the Heidelberg Catechism:

> Why was it necessary for Christ to suffer death?
>
> Because, by reason of the justice and truth of God, satisfaction for our sins could be made no otherwise than by the death of the Son of God.[12]

In a chapter opposing the "imputation of the active obedience of Christ," Shepherd proposes that "it would be better not to use the word [*merit*] at all," that is, regarding also the suffering and death of Jesus Christ, not only regarding the active obedience of Christ.[13] The liberated Reformed defender of Shepherd, Ralph Boersema, is correct in describing Shepherd's theology as the total rejection of the meritorious nature of the whole of Christ's saving work, both active and passive: "Shepherd's concern is the lack of biblical evidence for a works/merit principle of justification…He…fails to see a works/earn principle in Christ's obedience for our justification."[14]

Boersema is in full agreement with Shepherd in rejecting merit as the nature of the saving work of Jesus Christ. Boersema rejects "the concept of earning merits in order to present value to God with a view to being accepted by him," in its entirety. Significantly, the liberated Reformed theologian proposes that a theology of merit regarding the work of Christ is in conflict with the gospel of the love of God. "God loves man and man relates to him in love that only seeks his glory. True love is not *quid pro quo* goodness given in exchange for goodness." Christ did not purchase the kingdom of heaven for his people, that is, by earning it for them. "He inherited the Kingdom for us rather than purchasing it."[15]

---

12 Heidelberg Catechism Q&A 40, in Schaff, *Creeds of Christendom*, 3:320. See also the Belgic Confession 20, in ibid., 3:405–6.

13 Shepherd, "The Imputation of Active Obedience," in Sandlin, *A Faith That Is Never Alone*, 277.

14 Boersema, *Not of Works*, 106.

15 Ibid., 140.

Boersema and the men of the federal vision explicitly deny that Christ "purchased" eternal life for his people. They state that this denial of redemption is the meaning of their rejection of merit. Thus Boersema and the men of the federal vision make plain to the least sophisticated Reformed believer, to say nothing of all Reformed theologians, that their theology is the denial of the biblical gospel of redemption. Redemption in the Bible is the purchase, or buying, by the payment of a price—*to the just God*—of sinners who are indebted to God on account of their sinfulness and sins. To deny purchase is to deny redemption, and to deny redemption is to deny the Christian gospel at its heart. This denial is the necessary implication of the rejection of merit as the nature of the saving work of Jesus Christ.

Every child of the Reformation, and especially every Reformed Christian, must wonder in amazement at the appearance, defense, and promotion of the theology of the new perspective and of the federal vision in evangelical, Reformed, and Presbyterian circles.

Concerning the "merits of Jesus Christ," leading federal vision theologian James B. Jordan dismisses the confession of them by Protestant theology "as a hangover of medieval theology." Jesus' work was not meritorious, neither his active obedience nor his passive obedience. "Nowhere [in scripture] is Jesus' accomplishment spoken of as earning salvation."[16] "There is no 'merit' theology in the Bible."[17]

Inexcusably misreading Calvin on Christ's meriting, as though the reformer repudiated merit in favor of divine mercy (and thus playing the entire community of contemporary Reformed students of Calvin for fools), Rich Lusk concludes, with specific

16 James B. Jordan, "Merit Versus Maturity: What Did Jesus Do for Us?" in Wilkins and Garner, *The Federal Vision*, 192.

17 Ibid., 195.

reference to the work of the sinless Jesus Christ, that "meriting something from God is absurd."[18]

Lusk indicates that his and the federal vision's rejection of Christ's meriting is an aspect of their denial of justification by faith as the imputation to the believing sinner of Christ's righteousness, passive as well as active:

> Justification requires no transfer or imputation of anything. It does not force us to reify "righteousness" into something that can be shuffled around in heavenly accounting books...My in-Christ-ness makes imputation redundant. I do not need the moral content of his life of righteousness transferred to me...I am not justified by a legal transfer of his "obedience points" to my account...[This doctrine of justification] could leave adherents exposed to the infamous "legal fiction" charge...It could become, as Wright has said, "a cold piece of business."[19]

In *A Faith That Is Never Alone*, Lusk makes unmistakably plain that the federal vision's repudiation of the meritorious nature of Christ's saving work extends to the entirety of the work of Christ—passive as well as active obedience. He makes plain also the close relationship between this repudiation of merit and the federal vision's heresy of rejecting justification as the

18 Lusk, "A Response to 'The Biblical Plan of Salvation,'" in Beisner, *The Auburn Avenue Theology*, 145. This is Lusk's conclusion based on his reading of Calvin as a theologian who "virtually refines it [merit] out of existence by subordinating merit to mercy." This is Lusk's understanding of Calvin's statement in one place that "it is absurd to set Christ's merit against God's mercy...Apart from God's good pleasure Christ could not merit anything" (Ibid., 144–45). What Calvin is teaching is not that mercy dispenses with the necessity of Christ's meriting, but that the mercy of God *provides* the necessary merit and the one who alone can merit with God. Thus there is no conflict between mercy and merit.

19 Ibid., 142.

imputation of Christ's righteousness to the account of the guilty but believing sinner. Lusk denies the doctrine that teaches that

> through his active (lifelong obedience) and passive obedience (suffering on the cross), Jesus accumulated merits in his account. Those merits are imputed to our accounts when we trust him. Because the merits of Christ have been transferred to us, God declares us justified. When the Scripture says, "faith is counted for righteousness," it really means that by faith, God transfers Christ's righteousness to us in order to declare us just.[20]

Such a doctrine is "not *exactly* what Paul means when he speaks of imputation."[21] "Exactly" in the preceding quotation is more deception by the federal vision theologian. In what Lusk immediately goes on to say about Paul's doctrine of imputation in Romans, it is evident that according to the federal vision the classic, creedal doctrine of justification is not *at all* what Paul means when he speaks of imputation. "In *none* of these instances [the texts in Romans 4 that teach imputation] does imputation mean that the righteousness of Christ is *transferred* to believers."[22] "He [Jesus] does not transfer righteousness or merits to our accounts."[23]

Federal visionist heretic P. Andrew Sandlin is sweeping in his rejection of merit, including therefore the meritorious work of Jesus, whether his active or his passive obedience: "God's relationship to man is not characterized by legality and merit."[24]

---

20 Lusk, "From Birmingham, with Love," in Sandlin, *A Faith That Is Never Alone*, 124–25.

21 Ibid., 125.

22 Ibid., 127.

23 Ibid., 138.

24 P. Andrew Sandlin, "The Gospel of Law and the Law of Gospel: An Assessment of the Antithetical Gospel-Law Paradigm," in *A Faith That Is Never Alone*, 243.

This wholesale rejection of merit is not only the perversion of the Reformation's doctrine of justification. It is also the denial of the cross of Jesus Christ and of God, who *is* righteousness, or justice. Since God *is* his perfections, Sandlin's sweeping statement amounts to declaring that God's relationship to man is not determined by who and what God is.

Merit of Christ in the Creeds

The first line of defense of the gospel of merit, and thus of the truth of imputed righteousness, is the Reformed and Presbyterian creeds.

As a minister of the Church of England, Wright is bound by the Thirty-Nine Articles of the Church of England. Article 11 exposes Wright as not only a heretic but also as a rebel against the authority of his own creed.

> We are accounted righteous before God, only for the merit of our Lord and Saviour Jesus Christ by Faith, and not for our own works or deservings. Wherefore, that we are justified by Faith only, is a most wholesome Doctrine, and very full of comfort, as more largely is expressed in the Homily of Justification.[25]

The men of the federal vision are mostly Reformed or Presbyterian theologians. The Presbyterians among them are silenced, or ought to be silenced, by the Westminster Standards. Explaining Christ's intercession, the Larger Catechism expressly affirms "the merit of his [Christ's] obedience and sacrifice on earth" and the application of this merit to all believers.[26]

The Westminster Confession of Faith attributes the perseverance of the saints to the "efficacy of the merit...of Jesus

---

25 Thirty-Nine Articles of the Church of England 11, in Schaff, *Creeds of Christendom*, 3:494.

26 Larger Catechism A 55, in *The Westminster Standards: An Original Facsimile* (Audubon, NJ: Old Paths Publications, 1997), 14.

Christ."[27] This merit of Jesus Christ, according to the Westminster Confession, is imputed to believers in the saving act of justification: "imputing the obedience and satisfaction of Christ unto them."[28] The judicial ground of this justification is the meritorious obedience of Christ on behalf of the elect believers. He earned, or merited, their deliverance from punishment and their reception of eternal life.

> Christ, by his obedience and death, did fully discharge the debt of all those that are thus justified, and did make a proper, real, and full satisfaction to his Father's justice in their behalf. Yet inasmuch as he was given by the Father for them, and his obedience and satisfaction accepted in their stead, and both freely, not for any thing in them, their justification is only of free grace; that both the exact justice and rich grace of God might be glorified in the justification of sinners.[29]

In this doctrine of the work of Christ as meritorious, the Westminster Confession speaks of Christ's "obedience" and "death" as comprising his meritorious work of salvation. Thus the creed would seem to be distinguishing Christ's saving work as both active obedience and passive suffering. Regardless of this distinction, the creed certainly does describe the saving work of Christ as meritorious in the stead of and on behalf of his elect people. His work discharged a debt. This is earning, or meriting, salvation from the guilt of sin. His work was a "proper, real, and full satisfaction to his Father's justice." This is earning, or meriting, full salvation, including eternal life. And the purpose of the meritorious work of Jesus was to glorify "both the exact justice

27 Westminster Confession of Faith 17.2, in Schaff, *Creeds of Christendom*, 3:636.

28 Westminster Confession of Faith 11.1, in ibid., 3:626.

29 Westminster Confession of Faith 11.3, in ibid., 3:626–27.

and rich grace of God." Not only God's grace and mercy! But also his "justice"—his "*exact* justice"!

The three forms of unity, which authoritatively define the Reformed faith, are as insistent upon the meritorious nature of the saving work of Jesus Christ as are the Westminster standards. Answer 21 of the Heidelberg Catechism posits "Christ's merits" as the only judicial ground of the salvation that the elect child of God receives by means of faith.[30]

According to article 22 of the Belgic Confession, true faith in Jesus Christ "embraces Jesus Christ with all his merits." The article affirms that through the faith of the believers Jesus imputes "to us all his merits, and so many holy works, which he hath done for us and in our stead." Thus by the imputation to us of his merits, Jesus is "our Righteousness."[31] The mention of "holy works," in addition to "merits," makes the active obedience of Christ part of the righteousness of the Savior that is imputed to the believers in justification.

Also the Canons of Dordt confess, and have every Reformed Christian confess, that the saving work of Jesus Christ was meritorious and that justification consists of the legal "transfer" of Jesus' merits to the account of the believing sinner. "We by faith, inasmuch as it accepts the merits of Christ, are justified before God and saved."[32] The Canons condemn the doctrine "that Christ, by his satisfaction, merited neither salvation itself for anyone, nor faith, whereby this satisfaction of Christ unto salvation is effectually appropriated."[33]

---

30 Heidelberg Catechism A 21, in ibid., 3:313.

31 Belgic Confession 22, in ibid., 3:407–8.

32 Canons of Dordt 2, error 4, in *Confessions and Church Order*, 165. Appealing to Romans 3:24–25 in support of this doctrine of justification as the imputation of the merits of Christ, this article in the Canons condemns the explanation of Romans 3 and 4 by the new perspective and the federal vision.

33 Canons of Dordt 2, error 3, in ibid., 165.

Telling against the federal vision is that this article of the Canons goes on to acknowledge that even the Arminian heresy recognizes that Christ's saving work was meritorious in a certain respect. It "merited" for the Father the right to prescribe new conditions by the fulfillment of which sinners might save themselves. Even the Arminians, although corrupting the truth of the doctrine, did not dare to go so far as to deny the meritorious nature of Christ's saving work.

Such is the fundamental importance of the "merit...of Christ" for salvation, according to the Canons, that it is a reason that saints do not fall away from Christ and perish everlastingly. "With respect to God, it is utterly impossible [that the elect saints totally fall from grace and faith], since...the merit...of Christ [cannot] be rendered ineffectual."[34] With the denial of the meritorious nature of Christ's work must be expected, therefore, the denial of the perseverance of saints, exactly what we find in the theology of the new perspective and of the federal vision. These enemies of the Reformed faith insist on the possibility *and reality* of the apostasy of men and women who once were savingly united to Jesus Christ.

For Reformed Christians the creeds are authoritative. The men of the federal vision *may* not contradict them. Nor may Reformed theologians carry on polite theological debates with the men of the federal vision as though the issues raised by the heresy were merely academic, as was done at the "colloquium" that gave birth to the book *The Auburn Avenue Theology, Pros and Cons: Debating the Federal Vision*.[35] Orthodox Reformed

34 Canons of Dordt 5.8, in Schaff, *Creeds of Christendom*, 3:594.

35 The book, published by Knox Theological Seminary, is a collection of papers presented at a "colloquium on the federal vision" in 2003 at the seminary. The editor of the book thanked "all fourteen of the participants" in the colloquium, half of whom were some of the most vehement promoters and defenders of the heresy of the federal vision, for their work in the colloquium, which all of them did "out of their love for the

theologians must expose and condemn the federal vision as heresy. Reformed churches must not debate the men of the federal vision but discipline them, as article 80 of the Church Order of Dordt requires: "Among the gross sins which are worthy of being punished with suspension or deposition from office, these are the principal ones: false doctrine or heresy."[36]

Cornelis P. Venema is guilty of both of these fatal errors in his examination of the heretical teaching of N. T. Wright. He notes that Wright pleads, understandably, that his theology of justification be judged in the light of scripture, setting aside the creeds of the evangelical and Reformed churches.

> Wright maintains that we need to take a "fresh" look at the biblical and especially Pauline texts without the encumbrance of the traditional formulations and confessional

---

Bride of Christ, and they are to be commended" (acknowledgments). The critics of the federal vision were mild in their criticism of the heresy, appreciative of many aspects of the false doctrine, and full of praise for the men who propounded the federal vision. Typical is this line from one of the purported critics of the federal vision: "I appreciate much of the project which the Federal Vision has undertaken, together with their very evident optimism, graciousness and sense of humor." His first and main criticism? "The advocates of the Federal Vision have sometimes overstated their case." The federal vision paper by Steve Schlissel to which the critic is responding is a "fine essay" (40–41). If this is the nature of the supposed criticism of the federal vision by prominent Reformed theologians, it is all over with creedal Reformed Christianity. Keeping in mind that the federal vision openly denies all of the doctrines of grace defended by the Synod of Dordt, and the fundamental Reformation doctrine of justification by faith alone as well, one imagines the president of the Synod of Dordt cordially declaring to Episcopius and his group of Arminian theologians, "We greet you as brothers motivated by the love of Christ and a desire for the welfare of Christ's bride, the Reformed Church in the Netherlands. Your polemic against salvation by grace alone is a 'fine essay.' I cannot speak highly enough of your mild demeanor and good humor. Now let us discuss these issues amicably—and endlessly." Contrast the actual dismissal of the Arminians by the angry president of the synod.

36 Church Order 80, in *Confessions and Church Order*, 402.

> (especially polemical) positions of the sixteenth-century Reformation. In this way, the contemporary church will honor the Reformation's emphasis upon *sola Scriptura*, while avoiding a slavish adherence to a reading of the apostle Paul that has been largely discredited by more recent historical and biblical scholarship.

So much for the creeds of the evangelical and Reformed churches: encumbrances expressing "slavish adherence to a reading of the apostle Paul." A brazen, if effective, way to decide the controversy at the outset: the Reformation's doctrine of justification is "largely discredited by more recent historical and biblical scholarship." And Venema allows Wright thus to exclude the creeds from the discussion. Venema makes no appeal to the creeds whatever.

"Discussion" is all that Venema's treatment of Wright's assault on the Reformation's and its creeds' doctrine of justification amounts to. There is no Luther-like exposure and condemnation of Wright's heresy.[37] Although it denies justification as the imputation of the righteousness of Christ by faith alone, the theology of Wright and the new perspective is merely "inadequate."[38] The strongest criticism of the new perspective is implicit: "The older perspective of the Reformation will ultimately prove to represent *more faithfully* what the apostle Paul boldly terms 'my gospel'" (Rom. 2:16).[39] The perspective of the new perspective on justification by faith is merely less faithful than that of the gospel of the Reformation and its creeds. If the defense of justification by faith alone is no stronger than that

37 Cornelis P. Venema, "What Did Saint Paul Really Say?: N. T. Wright and the New Perspective(s) on Paul," in *By Faith Alone: Answering the Challenges to the Doctrine of Justification*, ed. Gary L. W. Johnson and Guy P. Waters (Wheaton, IL: Crossway Books, 2006), 33–59.

38 Ibid., 55.

39 Ibid., 59; emphasis added.

of Venema, there soon will be no confession of the "older perspective" of the Reformation that will prove to be more faithful.

The creedal condemnation of the federal vision's rejection of the meritorious nature of Christ's saving work is solidly based on holy scripture. The biblical basis of this condemnation is not so much this or that text, although there are such texts, multitudes of them, as it is the overall doctrine of scripture concerning the nature of the suffering, death, and lifelong obedience of Jesus Christ. The obedient life and death of the Savior were not merely an evolutionary development of Jesus, and of the church in him, from a lower to a higher kind of human life, a somewhat miraculous advance from earthly life to spiritual, eternal life. By his life and death, Jesus did not merely "inherit" eternal life, as the federal vision is fond of saying, as the alternative to merit.

But Jesus *earned* deliverance from death, and he *merited* eternal life for himself as the representative of a guilty, undeserving people. He did indeed "inherit" eternal life, but he inherited eternal life *in the way and on the basis of meriting it.* This was necessary because, contrary to the old and new modernism, God is the God of justice. His justice requires that deliverance from the misery of sin be *earned* by the satisfying of his justice—exactly and in full. His justice also requires that the enjoyment of eternal life by an undeserving people be merited for them. They must have the *right* to life eternal, body and soul.

Salvation by grace *at the expense* of divine justice is not the gospel. It is liberalism or modernism, that is, the perversion of the gospel. The gospel is the good news that in the suffering and death of his own, dearly beloved Son in human flesh, God himself graciously satisfied his own justice.

The gospel is not the news that faith in Jesus Christ exempts one from fulfilling the demands of God's justice. But the gospel is the good news that by a sinner's faith in Jesus Christ God imputes, or legally reckons, to the guilty but believing sinner the righteousness of Jesus Christ, active as well as passive. The legal position of the believer before God the judge is that of one who has completely paid the debt of all his sin and who has perfectly fulfilled the will of God that he love God and the neighbor.

Merit of Christ in Scripture

This is the biblical testimony to the saving work of Jesus Christ, not in the odd text here or there, but in the massive, overall revelation of the nature of the work of the Savior. The meritorious nature of the saving work of the Messiah is the gospel of the massive, prominent testimony of the Old Testament scripture concerning the necessity of the atoning sacrifice. Rivers of blood ran through the nation of Israel, especially from her tabernacle and temple. Every drop cried out to the consciousness of guilty, believing Israelite sinners: "Your salvation requires the meritorious suffering and death of the Lamb of God in order to satisfy the justice of the righteous God of your salvation."

Revelatory of the significance of the sacrifices is the law concerning them in Leviticus 4:27–35. If an Israelite sinned and was "guilty," he had to bring an "offering" to the tabernacle. There he must "lay his hand upon the head of the sin offering." The priest would sprinkle the blood of the sacrificial animal on and at the bottom of the altar. Thus the "priest shall make an atonement for his sin that he hath committed, and it shall be forgiven him." All these bloody sacrifices typified the meritorious suffering and death of the Lamb of God, by which he took away the sins of the world.

> Surely he hath borne our griefs, and carried our sorrows: yet we did esteem him stricken, smitten of God, and afflicted. But he was wounded for our transgressions, he was bruised for our iniquities: the chastisement of our peace was upon him; and with his stripes we are healed. All we like sheep have gone astray; we have turned every one to his own way; and the LORD hath laid on him the

> iniquity of us all…for the transgression of my people was he stricken…thou [Jehovah God] shalt make his soul an offering for sin…by his knowledge shall my righteous servant justify many; for he shall bear their iniquities… he was numbered with the transgressors; and he bare the sin of many. (Isa. 53:4–12)

This work of the Savior is no mere development of himself from an earthly to a higher life. It is not a mere stage in his bland "inheritance" of eternal life. This is the bloody, awful work of suffering at the hand of a just God in order to merit with this God of justice deliverance from the guilt of sin and the right to eternal life by satisfying the justice of God as the substitute for guilty sinners.

The meritorious nature of the saving work of Jesus Christ is the gospel of the cross. At stake therefore in the controversy of evangelicalism with Wright and of reputedly conservative Presbyterianism and Reformed theology with the men of the federal vision is the truth of the cross of Christ, nothing less. To deny that the work of Jesus was meritorious in nature—earning with God salvation for all those for whom he lived, suffered, and died, including payment of sin's debt and acquiring the right to life eternal—is, by virtue of this denial, denial of the cross of Christ.

According to Acts 20:28, in the death of Jesus God "purchased" his church "with his own blood." To purchase is to earn, or merit, the deliverance of the church from the ruling power of sin, from death as punishment, and from everlasting hell and to earn, or merit, the right of the church to holiness, to spiritual life already now, and to heaven by the payment of a price deserving this great salvation. The price paid by Jesus was the blood—the *life's* blood—of God himself in the human nature of the eternal Son become flesh.

To deny the meritorious nature of the lifelong suffering and of the death of Jesus is to deny the cross as God's "purchase" of his church at this expensive price, graciously paid by God himself in our flesh.

Second Corinthians 5:21 teaches that the cost to Jesus, and to God, of our becoming the righteousness of God was that Jesus was "made...sin for us." To him (legally) was imputed by God all the multitude of the sins of the numerous elect church, so that especially on the cross, in the judgment of God, Jesus was nothing but a massive, human lump of sin. This demanded the appropriate punishment: eternal hell (concentrated into six hours). By the payment of this price, by himself in the beloved Son, who is personally God, God merited, or earned, "for us" release from this dreadful death sentence and the right to spiritual and eternal life.

To deny the meritorious nature of the death of Jesus Christ is to deny this substitutionary nature of the cross of Christ. In this case, whatever the cross may have been, it was not God's making Jesus sin for us. Neither does it make us the righteousness of God by the imputation of the righteousness of the cross. This is the cross-denying, hopeless "gospel" of the new perspective and of the federal vision.

Galatians 3:13–14 and 4:4–5 are the clear and decisive apostolic doctrine of the cross, indeed also of the lifelong suffering of the Savior. Such is the clarity and decisiveness of the passages that the cross of Christ was meritorious atonement that in his visceral opposition to this doctrine Wright is stirred to damn the right understanding of the passages, and thus creedal Protestant Christianity, as "nonsense."[40] Not merely mistaken, but nonsense!

Galatians 3:13–14 proclaims the glorious gospel that "Christ hath redeemed us from the curse of the law, being made a curse for us." The positive benefit earned by this redemption is "that

40 Wright, *Climax of the Covenant*, 150.

the blessing of Abraham might come on the Gentiles through Jesus Christ; that we might receive the promise of the Spirit through faith." The suffering and death of Jesus Christ were the deliverance of those for whom he died from the curse of the law and the obtaining for them of the blessing of eternal life by the Spirit. This deliverance from curse to blessing was *redemption*—the payment of the price required by the true God, who, contrary to the idolatry of the new perspective and the federal vision, is the God of justice. Christ's saving work therefore, especially in dying, was a meriting, an earning, a deserving, by satisfying God's justice.

And the price was high: Christ's "being made a curse for us."

Galatians 4:4–5 teaches that the very purpose of God in the incarnation and birth of his Son was the meriting of deliverance from the condemning function of the law and the earning of the right to become the children of God. "God sent forth his Son, made of a woman, made under the law, to redeem them that were under the law, that we might receive the adoption of sons."

Denial of the meritorious nature of the saving work of Christ, or casual dismissal of this truth as unhelpful and expendable, is denial or dismissal of the cross as redemption. Rejection of the truth underlying redemption, namely, the righteousness of God, which demands that salvation be merited, makes God out for a fool in going through the trouble of sending forth his own Son, made of a woman, made under the law. No believer whose heart has been touched by the greatness of the grace of God toward him in the incarnation of God's Son, in order to redeem him from the curse of the law, will lightly accede to Shepherd's suggestion that we dispense with the meritorious nature of the death of Jesus Christ.

With appeal to no other passage of the New Testament setting forth the suffering and death of Jesus Christ as meritorious, 2 Peter 2:1 reveals the nature of Christ's saving work, especially his death, as his buying of sinners: "the Lord that bought them."

Ignoring the controversy over the text's acknowledgment that the heretics *claimed* that Christ bought them, the text teaches that the nature of the death of Jesus Christ the Lord was that it was Christ's buying of humans. Jesus paid the price for the salvation of those sinners for whom he died. He earned, or merited, their salvation. Buying is earning, or meriting.

Denial of the meritorious nature of the saving work of Jesus Christ leaves all sinners unbought, unredeemed, and therefore still rightly the slaves of sin and Satan and justly doomed. No one has the right to saving union with Jesus Christ, to friendship with God, or to eternal life.

Possibility and Necessity of Jesus' Meriting

Jesus merited with God. As the genuinely human head of his people, conceived and born into the lowly condition of the human race that had fallen into sin and plunged itself into death, although without sin himself, and having made himself responsible for the guilt of his people, he earned the right to exalt himself, as a genuine human, to the highest level of life and glory possible for a human. This is the reward merited by Jesus that is described in Philippians 2: "Wherefore," because he humbled himself and became obedient unto death, even the death of the cross, "God also hath highly exalted him, and given him a name which is above every name" (vv. 8–9).

As the head of his guilty people, Jesus merited not only for himself, but also for them. He earned for them deliverance from the dishonor of the race that plunged itself into the shame of sin and death by Adam's disobedience. He merited also for them the bestowal of "the image of the heavenly" that far exceeds the glory of Adam in paradise (1 Cor. 15:35–58).

Mere man cannot merit with God. The reason is not only that all the deeds of mere men are defiled with sin, so that they deserve punishment. But the reason is also that meriting requires that one perform more than is commanded him, more than he owes to God. This is the word of Jesus in Luke 17:10: "So likewise ye, when ye shall have done all those things which are commanded you, say, We are unprofitable servants: we have done that which was our duty to do." Mere man owes God perfect obedience. Perfect obedience on the part of mere man could not merit.

Jesus could merit. First, he paid to God obedience that he himself personally did not owe. Freely, willingly, he who is the second person of the Trinity became a man. Freely, he subjected himself to the penalty of death and damnation owed to God by the elect human race of which he had voluntarily become the head. To this penalty he himself was not liable. Freely, graciously, he took upon himself, as a genuine human, the obligation to obey the law of God perfectly in the stead of and on behalf of the disobedient people of whom he was the representative head. This duty was not his obligation naturally, he being as to his person God the Son.

Jesus could and did merit, second, because he is God as to his person and divine nature. Mere man can never merit with God, contrary to the heresy of the Roman Catholic Church. But God can merit with God. God the Son can merit with God the Father.

To the objection of the new perspective and of the federal vision that it is contrary to the relationship of Father and Son—a relationship of love—to represent the redeeming work of Jesus as meriting with the Father, the reply is that in reality this objection is objection against the entire mediatory work of Jesus as Savior. Federal vision theologian Rich Lusk makes this objection against the doctrine of the meritorious nature of the saving work of Jesus Christ. He charges, as a grievous fault of the theology of merit, that it regards Jesus as "a dutiful servant who has to earn favor." Lusk then asks a series of rhetorical questions that are intended to expose the theology of merit as utterly erroneous: "Is this really the way the beloved Son related to his Father during his ministry? As an employee earning wages? As a hired gun fulfilling the terms of a contract?" Lusk's conclusion concerning Jesus' meriting is this: "Jesus *never* had to earn the favor of God. He was never a 'Dutiful Employee' but *always* a 'Beloved Son.'"[41]

To this appeal by the federal vision to God's fatherhood regarding Jesus as dispensing with merit and to this heresy's appeal to divine love as rendering justice unnecessary, if not ungodly, the reply is that in reality this objection is against the entire mediatory work of Jesus as Savior from sin. Is it not, on the thinking of the new perspective and of the federal vision, contrary to the relation of Father and Son that the Father should make the Son the object of his punitive wrath from the very conception and birth of the Son? Is it not contrary to the relationship of Father and Son that the Father should pour out upon the Son, on the accursed tree, all the vials of his wrath, so that the Son must cry out, in the extremity of his anguish, "My God, my God [not 'My Father'], why hast thou forsaken me?" Is it not contrary to the relationship of Father and Son, as to the Father's infinite love for his Son, that the Father should condemn the Son to the misery of eternal hell?

By this objection of the new perspective and of the federal vision against the truth of the meritorious nature of the redeeming work of Jesus Christ, these heretical movements within evangelicalism and within reputedly conservative Presbyterian and Reformed churches clearly identify themselves as foes of the redeeming ministry and redemptive work of Jesus Christ at their very heart.

Jesus the eternal Son could and did merit with his Father in his human nature, in his genuine manhood, as a real man. This meriting was the very mission on which his Father sent him and the very mission on which the eternal Son came into our world

41 Lusk, "A Response to 'The Biblical Plan of Salvation,'" in Beisner, *The Auburn Avenue Theology*, 137.

as the man Jesus. "God sent forth his Son...*in order to* redeem them that were under the law" (the literal Greek text of Gal. 4:4–5, emphasis added). This meriting was the office of Jesus as the Messiah, the Christ.

Opposition to the meritorious nature of the saving work of Jesus by the new perspective and the federal vision is no minor theological squabble. It is the denial of the redemptive work of Jesus. It is the denial of Jesus as the Christ of God. It is the old liberalism dressed up for the seduction of contemporary evangelicals, Presbyterians, and Reformed. According to theological liberalism, old and new, God is only love, without justice. Love saves at the expense of justice, which is the disparagement of love and the denial of justice. The justice of God is obnoxious to liberal, that is, unbelieving, theology.

The Reformed faith, on the contrary, finds the necessity of all of Christ's humbling of himself, especially his death, in the "justice and truth of God":

> Why was it necessary for Christ to suffer death?
>
> Because, by reason of the justice and truth of God, satisfaction for our sins could be made no otherwise than by the death of the Son of God.[42]

42 Heidelberg Catechism Q&A 40, in Schaff, *Creeds of Christendom*, 3:320.

Chapter Nineteen

THE MERIT OF CHRIST'S ACTIVE OBEDIENCE

The establishing beyond all doubt that the work of Jesus Christ was meritorious leaves still the question, emphatically raised by the new perspective and the men of the federal vision, whether the active obedience of Christ was meritorious, as well as the passive obedience, or only the passive obedience.

The distinction between the two aspects of Christ's obedience is theological, not explicitly biblical. The theological distinction refers to Christ's obedience in all his ministry to the will of God (his active obedience) and his obedience in suffering the punishing wrath of God against the sins of God's elect people, especially in his crucifixion (his passive obedience). N. T. Wright and the men of the federal vision promote their wholesale rejection of the meritorious nature of Christ's redemptive work, including his suffering and death, by a noisy attack on Christ's active obedience. By exposing the teaching of an active obedience of Christ as unbiblical, they intend to weaken, if not negate, also the truth that Christ's passive obedience was meritorious.

Norman Shepherd is guilty of this duplicitous method of denying the meritorious nature of the work of Christ. In the book *A Faith That Is Never Alone*, Shepherd argues at length that neither Calvin, nor the Reformed confessions, nor the Bible clearly and incontrovertibly teaches the active obedience of Christ as meritorious. The very title of his article is crafted to leave the impression that Shepherd's controversy is with a meritorious active obedience of the Savior. The title is, "The Imputation of Active Obedience."[1] Shepherd concludes his study of the issue raised in the title of his article by asserting that he has effectively challenged the doctrine of "the imputation of the *active* obedience of Christ for the justification of sinners."[2]

Likewise, Shepherd's defender Ralph F. Boersema, although in reality denying merit altogether regarding Christ's saving work, is at pains to leave the impression that the issue is the meritorious nature of Christ's active obedience. In the chapter titled, "Imputation of Christ's Active Obedience?" Boersema contends that Christ's "active obedience was not a means of earning the inheritance for us. An inheritance is a gift not a purchase! His active obedience was not imputed to us for righteousness," that is, it was not part of the meritorious work of Christ on our behalf.[3]

Rich Lusk also is outspoken in his rejection of the active obedience of Christ being part of the righteousness imputed to the believer (although Lusk objects to ["legal"] imputation as such): "The imputation/transfer of the active obedience of Christ... never really finds a home in Paul's description of salvation."[4]

Rather than having been meritorious, the active obedience of Christ has only the significance that it enabled Christ to offer the perfect, sinless sacrifice to God. Ignoring that—in the end the men of the federal vision oppose the meritorious nature of the work of Christ in its entirety—their deceptive argument proceeds by a strong rejection of the merit of Christ's active

---

1 Shepherd, "The Imputation of Active Obedience," in Sandlin, *A Faith That Is Never Alone*, 249–278.

2 Ibid., 278; emphasis added.

3 Boersema, *Not of Works*, 121.

4 Lusk, "From Birmingham, with Love," in Sandlin, *A Faith That Is Never Alone*, 136.

obedience. Ostensibly, they reject the merit of his active obedience in favor of the merit of his passive obedience, that is, his suffering and death.

Testimony of the Creeds

The orthodox Reformed response to the denial of the active obedience of Christ must be and is that also Christ's active obedience was meritorious. The fact is that the active and passive obedience of Christ simply cannot be so sharply distinguished as they are in the theology of the federal vision, and perhaps in Reformed theology itself. First, the so-called passive obedience of Christ cannot be restricted to Jesus' cruel suffering and shameful death at the very end of his ministry. As the Heidelberg Catechism teaches in answer 37, the meaning of the confession in the Apostles' Creed, "He suffered," is that

> *all the time he lived on earth*, but especially at the end of his life, he bore, in body and soul, the wrath of God against the sin of the whole human race, in order that by his passion, as the only atoning sacrifice, he might redeem our body and soul from everlasting damnation, and obtain for us the grace of God, righteousness, and eternal life.[5]

The suffering of Jesus Christ was meritorious. "He bore…the wrath of God against…sin…in order that…he might redeem… and obtain." It was lifelong: "all the time." This meritorious suffering pervaded all his life and actions: "in body and soul."

Second, the so-called passive obedience was intense and strenuous activity on the part of Jesus. Jesus was not passive in his lifelong suffering. Actively, he accepted, entered into, and willingly endured the suffering. Actively, he bore the cross.

5 Heidelberg Catechism A 37, in Schaff, *Creeds of Christendom*, 3:319; emphasis added.

Actively, he descended into hell. Actively, he subjected himself to the torments of hell in body and soul. At the end of the six hours, hell had exhausted itself in Jesus. No flame flickered that he had not actively bid burn itself out in him. Regardless of the theological distinction and its usefulness, active and passive have no objective, clearly defined reality in the ministry of Jesus.

Third, the life and ministry of Jesus Christ were one. They were one, whole and entire, massive act of obedience to the will of God. This one obedient life and ministry merited both deliverance from damnation and the right to life eternal. All of that life, including both the active doing of God's will, for example, the exhausting labor of teaching the truth and the passive suffering of God's wrath, was one gigantic reality of obedience on behalf of and in the stead of a people guilty of disobedience.

Fourth, the justice of God required of the representative head of the elect, new human race the perfect fulfillment of his will for humans, as well as the suffering of the punishment due to them for their sin.

In justification the totality of the obedience of Jesus Christ, active as well as passive (if we are determined to distinguish), is imputed to the believing sinner. It is legally with the justified sinner not only as if he had suffered fully the punishment deserved by his sinfulness and sin, but also as if he had perfectly kept all the commandments of God and broken none of them.

The fact that justification includes the imputation to the sinner of the active obedience of Christ, so that the legal standing of the sinner before the judgment seat of the just God is as though the sinner had perfectly obeyed the law of God, is the clear testimony of another Reformed confession, the Reformed Form for the Administration of the Lord's Supper: "The perfect righteousness of Christ is imputed and freely given him [everyone who believes] as his own, yea, so perfectly as if he had satisfied in his own person for all his sins *and fulfilled all righteousness*."[6] The form refers to two aspects of the righteousness of Christ that is imputed to believers: satisfaction for sins and fulfillment of all righteousness.

The major Reformed creeds emphasize the oneness of the life and ministry of Christ as meritorious obedience, including both the active obedience of his life and the passive obedience of his death. Questions 60 and 61 of the Heidelberg Catechism include the "holiness of Christ" with his "satisfaction" as the meritorious righteousness that is imputed to the believer by faith. Christ's holiness was his consecration of himself to God in perfect love, taking form in obedience to the divine law not only in all his actions, but also in all his thoughts and desires. Not only is his "satisfaction" imputed to the believer, that is, according to the theological distinction, his passive obedience, but also his "holiness," that is, his active obedience. The benefit of this imputation is not only that the state of the believer is "as if I had never committed nor had any sin," that is, forgiveness, but also as if "I...had myself accomplished all the obedience which Christ has fulfilled for me."[7]

Let him who dares strip any aspect of the life and ministry from the holiness of Christ, the servant of Jehovah. All the obedience of his one, entire life and ministry is the righteousness of the justified believer.

Similarly, article 22 of the Belgic Confession describes the entirety of the saving work of Jesus Christ as meritorious and affirms that the whole of it is imputed to the believer. It is

---

6 Form for the Administration of the Lord's Supper, in *Confessions and Church Order*, 268; emphasis added. This form is an authoritative creed in all Reformed churches that stand in the tradition of the Dutch Reformed churches. This same form testifies that believing "remembrance" of Jesus Christ in the sacrament includes that, in addition to assurance of Christ's suffering and death for us, one is "confidently persuaded...that He hath fulfilled for us all obedience to the divine law and righteousness" (Ibid., 270).

7 Heidelberg Catechism Q&A 60–61, in Schaff, *Creeds of Christendom*, 3:326–27.

enough to silence the men of the federal vision that the article affirms that Jesus Christ imputes to us "all his merits, and so many holy works, which he hath done for us and in our stead." Not solely his suffering is imputed, but also "so many holy works," all of which are his "merits…for us and in our stead." Thus he is "our Righteousness."[8]

Conclusive as these lines are regarding the question whether in justification also the active obedience of Christ is imputed to the believer, the article is even clearer and stronger. Justifying "faith…is an instrument with which we embrace Christ our Righteousness." The truth is that Jesus Christ himself in the entirety of himself, God and perfectly holy man, and in the whole of his obedience to the Father, active and passive, is one, enormous, infinite mass of merit. All of this faith embraces, because it embraces Jesus himself, so that all this merit becomes the righteousness of the believer by imputation. Nothing that makes up Jesus Christ—nothing!—including his glorious active obedience to the will of his Father, is or may be deleted from "all His merits" that become the elect believer's by faith.

Imputed to the believer for righteousness with God is the one, whole, massive, meritorious Jesus Christ. The self-righteous men of the federal vision evidently can get by with less. As for me, I am in great need of all of him, as my righteousness with God the just judge.

Against the opposition of the new perspective and of the federal vision to the meritorious nature of Jesus' saving work stand the Canons of Dordt in many articles. Defending sovereign, gracious election as the source of salvation against the error of making faith the "condition" of election, the Canons charge that this error makes "the merits of Christ…of none effect."[9]

The grand defense of effectual, limited atonement, in the

8 Belgic Confession 22, in ibid., 3:408.

9 Canons of Dordt 1, error 3, in *Confessions and Church Order*, 160.

second head of doctrine, describes the redemption of the cross as "merited" and charges the heresy of universal atonement as the "despising…of the merits of Jesus Christ."[10] The same head of doctrine condemns those who "teach that Christ, by His satisfaction, merited neither salvation itself for anyone, nor faith."[11]

The fifth head of doctrine of the Canons, confessing the perseverance of elect saints, finds the impossibility of the falling away of saints in its being "impossible" that "the merit…of Christ be rendered ineffectual."[12]

Those in Reformed churches who today oppose the theology of the merit of Christ's redemptive work, or even minimize the importance of proclaiming that work as meritorious, are opposing the Reformed creeds. Thus they are refuted, and their theology is condemned. The Reformed churches of which they are faithless members must not debate them, especially not in a friendly, supposedly scholarly fashion. But the churches must discipline them as the heretics they are and plainly show themselves to be.

Testimony of Scripture

In thus proclaiming the saving work of Jesus Christ as one, undivided, meritorious whole, the Reformed creeds express the teaching of scripture. One such passage is Romans 5:12–21. There is comparison between Adam and Christ as covenantal heads. As Adam earned death for all the race, whom he represented, so Christ earned life for the elect race, whom he represented. Meriting is on the foreground in the passage. Adam not only infected the race with sinfulness, in that the race "inherits" sin from Adam. But the sin of Adam is "imputed" to all humans, and therefore death righteously "passed upon all

10 Canons of Dordt 2, error 1, in ibid., 164.

11 Canons of Dordt 2, error 3, in ibid., 165.

12 Canons of Dordt 5.8, in Schaff, *Creeds of Christendom*, 3:594.

men" (v. 12). The human race *deserves* death because it is guilty of Adam's disobedience.

Likewise, Jesus Christ merited eternal life for his church. The meritorious obedience of Jesus "constitutes" (the meaning of the Greek word translated as "made" in verse 19 in the King James Bible, referring to a legal action) his many people righteous, just as the disobedience of Adam constituted the entire race sinners. As righteous by the meritorious work of Jesus, the elect race is worthy of eternal life.

The second noteworthy feature of Romans 5 is that it describes the meritorious work of Jesus Christ as his "obedience": "By the obedience of one shall many be made [legally constituted] righteous" (v. 19). The Holy Spirit does not specify the passive obedience, the suffering and death, but attributes the righteousness of the justifying work of Jesus to his "obedience."

This is not to deny that on the foreground, as the outstanding, fundamental aspect of the obedience of Christ, also in Romans 5, are Jesus' suffering and death. What is significant is that scripture views that death as *obedience*. The death of Christ becomes the righteousness of the believer not simply inasmuch as it was payment of the debt, suffering of the punishment due, or even satisfaction of offended justice. The death of Christ is the righteousness of the believer inasmuch as it was obedience to the will of God, which will the sinner is guilty of disobeying, beginning already with the sin of Adam. "By one man's *disobedience* many were made [constituted] sinners" (v. 19, emphasis added).

Also Hebrews 10:1–14 emphasizes that the ministry of Jesus Christ, culminating in his sacrifice of himself in fulfillment of the typical sacrifices of the Old Testament, was essentially Jesus' performance of the will of God. The entire ministry of Jesus was a matter of obeying God's will: "Lo, I come to do thy will, O God" (v. 9; see also v. 7).

The Reformed faith stands on solid biblical ground when it includes the entire ministry of the Savior, active and passive obedience, in the substitutionary work of righteousness that is imputed to the believer by faith.

It must be apparent to even the dullest theological mind that the men of the federal vision entertain the strongest aversion to the basic biblical and Reformed truth of justification as imputation—the act of God consisting of a legal reckoning of the obedience of Christ, whether active or passive, to the account of the guilty but believing sinner. It is this aversion that underlies the questioning of, and even attack on, the "merit" of Christ's work.

Federal Vision "Maturing"

Striking and significant in the theology of the federal vision is its substitution of "maturing" for meriting. This is the explanation, first, of Jesus' own advance from the lowly state into which he was born unto the exalted state of heavenly glory in his resurrection. According to James B. Jordan, Jesus did not earn this state of glory. Rather, he "matured to the point of being fit for it [glory]."[13] Jordan applies his new "maturation" theology to our salvation: "What we receive is not Jesus' merits, but His maturity."[14]

Rich Lusk spells out the federal vision heterodoxy of maturing into righteousness. Having rejected the Reformed creedal orthodoxy of Christ's meriting eternal life for himself and his people, Lusk has Jesus maturing into eternal life, and his people maturing with him, although his people must exert themselves to share in this maturity. "Jesus becomes the first mature man… The incarnate Son has matured into full Father-like-ness… Because of His maturation, the church is now called to grow up into maturity as well."[15]

---

13 Jordan, "Merit Versus Maturity," in Wilkins and Garner, *The Federal Vision*, 193–94.

14 Ibid., 195.

15 Lusk, "A Response to 'The Biblical Plan of Salvation,'" in Beisner, *The Auburn Avenue Theology*, 139.

This, it must be remembered, is the federal vision's re-doing, more accurately undoing, of Jesus' meriting eternal life for himself and his people and of his imputation of righteousness to believers by faith in him.

Although the word and notion of maturation are the favorite replacements of the truth of meriting for many of the men of the federal vision, others prefer to replace meriting with inheriting. This is true of Ralph Boersema. Defending the theology of Shepherd, Boersema rejects the thought that Christ earned, or merited, the kingdom of heaven for his people. Rather, Christ "inherited the Kingdom for us rather than purchasing it."[16]

One last, grievous error of the theology of the federal vision that contributes to its rejection of merit on the part of Jesus Christ, which then is imputed to the believer, must be noted. The men of the federal vision argue that because Adam's obedience in paradise was not, and could not be, meritorious, Christ's obedience also was not meritorious.

The men of the federal vision take issue with the popular, if not prevailing, thinking among Reformed theologians that Adam might have merited the higher, eternal life that Christ has now won for the church by Adam's obedience to the "probationary" prohibition against eating the fruit of the tree of the knowledge of good and evil. The vigorous argument of the men of the federal vision is that, since Adam's obedience would not have been meritorious, the obedience of Jesus Christ likewise was not meritorious.

> In the Garden of Eden, before sin entered the world... God did not offer eternal life contingent on man's merit or achievement or good works. In fact, the narrative of Genesis 1–2 asserts nothing whatever, explicitly or

16 Boersema, *Not of Works*, 140.

implicitly, about man's meriting or achieving eternal life, and neither does any other Biblical text.[17]

From their postulate that Adam could not merit, the men of the federal vision conclude that neither could Christ merit eternal life.

Here the controversy of the Reformed faith over the meritorious nature of Christ's saving work becomes murky. On the one hand, some who defend the meritorious nature of the obedience of Christ base this conviction on the notion that Adam might have merited the higher, eternal life for himself and the human race by obeying the command not to eat of the forbidden fruit. So much is this so, that the Presbyterian Meredith Kline declares that "if the first Adam could not earn anything, neither could the second."[18]

On the other hand, the men of the federal vision argue that, since Adam could not merit, neither was the work of the second Adam meritorious. "If the first Adam was not required to earn merit through works, then the active obedience of the last Adam need not be regarded as meritorious either."[19]

These two doctrinal positions seem to put Reformed orthodoxy between a rock and a hard place. Either we must acknowledge that Adam could have merited eternal life, or we must deny the meritorious nature of the work of Christ. These two positions are only seeming alternatives, however. Reformed orthodoxy responds, or ought to respond, to this either/or with "a plague on both your houses."

First, Adam the first—mere earthly Adam—could not merit with God. Mere man can never merit with God. He can never

17 Sandlin, "The Gospel of Law and the Law of Gospel," in Sandlin, *A Faith That Is Never Alone*, 223. See also Lusk, "A Response to 'The Biblical Plan of Salvation,'" in Beisner, *The Auburn Avenue Theology*, 121–26.

18 Meredith Kline, quoted in Lusk, "A Response to 'The Biblical Plan of Salvation,'" in Beisner, *The Auburn Avenue Theology*, 137.

19 Lusk, "From Birmingham, with Love," in Sandlin, *A Faith That Is Never Alone*, 142.

do more than his duty. By refraining from the fruit of the tree of the knowledge of good and evil, Adam would only have been confirmed in the state in which he had been created, a joyful, earthly life in paradise. And the human race would have enjoyed this earthly life with father Adam.

Reformed and Presbyterian theology has been seriously wrong in what is generally considered to be the traditional doctrine of "the covenant of works" with Adam. Herman Hoeksema and the Protestant Reformed Churches have been calling this error to the attention of the Reformed churches for many years.[20] Now the error contributes to the promotion of grievous heresy: the denial of the meritorious nature of Christ's work and of justification by faith alone. Effectively refuting the doctrine that Adam might have merited eternal life—the alleged ground of the doctrine that Christ merited eternal life—the men of the federal vision conclude triumphantly that thereby they have also refuted the doctrine that Christ merited eternal life.

The plague on the second house consists of affirming that, although indeed Adam could not merit the eternal life that Christ has earned for himself and his elect church, Jesus Christ *could* merit and did. He who is "the Lord from heaven," as 1 Corinthians 15:47 describes him, in distinction from the "first man...of the earth, earthy," had the unique qualifications to earn the highest, eternal life.

The objection by the men of the federal vision against Christ's meriting on the ground of Adam's not meriting is therefore empty. What further weakens the already impotent argument of the federal vision is that, despite its contention that Adam could not have *merited* eternal life, the federal vision

20 Hoeksema, "The Covenant with Adam," in *Reformed Dogmatics*, 214–26. For a more recent critique of the doctrine of the covenant with Adam as a conditional contract by which Adam might have merited eternal life, see my "The Covenant of Creation with Adam."

affirms that Adam might *otherwise have obtained* for himself and the entire human race the high, glorious, eternal life that Jesus Christ has merited for the church.

According to the federal vision, by obeying the command not to eat of the tree of knowledge Adam would have "matured into" the eternal life or "inherited" eternal life. Rich Lusk speaks for the men of the federal vision:

> His [Adam's] glorious starting position was a free blessing; the mature, eschatological life he was implicitly promised upon condition of perfect, faithful obedience would have been a gift as well. He was a favored son awaiting an inheritance, not an employee seeking an earned wage.[21]

Ignoring that obtaining eternal life by fulfilling a "condition" is, in fact, earning, the federal vision has no objection to Adam's obtaining for himself and the race the eternal life that Christ has won for the church. The only concern of the federal vision is the manner in which Adam might have done this: fulfilling a condition rather than meriting (as though this distinction amounts to a difference).

The *grievous* error of Lusk and the federal vision is their failure to realize that Adam could not have obtained eternal, heavenly life by any means or in any way whatever. Only Jesus Christ could take the human race higher than the life of the earthly paradise of Genesis 1 and 2. Only Jesus Christ could realize the most glorious, eternal life for humans. Only Jesus Christ is God the Son in human flesh. Only Jesus Christ could *earn* this highest, most glorious life for humans by his unique obedience.

Once and for all, Reformed theology must renounce its

21 Lusk, "From Birmingham, with Love," in Sandlin, *A Faith That Is Never Alone*, 142.

erroneous doctrine of Adam's possibly obtaining for all humans what Jesus Christ has obtained, by meriting, for the human race of the elect out of all nations. If the contemporary heresy of the federal vision does nothing more than occasion a critical re-examination of the traditional theory of a covenant of works with Adam whereby Adam might have earned eternal life, a good purpose of God with the federal vision will have been accomplished.

Reformed theologians might well be motivated to conduct this critical re-examination of the traditional theory of a covenant of works by the clear, powerful testimony of Colossians 1:13–29. God never purposed that Adam take the race into a higher, eternal life. God eternally decreed that, in the elect of all nations, the human race be exalted into the highest life and glory in and by Jesus Christ. This must and can only take place "through the blood of his cross," and therefore in the way of the fall of Adam. Not for Adam, even theoretically, were all things created in the beginning. Not upon Adam, even theoretically, did the resurrection of the creation into the glorious new creation and the glorification of the human race depend.

But on God's "dear Son," who is "the image of the invisible God," did all this glorification depend. The foundation of all this purpose of God is "redemption through his blood," merit imputed to the elect by faith, and by faith alone.

This is the heart of the Reformed faith, of Protestant Christianity, and of the gospel of grace of holy scripture.

For this, we contend against the new perspective on Paul and the federal vision.

Notice of Rejection of the Merit of "Active Obedience"

In all this contention over the active obedience of Christ, we are determined not to lose sight of the basic issue in the fight: justification by faith alone, against the false doctrine of justification by faith *and works*. In all their opposition, supposedly, to the merit of Christ's active obedience, the men of the federal vision are in reality opposing the truth of justification by faith alone, without works. The federal vision is not, at bottom, foe of the active obedience of Christ. It is foe of the Reformation, creedal, and gospel truth of justification by faith alone. Its fundamental theology is the Roman Catholic and semi-Pelagian heresy of justification by works.

Cautious as the men of the federal vision are, emphasize the rejection of *active* obedience as they do, in the end they cannot restrain themselves from making their heresy clearly evident, evident in so many words. First, they explain Romans 2:13 as teaching not what would have to be the case if justification were by the law, as Paul's heretical enemies were teaching, but what is actually the case. The text reads: "For not the hearers of the law are just before God, but the doers of the law shall be justified." Rome has always appealed to the text in support of its doctrine that the sinner is, in fact, justified by faith and by his own good works. The men of the federal vision agree.

With the entire Reformation, Calvin explained the text as hypothetical: if, as the Roman heresy teaches, justification is by works, it is not enough for the sinner to *hear* the law, but he must also *do* it, that is, obey the law perfectly. This, of course, is impossible for any sinner. Calvin wrote:

> To refute this mistaken impression [of the Jews in Paul's day, of the Roman Catholic Church in Calvin's day, and of the federal vision in our day] he asserts that the hearing or the knowledge of the law is not of such consequence as to afford righteousness, but that works must be brought forth in accordance with the saying, "He that doeth them shall live in them" (Lev. 18:5). The sense of this verse, therefore, is that if righteousness is sought by the law, the law must be fulfilled, for the righteousness of the law consists in the perfection of works...We can

> prove from this passage that no one is justified by works. If only those who fulfil the law are justified by the law, it follows that no one is justified, for no one can be found who can boast of having fulfilled the law.[22]

Calvin added, "Those who misinterpret this passage for the purpose of building up justification by works deserve universal contempt."[23]

Interpreting the text as teaching justification by works and thus making himself, and the theology of the federal vision on behalf of which he writes, the object of contempt, P. Andrew Sandlin has written: "He [Paul in Romans 2:13] acknowledged the life-giving power disclosed in the law by which a man is justified...(Rom. 2:13)...Nor is the law a rigorous code that one can never hope to meet."[24]

Second, with Rome and in opposition to Calvin and the Reformation, the men of the federal vision explain scripture's exclusion of works of the law in Romans 3:28 as merely the exclusion of *certain kinds* of works, not the exclusion of all works. The text reads: "We conclude that a man is justified by faith, without the deeds of the law." Rome has always explained the text as excluding only the ceremonial works of the Old Testament, which the Jews of Paul's day practiced and on which his Jewish adversaries insisted, not all works absolutely. On behalf of the Reformation, Calvin explained the text, rightly and as the text itself demands, as excluding all human works from God's justifying verdict upon the guilty sinner.

> Justification [as taught in Romans 3:28] is free in such a way as to make it quite evident that no merit of works can

22 Calvin, *The Epistles of Paul the Apostle to the Romans and to the Thessalonians*, 47.

23 Ibid.

24 Sandlin, "The Gospel of Law and the Law of Gospel," in Sandlin, *A Faith That Is Never Alone*, 238.

> at all be associated with it...It is quite absurd to restrict them [the "deeds of the law"] to ceremonial observances. It is also an erroneous misrepresentation to mean by the works of the law the works of the letter which are done without the Spirit of Christ.[25]

The federal vision sides with Rome in its explanation of Romans 3:28 and the other passages in Romans that exclude all works of the sinner himself from the divine act of justification. "'Works of the law' *denotes not the revelatory law, but a perversion of the law by the self-righteous, a Law without Christ.*"[26] Significantly, Sandlin then enlists on behalf of his doctrine of justification by faith *and by genuine good works* the doctrine of the conditionality of salvation, as taught and defended by such as Sinclair Ferguson.[27] Here Sandlin is right: the theology of a conditional salvation—the condition being faith—is, in fact, a form of the false "gospel" of salvation by works. The true gospel of grace is the good news of unconditional justification and salvation, that is, the good news that salvation does not depend upon the sinner but upon God alone.

Third, the federal vision bluntly asserts that the justification at the final judgment will be based not only on Jesus' work for his people, but also on his people's own good works. Arguing for a justification at the final judgment that will be based on the sinner's good works (*with significant appeal to Romans 2:13)*,

---

25 Calvin, *Epistle...to the Romans*, 79.

26 Sandlin, "The Gospel of Law and the Law of Gospel," in Sandlin, *A Faith That Is Never Alone*, 220. The emphasis is Sandlin's.

27 Ibid., 221. In defending the conditionality of the covenant, implying the falling away of saints—the denial of the perseverance of saints—Don Garlington is forced to take note of the confession of perseverance by the Canons of Dordt in the fifth head. His resolution of the problem of the Canons' contradiction of his doctrine of the falling away of saints is the condemnation of the Canons: "The 'five points' of [the Canons] are schematized and tend to be artificial" (Garlington, "Covenantal Nomism and the Exile," in Sandlin, *A Faith That Is Never Alone*, 391).

Rich Lusk has written: "Paul never says that a bare faith will be sufficient at the last day…Instead, he says the goal of final salvation remains contingent on conditions which are yet to be fulfilled."[28] So important will our own good works be for our justification in the final judgment that they "will be the *decisive* factor."[29] In the final judgment our good works will not be "merely verification of salvation." It is "better to call works a *condition* of final justification."[30]

Then—if not forgetting himself, certainly forgetting the Reformed creeds and the Protestant Reformation—in his obsession with promoting the heresy of justification by works, Lusk boldly and unambiguously exclaims, "The works that justify at the last day are the works that flow out of…faith."[31] These, of course, are the sinner's own good works. Making plain what he and the other men of the federal vision mean by their declaration that justification is by a "working faith," Lusk states that "faith and works justify conjointly…Final justification is by faith and works together."[32]

Attack on the active obedience of Christ as meritorious is merely a ploy on behalf of rejection of the meritorious nature of all of the work of Christ, including his suffering and death. Rejection of the meritorious nature of the work of Christ is the Trojan horse by which the heresy of justification by the works of the sinner himself is introduced into the Reformed and Presbyterian city of God.

Stripped of all its deceptive wording and argument, the theology of the federal vision is that, regardless of the truth of justification with respect to the provisional justification in time

---

28 Rich Lusk, "Future Justification," in Sandlin, *A Faith That Is Never Alone*, 317–18.

29 Ibid. The emphasis is Lusk's.

30 Ibid., 342. The emphasis is Lusk's.

31 Ibid., 343.

32 Ibid., 354.

and history, the final, ultimate, decisive justification in the day of Christ is by the good works of the sinner himself. Whatever role faith may play in the final judgment, good works are determinative of righteousness with God and of eternal salvation. This is another reason the men of the federal vision are so determined to deny the active obedience of Christ as having been meritorious. If his active obedience was meritorious, there would be no place at all for the sinner's own good works as the basis of his justification in the final judgment. Whatever Christ's passive obedience—his suffering and death—may have accomplished, the sinner's own active obedience plays the decisive role in the final, all-determining judgment in the day of Christ. For the federal vision justification is by the good works of the sinner himself.

The issue in the controversy of the Reformed faith with the federal vision is the gospel truth of justification by faith alone.

By faith alone without our own works.

Chapter Twenty

THE REWARD OF GRACE

A prominent argument on behalf of the meritorious nature of the good works of believers that we did not consider in the previous chapter is the biblical teaching that God rewards the good works of his people. One of the main arguments of the Roman Catholic Church on behalf of their contention that the good works of the faithful merit with God and that therefore justification is not by faith alone, but by faith and good works, is the undeniable biblical teaching that God rewards good works. For this reason the Heidelberg Catechism concludes its explanation and defense of justification by faith alone with the question, "How is it that our good works merit nothing, while yet it is God's will to reward them in this life and in that which is to come?"[1]

Rome's argument is simple and clear. The Bible teaches the reward of good works. Reward implies that these good works merit. If good works merit with God, justification is not by faith alone and of grace alone, but by faith and the works and worthiness of the sinner. In short, the biblical truth of the reward of works exposes the doctrine of justification by faith alone as erroneous. In defense of Rome's doctrine of justification by

1 Heidelberg Catechism Q 63, in Schaff, *Creeds of Christendom*, 3:327.

works, against the Protestant Reformation, the Council of Trent decreed:

> Life eternal is to be proposed to those working well *unto the end*, and hoping in God, both as a grace mercifully promised to the sons of God through Jesus Christ, and as a reward which is according to the promise of God himself, to be faithfully rendered to their good works and merits.[2]

In support of this appeal to the biblical teaching of the reward of good works, as grounding Rome's doctrine of the merit of good works and thus its doctrine of justification by faith and works, Trent appealed to the passages of scripture that teach the reward of good works, including Matthew 10:42, 1 Corinthians 4:5, and Matthew 16:27.

The Reformed faith does not, of course, deny that God will reward, and indeed does already in this life reward, the good works of his elect and justified people. In many places the Bible teaches that God will reward the good works of his people, especially those that consist of suffering for Christ's sake, but also such a seemingly insignificant work as giving a cup of cold water to the thirsty neighbor in the name of Jesus Christ.

Such is the prominence of the matter of the reward of good works in the controversy over justification and such is the importance of the truth of the reward for the Christian life that the subject is worthy of a chapter devoted to it in a book on justification.

In Matthew 5:10–12 Christ promises a great reward to the citizens of the kingdom of heaven for their suffering of reproach and persecution for his sake: "Rejoice and be exceeding glad: for great is your reward in heaven."

Revelation 11:17–18 promises that in the final judgment

2 Canons and Decrees of the Council of Trent, Sixth Session, Decree on Justification 16, in ibid., 2:107.

God will give a reward to his servants, to the prophets, to the saints, and to those who fear his name.

In Matthew 16:27 Jesus promises that he will reward every man according to his work.

Matthew 25:21, 23 has the Lord rewarding his "good and faithful" servants for their good works by making them rulers over "many things" in the new world.

Verses 31–46 of Matthew 25, the account of the final judgment, teach that Christ the judge will reward the sheep on his right hand for their works of feeding Christ's hungry brothers and sisters, showing them hospitality, visiting them in prison, and other acts of charity.

Hebrews 6:10 assures the struggling Hebrew Christians that God is not unrighteous "to forget your work and labour of love, which ye have shewed toward his name, in that ye have ministered to the saints."

In a significant passage especially for ministers of the word and sacraments, Paul applies the truth of the reward of good works to pastors. Every preacher will receive his own reward from Christ according to his own labor (1 Cor. 3:8). In this context the apostle warns some ministers, who are regenerated children of God but whose work is shoddy, that they will be saved, but their work will be burned and they will suffer loss, evidently loss of an element of the reward that Christ will give to diligent ministers (v. 15).

The letters to the seven churches in Revelation 2 and 3 are full of promises of Christ's reward of faithful work, both by the church and the individual member. There are also warnings of recompense of unfaithfulness.

These are only a few of the passages that teach the divine reward of good works. The sheer number of such passages indicates the importance of the truth of good works in the Christian gospel and regarding the Christian life.

Nature of the Reward

As to the nature of the reward, that is, what it consists of, scripture makes plain that the reward will be eternal life itself in the resurrection body and soul in the new creation. The reward will be the coming perfect salvation, nothing less—the bliss of communion with God in the presence of Jesus Christ and the glory of reigning with Christ over all things. For the sheep on Christ's right hand in the final judgment, the reward of their good works will be inheriting the kingdom and "life eternal" (Matt. 25:34, 46).

Romans 2:6–11 teaches that God will render to those "who by patient continuance in well doing seek for glory and honor and immortality" the reward of "eternal life."

To appeal to no other passage, Colossians 3:23–24 explicitly identifies the reward of good works as "the inheritance": "ye shall receive the reward of the inheritance."

Because the Bible teaches that the reward of the good works of the saints is eternal life, the implication of the Roman Catholic doctrine of a *merited* reward is that good works merit, or earn, eternal life with all its bliss and glory. If our good works merit the reward, the boast of all those who are saved will forever be, "I earned this salvation by my own good works." They will shout in the presence of God and in the face of Jesus Christ on the world's last day, and eternally, "Salvation is of me," rather than, "Salvation is of the Lord."

God forbid!

The truth of the reward includes one other important feature. There will be degrees of the glory of eternal life and of the blessedness of perfected salvation. These degrees of bliss and glory will be commensurate with the good works that God's people performed in their earthly lives. According as they worked out of love for God and the neighbor and in accordance with the good works they performed, they will receive from Christ the judge more splendid glory, more honorable responsibility, a higher place in the everlasting kingdom of Christ in the new creation.

All elect, justified, and sanctified Christians will receive the same salvation and eternal life. All will be perfectly blessed and blissful. All will be glorious. And the bliss and glory will be the reward of the good works that all performed. For in the final judgment it will become evident that all performed good works in some way, even though it may have been confessing Christ with one's dying breath, as was the case with the malefactor who was crucified with Christ. But there will be differences of degrees of glory, just as there will be degrees of shame and suffering in hell, according to the wicked works of the reprobate.

The punishment of the man or woman who rejected Christ in unbelief, even though he or she was born and raised in the sphere of the covenant, will be more severe than the punishment of the pagan, who only despised the revelation of God in nature. Jesus warned the scribes and Pharisees that theirs would be "the greater damnation" (Matt. 23:14). "According to her works," Babylon will receive "double" punishment. This very severe punishment is expressly called Babylon's "reward": "*Reward* her even as she rewarded you, and double unto her double according to her works" (Rev. 18:6, emphasis added).

As there will be degrees of shame and suffering in hell, according to the evil of the works of reprobate sinners, so also will there be degrees of glory and bliss enjoyed by the elect saints. These degrees of glory and bliss will correspond to the good works of the saints. The prophets and apostles will be more glorious than we. The minister who worked sacrificially and diligently in the office of the ministry will be more glorious than the one who too much sought his ease and comfort, giving his work of sermon preparation, catechism instruction, and visiting the needy a "lick-and-a-promise."

For the rest it is appropriate that one not attempt to make specific application of the truth of the reward of good works.

Many who were first in this life will be last in the life to come. Some who were last in the kingdom in history will be first in the kingdom in its eternal form. Rewarding his people will be part of the great work of Christ as judge. Only he has the necessary knowledge to reward rightly. Many laymen and laywomen who received little attention in the church in history will be more glorious than many a minister who did receive the praise of men. The wife and mother who bore patiently with a rough husband or even an unbelieving husband, for God's sake, raised her children in the fear of God, and prayed day and night, although taken for granted by her fellow saints, will be more glorious than many a professor of theology.

Because the quality and the circumstances of the work count for much with Christ, and not simply the quantity, the evildoer on the cross who confessed Christ—who *alone* confessed Christ when the Savior was denied and despised by all others—although that evildoer had but one good work, may well be more glorious in the new world than many who rather matter-of-factly, though not insincerely, confessed Christ their lives long in propitious circumstances.

An example that illustrates the truth of degrees of glory is that of glasses filled with wine. (I choose wine because the parable of the talents in Matthew 25:21 represents the reward of eternal life as entrance into the joy of our Lord, and wine is the symbol of that joy). When the multitude that no man can number receive eternal life in body and soul in the day of Christ, all the glasses will be full of wine. But the glasses will not all be the same size. Some will be larger and more capacious than others.

That the reward of good works includes degrees of glory for the blessed is clearly and repeatedly taught in the Bible. It is the teaching of all the passages that promise a reward according to one's works. Christ announces that at his coming, obviously in the final judgment, he will "reward" every man "according as his work shall be" (Rev. 22:12). If this passage could be explained as referring to the reward that corresponds to the two basic conditions of humans, holy by faith in Jesus and unholy because of unbelief, Luke 19:11–27 certainly teaches the reward of degrees of glory among those who are saved. One faithful servant of Christ is rewarded with rule over ten cities according as he had gained "ten pounds" for the Lord. Another faithful servant is rewarded with rule over five cities according as he had gained "five pounds" for the Lord. As has already been noted, 1 Corinthians 3:8 promises ministers in particular that "every man shall receive his own reward according to his own labour."

This then is the truth about the reward of good works. There certainly will be a reward of the good works of the children of God. The reward will be eternal life in varying degrees of bliss and glory. Both eternal life itself and the varying degrees of bliss and glory will correspond to, and marvelously accord with, the good works that the elect believers did in their earthly lives.

Non-Meritorious

This reward, however, will not have been merited, or earned, by the good works of the children of God. When we receive the reward, we will not receive it as something we deserve by virtue of our good works. If this were the case, we would merit eternal life itself, inasmuch as the Bible teaches that the reward is nothing less than eternal life. Nor will the degree of glory be what the child of God has earned by his works. When the apostle Paul is sitting on his throne, very near the Lord Jesus himself, the apostle will not say or even think, "This is what I deserve by all my apostolic labors and by my abundant suffering on behalf of the Lord Jesus." In fact, the great apostle never worked or suffered with the purpose of meriting either salvation or a high degree of glory.

When Christ the judge bestows the reward on his people, he will not be paying wages for which his people obligated him by their working. The Reformed faith denies neither the good works of believers nor God's reward of these good works. But it denies that the reward is merited. "We do good works, but not to merit by them (for what can we merit?)."[3]

What then is the explanation of the reward of good works? If the explanation is not merit, what is the explanation?

The Heidelberg Catechism considers the Roman Catholic argument against justification by faith alone and for her doctrine of justification and salvation by meritorious works in question 63: "How is it that our good works merit nothing, while yet it is God's will to reward them in this life and in that which is to come?" The response of the Catechism and its explanation of the reward of good works is, "The reward comes not of merit, but of grace."[4] The reward of good works is a *gracious* reward. Therefore, the reward of works is in perfect harmony with the biblical teaching of justification by faith alone and salvation by grace alone.

The Belgic Confession expresses the same truths, namely, that God rewards the good works of his people and that the reward is a reward of grace: "We do not deny that God rewards good works, but it is through his grace that he crowns his gifts."[5] "Crowns his gifts" is not only a lovely figure, but also a doctrinally exact explanation. In rewarding our good works, God places the crowning grace upon the grace of our performance of good works. Grace for grace!

When the Reformed faith denies that the reward will be meritorious, the meaning is that good works do not deserve the reward; that good works do not obligate God or put him into the believer's debt; that good works are not in any respect whatever the believer's contribution to God, as though the believer by these works is giving to God something of his own, something

---

3 Belgic Confession 24, in ibid., 3:411.

4 Heidelberg Catechism Q&A 63, in ibid., 3:327.

5 Belgic Confession 24, in ibid., 3:412.

that God has not himself given to the believer; and that the reward is not payment earned.

The Bible, which certainly teaches a reward of good works, also teaches that the reward will be gracious, not merited. This the Bible teaches in the following prominent truths. First, the elect, believing saint is conceived and born dead in sin by nature, incapable of any good, whether the ability to perform good works or the ability of a free will, that is, the ability to choose for God and the good. By nature the believer has nothing, absolutely nothing, that he can contribute of himself to God and his kingdom.

> And you hath he quickened, who were dead in trespasses and sins…[You] were by nature the children of wrath, even as others…When we were dead in sins, [God] hath quickened us…by grace ye are saved…For by grace are ye saved…not of works…For we are his workmanship, created in Christ Jesus unto good works, which God hath before ordained that we should walk in them. (Eph. 2:1–12)

Second, the ability to know, love, will, and do the good is the gift of God to his child, by the regenerating Spirit of Christ, in pure divine grace (John 3:3–8; Rom. 8:1–10). God must create us "unto good works," according to Ephesians 2:10: "created in Christ Jesus unto good works." That is, God must perform a work upon us and in us that is comparable to his marvelous work of creating the universe in the beginning. Otherwise, we would not be able to perform one very small and insignificant good work. It is important in Ephesians 2:10 also to notice that good works do not precede salvation, described in the text as a new creation, or condition our salvation or earn salvation. We do not work in order to be saved. But we are saved in order to work. Good works are the result and fruit of gracious salvation. This relationship of salvation and good works is crystal clear in

Ephesians 2. For the teaching that good works earn or condition salvation, there is no excuse.

Third, not only does the Spirit of Christ give the elect child of God the ability to do the good, but the Spirit of Christ actually works the willing and doing, so that the performance of good works is the almighty doing of the Spirit in and through the believing child of God. According to Philippians 2:13, "It is God which worketh in you both to will and to do of his good pleasure." The Greek original of the text is, if this is possible, even stronger: "It is God which worketh in you both the willing and the doing." This is not a denial that the believer himself truly does the good works, what verse 12 refers to as the working out of one's own salvation. Neither is this a minimizing of the importance and worth of the activity of the believer in performing good works. It is, however, the clear and powerful reminder that all the believer's good works originate in the grace of God and that even the believer's doing of the works is the product of the working of divine grace in him.

Fourth, the ultimate source of all the good works of every believer is the gracious, eternal counsel of God. Ephesians 2:10, quoted above, teaches that not only has the believer been created unto good works, but also that God has ordained beforehand all the good works that every believer performs: "unto good works, which God hath before ordained that we should walk in them." In the eternal decree of election, in which God chose each member of his church unto salvation, he also ordained all the good works that each of them would perform in his or her lifetime.

It is not so that God merely ordained that all of his children would perform good works, leaving it up to them or their circumstances to determine what and how many those good works would be. But he ordained all of the particular good works that each of them would perform. He ordained that Ruth would cleave to Naomi and, in spite of all the hardships attendant on a widowed Moabite's becoming part of the nation of

Israel, declare, "Thy God shall be my God," thus becoming the great-grandmother of Jesus. He ordained that Paul would withstand Peter to his face at Antioch because of Peter's compromise of the gospel of salvation by (unconditional) grace. He ordained that Luther would stand against the whole world at the Diet of Worms and make his glorious testimony before the princes of this world. He ordained that the Christian woman, treacherously abandoned by her faithless husband, would remain unmarried as long as her husband lives, in obedience to the word of God concerning marriage.

Ephesians 2:10 teaches that our good works are not our contribution to God, but his gift to us. Inasmuch as the decree of election, in which God ordained not only us but also all our good works, is a gracious decree, his ordaining of our works is a gracious gift of these works to us.

The Belgic Confession puts into the mouths of Reformed Christians that a reason they do not perform good works "to merit by them" is that "we are beholden to God for the good works we do, and not he to us." The biblical basis for this confession is Philippians 2:13.[6]

Here we must notice something about a life of good works that all too often we forget. Serving Christ by our good works is a privilege, not only our duty or calling. We are indebted to God that we may and can perform good works. It is not the case that we are indebted to God for forgiveness, peace, and hope, but that God is indebted to us for the good works we perform. Good works are an aspect of his salvation of us, and we are indebted to him for the right and ability to do them.

What, after all, is the alternative to a life of good works? The shame, folly, vanity, and misery of a life of evil deeds in slavery to the devil! Surely every pastor has seen at close range the devastating, painful effects on sinners and the destructive consequences

6 Belgic Confession 24, in ibid., 3:411–12.

on that slice of the earthly sphere of life that they occupy of the life of disobedience of these sinners. How the family life, the social life, and the personal life of the drunkard suffer unmitigated misery! How the fornicator destroys his or her accomplices, scatters his or her offspring to the winds, fatally weakens society as he or she undermines its very foundation, and comes at last to ruin himself or herself! At best, the earthly life of the ungodly, regardless how comfortable, is a life of vanity. Over it hangs the certainty of death. It ends in the grave. God impresses on the soul of the ungodly, all his life long, the terrifying reminder, "Remember, O man, you must die." That a life of good works is a life of deprivation and joylessness, whereas a life of sin is pleasant, fulfilling, and glamorous, is not the least of Satan's deceits.

The one who performs good works has the right and privilege of serving the one, true God and his glorious Son. He has the right and privilege of living a meaningful, worthwhile, and happy life in the world. By such a life he escapes the shame and misery that attend and destroy a life of evil works. This says nothing yet about the reward in the life to come.

That our good works are God's gift to us and a privilege for us is true regarding all our good works, including bearing reproach, enduring hardship, and suffering persecution for God's sake. Concerning suffering, Philippians 1:29 says that unto us Christians "it is *given*...to suffer for his [Christ's] sake" (emphasis added).

This truth of our good works being God's gift to us, not our contribution to God, must live in our consciousness more than it does, altogether apart from our controversy with Rome and others about meritorious good works. All too often we find ourselves thinking that we are doing something for God, especially when the way and work become difficult and costly. The truth is that God is graciously privileging us to work some little thing on behalf of his Son. We must thank God for the privilege of performing the good works that fall to our lives.

In passing I observe that Reformed Christians must learn from Ephesians 2:10 the importance of our doing good works. So important is this that God ordained the good works that we should perform. The text is the death of the antinomian heresy, that is, the doctrine that salvation by grace implies the license to sin or, at least, carelessness concerning obedience to the law of God on the part of the graciously saved sinner. If salvation is God's creation of his people unto good works and if when he ordained his people unto eternal life he also ordained good works for them to walk in, a life of good works is important to God and necessary for his people.

That good works do not merit is in no way the minimizing of the importance of good works in the lives of the saved. The preaching that condemns the doctrine that good works merit may not leave the impression that the exhortation to good works is suspect in the Reformed religion, and then fail to give the exhortation.

That we have no right to perform good works, having lost this right in the fall of Adam, so that by nature every human deserves only to serve Satan with the cruel service of the slave-labor of sinning, points to another way in which it is true that the reward of our good works is gracious. Christ Jesus earned for his people the right to perform good works. It cost God his own Son to get for us the right to live lives of sanctification, that is, lives of good works. "[Jesus Christ] gave himself for us, that he might redeem us from all iniquity, and purify unto himself a peculiar people, zealous of good works" (Titus 2:14). If the foundation of zeal for good works is the cross of Christ, God's reward of the good works of his people is a reward of grace.

Other important scriptural, confessional, and experiential considerations verify the Reformed confession that the reward of good works is not a merited reward but a reward of grace. One is that every one of the good works of God's child is defiled and tainted with sin, whereas God demands sinless perfection. Were

God to judge any one of his children strictly on the basis of the merit of his good works, his good works would damn him. Not only would his completely sinful works damn him, but also his imperfect good works would damn him.

This is the confession of the Reformed faith in question 62 of the Heidelberg Catechism: “But why can not our good works be the whole or part of our righteousness before God?” This is the same as to ask, “Why cannot our good works *merit*?” The Catechism answers, “Because the righteousness which can stand before the judgment-seat of God must be perfect throughout, and wholly conformable to the divine law; whereas even our best works in this life are all imperfect and defiled with sin.”[7]

The Belgic Confession binds the same truth on the consciences of all believers:

> Though we do good works, we do not found our salvation upon them; for we can do no work but what is polluted by our flesh, and also punishable; and although we could perform such works, still the remembrance of one sin is sufficient to make God reject them.[8]

Merit Exposed by Romans 7

This teaching of the Catechism is solidly based on Romans 7. Here the apostle, speaking of himself not only as a sanctified child of God, but also as undoubtedly one of the holiest humans who has ever lived, cries out, “I am carnal, sold under sin…In me (that is, in my flesh), dwelleth no good thing: for to will is present with me; but how to perform that which is good I find not…O wretched man that I am! who shall deliver me from the body of this death?” (vv. 7–25). Here is no boastful claim to meritorious good works. Here is the lament that every work the sanctified apostle of Jesus Christ performed was defiled

7 Heidelberg Catechism Q&A 62, in ibid., 3:327.

8 Belgic Confession 24, in ibid., 3:412.

by sin, imperfect, and therefore in respect of the imperfection not a "good thing." Here is the deathblow to every doctrine that teaches justification by faith and by the good works of the sinful saint himself. Works defiled with sin cannot justify sinners. A "wretched man" cannot produce a single work that meets the standard of the God who is righteous.

By their doctrine of justification by the good works of the sanctified sinner, N. T. Wright and the men of the federal vision are compelled to interpret Romans 7 as the confession not of the regenerated, believing, sanctified Paul and of all the saints with him, but of the unregenerated unbeliever, who is still attempting to acquire righteousness by observance of the law (Torah). Obviously, the man or woman of Romans 7 has no good works with which to contribute to his or her justification. With exegesis of Romans 7 that can only be described as tortuous, if not absurd, Wright explains Romans 7, especially the second half of the chapter, this way:

> In...Romans 7...Paul describes Israel as being in the flesh, in Adam, so that when Israel embraces Torah [the law] all it can do is condemn her....Here Paul uses the autobiographical device, the "I," not least to avoid giving the appearance of criticizing his fellow-Jews as though from a distance. The plight he describes is that which, from his Christian standpoint, he realizes he had been in as a zealous Pharisee.[9]

Wright's "autobiographical device" is the assertion that in Romans 7 the apostle is not speaking of himself in his own

---

9 Wright, *What Saint Paul Really Said*, 144. See also 226–30 in his *The Climax of the Covenant*, where Wright adds that in Romans 7 it is also Adam and Cain who speak—anyone but Paul, as the chapter conclusively makes plain. We criticize Wright not only as a heretic, but also as a willful exegete of holy scripture. A willful exegete is one who deliberately corrupts scripture to support his heresy.

person, despite his use of the first-person pronoun, "I." The "I" is merely a device by which he refers to others, so that, in reality, others are speaking in the passage. Whoever is speaking is not a regenerated, believing child of God but an unregenerated, ungodly unbeliever. "Autobiographical device" is Wright's exegetical device that makes it possible for him to explain Romans 7 as permitting justification by the good works of the believer.

What Wright either does not notice or does not mind is that this interpretation of Romans 7 commits him, his new perspective on Paul, and the men of the federal vision who follow his explanation of Romans 7 to the Arminian heresy of the free will of the unregenerated sinner. Romans 7 ascribes to the one who is speaking a will to do the good and a will that detests the evil (vv. 15–16, 18–20); a "delight in the law of God" (v. 22); the ardent desire to be delivered from sin (v. 24); and trust in Jesus Christ (v. 25). If the one speaking in Romans 7 is an unregenerated unbeliever, whether unconverted Paul, or fallen Adam, or Cain, or a Pharisee, unsaved unbelievers have a will that not only *can* choose but also *does choose* God, Christ Jesus, and the good. The Roman Catholic Church will be happy to hear it. Pelagius and Arminius would have been delighted to agree. Wright's exegesis of Romans 7 was theirs. In fact, Arminius was first found out as the heretic he was exactly by this interpretation of Romans 7.

That the apostle employs no device in Romans 7 is abundantly plain on the surface of the passage. The passage is the intensely personal lament of an anguished and broken heart: "I am carnal, sold under sin...The good that I would I do not: but the evil which I would not, that I do." The climax is the lament: "O wretched man that I am!" Not Cain, but "I." Not that I used to be in my unconverted, Pharisaical state, but that I "*am*." And then the cry of hope out of the depths, which God gives only to the born-again, penitent, believing son or daughter: "Who shall deliver me...?" "*Me*"—the sanctified apostle, toward the end of his holy life.

The good works of the holiest saint, the apostle Paul, need forgiveness of their imperfection and sinful taint. God graciously does forgive the good works of his saints regarding their imperfections and sinful taints, as well as their completely evil works.

Who can speak of merit in light of Romans 7, to say nothing of his experience of the imperfection of his best works? God's acceptance and reward of our good works is grace.

Against a meritorious nature of our good works is also this obvious reality that the reward of them is much greater and more glorious than any and all of the good works. There is no equivalence between the works and the reward, as there ought to be if the reward is merited. The reward is eternal life and sharing the glory of the exalted Christ in body and soul in a marvelous new creation forever. When the holiest of believers looks at his few, puny, insignificant good works, all of which grace has produced in him and all of which he defiled by not loving God and the neighbor with the fervor and purity that were required of him, he can only marvel at the sheer grace of God in promising him a reward, and such a reward, for these trifles.

The idea of marching into the courtroom of the final judgment waving these little, defiled things as deserving what awaits him is to him (and this also is grace) not only the height of wickedness, but also the height of absurdity. It is as though one should offer to the brain surgeon, who has accomplished a long, delicate, successful, life-saving surgery, a bouquet of wilted flowers as payment for the surgery.

This is the grievous error of Wright and the men of the federal vision. Although they grudgingly grant the possibility that justification in time may be by faith alone, they insist that the justification of the final judgment is by faith *and the good works* of the one who is justified. This, of course, is the justification that finally matters, the decisive justification. Wright affirms "the final justification of God's people, on the basis of their whole life. This will take place at the end."[10]

Norman Shepherd explains Romans 2:13 ("the doers of the law shall be justified") as teaching that "in the Day of Judgment 'it is those who obey the law who will be declared righteous.'"[11] What is intended is that the good works justify with faith.

The new perspective and federal vision theologian Don Garlington thinks that "all of the judgment texts...base final forensic acquittal on 'works'"—the justified sinner's own works.[12]

Rich Lusk speaks for the federal vision when he proclaims that "works are the criterion of the final judgment." These works are the good works of those who will be justified. Lusk adds that "works will be the *decisive* factor."[13]

The Belgic Confession denies that the good works of the believer are of any "account" in the divine act of justification, whether this justification be God's present declaration that the believer is righteous or the declaration in the final judgment: "[Good works] are of no account towards our justification. For it is by faith in Christ that we are justified, even before we do good works."[14]

The truth of the reward of our good works is that God, out of pure grace, is pleased to reward his gift to us and in us. This pleasure is not because God is indebted to us by our works, but because he is surpassingly gracious, always giving, always giving more, until his grace bids fair to take our breath away, or better, arouses us to sing and shout his praises everlastingly and to

---

10 Wright, *Paul*, 121.

11 Shepherd, "Faith and Faithfulness," in Sandlin, *A Faith That Is Never Alone*, 66.

12 Don Garlington, "The New Perspective, Mediation, and Justification," in Sandlin, *A Faith That Is Never Alone*, 295.

13 Lusk, "Future Justification," in Sandlin, *A Faith That Is Never Alone*, 318. The emphasis is Lusk's.

14 Belgic Confession 24, in Schaff, *Creeds of Christendom*, 3:411.

show forth our thankfulness by confession of his grace (including controversy with all theologies that compromise grace) and by a holy life. He rewards our works, never overlooking a single one, although when we stand before Christ in judgment we do not remember them. “Lord,” respond the righteous to the King in the final judgment, when the King announces his reward of their good works, “when saw we thee an hungred, and fed thee? or thirsty, and gave thee drink?” and so on (Matt. 25:31–46).

Lest the reward of good works cause the saints to stumble into the error of merit, scripture is careful to guard the truth of grace in the matter of the reward, in the passages that teach the reward. Matthew 25:31–46 demonstrates this carefulness. This is the passage that teaches that the perfected kingdom is the reward of the sheep on Jesus’ right hand. Against the danger that the believing saints suppose that their good works merit the reward, Jesus says, “Ye blessed of my Father, inherit the kingdom prepared for you from the foundation of the world” (v. 34). The saints will “inherit” the kingdom. Inheriting a great good is receiving it simply because of the graciousness toward the recipient on the part of the one who wills the good. Fathers do not will their goods to their children because the children earned the goods, but because the father freely loves his children.

In addition, Matthew 25 describes the kingdom inherited by Jesus’ disciples as prepared for the disciples “from the foundation of the world” (v. 34). The kingdom is given to Christ’s people in the eternal decree of election, before they ever did one good work. In the decree the kingdom is not prepared for those to whom it is willed on the basis of their (foreseen) works, for the decree itself ordained the good works for these persons (see Eph. 2:10).

Not our good works but the obedience of Christ for us and in our stead, especially his satisfactory suffering and death, merited for us the reward of eternal life and glory. We have this merit not by working but by believing on him, by believing only. His work was well deserving of the reward for himself and for us, for he is the eternal Son of God in human flesh. His obedience has infinite worth and value. He who is the form of God humbled himself even to the accursed death of the cross out of perfect love for God, whose will he fulfilled, and perfect love for his chosen people, whose life and glory he merited.

Pleading the merits of Jesus Christ, and those only, let us stand daily in the courtroom of God; let us enter the judgment at the moment of death; and let us appear one day before the Christ of God on his great, white throne in the final judgment. Only if the merits that render us righteous before God are those of Jesus for us and on our behalf do we have assurance of our salvation, now, at death, and in the final judgment. The false doctrine of justification by the merits of one's own works robs the one who believes this doctrine of all assurance of salvation.

In the controversy over merit, assurance of salvation was of great importance to the reformers, as is evident from the Reformed creeds. Repudiating the merit of the good works of the believer, the Belgic Confession concludes:

> Thus, then [if our works are meritorious and therefore the foundation of our salvation], we should always be in doubt, tossed to and fro without any certainty, and our poor consciences would be continually vexed if they relied not on the merits of the suffering and death of our Savior.[15]

Other Aspects of the Reward

More should be said, if very briefly, about the reward of good works than only that it does not contradict the gospel truth of justification by faith only. First, the promise of a reward is intended by God to be an incentive to perform good works.

---

15 Belgic Confession 24, in ibid., 3:412.

The reward is not the only incentive. It is not even the most important and powerful incentive. Surely gratitude, a gratitude that seeks to glorify God, is the chief motive of the Christian life of obeying the law of God and serving God. Nevertheless, the prospect of the reward is an incentive, and a necessary one.

It is a danger that the Reformed child of God becomes so "spiritual" that he discounts and even discards the incentive to a life of good works that consists of anticipation of the reward. Christian parents can make the same mistake in raising their children. "Why reward them for their obedience?" such parents ask; "they owe obedience to their parents." That children owe their parents obedience is true. But rewards have their proper place in child-rearing to help the children pay this debt. There are parents who threaten their children to accomplish their obedience, but who never reward. This is a mistake. God's rearing of his children ought to be the example to Christian parents. God rewards, even though his children owe him their obedience, and even though their obedience is his own work in them.

Especially are the truth and reminder of a future reward a necessary encouragement to the child of God when he suffers and is tempted to become discouraged. Then Romans 8:17–18 must come to the rescue: "If so be that we suffer with him, that we may be also glorified together. For I reckon that the sufferings of this present time are not worthy to be compared with the glory which shall be revealed in us."

A second truth about the reward that is not directly related to the reward's not being meritorious concerns the correlation of the good works to the differing degrees of the reward. As has already been shown, there will be such correlation. There will be differing degrees of bliss and glory commensurate with the lives of good works of the saints. This correlation must not be conceived as merely external and formal. That is, the correspondence between good works and reward is not merely that God numbers the good works of his child, notes their value, and gives the man or woman a place in heaven that accords with the number and value of the works.

But the correspondence of works and reward is more internal and necessary. One's work in the covenant and on behalf of the kingdom on earth expands his capacity for glory in the coming world. The more one gives himself to God and the neighbor, the more one is zealous for the truth, and the more one suffers for Christ's sake, the greater becomes his spiritual capacity for the life and glory that await.

A word is in order concerning suffering for Christ's sake. We must not shrink from suffering; we must not despise suffering; we must not underestimate the value for ourselves of suffering. Not if it is suffering for the sake of Christ. Suffering actually prepares us for the bliss and glory that lie in store for us. In part this is the reason Christ left some of his afflictions "behind" for his people. In part this is the reason the apostle could "rejoice in my sufferings for you" (Col. 1:24). Whether it is by suffering for Christ's sake or by other good works, every child of God is being fitted in this life for the degree of bliss and glory that God has ordained for him or her.

Yet one more important aspect of the reward of grace is that for the most part the reward is future. God will give it and the saint will receive it at the return of Christ and as an element of the final judgment. There is reward of good works already in this life, especially the sense of God's approval, his "Well done, good and faithful servant," at the end of the day. But it is also true that often in this life the holy life of the child of God is unnoticed and unappreciated. More discouraging still, his good works are often unfruitful, or so it seems to him. He gives a cup of cold water in the name of Jesus, whether to a thirsty unbeliever or to a thirsty member of the church. Nevertheless, the unbeliever persists in rejecting Christ and the church. Regardless of the cup of cold water, the member of the church forsakes the church.

Indeed, the holy life of the child of God is often scorned. For it the believer is often persecuted.

Not in this life but in the life to come we have our reward. For the coming life of eternity, therefore, we long. In hope of that coming life, we labor, endure, suffer, and abound in good works.

"Come, Lord Jesus, with the reward of grace!"

Chapter Twenty-One

PAUL AND JAMES

With this topic in our study of justification we come to the most popular and seemingly weightiest objection to the Reformation, creedal, and biblical doctrine of justification by faith alone. All of the foes of the gospel truth of justification, Rome, Arminianism, the federal vision, and others, appeal to scripture against the truth of justification. The passage of scripture to which they appeal is James 2, particularly verses 14–26:

> Was not Abraham our father justified by works, when he had offered Isaac his son upon the altar?...Ye see then how that by works a man is justified, and not by faith only. Likewise also was not Rahab the harlot justified by works, when she had received the messengers, and had sent them out another way? For as the body without the spirit is dead, so faith without works is dead also.

Seemingly, the Bible explicitly denies the fundamental Reformation doctrine that the guilty, shameful sinner is justified by faith alone, that is, altogether apart from and without good works that he himself performs.

At the time of the Reformation, the Roman Catholic Church and the theologians who rose to her defense incessantly quoted this passage against Luther. They so exasperated Luther by their refusal to enter into the interpretation of the passage in light of the teaching about justification elsewhere in the Bible, especially Romans and Galatians, contenting themselves with mere quoting of the passage in James, that on one occasion Luther rashly dismissed the book of James as a "right strawy epistle," a judgment that he did not maintain.[1]

Still today this passage is Rome's main defense of its doctrine of justification by faith and good works, as well as its chief refutation of the Reformation doctrine of justification by faith alone. Also the Arminians appeal to this passage as supportive of their teaching that one's righteousness with God includes his own good works. In recent times the men of the federal vision likewise appeal to James 2 in support of a doctrine of justification that maintains, like Rome and Arminianism, that the righteousness of the sinner with God includes not only the death of Christ for him but also the good works he himself performs by the grace of the Spirit within him.

Obviously, the right explanation of James 2 is required for the proclamation and maintenance of the gospel truth of justification. Basic to this right explanation are three principles that govern all interpretation of scripture. First, scripture interprets scripture. Any particular passage of scripture must be interpreted in light of the rest of scripture, especially those passages that bear directly on the passage under consideration. Second, scripture is one unified, harmonious word of God. Scripture does not contradict itself by teaching a truth in one place and teaching its opposite in another place. Third, every passage of scripture must be explained in the light of its context.

All of these principles of biblical interpretation are implications of the fundamental truths that scripture is breathed forth of God so that it is divine, not human, and therefore not to be criticized (2 Tim. 3:16; John 10:35) and that God gave

---

1 Quoted in G. C. Berkouwer, *Faith and Justification* (Grand Rapids, MI: Eerdmans, 1954), 130.

the scripture to be understood by the believer. Apart from these truths concerning the Bible and the implications of interpretation that flow from them, scripture is flawed and fallible, and no understanding of the biblical revelation is possible.

Today, even in reputedly conservative churches, theologians neither believe nor practice these principles. Under the guise of "perspectivalism" and "paradox," theologians affirm contradictions in the Bible, for example, that the teaching of James on justification simply contradicts the doctrine of Paul in Romans and Galatians. We should make no effort to harmonize Paul and James. The effort would be futile. The doctrine of Paul and the teaching of James are different "perspectives" on one and the same truth. They are different *contradictory* perspectives on justification. A Presbyterian, Reformed, or evangelical minister ought to preach Paul one Sunday and James the next Sunday without any effort to show their agreement. The minister should not attempt to show their agreement, because they do not agree.

Of course, the result is that James' "perspective" gains the upper hand, and soon Paul's "perspective" is never again heard in the Presbyterian, Reformed, or evangelical church. The end of this "paradoxical perspectivalism," if not the purpose, is ecumenical conversation with Rome, and soon the return of penitent Protestants to the Roman Catholic Church, where they trust for their salvation in their own and the saints' good works for their righteousness with God and are damned.

Rome's Harmony of Paul and James

In the past the Roman Catholic Church was not as unbelieving about the Bible as are the contemporary theologians in the reputedly conservative Presbyterian and Reformed churches. At least Rome attempted to harmonize James and Paul. Rome harmonized the two writers of holy scripture by insisting that both meant the same thing with justification: the forensic (legal) declaration of God's giving the sinner (legal) standing with God as forgiven and right with God the judge. But James and Paul had two different kinds of works in view. When Paul in Romans 3 and 4, in Galatians, and in fact throughout all his epistles denied that the sinner is justified by works, he was referring only to ceremonial works, to typically Jewish works, for example, circumcision. When James affirmed justification by works, he had genuinely good works in mind, that is, good works that a renewed, believing child of God performs by the grace of the Spirit in him and, let it not be overlooked, works that the child of God performs by the power of his own free will.

According to Rome therefore, justification (as God's legal acquittal of the sinner and granting the right standing with God that deserves eternal life) is partly based on the death of Christ and partly based on the sinner's own (truly) good works, which he does with the help of the Holy Spirit. The righteousness of the justified sinner is partly the obedience of Christ on the sinner's behalf and partly the sinner's own good works, which he performs with the help of grace. But no one is justified by ceremonial, Old Testamental, Jewish works.

Several aspects of the Roman doctrine of justification are noteworthy. First, Rome does harmonize Paul and James. Second, the agreement of Paul and James hinges on the assumption that both Paul and James speak of justification in the same sense but have two different kinds of works in mind. Third, on the Roman Catholic interpretation of James 2, justification is by faith and by good works. One's own good works done, to be sure, with the help of grace are in part one's righteousness with God. The forgiveness of sins, a right standing with God, and therefore eternal life depend not only on Christ's obedience in the stead of and on behalf of the guilty sinner, imputed to him by means of God-given faith, but also on what the sinner himself does and must do. In the language of Romans 9:16, salvation is "of him that willeth…[and] runneth."

Arminianism, which is the bastard offspring of Roman Catholicism, agrees with the Roman doctrine of justification and interprets James 2 as does the Roman Catholic Church, except that Arminianism emphasizes that faith—the act of believing—is especially the sinner's righteousness with God.

Of greatest significance to Reformed Christians today is that the men of the federal vision, denying the Reformation and the confessional doctrine of justification by faith alone, come down on Rome's side in the crucially important matters of explaining James 2 and, in the course of the explanation, of harmonizing James 2 and Paul. The men of the federal vision contend that Paul and James speak of justification in the same sense but have different works in view. Leading spokesman Norman Shepherd writes in the *Reformation and Renewal Journal*:

> As evangelicals we often try to dodge this attack [of Rome against the Reformation's confession of justification by faith alone] by saying that these verses [in James 2] are not talking about justification by faith in the forensic, soteric sense that Paul talks about it in Romans and Galatians. The Westminster Confession, however, does not use this dodge. Instead, the Confession acknowledges that *James is talking about faith and justification in the same sense that Paul uses these terms when he denies that justification is by works.*[2]

Shepherd therefore is compelled to harmonize Paul and James some other way. The only possible other way is having them refer to two different kinds of works, just as Rome argues.

As is well known, Luther cut off Rome's attempt to harmonize Paul and James by inserting *only* (German: *allein*) in Romans 3:28, so that the text would read, "Therefore we conclude that a man is justified without the works of the law, only

2 Shepherd, "Justification by Faith Alone," 80; emphasis added.

by faith." *Only*, which is not explicitly in the Greek text but is fully warranted, indeed implied, by the thought of the text, cuts off the possibility of explaining the text as merely ruling out ceremonial works from justification. *Only* or *alone*, both in Luther's translation of Romans 3:28 and in the confessions of the Reformed churches, for instance questions 60 and 61 of the Heidelberg Catechism, is decisive that *all* works of the sinner himself are excluded from justification and that Paul and James must be harmonized some other way than that proposed by Rome and by Shepherd.

Fully aware that Luther's *allein* in Romans 3:28 is the death-blow to his and the federal vision's explanation of James 2 as teaching forensic justification by faith and good works, Shepherd criticizes Luther's *allein* in the German text of Romans 3:28: "Luther inserted the word 'alone' into his translation of Romans 3:28 to make it read 'For we hold that one is justified by faith *alone* apart from works of the law.' This is the origin of the dogmatic formula, justification by faith alone. *However, his insertion actually distorts Paul's meaning*."[3]

Justification by faith alone is a *distortion* of the apostle's meaning in Romans 3 and 4!

According to Shepherd, Luther was wrong. With Luther the entire Reformation of the church in the sixteenth century was wrong. All the Reformed creeds, which teach justification by faith *alone*, are wrong. Justification is not by faith alone. Justification is by faith *and by good works*, just as Rome has always taught.

If both Paul and James speak of justification in the same sense—as God's declaration of the sinner's forgiveness and righteousness before him as just judge—the only way to harmonize Paul, who denies that justification is by works, and James, who affirms that justification is by works, is by explaining that the

3 Shepherd, "Justification by Faith Alone," 87; emphasis added.

two writers of holy scripture have different works in view. This is the explanation by Shepherd in his effort to harmonize Paul and James. The works that Paul has in mind when in Romans and Galatians he denies that a man is justified by works are the ceremonial works of the Mosaic law and works that are performed with the motive of meriting: "Paul is saying [in Romans 3:28] that the old covenant has been set aside. Justification comes...not by adherence to the provisions of the Mosaic covenant." Also, when the apostle rejected works for justification, he objected to the theology that makes "salvation a matter of human achievement." That is, the only works excluded by Paul from justification are those done with the motive of earning salvation.

Not content to corrupt the doctrine of the apostle Paul, Shepherd immediately misrepresents the doctrine of Luther, Calvin, and the entire Reformation in their gospel of justification by faith alone, that is, without works. In repudiating works in the divine act of justification, the reformers were merely refuting "the Roman Catholic doctrine of justification by faith *plus the merit of good works. We are not justified by the merit of our works but only by faith in Jesus Christ.*"[4] The Reformation therefore was not rejecting all works, but only works that are performed to merit with God.

The agreement of Paul and James then is this. Paul denies that the Old Testament works of obedience to the Mosaic covenant and works that are done to merit justify. But Paul agrees with James, who supposedly teaches that genuinely good works do justify, works that one does with another motive than to earn salvation. Paul agrees with James that justification is by faith and by genuinely good works. According to Shepherd, the gospel of Paul and James, very much like that of Shepherd himself and the federal vision but quite unlike the gospel of the Reformation

4 Shepherd, "Justification by Faith Alone," 87–88; emphasis added.

and of the Reformed creeds, is justification by faith and by genuinely good works.

That it is indeed the doctrine of the federal vision that Paul and James are to be harmonized by the explanation that they have different kinds of works in view and that therefore both teach justification by faith and works is evident from federal visionist Steve Schlissel. Writing in the book that authoritatively sets forth the federal vision heresy, Schlissel denies that Romans 3:28 has any and all human works in view. Rather, the reference in the text is to "Jewish" deeds. Other works of the believer, works done out of love for God and by the power of the indwelling Spirit of Christ, *are* included in justification, *are* included in justification in the sense of Romans 3 and 4: forgiveness of sins and a right, legal standing with God by divine verdict from the bench.

In Romans 3:28, according to Schlissel, the "'deeds of the law'...clearly has reference to a *Jewish thing*, and not to a Lutheran conception of the Law." Shrewdly, Schlissel avoids saying a Heidelberg Catechism, a Belgic Confession, or a Reformed conception of the law, although this is what he intends. Schlissel then draws the heretical conclusion: "the Law is 'obeyable,'" so that "truly responding to the Law...in faith does justify." The false gospel of the federal vision, which is no gospel, is justification by obeying the law, that is, by works![5] And in large part the alleged biblical basis is James 2.

Let us be forthright, as the federal vision is not. For the federal vision the Reformation was a gigantic mistake. All that struggle, suffering, and martyrdom were for nothing. In fact, Luther and the other reformers were heretics, and the Reformation was schism, as Rome has always charged. The great issue in the Reformation was justification by faith alone and the corresponding deeper truth of salvation by sovereign grace alone.

---

5 Schlissel, "Justification and the Gentiles," in Wilkins and Garner, *The Federal Vision*, 260–61.

Regarding this issue the Reformation was mistaken, a judgment that the federal vision bases largely on James 2.

Then we ought also to be honest, as the federal vision is not. All of us believing, Reformed, Protestant Christians must live in the terror of never knowing whether we have worked enough to satisfy God the judge. We must live and die without assurance of justification and salvation, as Rome has always correctly inferred from its damned doctrine of justification by works. At the same time let us raise our crest of pride. Our work is our righteousness with God. Christ's work is part of our righteousness. But our own is also part of our righteousness. And ours is decisive. Without our work Christ's is not enough to gain our righteousness and salvation. All of us may stride arrogantly into the divine judgment hall waving our pitiful, sin-tainted deeds as the ground of our claims to eternal life. And be damned eternally—on the ground of our best works!

What Christian can abide these notions? What Christian can abide the doctrine of justification by faith and by his own good works?

Against this heresy, as vigorous in the sphere of Christianity as ever it was, now promoted within the camp of conservative Reformed and Presbyterian Christianity, we confess that the elect, believing sinner is justified by faith alone without any works of his own whatever—ceremonial or moral, performed with or without the purpose of meriting, done in one's own strength or with the help of the Holy Spirit. Whether the word is inserted into the translation (which is perfectly acceptable) or understood as the thought of the text, Romans 3:28 teaches as the gospel truth of justification that one is justified by faith *alone.*

The Reformed Harmony of Paul and James

How then must James 2 be understood? And how are Paul and James to be harmonized?

Whatever James teaches in chapter 2 about justification is and must be in harmony with the teaching of Paul in Romans and Galatians. The Spirit of the inspiration of scripture cannot contradict himself, certainly not in God's revelation of himself as justifier and savior and of the way of the salvation of sinners. Romans and Galatians certainly teach justification as the legal act of God's acquitting the elect, believing sinner of his guilt and reckoning to the sinner the perfect obedience of Christ. This is evident beyond all doubt in the language of Romans 3 and 4 and in Galatians. Justification in these passages is a *counting* of righteousness to the believer (Rom. 4:3–5; Gal. 3:6); a *reckoning* of righteousness (Rom. 4:4, 9–10); an *imputing* of righteousness (Rom. 4:6, 8, 11, 22–24). In fact, these various words in the English Bible all translate the same Greek term, which expresses the legal transfer to one of a state (in this case righteousness before God the judge in a courtroom setting) that is not one's naturally.

A suitable example from ordinary human life is hard to come by in the nature of the case. In justifying the elect, believing sinner God does something wonderful, amazing, indeed unheard of in everyday earthly life. Biblically, the divine act of justification is a "mystery." But neither is an example from everyday life necessary. Romans 4:5 clearly explains the mystery of justification as the imputing of righteousness to a guilty sinner: "To him that worketh not, but believeth on him that justifieth the ungodly, his faith is counted [or reckoned, or imputed] for righteousness."

One appears in the divine courtroom as ungodly, only ungodly, nothing but ungodly, as concerns his legal standing before God the judge. He is guilty of the worst of all sins: ungodliness. Still more condemnable, and condemning, he himself is ungodly. Regarding his nature, that is, everything that he is in and of himself, soul and body, he is ungodly, and ungodly only. As ungodly he deserves the verdict of guilty and the carrying out of the verdict in suffering the penalty of death, eternal death in hell. But the judge, who is God, makes an amazing declaration from the judicial bench. He pronounces the believing but ungodly sinner just, or righteous, before himself and regarding his high and perfect standard of righteousness. By virtue of this divine declaration, or verdict, the elect sinner really becomes and truly is not guilty and perfectly righteous.

The explanation of this amazing verdict is nothing in the justified sinner himself, absolutely nothing. But the explanation is that the judge has legally made over, or imputed, to the sinner the perfect righteousness of another, namely, Jesus Christ, who is the sinner's head and legal representative by virtue of God's eternal appointment of Jesus Christ as the covenantal head of the justified sinner. The explanation of the amazing verdict is the wonderful grace of God in Jesus Christ.

This verdict is a reality, also in the sinner's consciousness, by means of the sinner's faith in Jesus Christ, which faith God has worked in the sinner's heart. The verdict of justification is not a reality because of, or by means of, or consisting in part of, the sinner's works. Romans 4:5 gives three reasons that the works of the sinner do not play a role in his justification, other than being the very reason he stands in need of justification. First, the justified sinner does not work in order to be justified. For justification he consciously and deliberately refuses to work: "to him that worketh not."

Second, the one who is justified is "ungodly"—ungodly, and ungodly *only*, in the matter of justification. All his works are ungodly regarding their possibly furnishing material for the divine declaration of righteousness, for even his best good works are defiled with sin.

Third, emphatically the text teaches that the elect sinner's "*faith* is counted for righteousness." Especially in light of the text's statement that God justifies those who do *not* work, the mention of faith clearly rules works out in the matter of justification: *not* works but *faith*, that is, faith *alone.* And faith is counted for righteousness, not as a work that itself deserves righteousness, nor as a work of the sinner that itself is righteousness with God. This would contradict everything the text and the passage in which it occurs teach concerning the grace of justification. To make faith itself, the act of believing on the part of the sinner, deserving of righteousness or itself the sinner's righteousness would be a form of righteousness by works, which the text denies. But faith is counted for righteousness regarding faith's *object*, who is Jesus Christ as the righteousness of God for guilty but believing sinners. Nor ought it to be regarded as strange that by faith the apostle would be referring to faith's *object*, namely, Jesus Christ. For faith is union with Christ, so that faith *is* Christ with respect to faith's object.

Romans 4:5 teaches and explains justification as the legal declaration of God upon and to the believing sinner imputing the righteousness of Christ to him. Justification in Romans and Galatians as this divine verdict imputing to the sinner the righteousness of Christ is by faith alone, apart from the believing sinner's good works. This truth is fundamental for the right harmonizing of Paul and James.

In addition, importantly, Romans and Galatians are also certainly referring to *all* works when they deny that justification is by works. Romans and Galatians are not referring merely to certain kinds of works, whether the works of obedience to the ceremonial law of the Old Testament (the Mosaic economy), or works performed with the motive of meriting salvation. The law to which Paul refers in Romans 3:28, when he writes that the sinner is not justified by the "deeds of the law," is not the ceremonial law of the Old Testament but the law by which is "the knowledge of sin" (v. 20). This law is the moral law of the ten commandments. It is the law that is inscribed on the fleshy tables of the heart of the child of God and that is the guide of the holy life of the justified sinner. Nevertheless, a man is justified without deeds of obedience to this moral law or any other form of the law of God.

In Romans 4 the Holy Spirit excludes *all* works and *every kind* of working from justification. Absolutely no limitation or specification of the works and working excluded from justification is stated or suggested in the passage, as though the Spirit had only certain kinds of works and workings in view. The passage simply excludes all works and workings of the sinner from justification: "to him that worketh not" (v. 5); "without works" (v. 6).

In Romans 4 the argument of the apostle demands understanding works and working as any and all works and working of the sinner himself, including works done with the help of grace and performed by the power of the Holy Spirit, that is, genuinely good works. The argument is that if even a regenerated child of God is justified by works "he hath whereof to glory" (v. 2). Regardless that the works are done with the help of grace, justification by these good works puts the sinner in a position to boast. Not only works of obedience to the ceremonial law or works done with the intention to merit, but also any work, if it is the ground and content of the righteousness of justification, necessarily puts the sinner in a position of boasting or glorying in himself. But no one is or may be in a position to "glory" or boast in himself in the matter of justification.

Verse 4 observes that if justification were at all by the sinner's own working, the reward would be "of debt," not "of grace." This must not be. Therefore, all works are excluded from justification. It makes no difference whether the works are works done in obedience to the ceremonial law, works performed with the motive of earning, or genuinely good works rising out of a thankful heart, justification by works would mean that the reward of eternal life would be a matter of debt rather than of grace. This would disannul the ultimate purpose of God in the salvation of sinners: the glory of himself by a gracious salvation.

In Romans 4:5 the apostle does not say, "But to him that worketh not, in obedience to the ceremonial law, his faith and his good works done in obedience to the moral law are counted for righteousness." But he says, simply and absolutely, "But to him that worketh not," that is, in the matter of becoming righteous with God. In order to be justified, one does not work at all.

The contrast in Romans 3 and 4 is not between working done to obey the ceremonial law and working done to obey the moral law, between works done in one's own strength and works done with the help of the Spirit, between works performed with the intention of merit and works done out of gratitude. But the contrast is between works and faith, between working for righteousness and believing in Christ for righteousness: "law of works"/"law of faith" (3:27); "by faith"/"deeds of the law" (v. 28); "works"/"believed" (4:2–3); "worketh"/"believeth" (v. 5); "law"/"faith" (v. 14).

Regarding justification as the legal act of God's forgiving sins and reckoning one to be in perfect conformity with the law of God, and having in mind any and all kinds of works, including those done with the help of grace, Paul declares in Romans 4:2 specifically concerning Abraham—regenerated, believing Abraham—that he was not justified by works, by any works of his own whatever: "For if Abraham were justified by works, he hath whereof to glory; but not before God." Rather than working for righteousness, Abraham, who is both the father and the exemplar of all the children of God, "believed God."

Three essential and perfectly clear truths about justification are the teaching of the Holy Spirit in Romans and Galatians. First, justification is by faith alone, without works. Second, the justification that is by faith alone is the divine verdict that actually accomplishes the sinner's righteousness with God, saving the sinner by delivering him from a state of guilt into a state of innocence. Third, the works excluded from this justification are all works of the sinner himself whatever, including the genuinely good works that a believer performs in thankfulness to God for gracious salvation.

Whatever may be the meaning of James 2, the passage cannot contradict this clear, authoritative doctrine of Paul concerning justification. That is, the Spirit who inspired both Romans 3 and 4 and James 2 cannot contradict himself, teaching in James 2 the opposite of what he teaches in Romans 3 and 4. When James 2:21 says that "Abraham our father [was] justified by works," the text cannot contradict Romans 4:2–3, which teaches that Abraham was justified *not* by works, but by faith only. James cannot speak of justification in the same sense as Paul does in Romans and Galatians. Or to say it differently, James describes an entirely different aspect of justification from what Paul describes in Romans and Galatians, namely, the legal act forgiving sins and imputing to the sinner the obedience of Christ.

James describes the believer's demonstration and proof of his free justification by faith alone. One who has been justified by faith alone will show this justification. He will show it to other humans. He will confirm his justification to himself. He will also show this justification to God his judge. He will show, or demonstrate, his justification by the good works that are always the fruit of justification. By his good works the justified sinner is not declared righteous legally, as though these works were the ground of his forgiveness and righteousness with God the judge, as though these good works were the content of his right standing before God, as though these good works constituted the sinner's worthiness to inherit eternal life. But the good works are his justification demonstratively. They show the reality of his justification by faith alone.

That James has in view a different aspect of justification than what Paul teaches in Romans and Galatians is evident from James 2 itself. James contends with church members who, although they profess to have faith, faith by which they are justified, in fact have a "dead" faith (vv. 17, 20, 26), a "faith" that produces no good works at all but is content to live impenitently in sin. James challenges this kind of church member: "Shew me thy faith without thy works [which is impossible], and I will shew thee my faith by my works" (v. 18). The subject in James

2 is the *showing*, or *demonstration*, of faith and therefore also the demonstration of justification.

James' doctrine is that the faith that justifies by itself alone also always works, for justifying faith is not a "dead faith," which is no faith at all, but a living faith. True, living, justifying faith is union with Christ, and union with Christ does and must bear fruit in good works of obedience to the law of God. Doing justice to James' terminology, James teaches that, regarding its clear and powerful demonstration, justification is by works. Paul, in contrast, teaches that, regarding the means by which the sinner is declared righteous by God the judge, justification is by faith, and by faith only.

James makes plain that he does not contradict but is in full agreement with Paul regarding justification's being by faith alone. In the midst of his impassioned contention with the antinomian abusers of gracious justification, James quotes Genesis 15:6, the text that figures so decisively in Paul's theology of justification by faith alone in Romans 4: "Abraham believed God, and it was imputed unto him for righteousness" (James 2:23; Rom. 4:3). Long before Isaac was born and therefore long before Abraham offered his son on the altar, which work, James says in verse 21, demonstrated his justification, Abraham was justified by faith—by faith *alone*. Faith was imputed to Abraham for righteousness, faith apart from any good work on Abraham's part, specifically the awesome good work of offering his son on the altar.

There is one other consideration in James 2 that proves beyond any contradiction that James does not teach justification in the sense of the legal verdict that constitutes the sinner righteous before God the judge. It is unfortunate that in the controversy over Paul and James regarding justification this consideration is seldom, if ever, noticed. This is the important, if not decisive, fact that James does not teach justification by faith *and works*, as the proponents of the heresy of justification by faith and works argue, supposedly on the basis of James 2. But James teaches justification *by works,* by works *alone.* Verse 21 asks rhetorically, "Was not Abraham our father justified by works?" Then the work of offering Isaac as a sacrifice is instanced. There is no mention of faith. The thought of James is that Abraham was justified by works *only.* Also, verse 24 states that "by works a man is justified, and not by faith only." James' justification is by works only, rather than by faith only. "Likewise also was not Rahab the harlot justified by works" (v. 25). Again, there is no mention of faith at all. The text teaches that Rahab was justified by works, and by works only.

A common but erroneous understanding of James 2, not only by Rome but also by the federal vision and also at times on the part of Reformed expositors of the passage, is that James 2 qualifies Paul's teaching that justification is by faith alone. Then the harmonizing of Paul and James consists of teaching that justification, as the forensic declaration of the believing sinner's righteousness in his consciousness, is by faith and by the sinner's own good works. But this is not the harmonizing of Paul and James. It is rather the contradicting of Paul. It is the fatal concession that Rome's doctrine of justification is right. It is the condemnation of the Reformation. It is the denial of the gospel of grace.

Such harmonizing of Paul and James is also a total misunderstanding and misrepresentation of James. James 2 does not qualify, that is, contradict, the doctrine of Paul. James does not teach, or allow anyone to teach, that justification *as the imputation of righteousness* is by faith and by good works. James teaches that justification is by works, by works *alone.* For James is not teaching justification as the forgiveness of sins and the imputation of the righteousness of Christ in the believing sinner's consciousness. James is teaching justification with regard to the demonstration of this saving act of God. Regarding its demonstration, justification is by works, by works *only.*

If James 2 teaches justification in the same sense that the doctrine has in Romans 3 and 4, James teaches forgiveness and righteousness with God not by faith and works, but by works only. Not only does this put James squarely in total opposition to Paul, it also makes James a flaming Pharisee and an outright Pelagian. James' doctrine of justification by works *only* demands the interpretation that James speaks of the demonstration of justification. Works are justification's demonstration. Works are justification's *only* demonstration. Faith is the only *means* of justification, but faith is not the demonstration of justification. Works are.

James teaches the truth that Jesus had earlier taught in Luke 7:47 concerning the sinful woman who loved him and anointed his feet with precious ointment, because he had forgiven her sins: "Her sins, which are many, are forgiven; for she loved much." Jesus did not mean that her sins were forgiven, that is, that she was justified, on the ground of her great love, that is, her good work. But her great love was proof and evidence of the forgiveness of her many sins. Her love was demonstration of her justification. That this was the meaning of Jesus' word in Luke 7:47 is put beyond any doubt by the second part of the text: "but to whom little is forgiven, the same loveth little." The good work of love is not the cause of justification, but justification's fruit and evidence.

James does not contradict the gospel of grace of Romans 3 and 4 and of the epistle to the Galatians. But James teaches and warns that the gospel of grace, particularly the truth of justification by faith alone, is no occasion for license. Rather, the full truth of justification is that the justified sinner will work, will work good works, will work deeds that are amazing, will work deeds of self-sacrifice and of help of the true church and her members, will work deeds that arise from the living faith that trusts the promises of God even when those promises seem impossible of fulfillment.

Our good works are not the conditions for justification, nor the basis of justification, nor the content of justification. They are the fruit and demonstration of justification.

This has always been the orthodox Reformed explanation of James 2 and of the harmony of Paul and James. In his commentary on James 2, Calvin wrote:

> When Paul says that we are justified by faith, he means no other thing than that by faith we are counted righteous before God. But James has quite another thing in view, even to shew that he who professes that he has faith, must prove the reality of his faith by his works. Doubtless James did not mean to teach us here the ground on which our hope of salvation ought to rest; and it is this alone that Paul dwells upon...We must take notice of the two-fold meaning of the word *justified.* Paul means by it the gratuitous imputation of righteousness before the tribunal of God; and James, the manifestation of righteousness by the conduct, and that before men, as we may gather from the preceding words, "Shew to me thy faith," etc.[6]

This understanding of the harmony between Paul and James is creedal for the Reformed churches. Even though article 24 of the Belgic Confession does not expressly refer to Paul and James, the mention of a "vain faith" indicates that the article has an eye on James 2, and the assertion that good works "are of no account towards our justification" makes plain that the article has Romans 3 and 4 in view. The article therefore authoritatively harmonizes Paul and James on justification.

> It is impossible that this holy faith can be unfruitful in man: for we do not speak of a vain faith, but of such a

6 John Calvin, *Commentaries on the Catholic Epistles*, trans. and ed. John Owen (Grand Rapids, MI: Eerdmans, 1948), 314–15.

> faith as is called in Scripture *a faith that worketh by love*, which excites man to the practice of those works which God has commanded in his Word. Which works, as they proceed from the good root of faith, are good and acceptable in the sight of God, forasmuch as they are all sanctified by his grace: howbeit they are of no account towards our justification. For it is by faith in Christ that we are justified, even before we do good works, otherwise they could not be good works any more than the fruit of a tree can be good before the tree itself is good.[7]

Relationship of Justification and Sanctification

Consideration of the relationship between Paul and James on justification, in light of the perennial appeal to James 2 by defenders of works-righteousness with the purpose to overthrow the truth of justification by faith alone, raises the important question of the relationship of faith and good works in the life of the regenerated child of God. In the language of theology, this is the issue of the relationship of justification and sanctification.

Always, those who deny or subtly compromise the truth of justification by faith alone do so, they say, because they fear that the doctrine of justification by faith alone fails to motivate church members to be zealous for a life of good works. Whether the enemies of justification by faith alone explicitly make the charge, as Rome has always done, or cleverly suggest this, as is the tactic of the men of the federal vision, their concern is that justification by faith alone cuts the nerve of holiness. If justification by faith alone does not cause those who believe it deliberately to behave wickedly, the doctrine diminishes the zeal for godliness of life. Since a life of holiness is obedience to the law of God, the fear of those who oppose the doctrine of justification by faith alone is that those who are taught this doctrine

---

7 Belgic Confession 24, in Schaff, *Creeds of Christendom*, 3:411.

will, at best, "sit loose to the law," or at the worst, hold the law in contempt.

The evil that is the fear or charge of those who oppose justification by faith alone, theology calls antinomism or antinomianism. This is the evil both in theory and in practice of rejecting the law of God—the ten commandments—as the authoritative, binding rule of life for the justified sinner. *Anti* means "against," and *nomos* is the Greek word for "law." With this rejection of the law as the rule of life invariably goes a lawless life.

Our interest here is not whether those who charge antinomianism against the doctrine of justification by faith alone do truly fear this evil or hypocritically use the argument in the interests of their real purpose, which is to corrupt the gospel of grace. Regarding the Roman Catholic Church, the charge against the Protestant doctrine of justification is ludicrous. No one should or can take the charge seriously. Rome interested in holiness of life? The Rome of the time of the Reformation with her profligate popes and priests, the church that was thoroughly worldly, interested in holiness? The Rome of our day, knowingly embracing the members of the violent Mafia, welcoming the adulterous Kennedys and other ungodly celebrities, covering up the buggery of her priests until the secular media exposed the depravity, and assuring multitudes of members that they have a good shot at heaven even though they go on impenitently in disobedience to all of God's commandments, as long as they go to confession regularly and perform prescribed deeds of satisfaction—Rome interested in holiness?

Regarding the Reformed and Presbyterian theologians in the movement that calls itself the federal vision, who present themselves as sincerely concerned about the lack of zeal for good works in the lives of many who confess justification by faith alone and whose own lives appear to be upright, it is noteworthy that the Bible never commends heretics for their sincerity, but rather condemns them for their corruption of the gospel of grace.

The issue is not the sincerity of those who oppose justification by faith alone because of professed concern for holiness. The issue is the gospel truth of justification by faith alone. We may grant that some Reformed and Presbyterian theologians who promote the theology of the federal vision are sincerely afraid that the Reformation doctrine of justification by faith alone fails to produce lives of good works. We need not challenge the sincerity of their conviction that only a doctrine that makes the sinner's own good works part of his righteousness with God, now and in the final judgment, will motivate the sinner to be more obedient to the law of God than otherwise he would be.

But we will recall that, no matter how hypocritically and even laughably, the Roman Catholic Church opposed the Reformation's gospel of grace for exactly this reason. Rome charged that justification by faith alone would lead to carelessness of life and even open immorality. To this charge the Heidelberg Catechism responds in question 64. Having explained the truth of justification by faith alone, the Catechism asks, "But does not this doctrine make men careless and profane?"[8]

The same fear, ostensibly, fuels the opposition to justification by faith alone on the part of the men of the federal vision. This fear accounts for their insistence that one's own good works are part of his righteousness with God, now and in the final judgment. Only if believing sinners are justified by faith and good works will they be motivated to live obedient, holy lives. This is a main concern, if not *the* main concern, of Norman Shepherd in his *The Call of Grace.* Knowing that one's own obedience to the law, one's own faithfulness in the covenant, is part of the righteousness of faith is necessary, according to Shepherd, to move confessing Christians to be holy. A theology of a conditional covenant and covenantal salvation, the conditions

---

8 Heidelberg Catechism Q 64, in ibid., 3:328.

being the sinner's act of believing and subsequent obedience to the law, is necessary to escape the error of antinomianism.

Already in the preface of his book, Shepherd is wondering "where and how," in light of the Reformed faith's confession of salvation by grace, "does human responsibility enter in?"[9] "Human responsibility" for Shepherd is conditions that humans must perform and upon which the covenant of God and its promises of salvation depend: "conditions were, indeed, attached to the fulfillment of the promises made to Abraham."[10] Only a conditional covenant with a conditional salvation can ward off the threatening evil of antinomianism. Only the preaching of a conditional covenant enables the Reformed preacher to "preach grace without being antinomian."[11]

Significantly, again and again Shepherd appeals to James 2 in support of his conditional theology. Just as is the Roman Catholic explanation of James 2:21, so for Shepherd the text means that "Abraham was considered righteous for what he did when he offered his son Isaac on the altar. His faith and his actions were working together."[12] "Considered righteous" is justification as the forensic—the legal—act of God rendering Abraham righteous, in the sense that justification has in Romans 3 and 4. Faith and actions working together for this divine consideration is justification by faith and works, exactly as Rome has always held.

The preaching of conditional salvation is a modern form of the preaching of justification by works. That Shepherd denies that the good works upon which the promises of God and salvation depend are meritorious is irrelevant. A work of the sinner upon which salvation depends is as much a denial of the gospel of grace as is a meritorious work. Behind this preaching of

9 Shepherd, *Call of Grace*, vii–viii.
10 Ibid., 14.
11 Ibid., 8.
12 Ibid., 16.

conditional salvation, now in the conservative Reformed and Presbyterian churches, is the fear that the doctrine of justification by faith alone and thus of salvation by grace alone does indeed make men careless and profane.

To condemn the men of the federal vision for their denial of justification by faith alone, out of a fear of antinomianism, without calling attention to the theological root of this denial would be inexcusable. The root of their denial of justification by faith alone is their emphatic teaching of a conditional covenant. According to the federal vision's basic covenantal doctrine, God graciously makes his covenantal promise to believers and all their children. Thus God graciously establishes his covenant with all the children, those who eventually perish as well as those who are eternally saved. But this gracious covenantal promise and covenant of grace depend for their saving effect upon conditions that the children must fulfill. These conditions are faith and lifelong obedience.

Justification *in the covenant*, therefore, is by faith and works. A child's righteousness with God, especially in the final judgment, depends both on God's grace and, decisively, on the child's performance of the conditions, that is, the child's good works. A covenantal child's righteousness with God the judge is partly the obedience of Christ and partly the child's own obedience, including the obedience of believing. This insistence on the conditionality of the covenant and its salvation is motivated by the belief that only if children born to believing parents are convinced that God's covenant is dependent on their fulfilling the conditional works of faith and obedience will they live godly lives.

The federal vision's doctrine of justification by faith and works is the expression of the heresy of a conditional covenant. The federal vision boldly acknowledges, indeed proclaims, this root of its doctrine of justification. Many of the Reformed and Presbyterian churches and theologians decline to recognize this covenantal root of the federal vision and, in certain instances, refuse to condemn the federal vision because these theologians and churches share the theology of a conditional covenant that is the root of the false doctrine known as the federal vision.

Because the theology of Shepherd and the federal vision is the avowed, natural development of their doctrine of a conditional covenant, the theologians of the liberated Canadian Reformed Churches are loath to criticize the federal vision, and indeed they offer defense of its theology. It is well known that liberated Canadian Reformed theologian Jelle Faber angrily condemned the Orthodox Presbyterian Church for its dismissal—dismissal, not discipline—of federal vision theologian Norman Shepherd.

In an editorial in the Canadian Reformed magazine, *Clarion*, a professor at the theological college of the Canadian Reformed Churches, Prof. C. Van Dam, took sharp issue with the mild and misleading criticism of some of the doctrinal tenets of the federal vision by Mid-America Reformed Seminary. Van Dam criticized Mid-America's confession, contrary to the theology of the federal vision, closely linking covenant and election. Van Dam contended that the covenant of grace with believers' children is not governed by election: "To insist, as the *Testimony* [of Mid-America] appears to do, that the covenant is only made with the elect does not agree with Scripture." In a statement that could have been authored by Norman Shepherd, or John Barach, or any of the other men of the federal vision, Van Dam immediately added, "Whether in the end they [the children of believers] turn out to be unbelievers or not, the covenant is made with them and the accompanying promises are theirs."[13]

13 C. Van Dam, "Has Mid-America Reformed Seminary Changed its Course?," *Clarion* 56, no. 16 (August 3, 2007): 392. Given this opportunity, in the midst of a controversy over all the fundamental doctrines of the Reformed faith, to issue a stirring defense of the governing of the covenant, the promise of the gospel, and covenantal salvation by election—the

A little later Van Dam came out wholeheartedly in support of Shepherd and his theology, that is, the theology of the federal vision. "Shepherd is...fully committed to the Reformed faith." With specific reference to the root of Shepherd's and the federal vision's theology, Van Dam added, "His emphasis on the covenant is both refreshing and much needed." Van Dam took note of the theological source of Shepherd's and the federal vision's theology of justification by works: "For this covenantal emphasis he [Shepherd] freely acknowledged his debt to the theological studies and thinking coming out of the Liberation of 1944 [of the Reformed Churches in the Netherlands, liberated, largely under K. Schilder] in The Netherlands."[14]

Van Dam's conclusion of his critique of the theology of Shepherd and the federal vision is amusing: "The conflict surrounding Shepherd is not an issue with us."[15] It is not an issue with the Canadian Reformed Churches because the theology of the federal vision is the theology of the liberated and Canadian Reformed Churches.[16] Basic to the federal vision is the teach-

---

fundamental truth at issue in the controversy with the federal vision—the faculty of Mid-America fell flat on its face. It responded to Van Dam's liberated challenge to its apparent relating of covenant and election by election's governing of covenant and covenantal salvation by assuring Van Dam (and the liberated churches) that its *Testimony* only addressed certain narrow, limited issues occasioned by the federal vision. It assured Van Dam (and the liberated churches) that the *Testimony* did not reflect on the liberated confession that the covenant is "with believers and their children." By this language the faculty of Mid-America certainly meant to express agreement with the liberated doctrine that God establishes his covenant of grace with all the children of believers alike, reprobate as well as elect, the covenantal theology for which Van Dam had expressly contended in his opening article ("Further Discussion," *Clarion* 56, no. 21 (October 12, 2007): 525).

14 Van Dam, "Reflections on a Conference," *Clarion* 57, no. 6 (March 14, 2008): 134.

15 Van Dam, "Reflections on a Conference," 134.

16 For a full-scale, enthusiastic defense of the theology of Shepherd and the federal vision as liberated orthodoxy by a liberated theologian, see Boersema, *Not of Works*.

ing of justification by faith and works. The root of the heresy, as of all the other heresies necessarily taught by the movement, is exactly what the movement has indicated by its name: *federal* vision—the doctrine of a conditional covenant.

The fear of the federal vision, as of the covenantal doctrine that is its root and essence, is that justification by faith alone threatens a responsible, zealous, holy life. Always the objection to the gospel truth of justification by faith alone is the fear, whether real or concocted, that the doctrine leads to carelessness of life and sheer lawlessness. Justification by faith alone is a danger to the Christian life of love for God and the neighbor in obedience to the good and holy law of God! Such is the fear and charge of the foes of justification by faith alone.

Let us do full justice to the alleged fear. Justification by faith alone means, and vigorously proclaims to the believing people of God, that the good works of those who believe the gospel from the heart add absolutely nothing to their righteousness with God and that their carelessness, sins, and immorality detract absolutely nothing from their righteousness with God. It means and openly teaches that God's verdict upon them, now and in the final judgment, depends not at all on their holiness and good works. Justification by faith alone is unconditional forgiveness and unconditional imputation of the obedience of another, even Jesus Christ. The righteousness of the guilty sinner with God has absolutely nothing to do with his own obedience to the law of God. Regarding his righteousness, and therefore the salvation that depends on this righteousness, the law is excluded, completely excluded (not regarding Christ's obedience to the law in his stead, but regarding any and all demands of the law on the sinner himself as conditions of righteousness and salvation).

"The righteousness of God *without the law*" (Rom. 3:21, emphasis added). "By *the works of the law* shall no flesh be justified" (Gal. 2:16, emphasis added). "By grace are ye saved...*not of works*" (Eph. 2:8–9, emphasis added).

What shall we say to the apparently anguished fear that Paul's dangerous doctrine in Romans 3 and 4 and in Galatians will, if not *must*, lead to the dreadful antinomianism described and combatted in James 2? How do we respond to Rome, the federal vision, and the advocates of a conditional covenant? Perhaps closer to home, how shall we respond to the member of our own congregation who, loudly espousing justification by faith alone, ignores the law of God and evidently claims the right to live like the devil?

Are we able to respond while maintaining firmly the doctrine of justification by faith alone? Or must we hedge on justification by faith alone at the critical point? Must we, to escape the admitted evil of antinomianism, corrupt the doctrine of justification by faith alone? Must we, no doubt ever so cautiously and deceptively, add the good works of the sinner to his righteousness with God? Must we scare the perceived antinomian into obedience by making his final justification dependent on his own good works? Ought we to make faith and its good works conditions unto righteousness and salvation? That is, in view of the antinomian heresy and way of life, should we deny the doctrine of justification by faith alone, or at least weaken the preaching of it in the congregation?

What is the response of the Reformed confessions to the fear of antinomianism? What is the response of scripture, that is, of God himself, to the fear, and why?

The fear, if fear it is, that justification by faith alone makes people careless or even profane, so that in order to achieve godly living and good works, the church must teach justification by faith and works or a conditional covenantal salvation, is an utterly mistaken and wicked fear. It is the fear of Uzzah that without his help the ark of the Lord would fall and be broken, so that he had to lay his unclean hands on that holy thing, the instant punishment of which presumptuous act was death and damnation (2 Sam. 6:1–11).

The fear that the biblical truth of justification needs the help of contemporary theologians to safeguard godly living is unbelief. Unbelief does not trust grace to save the elect believer to the uttermost, that is, to sanctify as well as justify, to deliver from the power of sin as well as from the guilt and shame of sin. Unbelief does not trust grace to save fully because it does not *know* the grace of God.

The fear that justification by faith alone makes people careless is essentially the same as the fear that the certain knowledge of one's own unconditional election and sure perseverance unto eternal life and glory must lead to a life of disobedience to the law, since one "will be saved anyway." Those churches that are willing to tolerate the corruption of the truth of justification in the interests, supposedly, of holy living ought to consider that both Rome's and the federal vision's corruption of justification is accompanied by the rejection of all the doctrines of grace: unconditional election; total depravity; the definite particularity of the atonement; and the preservation of saints, that is, the entirety of the gospel of grace.

Underlying the fear of salvation by grace alone is the notion that the real motivation to holiness of life and zeal for good works must be the conviction that one must himself earn his salvation, or that his salvation depends upon his own good works, or that failure to work means hell. The result in those who are driven by this foolish and wicked fear is that they try to live the Christian life like a slave or out of terror. Such motivations make all their attempted Christian life obnoxious to God. God cannot and will not be served acceptably in these ways. The Belgic Confession warns against this fear concerning the Christian life with its consequent illicit motivations of this life: "It is so far from being true, that this justifying faith makes men remiss in a pious and holy life, that on the contrary without it they would never do any thing out of love to God, but only out of self-love or fear of damnation."[17]

17 Belgic Confession 24, in Schaff, *Creeds of Christendom*, 3:410–11.

The biblical and Reformed response to the fear that justification by faith alone makes people careless and profane is that this is *impossible*. The teaching of this doctrine has never made one elect, believing person careless and profane, although it certainly has exposed the profanity of many nominal members of the church and even hardened them in their profanity, as they seized on this doctrine to excuse their careless lives and abused the doctrine. But these are reprobate, ungodly persons in the congregation whom God wills to harden with the preaching of the grand gospel truth of justification (Rom. 9:18). These are persons who abuse all the doctrines of the Christian faith. The fault is not in the doctrine but in themselves. The doctrine of justification by faith alone has made every true believer careful to obey the commandments of the law, that is, the doctrine has made them holy. All become devoted in grateful love to God their gracious justifier. All are "pronomian," not antinomian.

This is not to say that none of the justified has ever been tempted to abuse—not rightly use but abuse—the doctrine by living a careless life on the basis of the truth that he is justified by faith alone. The warning of James 2 makes clear that there were those in the Christian church already in its earliest days who were tempted to make the doctrine of justification by faith alone an excuse, if not a reason, for failing to sacrifice greatly for God's sake, when called to do so like Abraham, or for refusing to help the people of God in their need, as Rahab helped. But this is not right knowledge or application of the doctrine of justification by faith alone. Rather, it is misunderstanding. Nor is this lackadaisical attitude and life the product of justification by faith alone. Rather, it is the warring of the depraved nature against the truth of justification.

The Heidelberg Catechism explains why the fear that justification by faith alone makes humans careless and profane is unfounded: "It is impossible that those who are implanted into Christ by true faith should not bring forth fruits of righteousness."[18]

It is impossible that the divine act of the justifying by faith alone of the elect ungodly, apart from all his own works, should bring about, or lead to, or allow carelessness or profanity of life. First, the true faith by which one is justified is spiritual union with Christ. Spiritual union with Christ brings the life of Christ into the heart of the justified sinner. This sin-overcoming life of the risen Christ rules in the justified sinner, producing love for God and love for the neighbor. One can no more be united to Christ by the faith that justifies and not bring forth the fruits of good works than a branch can be grafted into a tree and not bring forth, by the life of the tree, leaves, blossoms, and fruit.

The faith that is the means of justification is always also the faith that is the means of sanctification, God's work of making the elect sinner holy, so that he obeys the law and performs good works. At the great Jerusalem synod, the issue was exactly that which concerns us now, namely, whether Paul's doctrine of justification by faith alone is not a dangerous doctrine regarding the Christian life of holiness, so that the converts, especially the loose-living Gentile converts, should have the law imposed on them for righteousness and some conditions unto salvation added to the gospel. There Peter declared that men are sanctified by faith alone, as they are justified by faith alone: "purifying their hearts by faith" (Acts 15:19).

The same Christ who justifies us by faith alone sanctifies by his Holy Spirit those whom he justifies. He is a complete savior. He saves not only from sin's guilt but from sin, which is also a corrupting, destroying power. This is the answer of question 86 of the Heidelberg Catechism to a question very much like question 64. "Since, then, we are redeemed from our misery by grace through Christ, without any merit of ours, why must we

18 Heidelberg Catechism A 64, in ibid., 3:328.

do good works?" The mention of merit indicates that the Catechism again confronts Rome's fear or charge that unless the church puts the members on the footing with God of earning their salvation by their own good works, the members will not feel it necessary to do good works. The answer of the Catechism is, "Because Christ, having redeemed us by his blood, renews us also by his holy Spirit."[19]

Christ is not half a savior, delivering sinners from guilt but leaving them under the rule of sin as a destructive power. Having justified, he always also at once sanctifies. He taught this in his saving word to the adulterous woman in John 8:11: "Neither do I condemn thee" (free justification, consisting of and based on nothing in the woman herself); "go, and sin no more" (the efficacious word that makes her holy, following the word of justification but accompanying that word).

Second, it is impossible that justification by faith alone makes one careless because the Spirit at once carries out the work of Christ of sanctifying the justified sinner in this way, that by the very declaration of forgiveness and righteousness he makes the forgiven sinner *thankful* to his merciful Savior. The sinner experiences deliverance from the guilt of sin unto a right standing with God the judge as the greatest good. For this deliverance he is thankful. Such is his thankfulness that he loves the Savior and the God who gave him. In this love the forgiven sinner obeys the will of the gracious God.

The good works and holy life of the justified Christian are not a matter of the earning of a hired hand, or a matter of the forced labor of a slave, or a matter of the grim service of one in terror at the prospect of hell. They are the works and working of thankful love, willingly offered to the God of grace.

Those who corrupt the gospel of grace by works-righteousness, by a conditional covenant, or by a message of salvation by

---

19 Heidelberg Catechism Q&A 86, in ibid., 3:338.

human willing and working (Rom. 9:16) forget that motives of meriting, or repaying, or terror of punishment in case of failing to work sufficiently are not the only, or the best and most powerful, motives for work in earthly human life. Love is a motive for hard, sacrificial, even heroic working. Love is the best motive. Love is the most powerful motive. One example will suffice. What motivates the mother to care for her children, doing the dirtiest tasks, putting in the longest hours, and in reality sacrificing her own life in hundreds of ways for the lives and welfare of her children? There is not money to pay her. In fact, any mother worthy of the glorious title would spit on money if it were offered to her as payment for her work. The motive is not the expectation of payment. It is simply, but gloriously, love, love for her offspring for God's sake that will put forth every effort, labor long hours, make every sacrifice, and in a way, gladly give up her own life.

Love for God and for us moved the Christ to lay down his life as a sacrifice on our behalf.

Love for him, and for the God who gave him as our redeemer (as we realize in the gift of justification by faith alone), motivates us to serve him and God—gladly, willingly, freely, wholeheartedly, sacrificially—in thankfulness. Only this motivation of the Christian life is pleasing and acceptable to God. This motivation of the truly Christian life is worked and secured only by the gospel truth of justification by faith alone. Magnificently, the Heidelberg Catechism, in its third part, puts the entirety of the Christian life under the rubric of thankfulness for gracious salvation.

The response of the Reformed confessions to the fear that grace, particularly the grace of justification, leads to carelessness of life is the response of the Bible to this fear. To Paul's grand doctrine of justification by faith alone in Romans 3 and 4 comes the objection or expression of fear: "What shall we say then? Shall we continue in sin, that grace may abound?" That is, "But does not this justification by faith alone that you have been teaching lead to carelessness, indeed even to the damnable theology that the justified sinner could and should sin as much as possible in order to experience and show the exceeding greatness of the grace of forgiveness?" (Rom. 6:1).

Note well, first, that the right doctrine of justification will always occasion this objection, or charge, or statement of fear. If the fear is broached or the charge leveled, it is confirmation that we are teaching the right doctrine of justification. The Protestant Reformed Churches draw this charge in various forms: "They deny the responsibility of man! They are hyper-Calvinists!" Early on in my controversy with the theology of the federal vision, I wrote that no one would ever think of charging Shepherd and his colleagues with making people careless and profane by their doctrine of justification.

> Who would ever think of charging the justification doctrine of Norman Shepherd and his allies with antinomism? So full is their doctrine of conditions, law, and human works that it is simply inconceivable that anyone would ever think of saying, "You make void the law through faith! It is the implication of your doctrine that justified sinners continue in sin that grace may abound!"[20]

Noteworthy, second, is that in response to the objection or charge against his doctrine of justification by faith alone, Paul does not compromise or go back on the doctrine in the slightest. He does not respond, "Oh my, there is something to the fear. We may have a church full of licentious people if I maintain what I wrote in Romans 3 and 4. I better adapt my doctrine according to the fear. I will bring into justification the law and its commandments; I will demand good works as part of the sinner's righteousness, if not in this life, then in the final judgment;

20 Engelsma, *The Covenant of God and the Children of Believers*, 167–68.

I will insist on conditions that the sinner must fulfill." Nothing of the sort. The apostle maintains his doctrine fully and unapologetically. Indeed, he goes on in chapters 8 and 9 to ground gracious justification in gracious, unconditional predestination, which doctrine draws the charge or elicits the fear of spawning a wicked life even more, if this is possible, than does the doctrine of justification by faith alone.

Third, the response of Paul to the fear of a careless and profane life is that this kind of life is impossible for the justified sinner because the faith that justifies is union with Christ that *must* and *will* crucify the old man of sin and make people willing servants of Christ in a life of holiness. "How shall we, that are dead to sin, live any longer therein?...our old man is crucified with him, that the body of sin might be destroyed, that henceforth we should not serve sin" (Rom. 6:2–6).

This does not imply that the true church, as marked by the teaching of justification by faith alone, is not tempted by the antinomian heresy, if not in the gross form of "Let us sin that grace may abound," then in the lesser form of "We may be lax in obedience to the law because grace abounds." Neither is the justified sinner exempt from the temptation. Every pastor knows better. James 2 proves otherwise. The history of the church demonstrates that antinomianism is a perpetual danger. One of the evils present already in the churches of Asia Minor of Revelation 2 and 3 was antinomianism in its gross form. There was rejection of the law as the rule of a thankful life. There was open immorality on the ground of salvation by grace alone. That was the evil of the Nicolaitans, of those who held the doctrine of Balaam, and of the monstrous Jezebel, whose "gospel" was, "Let us know the depths of Satan."

The poet called attention to the danger, always, of the abuse of the doctrine of justification by faith alone, astutely observing that the danger is not the doctrine itself but the carnality of the abusers of the doctrine:

"All works, Great Men, Societies are bad.
The Just shall live by Faith..." he cried in dread.
And men and women of the world were glad,
Who'd never cared or trembled in their lives.[21]

In fact, I dare say, much of evangelical Christianity in North America has succumbed to this very evil. The law does not function as authoritative guide of the life of the people, nor is it preached as such. Members live openly and grossly immoral lives, especially sexually. Consider only the adultery of remarriage after divorce. There is no discipline of impenitent sinners. The response to rebuke is, "We are saved by grace. God is a graciously forgiving God." Apart from the antinomian nature of the response, by both preachers and members, the response is dubious in view of the fact that much of this evangelical Christianity has not preached the gospel of grace soundly, purely, and fully for years. For the most part these churches are Arminian, pietistic, and charismatic.

The message and church life of these churches are antinomian. "Let us sin that grace may abound!" At least, "Our impenitent lawlessness of life is permitted because we are saved by grace!"

Avowed antinomianism rears its ugly head also in some branches of Reformed Christianity. One such branch is churches that have been influenced by the German theologian H. Kohlbrugge. They object strenuously to demands in the covenant, to admonitions to godly living, and to the sharp preaching of the "must" of the law as the authoritative guide to the Christian life. Their treatment of the third part of the Catechism, which Catechism they profess to honor, is scanty and objectionable. For example, they explain the "must" of question 86 as meaning

21 W. H. Auden, "Luther," in *Collected Poems*, ed. Edward Mendelson (New York: Random House, 1976), 235.

"will," not "should" or "ought to." Admonitory preaching is condemned as "law-preaching."

Against the threat of antinomianism, the true church must faithfully preach justification by faith alone and salvation by grace alone, without compromise. But the church must preach justification in its whole truth, including God's purpose with justification, that the justified sinner be thankful and in this thankfulness obey the law of God. The church must preach justifying faith as union with Christ and therefore as a faith that also sanctifies and produces the fruits of good works (faith alone justifies, but faith is never alone). The church must preach the law as the rule of thankfulness and good works as the expression of this thankfulness. The church must preach Christ as the complete savior, delivering from the pollution of sin as well as from the guilt of sin.

The church must withstand to their faces those sometimes noisy opponents in the church who, in their misguided zeal for grace, object to admonitions, the "must" of the law, and the genuine responsibility of the Christian, that is, his obligation to do the will of God. When antinomianism appears, or to prevent it from appearing, the church must preach justification by works, not justification by faith *and* works, but justification by works in *the real, orthodox sense of James 2*. When antinomian members of the church spread their heresy in the church or brazenly and impenitently live lawlessly, the church must exercise discipline upon them.

Genuine Calvinism is as zealous on behalf of sanctification as it is on behalf of justification. Calvin was. The Reformed creeds are. So is the Bible.

But the two saving works of Jesus Christ, although intimately, indeed inseparably, related, are distinct.

In the interests of our thorough study of justification, I briefly explain both the distinction between and the relationship of justification and sanctification. Our interest is not here sanctification, but justification. Therefore, nothing like a complete explanation of sanctification should be expected.

There are good reasons for including its relationship to sanctification in a study of justification. First, scripture and the Reformed creeds teach the relationship between these two saving acts of God in Jesus Christ. Second, the heresy of justification by faith and works has always as a main component the confusion of the two works of God. Rome teaches justification not only as the imputation of righteousness, but also as the infusion of righteousness. The federal vision's heretical doctrine of justification by faith and works makes justification, especially in the final judgment, consist both of Christ's work for us and of our own good works, which, with more or less clarity and sincerity, they attribute to the work of Christ in us. The work of Christ in us is sanctification. Thus the federal vision deliberately confuses justification and sanctification. This confusion is not innocent. Sanctification in federal vision theology very much consists of the active contribution to his holiness of the sinner himself. In this way the justification, especially the final justification, of the sinner includes and even depends upon his own performance of good works and his good works themselves.

In his criticism of the Council of Trent, Calvin charged that the Roman Catholic heresy of justification by works, which Trent made official dogma, consisted of a confusion of justification and sanctification. He acknowledged the close relationship between justification and sanctification but insisted that the maintenance of the gospel of grace demands that they be distinguished. "It is not to be denied…that the two things, Justification and Sanctification, are constantly conjoined and cohere; but from this it is erroneously inferred that they are one and the same." To illustrate both the close relationship and the sharp distinction between justification and sanctification, Calvin appealed to the light and the heat of the sun: "The light of the sun, though never unaccompanied with heat, is not to be considered heat." About his figure but with application to its reality, Calvin then asked, "Where is the man so undiscerning as not to distinguish the one from the other?"[22]

Let us be clear about the theological terms and the saving works they describe. Justification (the root being *just* or *righteous*) is the act of God in Christ forgiving the elect sinner's sins and sinfulness and reckoning him righteous before God the judge by imputing to his account all the obedience of Christ in his stead. This obedience of Christ, which is imputed to the elect, believing sinner by means only of the sinner's God-given faith in Christ, is all Christ's doing of the will of God throughout all his life and ministry, but especially the obedience of his suffering and death at the end of his life, culminating in his death on the cross. By this act of God the sinner is perfectly just in the judgment of God in the sinner's own conscience, already in this life. This act of God is the subject of Romans 3–5, the book of Galatians, and other passages of holy scripture.

In sharp distinction from justification, sanctification is the work of God by the Spirit of Jesus Christ in the elect, believing, and justified sinner making him holy. The root of the Latin-based term *sanctification* is *holiness*. Holiness consists of cleansing from the defilement and power of sin and of consecrating one to God in love for him, so that one obeys God's law and performs the good works that God requires of him. Sanctification, like justification, is a work that God performs within the sinner by means of the sinner's faith (Acts 15:9). Unlike justification, sanctification is not perfected in this life. There is progress in this work. One becomes increasingly holy, although "even the holiest men, while in this life, have only a small beginning of this obedience."[23] Sanctification is the subject in Romans 6, 12–16; Ephesians 4–6; 2 Thessalonians 2:13; James; and many other passages of scripture.

22 Calvin, "Antidote to the Council of Trent," in *Calvin's Tracts*, 3:115–16.
23 Heidelberg Catechism A 114, in Schaff, *Creeds of Christendom*, 3:349.

These two works of God in Christ have in common that both are works of salvation from sin. But they are and must be sharply distinguished. First, justification is a legal act in the consciousness of the believing sinner, declaring him righteous before God by a verdict, as in a courtroom. Sanctification, in contrast, is a work of spiritual power in the believing sinner's heart, mind, soul, and body, making him holy, or good. Justification removes sin's guilt and effects the legal state of innocence. Sanctification overcomes the ruling power of sin in one's life and accomplishes the victory of holiness. Justification releases the sinner from the bondage of guilt. Sanctification releases the sinner from the bondage of the ruling power of sin.

Second, justification *imputes*, or reckons, Christ's righteousness to the sinner's account, or standing, before God the judge. Sanctification *infuses* Christ's obedience into the sinner. The distinction between the two acts of God is the difference between imputing and infusing. Whatever church or theologian explains justification as the infusing of righteousness, even in part, thereby corrupts the gospel truth of justification.

Third, justification reckons to the sinner's account Christ's obedience to the law in that sinner's stead, so that the sinner is freed from the obligations to keep the law for his righteousness and to suffer the law's penalty for his unrighteousness. Sanctification writes the law of God upon the sinner's heart, so that he begins victoriously to obey the law.

Fourth, justification delivers the sinner from the guilt of sin, the liability to divine punishment and the sense of shame. Sanctification delivers the sinner from the ruling power of sin and thus from the pollution of sin. The justified adulterer is freed from the punishment of death and the haunting shame of his deed. He stands consciously before God, his wife, society, and his own conscience as one who has perfectly and always obeyed the seventh commandment. The sanctified adulterer is no longer ruled by lust, fights against lust whenever it arises from his sinful nature, and heartily wills never again to commit the deed, whether in thought or in deed, but to live chastely.

Fifth, justification blesses the sinner with peace with God in his conscience. Sanctification blesses the sinner with the power to love God and the neighbor.

Sixth, justification is a perfect act of salvation upon the believing sinner by Christ in this life. Sanctification, although a victorious work of Christ upon the believing sinner already in this life, is never perfect in this life but is progressive. When Christ justifies the believing sinner through his faith, he fully pardons all his sins and decisively reckons to the sinner all Christ's obedience on the sinner's behalf. The blessing of justification for the sinner is that he is conscious and assured of perfect righteousness with God. Consciously, he stands before God the judge as one who has never had nor committed any sin but is perfectly innocent with the full obedience of Jesus Christ, his representative. One is not increasingly justified. One is not justified more and more. When the judge declares concerning one who is on trial that the defendant is not guilty, the verdict is a perfectly accomplished verdict, and the consciousness of the one who has been acquitted is that of perfect innocence regarding the demands of the law.

Sanctification, in contrast, is never perfect in this life. The sanctified sinner is never completely delivered from the power and pollution of sin (contrary to the false and foolish teaching of the perfectionists. Regarding the folly of this teaching, the story comes down in church history that when a man claimed perfection of holiness, another responded, "I will believe this after I have talked to your wife"). Sin no longer rules in the sanctified sinner, according to Romans 6, but sin does remain in him, powerfully so, so that he has yet a sinful nature (which is sin), commits sin (contrary to his will, as Paul teaches in Romans 7), and corrupts even his best works with sin as long as he lives.

Nevertheless, there is, and ought to be, progress in holiness in every child of God throughout his life. The Heidelberg Catechism insists on this progress in explanation of the necessity of sharply preaching the ten commandments to the congregation: "that…[we may] become more and more changed into the image of God, till we attain finally to full perfection after this life."[24] This confessional statement indicates that perfection of sanctification comes at death and ultimately at the resurrection of the body, when the body shares with the soul the perfect holiness of Christ. The Catechism teaches that a reason the believer does not fear but even longs for death is that at his death the Spirit of Christ finally abolishes his sinful nature and the power of sin in him. "Why must we also die? Our death is…only a dying to sins."[25]

Thus the Reformed confessions sharply distinguish these two eminent works of salvation.[26]

The distinction is biblical. Romans 3–5 teach justification as the legal act of God in Christ perfectly delivering from guilt, on the basis of Christ's life and death, so that the sinner has peace with God. Romans 6–7, the first part of 8, and 12–16 teach sanctification as the Spirit's work in the justified sinner of actually delivering him from the ruling power of sin, although not perfectly in this life (see especially chapter 7), so that he victoriously lives a life of love for God expressed by obedience to God's law.

It is the fatal error of the Roman Catholic Church and today, amazingly, of reputedly conservative Reformed and Presbyterian churches that they confuse and confound justification and sanctification. These are the churches that produce, tolerate, and even defend the federal vision. They teach that the saving work

---

24 Heidelberg Catechism A 115, in ibid., 3:349.

25 Heidelberg Catechism Q&A 42, in ibid., 3:320–21.

26 See also the Belgic Confession 23–24, in ibid., 3:409–12, and the Westminster Confession 11, 13, in ibid., 3:626–30.

of justification is partly God's work of infusing in the sinner the righteousness of Christ, so that the sinner performs good works. Then on the basis of both Christ's death and the good works of the sinner himself, God forgives the sinner and declares him just. To say it differently, the error is to describe justification as God's work, with the sinner's cooperation, of *infusing* righteousness into the sinner, rather than as God's work of *imputing* righteousness to the sinner, which righteousness is all and only the *alien* righteousness of Jesus Christ. The result in the theology of the federal vision is the heresy of justification by faith and works.

The confusing and confounding of justification and sanctification always result in, indeed have the purpose of, making the sinner's own good works part of his righteousness with God in the fundamental act of justification.

Although the two saving works of God in Jesus Christ are sharply distinguished, they are also inseparably related. Our concern here is to do justice to the truth that justification is always accompanied by sanctification. As the Reformed tradition has always insisted, especially in relating Paul and James, although Paul's justification in Romans 3 and 4 is by faith alone without works, James' justification establishes that faith is never alone without works. First, whomever Christ justifies, he also sanctifies, for Christ is a complete savior from sin. He does not only deliver from the guilt and punishment of sin, but he delivers also from the ruling power and the pollution of sin, as his saving word to the adulterous woman in John 8:11 brilliantly illustrates.

Whom Jesus justifies, he also sanctifies—*at the same time*, not years later. This is the Reformed condemnation of one party in the "lordship controversy" in fundamentalist circles in North America. Many dispensationalists, consistently with their denial that the law of God is the guide of the holy life of New Testament Christians, teach that Christ can deliver from the guilt of sin without delivering from the ruling power of sin. That is, it is possible, and often the case, that Christ justifies the sinner but does not sanctify him. Christ is savior of some sinners, but not the lord of their lives. Thus they teach that Jesus is merely half a savior. In the language of John 8:11, it is often the case that Jesus says to a sinner, "Neither do I condemn thee," but refrains from saying for many years, if not forever in this life, "Sin no more."

With scripture the Reformed faith knows Christ as a complete savior, delivering all his own both from sin's guilt and from sin's ruling power. Answer 86 of the Heidelberg Catechism expresses the truth about the inseparable connection between justification and sanctification: "Christ, having redeemed us by his blood, renews us also by his holy Spirit after his own image."[27]

Second, so intimately related are justification and sanctification, so inseparable are they, so impossible is it that one be justified without also being sanctified, that in an important sense only those are justified who have already been sanctified. There is an important order of the two works of grace that has justification preceding sanctification. This is the order of Jesus' saving word to the adulterous woman in John 8. This is the order of the sinner's experience of the two saving works. First, his sins are forgiven, arousing thankfulness. Then sanctification moves the forgiven sinner to express his thankfulness in a life of love for God and for the neighbor.

But objectively sanctification precedes justification in the life of the elect sinner. Before one can believe in Christ as presented in the gospel and in this way be justified in his own consciousness, he must have been united to Jesus Christ by the Holy Spirit and regenerated. Only one who has been born again with the new life of Christ can possibly believe the gospel and believe on Christ as presented in the gospel. But regeneration is a renewing, sanctifying work of God in one's heart, one's spiritual center. Regeneration enables and empowers one to believe

---

27 Heidelberg Catechism A 86, in ibid., 3:338.

on Christ so that he can be justified. This holiness of the believing sinner does not at all enter into one's justification by faith alone. Nevertheless, only one already born again and thus made holy will believe and be justified by that faith in Christ. With reason Calvin treated sanctification and the Christian life before he treated justification by faith alone in his *Institutes*. It is therefore impossible that one is justified but lives an unholy, lawless life. In this regard too justification and sanctification are inseparably related.

But, third, the relationship and order of justification and sanctification are that consciously the one who has been justified freely by the blood of Christ will love his gracious Savior. Since love for Christ is the motive of the life of holiness, the order of the two great saving works of Christ in the experience of the elect sinner is justification followed by sanctification. To put the relationship differently, the Spirit of Christ makes us holy by justifying us by faith alone. But sanctification will always certainly follow justification, and at once, as it were spontaneously.

Here the touching history and parable of Luke 7:36–50 are revelatory. The sinful woman loved Jesus much (sanctification) because he had freely forgiven all her great debt (justification). Her love, expressing itself in good works, including sexual chastity, was not the cause of her forgiveness, nor at all the righteousness with which she was declared right with God, but the fruit, result, and evidence of her justification. It was the *certain* and *instantaneous* fruit and effect of her justification. It was also the goal of God with her justification. In justifying the elect sinner by faith alone, the peace of the sinner is not the ultimate purpose of God. The ultimate purpose of God is the sinner's holiness of life out of gratitude to God, for by a holy life God is glorified.

So far is it from true, therefore, that justification by faith alone makes people careless and profane, as is the charge always against the biblical doctrine of justification by faith alone, that, on the contrary, the one who is justified by faith alone will certainly perform good works. Only the one who is justified by faith alone will perform truly good works, for only works done out of thankful love to God for a purely gracious salvation, specifically a gracious justification, are acceptable to God as genuinely good. Works done out of terror, to escape hell, or out of a slavish desire to earn salvation or fulfill conditions upon which salvation is supposed to depend, which implies that Christ's work was not enough and that salvation after all is not by grace alone, are not pleasing to God but terribly displeasing to him. Such deeds are not good works at all.

One of our reasons then, and not the slightest, for our defense of justification by faith alone is our ardent desire that the people of God will be zealous for good works. They will be zealous for good works by believing and living the truth of justification by faith alone.

This zeal requires the orthodox understanding of the relationship of Paul and James.

Chapter Twenty-Two

JUSTIFICATION AND ELECTION

No treatment of the biblical and Reformed, that is, Reformation, gospel truth of justification by faith alone is complete without a consideration of the close, necessary, and significant relationship of justification and election. Lacking its source in the truth of God's eternal election, the doctrine of justification by faith will not be rightly confessed and cannot be maintained. Calvin warned that those who refused or failed to teach God's predestination, particularly his eternal election of some in distinction from others whom he reprobated, would necessarily lose the gospel truth of justification. With specific reference to God's election and reprobation, which he had just explained, Calvin wrote: "Unless these points are put beyond controversy, though we may ever and anon repeat like parrots that we are justified by faith, we shall never hold the true doctrine of Justification."[1]

Today too, Reformed, Presbyterian, and evangelical churches safely house any number of theological and ministerial parrots, repeating in their lectures and books, "justification by faith alone, justification by faith alone," who are silent about election and even vociferous in compromising the doctrine by their loud affirmation of a saving grace of God for all men without exception and a gracious desire of God to save all humans without

1 John Calvin, "The True Method of Giving Peace to Christendom and Reforming the Church," in Beveridge, *Calvin's Tracts*, 3:254.

exception, accompanied by their rejection of the decree of reprobation. It is no surprise then that in the churches where these parrots recite the orthodox doctrine of justification by rote, there appears and establishes itself today the open, bold denial of justification by faith alone by the federal vision. *Without discipline*! Often *with deliberate refusal to discipline*!

By election is meant God's eternal, unconditional, gracious choice in Christ of a definite number of certain persons (as the bride and body of Jesus Christ) unto salvation, accompanied by God's eternal and equally unconditional appointment of the others unto damnation (which damnation, or punishment, is on account of their unbelief and other sins). Election is the truth taught in Ephesians 1:4: "According as he [God] hath chosen us in him [Jesus Christ] before the foundation of the world, that we should be holy and without blame before him in love."

The Canons of Dordt confess the truth of election in 1.7:

> Election is the unchangeable purpose of God, whereby, before the foundation of the world, he hath, out of mere grace, according to the sovereign good pleasure of his own will, chosen, from the whole human race, which had fallen through their own fault, from their primitive state of rectitude, into sin and destruction, a certain number of persons to redemption in Christ, whom he from eternity appointed the Mediator and head of the elect, and the foundation of salvation.[2]

Election and Justification in the Creeds and Scripture

The Reformed confessions teach the close, necessary, and significant relationship of justification and election. Canons 1.7 goes on to affirm that in the eternal decree of election God "hath

2 Canons of Dordt 1.7, in Schaff, *Creeds of Christendom*, 3:582.

decreed...to bestow upon them [those whom he elected] true faith [and] justification."[3] Canons 1.9 teaches that "election is the fountain of every saving good [which includes justification]; from which proceed[s] faith [which is the instrument of justification]."[4]

In the chapter on justification, the Westminster Confession of Faith declares that "God did, from all eternity, decree to justify all the elect."[5] This creedal statement locates the source of justification in God's decree of election; makes justification the outstanding benefit of salvation that God purposed for those whom he elected; identifies the beneficiaries of justification, both in God's intention and in God's saving work in history, as the elect; and assures that all for whom God has purposed justification will be justified.

The close and significant relationship between justification and election affirmed by the Reformed confessions is solidly based on scripture. In Ephesians 1:5 Paul views the relationship in light of eternal election, or the predestination unto salvation: "having predestinated us unto the adoption of children by Jesus Christ to himself, according to the good pleasure of his will." Adoption unto children is a legal act of God in the consciousness of the believer, dependent upon and immediately following the believer's justification, if it is not an aspect of justification itself. However adoption is viewed, adoption implies justification, so that the apostle in Ephesians 1:5 makes justification the purpose of God in his predestination, or election, of his people in eternity. The text teaches that God predestinated us unto justification.

Likewise, Romans 8:30 teaches that justification was the end and certain saving effect in history of God's electing decree: "Whom he did predestinate...them he also justified." To read

3 Canons of Dordt 1.7, in ibid.

4 Canons of Dordt 1.9, in ibid., 3:583.

5 Westminster Confession of Faith 11.4, in ibid., 3:627.

the phrase correctly, one must emphasize the words "predestinate" and "them." It is as if the apostle is answering the question, whom does God justify? At the same time the phrase establishes that predestination purposed the justification of those predestinated. The intimate relationship of justification and election is indicated by the question and answer of verse 33: "Who shall lay any thing to the charge of God's elect? It is God that justifieth."

The relationship of justification and election is the very structure of the book of Romans. In chapters 3–5 the apostle sets forth, explains, and defends the gospel truth of justification by faith alone, the grand theme of the epistle. In chapters 8–11 he grounds this gospel truth and locates its source in God's gracious, eternal election. "Whom he did predestinate…them he also justified" (8:30). "For he saith to Moses, I will have mercy on whom I will have mercy, and I will have compassion on whom I will have compassion" (9:15). In light of the first eight chapters of Romans, God's mercy and compassion are especially his justifying the ungodly. This merciful and compassionate justification has its source and explanation, including the explanation as to the particular objects of the mercy and compassion, in God's eternal will to have mercy and compassion upon them, that is, his eternal, sovereign election of some.

According to scripture, as faithfully confessed by the Reformed creeds, the relationship of justification and election is that justification rightly understood implies and demands God's eternal election as its source. If justification is by faith alone, apart from any and all works and worth of the sinner; if justification by faith means that faith is the instrument of justification, not the cause or condition; and if faith itself, both as the power of believing and as the activity of believing on Christ for pardon and righteousness, is the gift of God to the sinner who believes, the sole explanation of the justifying of sinners (in distinction from others who do not believe and who are not justified, although they hear the same gospel as do those who do believe) is God's prior, eternal purpose of grace toward the sinners who believe and are justified, that is, God's eternal, sovereign, gracious election of them unto justification and salvation.

The explanation of the justification of a sinner cannot be anything in himself, for he is guilty and totally depraved, including that his will is a slave to sin. In himself the sinner lacks both the right and the ability to believe and, by believing, the capability of making himself the object of God's gift of justification.

The source and explanation of the sinner's faith itself, as of the justifying verdict of God through this faith, is God's eternal election of this sinner. The Canons of Dordt express this dependency of the faith that justifies on election:

> That some receive the gift of faith from God, and others do not receive it, proceeds from God's eternal decree... According to which decree he graciously softens the hearts of the elect, however obstinate, and inclines them to believe; while he leaves the non-elect in his just judgment to their own wickedness and obduracy. And herein is especially displayed the profound, the merciful and at the same time the righteous discrimination between men, equally involved in ruin; or that decree of *election* and *reprobation,* revealed in the Word of God.[6]

In biblical support of this statement of the dependency of faith, with its justifying function, the Canons adduce Acts 15:18 and Ephesians 1:11.

Justification and Election Experienced

Locating the source of his justification in God's eternal, gracious election is a matter of the justified sinner's own experience. It is also a matter of the greatest importance for the believing sinner's

---

6 Canons of Dordt 1.6, in ibid., 3:582.

assurance of the love of God for him and of his certain salvation. At the moment of his justification, the forgiven sinner—marvelously freed from the guilt and shame of his sinfulness and all his transgressions, liberated from the wrath of God, the curse of the law, and the bondage of Satan, to whom the doors of heaven swing open upon fellowship with God in Jesus Christ—cries out, "To whom and to what am I indebted for this grace of justification? Whence comes to me this forgiveness and the faith by which I am forgiven?" The gospel's answer in his own consciousness is, "From the prior gracious purpose of God toward me in his decree of election."

God wills not only that his people are justified by a verdict that bestows assurance of the declaration of righteousness, but also that they know and are assured of their eternal election, that is, of his eternal love for them. This is possible only if justification has its source in the decree, that is, if those whom he justifies are those whom "he did predestinate" (Rom. 8:30).

An aspect of this assurance of one's election is that the justified sinner realizes that his justification is due to electing love that was (and is) particular and discriminating. The decree that is the eternal source of the faith and justification of some also sovereignly rejects the others, appointing them to perish in their unbelief and other sins, unforgiven and unrighteous, worthy therefore of eternal damnation. This illumines to the justified sinner the sheer grace of the election that accounts for his faith and righteousness, humbles him, and increases his gratitude to the electing God.

> What peculiarly tends to illustrate and recommend to us the eternal and unmerited grace of election is the express testimony of sacred Scripture, that not all, but some only, are elected, while others are passed by in the eternal decree; whom God, out of his sovereign, most just, irreprehensible and unchangeable good pleasure,

> hath decreed to leave in the common misery into which they have willfully plunged themselves, and not to bestow upon them saving faith...And this is the decree of reprobation.[7]

No confessing Christian can avoid this aspect of the relationship of justification and election, although many try to do so. If in fact justification depends solely upon election, if election is the source of justification, if the explanation of the forgiveness of some sinners is God's election of them, it is necessarily implied that it proceeds from God's counsel that the others do not believe and are not justified. God has not elected them but reprobated them. God has decided that he will not give them faith and, by faith, the righteousness of Christ. This is the reality, the awesome reality, as Calvin expressed it, of eternal reprobation.

To deny reprobation, as many professed Protestants do, is to jeopardize the gospel truth of gracious justification. Denial of reprobation is necessarily the affirmation that justification depends upon the will and working of the sinner. Faith then lies within the natural ability of every sinner—his supposed free will—and justification therefore depends upon the sinner himself, whether his work of believing, supposedly by this free will, or some other work. Denial of reprobation necessarily implies a teaching of justification by works.

The apostle Paul is deeply concerned to safeguard the gospel truth of justification by faith alone, with its ultimate purpose in the glorifying of God for the salvation of sinners (which is the heart of the message of the book of Romans). This explains Paul's inclusion of the truth of predestination in the second half of Romans 8 and in Romans 9–11. The treatment of predestination in this passage is not an isolated, dogmatical treatise on the subject. It is part and parcel of his setting forth and defense

7 Canons of Dordt 1.15, in ibid., 3:584.

of gracious justification with the necessary protection of the doctrine that only predestination affords. With good theological reason, the apostle asks not, "Who shall lay any thing to the charge of believers?" but, "Who shall lay any thing to the charge of God's *elect*?" (Rom. 8:33, emphasis added).

Such is the relationship of justification and election that justification magnifies the grace of election. God has so bound justification to election as justification's eternal, sovereignly gracious source in order that the true church in preaching the fundamental gospel truth of justification and the believer in experiencing this truth will proclaim, confess, and extol eternal election. God wills that the forgiven sinner do more than praise his justifying grace. God wills that the church and the believer do more than glory in the cross of Christ. God wills that the church and the justified believer know, confess, and magnify his election as the fountain of the cross, faith, and justification. Indeed, ignorance, silence, and much more denial of election will necessarily result in denial or corruption of the cross and of justification.

Only when, in the preaching and confession of the church, justification is traced to its source in God's gracious election is the grace of God in the salvation of his people faithfully and truthfully confessed to the glory of God. Regardless that a church or a professing believer begins well by affirming justification by faith alone, if this church or professing believer refuses to preach or confess election as the source of justification, that church or professing believer will in the end be unable to maintain justification by faith alone. That church or professing believer will fall away to the heresy of justification by faith and works. Reluctant, for whatever reason, boldly and continually to preach or confess a justification *of which the source and explanation is God's eternal election*, they will eventually preach or confess that the source and explanation of justification is the sinner himself—his work of believing as a matter of his free will and his other good works.

Although the main doctrine of the Reformation, for Calvin as for Luther, was justification by faith alone, the deepest concern of the Reformation, for Luther as for Calvin, was not justification by faith alone but salvation in Christ by the sovereign grace of God, having its source in eternal election, accompanied by eternal, sovereign reprobation. That Luther softened somewhat this concern in the latter stage of his ministry, under the influence of Philip Melancthon, was fatal to subsequent Lutheranism—fatal regarding subsequent Lutheranism's confession of justification by faith alone.

The reason for the heretical Roman Catholic doctrine of justification is that church's detestation of the truth of predestination. In the very midst of Rome's repudiation of the truth of justification by faith alone are both her statement that she is well aware of the relationship between predestination, that is, election, and justification and her expression of detestation of the doctrine of election.

> No one, moreover, so long as he is in this mortal life, ought so far to presume as regards the secret mystery of divine predestination [election], as to determine for certain that he is assuredly in the number of the predestinate; as if it were true, that he that is justified, either can not sin any more, or, if he do sin, that he ought to promise himself an assured repentance; for except by special revelation, it can not be known whom God hath chosen unto himself.[8]

Because the Arminians rejected the truth of sovereign, unconditional election, they also denied the particular, limited atonement of the cross, which merited both faith and justification for the elect. This heresy required Arminian theology to

8 Canons and Decrees of the Council of Trent, Sixth Session, Decree on Justification 12, in ibid., 2:103.

corrupt the doctrine of justification. Justification in Arminian theology is not the imputation of the obedience of Christ to elect sinners by means of faith. Rather, it is God's regarding the sinner's faith itself and the obedience of faith as the sinner's righteousness with God, which faith and obedience have their fountain in the free will of the sinner, according to Arminian theology. Universal, conditional election demands universal atonement. And universal atonement requires a conditional justification, that is, a justification consisting of and conditioned by the sinner's act of believing. This heretical doctrine of justification, originating in a false doctrine of election, the Canons of Dordt condemn:

> The Synod *rejects* the errors of those…who teach that the new covenant of grace, which God the Father, through the mediation of the death of Christ, made with man, does not herein consist that we by faith, inasmuch as it accepts the merits of Christ, are justified before God and saved, but in the fact that God, having revoked the demand of perfect obedience of the law, regards faith itself and the obedience of faith, although imperfect, as the perfect obedience of the law, and does esteem it worthy of the reward of eternal life through grace.

Rightly, the article goes on to say that this is the proclamation of "a new and strange justification of man before God, against the consensus of the whole church."[9]

The Federal Vision on Justification and Election

Ultimately, the cause of the heretical doctrine of conditional, and therefore losable, justification taught by the federal vision is its

---

9 Canons of Dordt 2, error 4, in *Confessions and Church Order*, 165. In light of the refusal of both the federal vision and of liberated theology to allow election to govern the covenant and its salvation, it is worthy of note that here the Canons defend election as the fountain of the "new covenant of grace" against the Arminian rejection of the government of covenantal salvation by election.

doctrine of conditional, and therefore losable, election. According to the federal vision, this conditional, losable justification, which is rooted in conditional election, especially characterizes the sphere of the covenant. God has elected all the baptized children of believing parents. According to this universal, conditional, losable election, he also justifies all the baptized children. But this justification is conditional. If the children do not fulfill the condition of believing, and do so to the very end of their lives, they will lose their justification and be condemned eternally.

The first chapter in the book that is the quasi-official statement of federal vision theology is titled "Covenant and Election." Federal vision theologian John Barach explains the theology of the federal vision as teaching that at their baptism God establishes his covenant of grace with all the baptized children alike. To all he makes the covenantal promise. With them all he establishes his covenant of grace. He "truly brings those people into His covenant, into union with Christ. They are 'in Him,' to use Jesus' words in John 15. They share in His blessings."[10]

These blessings include justification. The promises made to all the children at their baptism, promises that God also begins to fulfill with all the baptized children, include "adopt[ion]... as His children" and the "wash[ing] away [of] our sins."[11] But this justification and all the blessings of salvation promised and begun to be bestowed at baptism are conditional. They depend for their continuance and for their realization of eternal life upon the child's fulfilling the conditions of believing to the end and obeying the law of God. "That covenant relationship is conditional. It calls for repentance and faith and new obedience... Life in the covenant is [conditional]."[12]

10 Barach, "Covenant and Election," in Wilkins and Garner, *The Federal Vision*, 37.

11 Ibid., 41.

12 Ibid., 37.

The explanation for the conditionality of the justification of all the baptized children is the conditionality of God's election of them. He chose all the children unconditionally unto salvation, but their continuing in salvation, including justification, and finally enjoying eternal life are conditional. This is a conditional election. An election unto salvation that depends upon the child's continuing faith and obedience for bringing the child into eternal life and glory is a conditional election.

It is this heretical doctrine of election that accounts for the federal vision's heretical doctrine of justification. It explains why in federal vision theology justification can be lost. One is justified for a while but still may perish under God's condemnation. It explains why justification in federal vision theology is by works. An election that depends on the sinner's faith and good works as conditions demands a justification on account of faith (as a work of the sinner) and the sinner's other good works.

In his ground-breaking book advancing the theology of the federal vision in conservative Reformed and Presbyterian circles, Norman Shepherd argued for an election unto salvation that is ruled by the covenant, rather than the ruling of the covenant of grace by election. He explained what such a doctrine of election amounts to. It is a doctrine that makes the eternal, sovereign, efficacious decree, to which Shepherd paid lip service, an irrelevancy. The only election that matters is a decree of God that appoints all baptized members of the visible, instituted church, if not all humans without exception, unto salvation. But this decree is conditional. It depends for its success in the salvation of sinners upon the sinners' faith and lifelong obedience. It can, and does in many instances, become reprobation, which like election is conditioned upon the sinner's faith or unbelief. Examples of this conditional covenantal election that becomes reprobation, according to Shepherd, are Saul and Judas Iscariot. Once elected by God with his worthless but all-important covenantal election, they became reprobate by failing to perform the conditions of faith and obedience.

Demonstrating that his covenantal election, for all its God-dishonoring weakness, is nevertheless a real choice of sinners unto salvation, Shepherd explained John 15:1–8, the passage concerning the cutting off from the vine of branches that do not bear fruit, as teaching that those who are cut off were originally truly joined to Christ in a saving union, according to God's covenantal election, just as truly as are the humans who bear fruit and persevere unto eternal life. God's covenantal election unto salvation of those who perish is a failure. It is this election, remember, that truly matters.

Lest any exonerate Shepherd by supposing that this inefficacious election is, in Shepherd's theology, not the election taught in scripture but only the invention of Shepherd with the help of the liberated Reformed, Shepherd contended that the conditional election of his federal vision theology is that taught in Ephesians 1. The election that is "in [Jesus Christ]" from "before the foundation of the world" with the divine purpose that the elect be "holy and without blame" and that was decreed "in love" for the elect, the election that had as its ultimate purpose "the praise of the glory of his grace" and that is realized by "redemption through his blood," proves to be an utter and inglorious failure in many instances. Indeed, this election becomes reprobation.[13]

Because in the theology of Norman Shepherd election is conditional, so also is the redemption of the death of Christ and justification. An election that depends on the sinner demands a conditional death of Christ and a conditional justification.[14]

---

13 Shepherd, *Call of Grace*, 79–91.

14 The fundamental importance of his and the federal vision's false doctrine of election for their heretical doctrine of justification makes the omission of a critique of this doctrine of election in the examination of the federal vision by the theologians of Westminster West inexcusable. This

In addition to the rank heresy of his conditional covenantal election, Shepherd sins also by inventing a new election that differs from the eternal, unchangeable decree taught by the Canons of Dordt in 1.7. The Canons of Dordt, which binds Shepherd in the Christian Reformed Church, forbids him to invent a "covenantal election":

> There are not various decrees of election, but one and the same decree respecting all those who shall be saved both under the Old and New Testament; since the Scripture declares the good pleasure, purpose, and counsel of the divine will to be one, according to which he hath chosen us from eternity, both to grace and to glory, to salvation and the way of salvation, which he hath ordained that we should walk therein.[15]

Although the federal vision is known, or at least ought to be known, as heresy with respect to the doctrine of justification, its fundamental error is its false doctrine of election. In federal vision theology, election is not the "fountain of every saving good; from which proceed faith [and therefore also justification], holiness, and the other gifts of salvation, and finally eternal life itself, as its fruits and effects."[16] That in federal vision theology election is not

---

omission is a serious, if not fundamental, weakness of the examination (see *Covenant, Justification, and Pastoral Ministry: Essays by the Faculty of Westminster Seminary California*, ed. R. Scott Clark [Phillipsburg, NJ: P&R, 2007]). One of the writers calls attention to this omission: "no essay touches directly the question of the relation between covenant and election" (23). Is one overly suspicious in wondering whether theologians themselves committed to the doctrine of the well-meant offer and to the doctrine of a conditional covenant of grace with all baptized children alike of believing parents, that is, to the doctrines of preaching and of covenant that are not governed by election, are little disposed and little capable of opposing the theology of the federal vision with a strong doctrine of election, accompanied by an equally strong doctrine of reprobation?

15 Canons of Dordt 1.8, in Schaff, *Creeds of Christendom*, 3:583.

16 Canons of Dordt 1.9, in ibid.

the "fountain" of every saving good, particularly justification, *in the covenant* in no wise absolves this heresy from the condemnation of the Canons. The Canons do not confess that election is the fountain of every saving good *except the saving good of the covenant.* Election is the fountain of every saving good also in the covenant of grace, regarding specifically the salvation of baptized children of believers. The doctrinal sin of the federal vision, therefore, is its refusal to confess that election governs *covenantal* salvation. The weakness of the Reformed and Presbyterian community of churches in condemning the federal vision and in disciplining its advocates is the prevailing weakness of these churches regarding confessing and preaching God's predestination, the subject of the first head of doctrine of the Canons of Dordt.

Oh, That "Dangerous" Doctrine of Election

The men of the federal vision openly confess that their theology owes much to, indeed is the legitimate development of, the covenantal doctrine of the liberated Reformed churches, the fathers of which were Klaas Schilder and Benne Holwerda. Thus it is no surprise that the theology of these churches lends itself to the doctrine of justification by a faith that is a condition to justification, rather than faith that is the means of justification, and by the good works of the sinner. Like its daughter theology the federal vision, liberated theology makes justifying faith in the covenant a condition. The covenantal promise of justification and salvation, God gives to all baptized children alike. But the promise is conditional. It depends for its realization upon the child's performance of the condition: faith and faith's works. Therefore, some to whom the gracious covenantal promise is given perish.

The explanation of this conditional covenantal justification and salvation is that election does not govern the covenant and its salvation. How the liberated theologians rage against the relationship of covenant and election that has election governing the covenant. But if election—God's will—does not govern the covenant and its salvation, including justification, the will of the baptized child does govern the covenant. Hence justification is by faith *as a condition* and by works! Liberated theology is essentially the application of Arminianism, the Arminianism combatted and condemned by the Canons of Dordt, to covenantal salvation.

In his recent defense of Shepherd and the theology of the federal vision, liberated theologian Ralph F. Boersema has made perfectly clear that the federal vision is the legitimate, and to Boersema *lawful*, development of the theology of the liberated Reformed.[17] Boersema acknowledges and approves that Shepherd and the federal vision explain James 2:24 as teaching "justification in the same forensic sense as Paul."[18] This acknowledgment, by itself alone, condemns Shepherd's, the federal vision's, Boersema's, and evidently the liberated Reformed's doctrine of justification as the heretical doctrine of the Roman Catholic Church, which the Reformation and all the Reformed creeds damn as the heresy exposed in Romans 3–5.

If James teaches justification in the same forensic sense as Paul, James teaches that God declares the believing sinner righteous not by faith alone, but by the sinner's own works. If James teaches justification in the same forensic sense as Paul, the ground of justification as a forensic forgiveness of sins and as the reckoning of the sinner to be righteous is not the obedience of Christ alone but the obedience of the sinner himself. The Reformation, it will be recalled, explained James 2 as speaking of justification in a different sense than that of Paul in Romans 3–5. The Reformation explained James 2 as teaching the demonstration of justification.

Correctly, the liberated theologian describes Shepherd's doctrine of justification, which Boersema *defends*, as teaching that "works are necessary for justification":

---

17 Boersema, *Not of Works*.

18 Ibid., 42.

> What some people don't like is that Shepherd says that works are necessary for justification. They say that works are the fruit and evidence of faith and always follow faith, but Shepherd says more than that. For him, works are not only necessary for sanctification, but also for justification.[19]

What Boersema intends by the necessity of works for justification is evident from his explanation of Romans 2:13. He denies that the phrase "the doers of the law shall be justified" is to be "understood hypothetically in the sense that there are no persons who fall into that class." On the contrary, the text teaches a reality: justification is by the doing of the law. Justification is, in reality, by works, not by faith.[20]

Such a justification is conditional. This fundamental element of salvation depends upon the will and working of the sinner himself. Boersema enthusiastically avows this doctrine: "Many Scripture passages...condition our eternal well-being on what we do." Boersema states that by our "eternal well-being" he has specifically in mind our justification: "works are necessary for justification."[21]

The source of his liberated doctrine of justification by works, a justification that can therefore be lost and become condemnation, is for Boersema the characteristic liberated refusal to confess that the source and fountain of covenantal salvation is God's eternal election.

> This covenant love is that of a Father for his children and is bestowed on all members of the covenant people. It is not addressed only to the elect, nor does it merely bring a people into the pale of the Gospel. Baptism

19 Ibid., 214.
20 Ibid., 198–201.
21 Ibid., 187.

symbolizes union with God in Christ, not just the offer of union. [22]

Boersema contends that the covenantal promise; covenantal salvation, including justification; and the covenant itself are conditional. Specifically for Boersema and the liberated Reformed churches, the ultimate explanation is that election, election unto *covenantal* salvation, is conditional. "God works out his calling and election through a historical process. In that process some are among the chosen for a time and later reprobate."[23] According to liberated theology, "the covenant is not unconditional."[24] The covenant is not unconditional because it and its salvation do not have their "fountain," in the word of the Canons, in God's unconditional election.

The issue in the contemporary conflict over justification in the nominally conservative Reformed, Presbyterian, and evangelical churches is not justification but election. Denial that election is the fountain of covenantal salvation necessarily opens up these churches to the heresy of justification by works. Rejection of predestination assures the presence and flourishing in these churches of the false doctrine of conditional justification, that is, justification that depends upon the sinner's work of believing and his other works.

Reformed churches and theologians today are afraid of election. They are afraid of election's being the fountain from which all salvation, in particular the fundamental blessing of justification, flows. They are afraid of the gracious, sovereign, irresistible will of God. They are afraid that this will of God (and all the gracious acts of God that flow from it) will make elect sinners careless and profane. They are afraid that election will fail to make elect sinners sufficiently holy. They are afraid that election

---

22 Ibid., 137.

23 Ibid., 101.

24 Ibid., 85.

will weaken the elect sinner's sense of his responsibility. Election is a "dangerous doctrine." Or so they say. If they are honest about their fear, their fear is sinful. The name of this fear is unbelief.

The Bible and the Reformed creeds expose this alleged fear as false. In reality, what troubles the foes of election, particularly as the fountain of justification, is that election leaves no place for their determination that the will of the sinner himself shall be the source of all his salvation, particularly his justification. God's election as the fountain of justification decides that justification is by faith alone, without the works of the sinner. Heretics desire that justification be by the works of the sinner.

Election is indeed a dangerous doctrine. It is dangerous, indeed fatal, to the doctrine of justification on the basis of faith and to the doctrine of justification by works.

Election is not dangerous in the thinking of the elect believer, no more than it was to Paul or to the Synod of Dordt. On the contrary, it is assuring. It is assuring as the fountain of justification. It lives in the believing sinner's consciousness that he is righteous before God by faith, not because he performed the condition of believing and certainly not because he performs good works, but because God eternally chose him in love.

God's justification of the believing sinner is gracious. It is gracious inasmuch as it is by faith alone, without the sinner's works. It is all the more gracious inasmuch as its origin is election. Not only does God justify the ungodly (Rom. 4:5). Not only does God commend his love toward us in that, while we were yet sinners, as the ground of our justification Christ died for us (5:8). But also the grace of justification is that its fountain, or ultimate source, is that God in love chose us who did not appear before him as righteous when he chose, but as unrighteous, that is, as those who had to be justified at the cost of the deliverance of his own Son to the death of the cross.

What grace is the grace of justification! Accentuated by election as its source!

There is no one less careless and profane, no one more responsible, no one more zealous in holiness of life, no one who loves God more ardently, than the sinner justified by faith alone, who lives in the knowledge that the fountain of his justification is God's gracious election.

Chapter Twenty-Three

JUSTIFICATION IN THE FINAL JUDGMENT

There awaits the elect of God in Christ yet one more dramatic expression and manifestation of their justification. Likewise, the reprobate ungodly face the terrifying prospect of yet one more dramatic expression of their condemnation. These are the justification and condemnation of the final judgment on the world's last day, at the bodily coming of Jesus Christ.

The Bible teaches, and the creeds of the Reformation confess, a future final judgment of all humans and of all angels. Matthew 25:31–46 and Revelation 20:11–15 prophesy and describe the event. The passage in Matthew concludes Jesus' instruction about the "end of the world" (24:3). The outcome of the final judgment will be that those humans called sheep by Jesus the judge and who are shown to be righteous in the judgment enter into "life eternal" (25:46). Those who are called goats and who are shown to be unrighteous "go away into everlasting punishment" (v. 46).

Revelation 20:11–15 foretells the "great white throne" judgment (v. 11). All humans will be judged. The result of the judgment for some will be that they will be cast "into the lake of fire" (v. 15). Revelation 21 teaches that the others will inherit a new heaven and a new earth in which they will dwell with God (vv. 1–8). Second Corinthians 5:10 teaches the reality and nature of the event: "For we must all appear before the judgment seat of Christ; that every one may receive the things done in his body, according to that he hath done, whether it be good or bad."

The Reformed creeds confess the final judgment. According to the Belgic Confession,

> our Lord Jesus Christ will come from heaven, corporally and visibly, as he ascended with great glory and majesty, to declare himself Judge of the quick and the dead…And then all men will personally appear before this great Judge, both men and women and children, that have been from the beginning of the world to the end thereof…Then the books…shall be opened, and the dead judged according to what they shall have done in this world, whether it be good or evil.[1]

The Westminster Confession of Faith sets forth, authoritatively, the Presbyterian belief concerning the final judgment.

> God hath appointed a day wherein he will judge the world in righteousness by Jesus Christ…In which day, not only the apostate angels shall be judged, but likewise all persons, that have lived upon earth, shall appear before the tribunal of Christ, to give an account of their thoughts, words, and deeds; and to receive according to what they have done in the body, whether good or evil.[2]

Final Justification

This awesome event will be a public expression and manifestation by God in Jesus Christ of the verdict of justification that the elect now hear in the gospel of righteousness by faith alone in Jesus. That is, the final judgment will be justification of the

---

1 Belgic Confession 37, in Schaff, *Creeds of Christendom*, 3:433–34.

2 Westminster Confession of Faith 33.1, in ibid., 3:671–72.

elect believer. The full truth of justification therefore includes the final judgment. That the truth of the final judgment of the elect believer is an aspect of the doctrine of justification is established simply by the nature of the final judgment. It will be divine judgment. It will be the thorough examination of those who are judged with a view to the declaration of their righteousness; a verdict from the judge of their righteousness; and the carrying out of the verdict upon the righteous by their welcome into an eternal life of glory.

Although this is little remarked, also the final judgment of the reprobate ungodly will be the expression and manifestation of the verdict of condemnation that they hear and know already in this life. Those who came under the preaching of the gospel heard their condemnation in the ringing verdict of the gospel upon them for their unbelief: "He that believeth not is condemned already" (John 3:18). But also those who never heard the gospel showed "the work of the law written in their hearts, their conscience also bearing witness," so that their thoughts accused them and the others (Rom. 2:15). Even the pagan stands condemned in his own conscience. The final judgment will only make public and final the condemnation already passed upon him, of which also he was conscious throughout his earthly life.

Such is the relationship of the final judgment and present justification by faith that if the final judgment of men takes the works of believers into account as the basis of God's judgment of believers and as the content of their righteousness, even in part, the final judgment nullifies the gospel truth of justification by faith alone. In this case, in the end, decisively, justification is by works, not by faith alone. This is the reason all the enemies of justification by faith alone, from the Roman Catholic Church to the federal vision, are so insistent that the final judgment will be by works, if not entirely, then decisively. The great battle over justification, whether by faith alone or by works, comes down in the end to the orthodox understanding of the final judgment.

The concern in this examination of the final judgment is the doctrine of justification. Other aspects of this grand, future event, important and interesting as they are, are outside our purview.

According to scripture and the Reformed creeds, the final judgment will be a real event. It will be a wonder. It will occur immediately upon the bodily coming of Christ on the clouds. Such is the importance of the final judgment that it will be the main purpose of Christ with his coming, as it will be the realization of the goal, or ultimate purpose, of God with all of history. Even the resurrection of the bodies of all men will be subservient to the purpose of God that he judge the world in righteousness. The Apostles' Creed has the church confessing that the final judgment is the main purpose of Christ with his coming again: "He shall come again *to judge the quick and the dead*." Article 37 of the Belgic Confession makes the resurrection of the dead the divine summons to appear in the heavenly courtroom. The thought of the Belgic Confession is that "all the dead shall be raised out of the earth" in order "personally [to] appear before this great Judge."[3]

The judge will be the incarnate Son of God, the man Jesus Christ. That the judge will be Jesus is fundamental not only for the glory of Jesus, but also for the right understanding of the judgment itself as concerns the elect believer. *Jesus* judges him, the one who obeyed for him, both in his life and in his death.

In the judgment the deeds of all humans will be exposed, including things done in secret, idle words, the thoughts of the mind, and the hidden motives of the heart. Christ will conduct the judgment, pronounce the verdict, and carry out the sentence *according to men's works*.

It is especially that the judgment will be according to works that is critical in the controversy over the final judgment regarding the gospel truth of justification. That the judgment will be according to works is clearly taught by scripture. Jesus has the judge,

---

3 Belgic Confession 37, in ibid., 3:433–34.

who is himself, saying to the sheep on his right hand, "Inherit the kingdom…for I was an hungered, and ye gave me meat," and so on (Matt. 25:34–40). To the goats on his left hand, the judge will say, "Depart from me…into everlasting fire…for I was an hungered, and ye gave me no meat," and so on (vv. 41–45). Second Corinthians 5:10 has all appearing before the judgment seat of Christ "that every one may receive the things done in his body, according to that he hath done, whether it be good or bad."

The Roman Catholic Church has always appealed to this aspect of the final judgment in support of its teaching that justification, now and always, is by faith and by the good works of the sinner himself. Rome's explanation of the biblical teaching that the final judgment of those who are saved will be according to works is that God's verdict upon them, "Forgiven and righteous!" is based in part on the good works that they did (with the help of grace, of course) and that the righteousness that earns eternal life and glory for them is partly their own obedience to the law of God. Since this is exactly Rome's explanation of the justification of the saints in this life, there is harmony between present justification and the justification of the final judgment. Always and in every expression of it, for Rome justification is by faith and by works. One of the canons that the Council of Trent added to its creedal explanation of the doctrine of justification is the following:

> If any one saith, that the good works of one that is justified are in such manner the gifts of God, that they are not also the good merits of him that is justified; or, that the said justified, by the good works which he performs…does not truly merit…eternal life, and the attainment of that eternal life…and also an increase of glory: let him be anathema.[4]

4 Canons and Decrees of the Council of Trent, Sixth Session, [Canons] on Justification 32, in ibid., 2:117–18. Although this canon does not explicitly mention the final judgment, it expresses Rome's doctrine that the favorable

The implication of Rome's doctrine of a final judgment dependent upon the works of the sinner is that all Roman Catholics live in terror concerning the outcome of their judgment. Forever unsure of their righteousness and salvation in this life, they are also unsure of the verdict upon them at the moment of death and in the final judgment. Roman Catholics face the coming final judgment with uncertainty. What will the judge pronounce upon them? What will the sentence be? What will be their eternal destiny? At best, the Roman Catholic can expect purgatory—a temporary hell in which almost all Roman Catholics satisfy the justice of God in some measure—itself the denial of justification by faith alone.

> If any one saith, that, after the grace of Justification has been received, to every penitent sinner the guilt is remitted, and the debt of eternal punishment is blotted out in such wise that there remains not any debt of temporal punishment to be discharged either in this world, or in the next in Purgatory…let him be anathema.[5]

Final Justification for the Federal Vision

Today Reformed and Presbyterian churches with a name for orthodoxy take their stand with Rome regarding justification, specifically regarding the justification of the final judgment. They do this by tolerating and even approving in their midst the federal vision and the theologians who are aggressively promoting the theology of the federal vision. These churches include especially the Orthodox Presbyterian Church and the Presbyterian Church in America. Also the United Reformed

---

verdict of the judge in the final judgment, upon which eternal life depends, is based on the meritorious works of the sinner who will be justified in the final judgment.

5 Canons and Decrees of the Council of Trent, Sixth Session, [Canons] on Justification 30, in ibid., 2:117.

Churches have had advocates of the federal vision arise in their bosom without disciplining the heretics, indeed in at least one instance exonerating the federal visionist. Already this book has demonstrated that the heresy of the federal vision is its denial of justification by faith alone. What remains to be shown is that a fundamental aspect of this denial of the biblical and Reformation truth of justification is the federal vision's aggressive rejection of the truth of gracious justification in the final judgment.

In support of its heretical doctrine of justification by works, the federal vision adduces a false teaching of the final judgment. Rightly regarding the final judgment as justification of God's people, the federal vision argues that the final judgment is the all-important, decisive justification of sinners. This coming justification, they teach, will be based on the good works of believers so that the righteousness of sinners that gains them access to eternal life in the new world will be their own obedience. Christ's obedience on their behalf will be part of their righteousness but not the whole of it, as justification by faith alone insists. On the basis of this doctrine of the final judgment as decisive justification, the men of the federal vision contend either that present justification is also by the good works of believing sinners, or that present justification is merely provisional, needing the final judgment by works for its verification and substantiation. The present justification by faith alone, if it is even a temporal reality, gives way to the final judgment as decisive.

However the men of the federal vision view present justification by the gospel, the final judgment is the all-important justification, and the justification of the final judgment is by works. It is not by faith alone, that is, the righteousness of believers in the final judgment that is the basis of their worthiness to enter heaven and to receive full salvation is not the obedience of Jesus Christ in their stead and on their behalf.

Their righteousness in that (decisive) phase of justification is their own good works (performed, of course, with the help of the grace of God).

Writing in the book that is a definitive exposition and defense of the theology of the federal vision, Don Garlington contends that God's "declaration [justifying sinners] on the last day [in the final judgment] is a forensic acquittal." He immediately adds that the final judgment and "all of the judgment texts...*base* final forensic acquittal on 'works.'" Thinking to mitigate somewhat this rank expression of works-righteousness, Garlington goes on to identify the works that are the believer's righteousness with God in the final judgment as works that are the "believer's 'fruit'...which is the inevitable product of faith."[6]

Federal vision theologian Rich Lusk becomes bold in confessing the heresy's doctrine of justification by works with particular reference to the final judgment. He acknowledges that the final judgment will be "justification...a future verdict, a final imputation (or reckoning)." With the deceptive language that is characteristic of the federal vision, as of every heresy, Lusk then denies that a "bare faith will be sufficient at the last day." No Reformed theologian has ever taught that believers are justified by a "bare" faith, whether now or at the final judgment. All orthodox theologians have taught that the faith that justifies is not bare but adorned with good works.

What orthodoxy teaches is that these works do not contribute to the righteousness of justification. Bare faith justifies, inasmuch as bare faith clings to and makes the believer's the rich righteousness of Jesus Christ, by imputation. By bare faith the believer, who is stark naked in the judgment regarding any good work of his own, is clothed with the righteousness of all the good works of Jesus Christ.

---

6 Garlington, "The New Perspective, Mediation, and Justification," in Sandlin, *A Faith That Is Never Alone*, 295; emphasis added.

It is part of Lusk's deceit that his apparent objection to bare faith is, in reality, merely the ploy by which he can introduce into the Reformed churches the heresy that the good works that always accompany faith are part of the righteousness of the justified sinner—the *decisive* part of this righteousness. In reality Lusk's objection is not to a doctrine of justification by bare faith, that is, a faith that does not work. He objects, as does the theology of the federal vision, to the gospel truth of justification by faith alone, that is, faith apart from its works.

Lusk makes plain his real objection to confessionally Reformed and biblical doctrine concerning justification as realized at the final judgment. The good works that always adorn true faith are "conditions" of the justification at the final judgment: "The goal of final salvation remains contingent on conditions which are yet to be fulfilled." What role the sinner's good works play in the final judgment, Lusk declares, "In the final installment of our justification, there is a very real sense in which works will be the *decisive* factor." Reformed theology should not "say that works are (merely) *evidence* in the final court scene." Rather, "it might be better to call works a *condition* of final justification." "Works...justify at the last day." Perverting the doctrine of James in James 2:24 but clearly setting forth his and the federal vision's heresy, Lusk concludes, "Faith and works justify conjointly," that is, the sinner is justified by faith and by works, in opposition to scripture's teaching in Romans 3–5 that the sinner is justified by faith without works.[7]

Like Garlington and all the men of the federal vision, Lusk would have his readers suppose that his doctrine of justification by works escapes the condemnation of the Reformation, the Reformed creeds, and scripture inasmuch as these good works are the fruits of faith and genuine good works performed by the power of the Holy Spirit. Apparently, the federal vision does

7 Lusk, "Future Justification," in ibid., 309–55; emphasis added.

not understand, or more likely ignores, as has been proved earlier, that the Reformation's objection to justification by works applied to *all* works of sinners themselves, indeed *especially* to the good works that believers perform by the grace of the Holy Spirit. More seriously, indeed damning, for the theology of the federal vision and for the men of the federal vision, the federal vision corrupts the gospel of grace by declaring that the apostle in Romans 3–5 and in the book of Galatians does not refer to *all* the works a believing sinner performs when he denies that justification is by works.

Of fundamental importance to the men of the federal vision, their theological fathers, and their supporters for their doctrine of justification by works in the final judgment is Romans 2:13: "For not the hearers of the law are just before God, but the doers of the law shall be justified." The right understanding of the text, both in its immediate context and in light of the apostle's emphatic denial in chapters 3 and 4 that anyone is justified by the law or by the works of the law or by works, is that the text declares what would have to be the case if sinners were to be justified by the law. In this case one would have to be a "doer" of the law and not merely a "hearer." A "doer" of the law would be one who kept the law perfectly, both in thought and desire as well as in speech and deed. Also, he would have to render perfect obedience to all the demands of the law. One "does" the law only if he obeys perfectly.

This is impossible for fallen humans. It is exactly this impossibility of obeying the law and thus being justified by the law that the apostle is establishing in Romans 2:13. The text does not teach a possibility: justification by doing the law. But it vehemently makes known the utter impossibility of justification by the law.

Those theologians who proclaim justification by works, like Rome before them, explain Romans 2:13 as teaching not only what is possible, but also what is required for justification.

Especially do they explain the text as teaching what is required for justification in the final judgment. According to them, the text refers to the justification of the final judgment. That future justification will be God's declaring righteous, that is, his acquittal from the guilt of sin and his verdict of righteous, those humans who have done the law. That future justification will be by works. The sinner's righteousness in the decisive, final judgment will consist of his own good works of obedience to the law. After all is said and done, in the most literal sense of this phrase, one will be justified by works.

Such is the significance of one's interpretation of Romans 2:13 as teaching actual justification by the works of the sinner himself in the final judgment that this interpretation clearly and definitely identifies the interpreter as a proponent of the contemporary heresy of justification by works in the Presbyterian and Reformed churches. This is the interpretation of the text by Norman Shepherd. The twentieth of his "Thirty-four Theses on Justification in Relation to Faith, Repentance, and Good Works," which he presented to the Presbytery of Philadelphia of the Orthodox Presbyterian Church in 1978, reads:

> The Pauline affirmation in Romans 2:13, "the doers of the Law will be justified," is not to be understood hypothetically in the sense that there are no persons who fall into that class, but in the sense that faithful disciples of the Lord Jesus Christ will be justified.[8]

Having argued at great length against the explanation that Romans 2:13 only describes what would have to be the case, but cannot be, if sinners are justified in the final judgment by their own good works, Rich Lusk states that the text teaches what actually will be true in the final judgment. That is, believing

8 Cited in and defended by Boersema, *Not of Works*, 198. See also Shepherd, "Faith and Faithfulness," in Sandlin, *A Faith That Is Never Alone*, 66.

sinners will be justified by their own doing of the law; their own works will be "a *condition* of final justification"; and in the final judgment these "works play a decisive role." In defense of this bold declaration of justification by works, Lusk then, significantly, appeals to James 2.[9] This is fundamental, if not official, federal vision theology: justification in the final judgment not by faith alone, but by works.

It is regarding Romans 2:13 that the more cautious, if not more clever, Richard B. Gaffin Jr. tips his theological hand. With mention of Romans 2:13, among other similar passages, Gaffin has written that his view is that "some of these passages and perhaps others are plausibly, even most likely, to be read as referring to an actual future justification for believers." Gaffin explicitly recognizes the importance of Romans 2:13 in the current controversy over justification by faith alone not only in the Presbyterian community, but also in his own Orthodox Presbyterian Church and indeed in the seminary in which he was an influential teacher, and this at the time Shepherd raised the issue of justification, whether by faith alone or by works.

Gaffin at first professes that he will leave it an "open question" whether Romans 2:13 teaches hypothetically what would have to be the case if believing sinners were to be justified in the final judgment by doing the law, or what will actually be the case. Whereupon the Orthodox Presbyterian theologian launches an extended argument against taking Romans 2:13 hypothetically! Lest anyone mistake his defense of justification by works, as is possible in the density of his writing, Gaffin concludes his argument with an appeal to James 2 as referring to justification in the same sense that it has in Romans 3–5. For Gaffin therefore, Romans 2:13 teaches that sinners will be, and must be, justified in the final judgment by their having done the law.[10]

---

9 Lusk, "Future Justification," in Sandlin, *A Faith That Is Never Alone*, 309–55.
10 Gaffin, *By Faith, Not by Sight*, 79–108.

This explains Gaffin's resolute and successful defense of Shepherd for years in the Orthodox Presbyterian Church and his equally determined defense in the church courts of the propagation of federal vision theology by John O. Kinnaird.[11] In view of Gaffin's prominent place in the Orthodox Presbyterian Church, especially as a longtime professor of theology at Westminster Seminary, this goes a long way to explain the heresy of justification by works that is now widespread in the Orthodox Presbyterian Church.

The truth is that Romans 2:13 does indeed refer to justification in the final judgment, as it also refers to justification in history. The teaching of the text is that if one, whether Gentile or Jew, is to be judged by the law, he must appear before the divine bar of judgment as a doer of the law, and not only as one who knows what the law is or as one who boasts of adherence to the law. Gentiles have a certain natural knowledge of the law, and some pride themselves in this knowledge. All that this amounts to is that the knowledge of the law accuses and condemns them (Rom. 2:14–15). The Jews have a far better knowledge of the law. They rest in the law because of their knowledge. They even claim to approve of the law. But they do not *do* the commandments of the law.

To be justified by the law, one must do it. This is impossible, as the apostle plainly will state in chapters 3 and 4. "Jews and Gentiles...are all under sin...There is none righteous, no, not one." The conclusion is that "by the deeds of the law," that is to say, the law or works, "there shall no flesh be justified in his sight." Sinners must have a "righteousness of God without the law." This is the "righteousness of God which is by faith of Jesus Christ" (Rom. 3:9–10, 20–22). This righteousness is not bestowed by working, but by believing on Jesus Christ, by believing *only*.

11 See Elliott, *Christianity and Neo-Liberalism*, 121–237.

This is the reality of justification now. This will be the reality of justification at the final judgment.

Not only are the men of the federal vision guilty of corrupting the gospel of grace, but they are also guilty of debasing the law. For them the law is merely the demand that one does the best he can, that one makes a small beginning in loving God and the neighbor. The law is satisfied with an imperfect life. In fact, the law regards one whose nature is totally depraved, who is guilty of many misdeeds, and who has never performed a single perfect work in all his or her life as a doer of the law, in the language of Romans 2:13. This is supposed to be the holy law of the God who is righteousness. The federal vision is as ignorant of the law as it is of the gospel.

Part of the duplicity of the men of the federal vision is their claim to represent the theology of John Calvin, as though justification by faith without works was the doctrine of Luther but not the doctrine of Calvin. Let them listen to Calvin regarding the fundamental text, Romans 2:13, and be exposed by Calvin for the heretics they are. In his treatment of justification in his *Institutes*, Calvin not only treated Romans 2:13, but also devoted an entire section to the text. This was necessary because Rome appealed to the text against justification by faith alone, just as the federal vision does today.

> Here [in Romans 2:13] the apostle is casting down the foolish confidence of the Jews, who claimed for themselves the sole knowledge of the law, even while they were its greatest despisers. Lest, then, mere skill in the law should please them so much, he warns that if righteousness be sought from the law, not knowledge but observance of it is sought. We assuredly do not question that the righteousness of the law consists in works, and not even that righteousness consists in the worth and merits of works. But it has not yet been proved that we

> are justified by works unless they produce some one man who has fulfilled the law...It is as if he [Paul] said [in Romans 2:13]: "Do you seek righteousness in the law? Do not claim to have heard it, something of little weight in itself, but bring works whereby you may declare that the law was not laid down for you in vain." Since they were all lacking in these works, it followed that they were bereft of boasting about the law. Paul's meaning, then, requires us, rather, to frame the opposite argument: the righteousness of the law lies in perfection of works; no one can boast that he has fulfilled the law through works; consequently, there is no righteousness arising from the law.[12]

We sinful men and women must consider the future tribunal as the revelation of the righteousness of God! The righteousness of God who even for the redemption of his elect, beloved people demanded the death of his dear Son! *God* will judge the world, including us who believe on him, exhibiting his awesome justice as the perfect standard of the lives and works of all humans and spirits. That judgment will expose our sins, our outright sins, in all their deservingness of damnation, and the grievous imperfection of all our good works that we did by his grace, which imperfect good works, if dealt with as the basis of our justification, would also damn us.

Have Reformed and Presbyterian theologians lost the knowledge of their own sinfulness? Have they no sense of the awesome holiness of God? Is God blinding them to these basic realities? One who contemplates standing before the holy God in judgment according to divine justice, all his life opened up, all his motives exposed, all his secret thoughts and desires made known, all the spoiling of his best works by a grievous coming

---

12 Calvin, *Institutes*, 3.17.13, 1:817–18.

short of perfect love of God and the neighbor, to say nothing of the words and deeds spoken or done in secret in outright violation of the law of God—such a man or woman makes up his or her sanctified, wise mind that on that great day and in that awesome courtroom he or she will raise one plea, and one only: "God be merciful to me the sinner!" That is, "Forgive me, and declare me righteous for the sake, *only* for the sake, of the perfect obedience of Jesus Christ, whom thou thyself hast given to be my righteousness, especially in his suffering and death."

One who has even the slightest knowledge of the holiness of God has his mind made up, in all sincerity, that he will bring into the final judgment absolutely nothing of his own obedience and no work of his own as his righteousness upon which the verdict of the Judge must depend. God may bring the believer's works up in that judgment, and he will, for he is exceedingly gracious to those who trust only in the obedience of the Son, whom God himself has provided to be the righteousness of those who had, and *have*, none of their own. In his amazing grace God may and will reward the works he himself has accomplished in and through his elect children. But in the final judgment the believer leaves all his works outside the courtroom regarding the verdict of righteousness. And rightly so! All his good works, being defiled by sin, are as filthy rags in the matter of justification (Isa. 64:6).

Exactly this gives the believer boldness in the final judgment, as it also gives him boldness in his daily judgment and in the preliminary judgment at the moment of death. Everyone who depends on his own works for a favorable outcome of God's judgment of him, whether in this life or in the final judgment, must live and die in terror. "Have I done enough? Is what I have done good enough for justification? Will not the awesome, penetrating righteousness of the divine Judge expose the wickedness, or at least the imperfection, of my best works, how self intruded into my best works when I ought to have been perfectly devoted to the glory of God? What will the verdict be? What will it be? And what will the outcome be? Eternal heaven or eternal hell?"

Everyone who trusts alone in Christ Jesus, depending only upon his perfect, satisfactory obedience for righteousness with God the judge in the final judgment—this is faith—will be justified by this faith. Everyone whose plea in the final judgment is only, "God be merciful to me the sinner," will go home, like the publican in Jesus' parable, into the presence of God his Father in the new world, justified. About this he has no doubt. For his righteousness is the obedience of Jesus Christ.

According to Works

What then of the repeated and emphatic teaching of the Bible that future justification in the final judgment will be according to works? "We must all appear before the judgment seat of Christ; that every one may receive the things done in his body, according to that he hath done, whether it be good or bad" (2 Cor. 5:10). To this biblical teaching the Reformed confession does full justice, obviously without any fear that this compromises in any way the gospel truth of justification by faith alone: "[In the final judgment] the dead [shall be] judged according to what they shall have done in this world, whether it be good or evil."[13]

Because a final judgment of the elect believer according to his works seemed to them to compromise the gospel of justification by faith alone, some Reformed theologians have denied that believers will be judged in the final judgment. The final judgment is only for the unbelieving ungodly. Those Reformed theologians argued that it would be improper for the sins of believers to be brought to view, whether to the view of the believer or to the view of the entire human race, inasmuch as these sins have been blotted out in the blood of Christ. They argued also that a judgment according to works contradicts the

13 Belgic Confession 37, in Schaff, *Creeds of Christendom*, 3:434.

truth of justification by faith alone, apart from works. Those theologians concluded that the final judgment is only for the reprobate ungodly.

Those theologians erred. The Bible clearly teaches that "we," that is, elect believers, must appear before the judgment seat of Christ and that there we will be judged according to our works (2 Cor. 5:10). This teaching of the apostle derives from Christ's account of the final judgment in Matthew 25. The sheep appear in the final judgment as well as the goats. The sheep are judged according to their works, feeding the hungry, giving drink to the thirsty, and so on (vv. 34–40).

Those who deny that the elect believer must appear in the judgment are guilty of several errors. They do not understand the main purpose of the final judgment. The main purpose is the public vindication of God regarding both the salvation of the church of God and the damnation of the enemies of God. Theology calls this purpose the "theodicy."

Neither do those who deny the final judgment of the believers understand the nature of the judgment regarding the elect believers. It is not at all terrifying, an ordeal to be dreaded, a huge embarrassment before the entire watching world. Rather it is an event the believer very much desires and anticipates. It will be his "day in court" for one who is righteous, who is perfectly confident of his unassailable righteousness, and who desires that the entire world shall recognize and acknowledge his righteousness.

The Heidelberg Catechism expresses the attitude of the believer regarding the impending final judgment: "What comfort is it to thee that Christ shall come again to judge the quick and the dead?" The prospect of the judgment is not a terror but a comfort. The comfort is not that the believer will be exempted from the judgment, but that

> in all my sorrows and persecutions, with uplifted head, I look for the self-same One who has before offered himself

> for me to the judgment of God, and removed from me all curse, to come again as Judge from heaven; who shall cast all his and my enemies into everlasting condemnation, but shall take me, with all his chosen ones, to himself, into heavenly joy and glory.[14]

Those who deny that the believer will appear in the final judgment, probably thinking that they do him a favor, are in fact depriving him of a great good.

Also, those Reformed theologians who deny that the believer will be judged in the final judgment completely misunderstand what it means that the believer will be judged according to his works. They suspect that this biblical phrase conveys a form of works-righteousness. (It may also be the case that some professing Reformed Christians are motivated to deny a coming judgment of members of the visible church because they are thorough-going, fully developed antinomians, having good reason to shrink from judgment.)

But judgment *according* to works differs fundamentally from judgment *on the basis of* works. The Bible teaches the former; it never teaches the latter. Judgment *on the basis of* works would be the doctrine of justification by works. This would make the good works of the believer his righteousness with God, at least in part. This would mean that the entrance into eternal life and glory would be based on the believer's own deeds. This would be the corruption of the gospel of grace.

The final judgment of the elect believer will be based on the obedience of Christ in the stead of and on behalf of the elect believer, and on the substitutionary obedience of Christ only, exactly as is the case regarding the believer's justification now. The only work that will be the believer's righteousness before God the judge in Christ will be Christ's lifelong obedience to the

14 Heidelberg Catechism Q&A 52, in ibid., 3:323–24.

law, especially Christ's atoning death, in the believer's stead, precisely as is the case regarding the believer's righteousness before God now. The justification of the believer in the final judgment will be gracious, purely gracious.

That this will be the nature of the final judgment of the believers is abundantly evident from scripture. First, this judgment will be justification, and justification is by faith alone apart from works, as Romans 3–5, the book of Galatians, and many other passages of scripture teach. God will not, God cannot, justify in one way now—by faith—and in another way then—by works. Were the believer's justification in the final judgment to be by his own works, he could accuse God of deceiving him all his life long, in that he justified the believer by faith alone.

Second, that the coming justification will be purely gracious, not at all based on the works of the believer, is indicated by the order of events on judgment day. The first event will be the resurrection of the dead. The elect believers will be raised in their new, glorious bodies, made like the body of Jesus Christ. In this glorious body they will stand in the final judgment, perfected saints, ready to inherit the new world. Before they are judged according to their works, they will have received the great good that was their hope all their earthly lives: the resurrection of the body. Whatever role their good works may play in the final judgment, it cannot be that the works are the basis of their perfect salvation, for they are perfectly saved before these good works ever come up in the judgment.

Third, two of the outstanding passages on the final judgment of the believers, Matthew 25 and Revelation 20, are at pains to teach that the public justification of the elect believers will be gracious, not at all based on the good works they performed, even though these works come up in the judgment. In Matthew 25 before the judgment even begins the King separates the people who are judged as sheep and goats (vv. 32–33). Sheep in the Bible is the name of those given by God to Jesus Christ in the decree of election, the name of those for whom Jesus died to secure their salvation. This election and this atonement are unconditional, not dependent upon the works or worth of the objects of election and beneficiaries of atonement.

Further, in Matthew 25, when the King calls the sheep into eternal life and glory, every phrase of the call expresses that their entrance into perfect salvation is mere grace. The sheep are "the blessed of my Father" (v. 34). They are not the hard-working, meritorious members of the human race. Christ binds upon their consciousness that they "inherit the kingdom" (v. 34). One inherits not by earning, not by doing anything at all, but by being the object of the gracious will of the testator. This inheritance, the King will assure those who enter upon their inheritance, has been "prepared for you from the foundation of the world" (v. 34). This phrase describes the saved as those whom God has eternally elected in a decree that is unconditional, sovereignly gracious, and free, not dependent upon the works of the ones who are chosen. The sole reason for the perfection of salvation, into which the sheep enter by way of the final judgment, is God's determination to bestow this salvation upon them in the eternal decree of election.

At the moment the believing child of God enters upon perfect salvation, Jesus himself preaches directly to him the gospel that he preached to him by means of the true church every Lord's day during his earthly life: "It is of *grace*; it is of grace *only*." Impressed upon the heart of the elect believer as he begins to enjoy the things that eye has not seen, ear has not heard, and it never entered into the heart of man to imagine is this truth: "God has given me this, has *given* me this."

The same is true of the teaching about the final judgment of the elect people of God in Revelation 20:11–15. The passage harmonizes with the teaching of the Bible everywhere that all humans will be judged in the coming judgment "according to their works" (v. 13). Nevertheless, verse 15 establishes that God's eternal election, which is sovereignly gracious, not based on the works of those who are elected, will be decisive for the favorable verdict of the Judge upon the elect humans in the final judgment: "Whosoever was not found written in the book of life was cast into the lake of fire." What determines that one is not cast into the lake of fire on the last day and therefore determines that one is welcomed into the new world of Revelation 21:1 is that his name is written in the book of life.

The writing of names in the book of life is God's eternal election of some humans to eternal life. God's election is unconditional. It is not due to the good works of those who are written in the book. On the contrary, a life of good works is due to the writing of one's name in the book. Since the subject of the passage is the final judgment, the truth is that the verdict of righteousness unto eternal life in this judgment is not due to or based on the works of those who are justified, but is due to eternal, gracious election.

What then is the meaning of an impending, final judgment according to works, over which truth so many stumble? According to works refers to a standard, not a basis. The Judge's verdict upon the believer, "Not guilty! Perfectly righteous!" will be in accord with the fundamental nature of the believer's life in the world by virtue of the sanctifying work of the Spirit within him: a life of love for God and the neighbor; a life of living unto Christ; a life of obedience to the law of God. To put it differently, the good works of the child of God will come up in the judgment, not as entering into, much less determining, the verdict of righteousness, but as demonstration and evidence of justification. God has truly justified these humans in their earthly lives. Throughout their lives, their good works manifested, indeed proved, their justification. In the awesome proceeding of the final judgment, these good works will serve the same purpose: they will come up as showing the reality of the justification that God will echo before the world. The final verdict will accord with the good works of those justified.

Also the sinful deeds of the believer will be brought to light, but only as covered with the blood of Christ, as atoned for and forgiven. They will be exposed as obliterated. As the Catechism confesses in answer 52, Christ has removed all curse from the believer, including the shame, regarding the sinfulness and sins of the believing child of God. Also in this respect, the final judgment does not disquiet the believer. Even the disclosure of the covered sins of the child of God serves to magnify the grace of God in the judgment. Such gross sinners does God save. So great is his mercy!

Thus the purposes of God with the final judgment will be achieved. God will be vindicated, that is, publicly shown to be just, particularly in the justification and salvation of the elect church of Christ. He displays the elect saints as righteous with a perfect righteousness—the lifelong obedience and atoning death of Jesus Christ, their covenantal head—and therefore worthy of eternal life. He demonstrates the reality of their righteousness by its fruits in lives of holiness and good works, especially, as Matthew 25 emphasizes, love of Christ in his needy people. As the (forgiven) sins of the saints will demonstrate beyond any challenge, both to the ungodly and to the saints themselves, who will see their sins in the judgment as they never saw them before, their justification will be shown to be gracious.

In the final judgment God will glorify himself in his believing, justified people. He will also glorify himself in his condemnation of the unbelievers, who did not obey his gospel, believe on his Son, or observe his law.

The Same Verdict, One More Time

In the final judgment we believers will hear the same verdict upon us that we now hear through the gospel by faith alone, only louder, only directly from the mouth of God who is Jesus

Christ, and with the whole world listening: "Righteous for the sake of Jesus Christ!"

We must hear the verdict one more time on that auspicious occasion, as we are about to enter the new world with its bliss and glory. Although the final judgment has the vindication of God as its main purpose, it has also a purpose regarding us. As we receive the fullness of salvation, as we are graced with unimaginable blessedness, as we behold the beatific vision of the face of God in Jesus Christ, we must be confident that we have a right to all this. We must be absolutely confident. Only the word of Christ, forever ringing in our ears, "Righteous for my sake!" will give this confidence.

This confidence is very much the assurance that not we ourselves and our works, but Jesus Christ and his work are our righteousness. The verdict pronounced from the great white throne on that day will convince us, beyond all doubting.

We go into the new world, our inheritance, and live there in bliss everlastingly, with this gospel truth in our hearts and on our lips: "Justified by faith alone."

BIBLIOGRAPHY

Arminius, James. *The Works of James Arminius.* Translated by James Nichols. Vol. 2. Reprint, Grand Rapids, MI: Baker, 1991.

Auden, W. H. "Luther." In *Collected Poems*, edited by Edward Mendelson, 235. New York: Random House, 1976.

Bavinck, Herman. *Reformed Dogmatics.* Edited by John Bolt. Translated by John Vriend. Vol. 3, *Sin and Salvation in Christ.* Grand Rapids, MI: Baker Academic, 2006.

———. *Reformed Dogmatics.* Edited by John Bolt. Translated by John Vriend. Vol. 4, *Holy Spirit, Church, and New Creation.* Grand Rapids, MI: Baker Academic, 2008.

Beisner, E. Calvin, ed. *The Auburn Avenue Theology Pros and Cons: Debating the Federal Vision.* Ft. Lauderdale, FL: Knox Theological Seminary, 2004.

Berkhof, Louis. *Systematic Theology.* 4th revised and enlarged edition. Grand Rapids, MI: Eerdmans, 1965.

Berkouwer, G. C. *Faith and Justification.* Grand Rapids, MI: Eerdmans, 1954.

Boersema, Ralph F. *Not of Works: Norman Shepherd and His Critics, The Justification Controversy Laid to Rest through Understanding.* Minneapolis, MN: NextStep Resources, 2012.

Brine, John. "A Defence of the Doctrine of Eternal Justification." London: A. Ward, 1732. Reprinted, Columbus, MS: Pinehaven Baptist Church, 1979.

Brooks, Thomas. "Heaven on Earth: A Serious Discourse, Touching a Well-Grounded Assurance." In *The Works of Thomas Brooks*, vol. 2. Reprinted, Edinburgh: Banner of Truth, 1980.

Buchanan, James. *The Doctrine of Justification.* Edinburgh: T. and T. Clark, 1867. Reprinted. Grand Rapids, MI: Baker, 1977.

Calvin, John. *Calvin's Tracts*, vol. 3. Translated by Henry Beveridge. Edinburgh: Calvin Translation Society, 1851.

———. *Commentaries on the Catholic Epistles*. Translated and edited by John Owen. Grand Rapids, MI: Eerdmans, 1948.

———. *Commentary on the Epistles of Paul the Apostle to the Corinthians.* Translated by John Pringle. Grand Rapids, MI: Eerdmans, 1948.

———. *The Epistle of Paul the Apostle to the Romans.* Translated by Ross Mackenzie. Grand Rapids, MI: Eerdmans, 1961.

———. *The Epistles of Paul the Apostle to the Romans and to the Thessalonians.* Translated by Ross Mackenzie. Grand Rapids, MI: Eerdmans, 1960.

———. *Institutes of the Christian Religion.* Edited by John T. McNeill. Translated by Ford Lewis Battles. 2 vols. Library of Christian Classics 20–21. Philadelphia: Westminster Press, 1960.

———. *Sermons on Galatians.* Audubon, NJ: Old Paths Publications, 1995.

———. *Tracts Relating to the Reformation.* Translated by Henry Beveridge. Edinburgh: Calvin Translation Society, 1844.

Clark, R. Scott, ed. *Covenant, Justification, and Pastoral Ministry: Essays by the Faculty of Westminster Seminary California.* Phillipsburg, NJ: P&R, 2007.

Colson, Charles, and Richard John Neuhaus, eds. *Evangelicals & Catholics Together: Toward a Common Mission.* Dallas, TX: Word, 1995.

The Confessions and the Church Order of the Protestant Reformed Churches. Grandville, MI: Protestant Reformed Churches in America, 2005.

Dabney, Robert L. *Lectures in Systematic Theology.* Grand Rapids, MI: Zondervan, 1972.

De Moor, J. C. *De Rechtvaardigmaking van Eeuwigheid* [Justification from eternity]. Kampen: J. H. Kok, 1905.

De Reuver, Arie. *Sweet Communion: Trajectories of Spirituality from the Middle Ages through the Further Reformation.* Translated by James A. De Jong. Grand Rapids, MI: Baker, 2007.

Dunn, James D. G. *The Theology of Paul the Apostle.* Edinburgh: T&T Clark, 1998.

"ECT: The Gift of Salvation." *Christianity Today* 41, no. 14 (December 8, 1997): 34–38.

Elliott, Paul M. *Christianity and Neo-Liberalism: The Spiritual Crisis in the Orthodox Presbyterian Church and Beyond.* Unicoi, TN: Trinity Foundation, 2005.

———. *A Denomination in Denial: An Evaluation of the Report of the Committee to Study the Doctrine of Justification of the Orthodox Presbyterian Church.* Westminster, MD: Teaching the Word, 2006.

Engelsma, David J. *Battle for Sovereign Grace in the Covenant: The Declaration of Principles.* Jenison, MI: Reformed Free Publishing Association, 2013.

———. *Covenant and Election in the Reformed Tradition.* Jenison, MI: Reformed Free Publishing Association, 2011.

———. "The Covenant of Creation with Adam." *Protestant Reformed Theological Journal* 40, no. 1 (November 2006): 3–42.

———. *The Covenant of God and the Children of Believers: Sovereign Grace in the Covenant.* Jenison, MI: Reformed Free Publishing Association, 2005.

———. "The Gift of Assurance: The Spirit of Christ and Assurance of Salvation." *Protestant Reformed Theological Journal* 42, no. 2 (April 2009): 3–46.

———. *Federal Vision: Heresy at the Root.* Jenison, MI: Reformed Free Publishing Association, 2012.

———. "Martin Bucer: 'Fanatic of Unity.'" *Mid-America Journal of Theology* 4, no. 1 (Spring, 1988): 40–42.

Faber, Jelle. *American Secession Theologians on Covenant and Baptism.* Neerlandia, Alberta, Canada: Inheritance Publications, 1996.

Gaffin, Richard B., Jr. *By Faith, not by Sight: Paul and the Order of Salvation.* Bletchley, Milton Keynes, Bucks, UK: Paternoster Press, 2006.

Girardeau, John L. *Calvinism and Evangelical Arminianism: Compared as to Election, Reprobation, Justification and Related Doctrines.* 1890. Reprint, Harrisonburg, VA: Sprinkle Publications, 1984.

Godfrey, W. Robert. "Westminster Seminary, the Doctrine of Justification, and the Reformed Confessions." In *The Pattern of Sound Doctrine: Systematic Theology at the Westminster Seminaries*, edited by David Van Drunen. Phillipsburg, NJ: P&R, 2004.

Goodwin, Thomas. *The Objects and Acts of Justifying Faith.* Marshallton, DE: National Foundation for Christian Education, n.d.

Greijdanus, S. *Galaten* [Galatians]. Korte verklaring der heilige schrift [Brief explanation of the holy scripture]. Kampen: Kok, 1922.

Grosheide, F. W., J. H. Landwehr, C. Lindeboom, and J. C. Rullmann, eds. *Christelijke Encyclopaedie voor het Nederlandsche Volk* [Christian encyclopedia for the Dutch people]. Vol. 2. Kampen: J. H. Kok, 1925.

Hewitson, Ian A. *Trust and Obey: Norman Shepherd & the Justification Controversy at Westminster Theological Seminary.* Minneapolis, MN: NextStep Resources, 2011.

Hoeksema, Herman. *Reformed Dogmatics.* Grand Rapids, MI: Reformed Free Publishing Association, 1966.

Holl, Karl. *What Did Luther Understand by Religion?* Philadelphia, PA: Fortress Press, 1977.

Johnson, Gary L. W., and Guy P. Waters, eds. *By Faith Alone: Answering the Challenges to the Doctrine of Justification.* Wheaton, IL: Crossway Books, 2006.

Kamphuis, J. *An Everlasting Covenant.* Launceston (TAS), Australia: Publication Organization of the Free Reformed Churches of Australia, 1985.

Kersten, G. H. *Reformed Dogmatics.* Translated by J. R. Beeke and J. C. Westrate. Grand Rapids, MI: Eerdmans, 1983.

Kuyper, Abraham. *Dictaten Dogmatiek.* Vol. 4. Grand Rapids, MI: J. B. Hulst, n.d.

———. *Lectures on Calvinism.* Grand Rapids, MI: Eerdmans, 1953. Originally published as *Het Calvinisme: Zes Stone-Lezingen* (Amsterdam: Hoveker & Wormser, n.d.).

———. *The Work of the Holy Spirit.* Translated by Henri De Vries. Grand Rapids, MI: Eerdmans, repr. 1973.

Leith, John H., ed. *Creeds of the Churches.* Richmond, VA: John Knox Press, rev. ed. 1973.

Lillback, Peter A. *The Binding of God: Calvin's Role in the Development of Covenant Theology.* Grand Rapids, MI: Baker, 2001.

Luther, Martin. *Luther's Works.* Vol. 25, *Lectures on Romans.* Edited by Hilton C. Oswald. Saint Louis, MO: Concordia, 1972.

———. *Luther's Works.* Vol. 26, *Lectures on Galatians 1535.* Edited by Jaroslav Pelikan. Saint Louis, MO: Concordia, 1963.

———. *What Luther Says.* Compiled by Ewald M. Plass. St. Louis, MO: Concordia, 1959.

MacLeod, A. Donald. "A Painful Parting, 1977–1983: Justifying Justification." In *W. Stanford Reid: An Evangelical Calvinist in the Academy.* Montreal: McGill-Queen's University Press, 2004.

M'Crie, C. G. *The Confessions of the Church of Scotland.* Edinburgh: Macniven & Wallace, 1907.

Mouw, Richard J. *He Shines in All That's Fair: Culture and Common Grace.* Grand Rapids, MI: Eerdmans, 2001.

Packer, J. I. *A Quest for Godliness: The Puritan Vision of the Christian Life.* Wheaton, IL: Crossway, 1990.

Robbins, John W. *A Companion to the Current Justification Controversy.* Unicoi, TN: Trinity Foundation, 2003.

Robertson, O. Palmer. *The Current Justification Controversy.* Unicoi, TN: Trinity Foundation, 2003.

Rutton, Tim. "A Troubling Order for the Catholic Church." *Los Angeles Times,* Wednesday, March 31, 2010.

Sanders, E. P. *Paul and Palestinian Judaism.* London: SCM/Philadelphia, PA: Fortress Press, 1977.

Sandlin, P. Andrew, ed. *A Faith That Is Never Alone.* La Grange, CA: Kerygma Press, 2007.

Schaff, Philip, ed. *The Creeds of Christendom with a History and Critical Notes.* 6th ed. 3 vols. New York: Harper & Row, 1931. Reprint, Grand Rapids, MI: Baker Books, 2007.

———. *History of the Christian Church.* Vol. 7, *Modern Christianity: The Swiss Reformation.* New York: Charles Scribner's Sons, 1892.

Schaver, J. L. *The Polity of the Churches.* 4th ed. Grand Rapids, MI: Kregel, 1958.

Schilder, Klaas. "The Main Points of the Doctrine of the Covenant: A Speech Given by Professor Dr. K. Schilder in the Waalsche Kerk in Delft, the Netherlands on August 31, 1944." Translated by T. van Laar. Canada: n.p., 1992.

Shepherd, Norman. *The Call of Grace: How the Covenant Illuminates Salvation and Evangelism.* Phillipsburg, NJ: P&R, 2000.

———. "Justification by Faith Alone." *Reformation & Revival Journal* 11, no. 2 (Spring 2002): 75–90.

Smeaton, George. *The Doctrine of the Holy Spirit.* London: Banner of Truth, 1958.

The Subordinate Standards...of the Free Church of Scotland. Reprinted, Edinburgh: William Blackwood & Sons, 1973.

Tamerius, Travis. "Sounding the Alarm: N. T. Wright and Evangelical Theology." *Reformation & Revival Journal* 11, no. 2 (Spring 2002): 11–34.

Turretin, Francis. *Institutes of Elenctic Theology.* Edited by James T. Dennison Jr. Translated by George Musgrave Giger. Phillipsburg, NJ: P&R Publishing, 1994.

Van Dam, C. "Further Discussion." *Clarion* 56, no 21 (October 12, 2007): 524–25.

———. "Has Mid-America Reformed Seminary Changed its Course?" *Clarion* 56, no. 16 (August 3, 2007): 390–93.

———. "Reflections on a Conference." *Clarion* 57, no.6 (March 14, 2008): 133–35.

Veenhof, C. "*De zaak waar het om gaat*" [The real issue]. In *Appel!* [Appeal!].

Voetius, Gisbertus. *Voetius' Catechisatie over den Heidelbergschen Catechismus* [Voetius' catechism on the Heidelberg Catechism]. Edited by A. Kuyper. 1662. Reprint, Rotterdam: Gebroeders Huge, 1891.

Waters, Guy Prentiss. *The Federal Vision and Covenant Theology: A Comparative Analysis.* Phillipsburg, NJ: P&R, 2006.

The Westminster Standards: An Original Facsimile. Audubon, NJ: Old Paths Publications, 1997.

Wilkins, Steve, and Duane Garner, eds. *The Federal Vision.* Monroe, LA: Athanasius Press, 2004.

Wright, David F. "Martin Bucer 1491–1551: Ecumenical Theologian." In *Common Places of Martin Bucer*, trans. and ed. David F. Wright, 42–46. Ap-

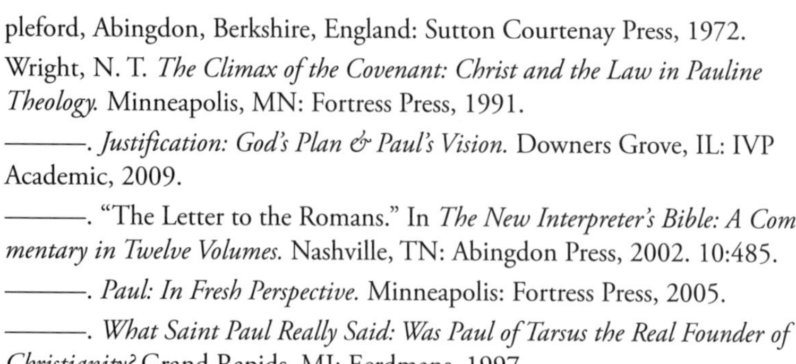

pleford, Abingdon, Berkshire, England: Sutton Courtenay Press, 1972.

Wright, N. T. *The Climax of the Covenant: Christ and the Law in Pauline Theology.* Minneapolis, MN: Fortress Press, 1991.

———. *Justification: God's Plan & Paul's Vision.* Downers Grove, IL: IVP Academic, 2009.

———. "The Letter to the Romans." In *The New Interpreter's Bible: A Commentary in Twelve Volumes.* Nashville, TN: Abingdon Press, 2002. 10:485.

———. *Paul: In Fresh Perspective.* Minneapolis: Fortress Press, 2005.

———. *What Saint Paul Really Said: Was Paul of Tarsus the Real Founder of Christianity?* Grand Rapids, MI: Eerdmans, 1997.

CREEDAL INDEX

SCRIPTURAL INDEX

RFPA publications
written by David J. Engelsma

Battle for Sovereign Grace in the Covenant: The Declaration of Principles

Better to Marry: Sex and Marriage in 1 Corinthians 6 and 7

Bound to Join: Letters on Church Membership

Christianizing the World: Reformed Calling or Ecclesiastical Suicide?

Common Grace Revisited: A Response to Richard J. Mouw's He Shines in All That's Fair

Covenant and Election in the Reformed Tradition

The Covenant of God and the Children of Believers: Sovereign Grace in the Covenant

A Defense of the Church Institute: Response to the Critics of Bound to Join

Federal Vision: Heresy at the Root

Hyper-Calvinism and the Call of the Gospel: An Examination of the Well-Meant Offer of the Gospel

Marriage: The Mystery of Christ and the Church

Prosperous Wicked and Plagued Saints: An Exposition of Psalm 73

Reformed Education: The Christian School as Demand of the Covenant

The Reformed Faith of John Calvin: The Institutes in Summary

Reformed Worship (coauthor with Barrett Gritters and Charles Terpstra)

Trinity and Covenant: God as Holy Family

Unfolding Covenant History: Judges and Ruth

RFPA publications
edited by David J. Engelsma

All Glory to the Only Good God: Reformed Spirituality

Always Reforming: Continuation of the Sixteenth-Century Reformation

Communion with God: Reformed Spirituality

Peace for the Troubled Heart: Reformed Spirituality

Righteous by Faith Alone: A Devotional Commentary on Romans

The Sixteenth-Century Reformation of the Church

The Reformed Baptism Form: A Commentary

The Rock Whence We Are Hewn: God, Grace, and Covenant